Mali

THE BRADT TRAVEL GUIDE

PUBLISHER'S FOREWORD

The first Bradt travel guide was written in 1974 by George and Hilary Bradt on a river barge floating down a tributary of the Amazon. In the 1980s and '90s the focus shifted away from hiking to broader-based guides to new destinations – usually the first to be published on these places. In the 21st century Bradt continues to publish these ground-breaking guides, along with other guides to established holiday destinations, incorporating in-depth information on culture and natural history alongside the nuts and bolts of where to stay and what to see.

Bradt authors support responsible travel, with advice not only on minimum impact but also on how to give something back through local charities. Thus a true synergy is achieved between the traveller and local communities.

*　　*　　*

Several years ago I received a laconic postcard from a friend in West Africa: 'Timbuktu hasn't changed much since I last saw it.' A comment on any other town would have been unremarkable, but Timbuktu has an almost mythical quality – it's hard to believe that it really exists. The same could be said for much of Mali: the Dogon villages, the Djenné Mosque and the River Niger, all brought to life here by Ross Velton and magnificently photographed by Ariadne Van Zandbergen. We had a long search for an updater whom we could trust to bring the guide thoroughly up to date, and I am particularly pleased that Jolijn Geels, whom I have known through her sensitive contributions to *Madagascar*, was available to do such an excellent job. She was aided by backpacker John Kupiec who regularly reaches places other travellers miss, along with naturalist Lyn Mair who added her authoritative stamp to the natural history section.

Hilary Bradt

23 High Street, Chalfont St Peter, Bucks SL9 9QE, England
Tel: 01753 893444; fax: 01753 892333
Email: info@bradtguides.com
Web: www.bradtguides.com

Mali

THE BRADT TRAVEL GUIDE

Second Edition

Ross Velton

Updated by Jolijn Geels

Bradt Publications, UK
The Globe Pequot Press Inc, USA

Reprinted May 2008
Second edition 2004
First published 2000

Bradt Travel Guides Ltd
23 High Street, Chalfont St Peter, Bucks SL9 9QE, England
www.bradtguides.com
Published in the USA by The Globe Pequot Press Inc, 246 Goose Lane,
PO Box 480, Guilford, Connecticut 06437-0480

British Library Cataloguing in Publication Data
A catalogue record for this book is available from the British Library

ISBN-10: 1 84162 077 7
ISBN-13: 978 1 84162 077 0

Photographs
Ariadne Van Zandbergen
Front cover Tuareg camel rider on the fringes of the Sahara

Illustrations Jolijn Geels, Carole Vincer
Maps Alan Whitaker

Typeset from the author's disc by Wakewing
Printed and bound in India by Nutech Photolithographers

Author

Ross Velton (rvelton@yahoo.com) has authored or co-authored over ten travel books on destinations ranging from Haiti to Walt Disney World, by way of Cap d'Agde, the world's largest nudist resort. In addition to his work for Bradt Travel Guides, Ross is an author for Rough Guides and a contributor to magazines and newspapers, including *The Times* and *The Independent*. He currently lives in Montreal, Canada.

UPDATER

When she lived in Surinam as a young child, a travel bug must have bitten **Jolijn Geels** (known in Mali as Julie) from the Netherlands, for she never could stay in one place for very long. After studying arts and culture, she lived in Spain and Scotland. A trip to Cameroon triggered her deep passion for Africa and she soon swapped her studio for hiking boots and a backpack. Since then she has travelled frequently to many corners of the continent, the Comoros Islands and Madagascar as a backpacker, tour leader and now as a contributor to this second edition of the Bradt guide to Mali.

Contents

LIST OF MAPS

KEY TO STANDARD SYMBOLS · Bradt

—·—	International boundary	⊠	Post office
------	District boundary	e	Internet access
�	National park	✚	Hospital, clinic etc
✈	Airport (international)	ö	Museum
✈	Airport (other)	⍾	Elephant concentration sites
═══	Paved roads (regional maps)	i	Tourist information
═══	unpaved roads (regional maps)	$	Bank
======	Track/4WD route	∴	Archaeological or historic site
━━	Railway	⊞	Historic building
----------	Footpath	⛫	Castle/fortress
⛴	Ferry	†	Church or cathedral
⛽	Petrol station/garage	↳	City wall
P	Car park	Ç	Mosque
🚌	Bus station etc	⋋	Stadium
⌂	Hotel, inn etc	▲	Mountain/hill Height in metres
Å	Campsite	⤫⤫	Border post
⇄	Direction of traffic (Town plans)	⦚	Waterfall
☆	Night club/casino	☀	Scenic viewpoint
⚲	Wine bar		
✕	Restaurant, café etc		

*Other map symbols are sometimes shown in
separate key boxes with individual
explanations for their meanings.*

Acknowledgements

DEDICATION
Dedicated to the remarkable women of Mali.

Ross Velton

I have depended on the support of many people to write this book.

One of my greatest debts of gratitude is to Odile, François and Martin Gil, Maverick, Jingle, Mr Sidibé and the others, whose welcome was always warm and unconditional. Thanks to Colette Martin-Chave for making the introductions and Fanny Couquaux for her moral support during a difficult time.

Various people in Mali were kind enough to give me their time and the benefit of their experience. Thanks to Maureen and Tore Rose, Martine Latraye, Oumar Balla Touré, David Rawson, Aminata Dramane Traoré, Violet Diallo and Dr Téréba Togola in Bamako; Amadou Camara in Djenné; Jean-Pierre Dougnon in Mopti; Lassana Cissé, Seydou Ouattara and Domo Guindo in Bandiagara; Daniel Thera and Gadioula Dolo in Sanga; Mamadou Baga Samaké in Douentza; Sister Anne-Marie Saloman in Gossi; Ali Ouls Sidi in Timbuktu; Mamadou Lamine Diakité in Kabara; Mamadou Bréma Keita in Sikasso; and the Coopérative des Transporteurs Routiers de Kayes in Kayes.

I also greatly appreciate the practical assistance provided by the Office Malien du Tourisme et de l'Hôtellerie (OMATHO), Air Afrique, Air Mali and Club Direct.

When travellers are on the road exploring unfamiliar places, they are ultimately dependent on the help and generosity of the local people. I thank everyone in Mali for their advice, friendship and hospitality.

The team at Bradt Travel Guides, and especially Tricia Hayne, should be acknowledged for commissioning and publishing this original guide. I also appreciate the hard work and constructive criticism of my editor, Janice Booth, and the advice of Bradt's most prolific author, Philip Briggs.

Moral support was provided, as always, by my mother and father.

Jolijn Geels

Of all the staff of OMATHO and the Mission Culturelle in various towns I am especially grateful to Ali Ouls Sidi and the delegation from the Mission Culturelle in Timbuktu; Mohamed Jean Pierre Tita and Sidi Mohamed ag

Idal in Kidal; Boubacar Hama Diaby in Djenné; Lassana Cissé in Bandiagara and Niang Madani in Ségou.

Many thanks to the very knowledgeable officials and professionals Lassiné Dembele and Baïkoro Fofana in Bamako; Issa Dicko in Essouk; and the guides Toka in Djenné; Youssouf Kangaye in Mopti; Sana Sibily in Timbuktu; Bemba Dabo and Sékou Coulibaly in Kita; Aboubacrine Berthe in Sikasso; Ibrahim Diakité in Gao; Dramane in Douentza, and most of all, my Dogon guide and friend Mamoutou A Guindo.

Thanks to Georgette van den Hoogen, Marja Oostwoud Wijdenes and Karen Crabbs in Bamako, Belinda Aked from the UK, and numerous Malians and fellow travellers for providing various kinds of assistance, transport, shelter and good company. My appreciation goes to Irene Saletan, Peter Udell, Hans Heitmann, Niels Wiedenhof, Trevor Marchand, Benny Verbercht, Barbara Keck and Geoff Nagle for sharing their experience through reports and emails. I would like especially to mention the adventurous John Kupiec from the USA, who wrote: 'a luxurious place for me to stay would be a farmers' haybarn in Ireland'. The extensive report of his ventures off the beaten track has proved invaluable for this second edition.

The pleasant cooperation of the team at Bradt Travel Guides – first of all with Hilary Bradt and Tricia Hayne – enabled me to enjoy every stage of the process. Thanks to Philip Briggs for many quick responses to my queries.

I owe a debt of gratitude to Herman Snippe, who like no other has to deal with the consequences of my passion for Africa.

Introduction

A brick had been thrown through a window of the Malian Consulate in Paris when I arrived to collect my visa on a bitterly cold December morning. Despite the chilling wind which had effectively refrigerated the building, the gaping hole in the glass had been left uncovered, while the consular staff, the lucky ones wearing heavy anoraks over their *boubous*, sat round a table drinking tea and discussing how best to solve the problem. 'Fools,' I thought.

Two months later on a dusty street in Bamako, a young lad stood accused of stealing a taxi driver's transistor radio. An expectant crowd had gathered as accuser and accused squared off to exchange threats, counter-threats, insults, evil looks and, at the critical moment of the confrontation, saliva. At this point a fistfight seemed to be the natural and inevitable progression; how could either side back down now after such an insult? But both sides did back down. Chairs were called for, a team of self-appointed mediators sprang from the crowd of onlookers, and the protagonists sat down to discuss their problem rather than fight it out.

I remembered the staff at the consulate in Paris and realised that I had been wrong to criticise their inaction. Now, having spent some time in Mali, I understood that they had been taking action – not in the Parisian way, but in the Malian way. For this is a country with its own, unique dynamic. Like the great river which winds its way through Mali's vast Sahelian and Saharan landscapes, the pace of life is slow and forceful. Newly arrived travellers still in the Western groove may find this frustrating at first, but give it a while and the charm and sense of humour of these mild-mannered people will win you over.

The tourist attractions in Mali speak for themselves and need no introduction. Grim stories about uncomfortable bus journeys in searing heat and annoying guides, which are hardly original in West Africa, might put you off visiting Mali – and buying this book! So I have opened on safe ground by introducing some of the most gentle and welcoming people in Africa. The rest is for you to discover.

ABOUT THIS BOOK

I hope that I have followed the many Bradt authors before me who have given their readers well-balanced and thought-provoking background information to the country they are about to visit. I also hope that I have produced a practical and user-friendly guide that will save you time and perhaps a little money. I have written it for travellers who are serious about exploring this country independently, using public transport and finding their own places to stay and things to do. This guide is not simply a listing of all the hotels and restaurants in Mali, nor is it by any means comprehensive. I have tried to point you in the right direction by giving you a few ideas and supplying what I think is useful information. The actual exploring and discovering is up to you.

The guide itself divides Mali into regions, which are then divided into towns and other places of interest. When I travel, I find that one of the most time-consuming and frustrating things can be finding out how to get from A to B. With this in mind, I have tried to make the *Getting there and away* section for each town as detailed and specific as possible. Where there is no map, I hope that my directions are clear and simple. Accommodation is another important consideration when travelling. At the very least, it should be safe and preferably clean. Since the first-time visitor has no way of knowing whether or not this is the case, I have placed a strong emphasis on the *Where to stay* sections.

Prices

One of the biggest drawbacks of a guidebook is how quickly it dates. This is especially true where prices are concerned. It may be that by the time you visit Mali few of the prices are as they are quoted in this guide. Nonetheless, I have chosen to be as specific as possible about the price of things. Even if they are not spot on when you arrive, they will give you a good idea of how to plan your holiday budget.

Spellings

You can virtually guarantee that for every place name, ethnic group, culinary speciality or important historical figure there will be an alternative spelling. In some cases – Timbuktu, for example – more than one other version exists. This is hardly surprising in a country where French is the official language and over 30 other indigenous languages are spoken. All spellings in this book are randomly chosen. In many cases I have opted for the French spelling of a word, although sometimes – Timbuktu is, once again, a good example – other spellings are more easily recognisable to the English-speaker. In no case, however, do I expect you to confuse one name or word for an entirely different and unconnected one.

Part One

General Information

MALI AT A GLANCE

'Where are you going on holiday this year?'
'Mali'
'Wow, Bali. That should be nice.'
'No, Mali.'
'Where's that?'
'In West Africa. It's where you'll find Timbuktu.'
'Is that the capital?'
'No, that's...hmm...that's...well, that's not Timbuktu.'

Area 1,240,190 km² (second largest country in West Africa and five times as large as Great Britain)
Population 11.63 million (July 2002 census)
Main languages French and Bambara
Capital Bamako (population 953,600)
Other main towns Ségou (102,200), Mopti (115,500), Sikasso (127,900), Gao (39,000)
Principal tourist attractions Dogon country, River Niger, Sahara desert, Timbuktu
Climate Hot and dry; semi-tropical in the extreme south
Time GMT
Money CFA franc = 100 centimes
Measures Metric system
Political system Multiparty republic
Head of state (President) Amadou Toumani Touré
Head of government (Prime Minister) Ahmed Mohamed Ag Hamani
Territorial divisions Eight regions: Kayes (First Region), Koulikoro (Second Region), Sikasso (Third Region), Ségou (Fourth Region), Mopti (Fifth Region), Gao (Sixth Region), Tombouctou (Seventh Region – French spelling) and Kidal (Eighth Region), which are divided into *cercles* and subdivided into *arrondissements*. Bamako is governed by the autonomous District of Bamako.
GDP $9.7 billion (2002)
GDP per head $900 (2002)
Foreign debt $3.3 billion (2001)
Consumer price inflation 4.5% (2002)
Life expectancy 46.5 years

Economist Intelligence Unit, Encyclopaedia Britannica and CIA's World Fact Book

Background Information

HISTORY

It is only really in the past 40 years that we have been able to talk about the history of Mali, the nation state. Previously, this land in the middle of the western Sudan had been the stomping ground of some of Africa's greatest empires and kingdoms, heroes and villains. Ask a Malian today about the history of her country and you will be regaled with stories of Soundiata Keita, Kankan Moussa and the great Mali Empire – a name the country adopted when it won its independence in 1960. The fact that this empire, along with others such as Ghana and Songhay, actually spread across the modern-day boundaries of several West African states does nothing to diminish the feeling that this is *Mali's* history and every Malian is very proud of it.

Early times

The earliest discoveries of the existence of man were made in East Africa at Olduvai Gorge (Tanzania), Lake Turkana (Kenya) and the River Omo (Ethiopia). These finds have been attributed to a period known as the Early Stone Age, dating back over two million years. This was a time when man was beginning to dominate animals through the use of rudimentary tools and weapons chipped out of stone, although his physical appearance was still some way between primates and modern man. There is scant evidence of Early Stone Age people in West Africa, and even less in Mali itself.

About 30,000 years ago man's body had adopted the form recognisable in all races of mankind today. He had become clever at making tools and gradually shifted from hunting and gathering to actually producing food – in other words, farming.

Agriculture began in Africa about 7,000 years ago in the Late Stone Age or Neolithic period. At this time, the Sahara was covered with grass and trees and, according to early rock paintings and engravings, supported elephant, hippopotamus and giraffe populations – animals which could not possibly survive there nowadays. Later drawings, such as those found in the Adrar des Ifôghas in the northeastern corner of Mali, depict domesticated animals and men hunting, farming and cattle-rearing. Further evidence of a rich and fertile Sahara supporting a dense human population was found to the west of the Adrar at the oasis of Asselar, where the fossilised remains of a man dating back to the Neolithic period were unearthed. However, the

Sahara was gradually drying out and the grass was disappearing, forcing the farmers and pastoralists to migrate southwards into moister savanna areas such as the Niger Inland Delta.

The arrival of the Iron Age in West Africa between about 500 and 400BC was of immense significance. Iron tools made agriculture more efficient and, consequently, food was more abundant. Mere survival became less of a day-to-day concern, giving people the opportunity to indulge in other activities. Craftsmen, traders, clerics and rulers emerged from the crowd, societies developed, and the foundations were laid for the economic, political and cultural changes which were to take place in the region during the first millennium. The knowledge of iron-smelting was probably imported to West Africa by the Phoenicians of Carthage (in modern-day Tunisia) across the trade routes of the Sahara.

Trans-Saharan trade

The earliest trade route used by the Phoenicians and Berber traders from North Africa was via Ghat (in modern-day Libya), crossing the Hoggar Mountains and following the River Niger down to Gao. A western route, meanwhile, linked southern Morocco to the Upper Niger. Initially, horse-drawn carts were used to transport goods across the Sahara between North and

West Africa. However, by about the beginning of the Christian era camels had been introduced to Africa, making trans-Saharan trade more practical and profitable (camels could travel further with less water and carry greater loads). It is at around this time that gold became the main commodity of trans-Saharan trade. Originating in the forests of West Africa, gold was carried in great quantities across the desert to North Africa, where it formed the basis of the Arabic monetary system. Ivory, ostrich feathers and leather also interested the Arabs and, in time, slaves were to become as popular. Meanwhile, salt from mines in the Sahara was in great demand in West Africa, as were horses, and metals such as copper. Trans-Saharan trade could not have developed into the big business it had become by the end of the first millennium without the presence of a dominant power in the western Sudan able to ensure the stability and security of the region so that trade could prosper.

The Ghana Empire

The kingdom of Ouagadou was probably founded some time during AD400 by the Soninké, who lived in the northern part of the lands dominated by the Mande peoples of the western Sudan. However, the first accounts of this kingdom were provided by Arab geographers and chroniclers in the 11th century when Ouagadou had developed into a fully fledged political state covering much of what is now northwestern Mali (and parts of southern Mauritania) and known to the Arabs as the Ghana Empire. The trans-Saharan trade in gold was the impetus for Ghana's ascendancy and the reason why it dominated the region until the 12th century. Control of the gold fields of Bambouk and Buré was the key to Ghana's economic prosperity, which was derived primarily from taxes on all gold passing through the empire on its way to North Africa. The Arab chronicler, El Bekri, writing in 1067–8, describes Ghana's ancient capital, Koumbi Saleh (in modern-day southern Mauritania), as two towns several kilometres apart: one for the king and his court and another for visiting Arab traders. The rulers of Ghana were essentially animist, believing that natural objects possess souls, but they were also receptive to Islam. This had the dual advantage of enabling them to command the respect and allegiance of subjects who followed the ancestral religion, while at the same time not alienating Muslim merchants and thus jeopardising trade. The result by the middle of the 11th century was an empire in which rulers exercised a degree of central authority over a network of smaller states hitherto unseen in the western Sudan, and a climate in which the gold trade could – and did – thrive.

In the early 11th century, just as the Ghana Empire was at its zenith, a group of Islamic reformers known as the Almoravids was formed in the western Sahara. Before too long, this group split in two and the southern faction, led by Abu Bakr Ibn 'Umar, turned its attentions towards the infidels of Ghana. Almoravid raids disrupted trade from 1062 onwards, and in 1076 the Almoravids conquered the Ghana Empire. A Muslim king was installed and many Soninké were converted to Islam. Those who resisted conversion fled to

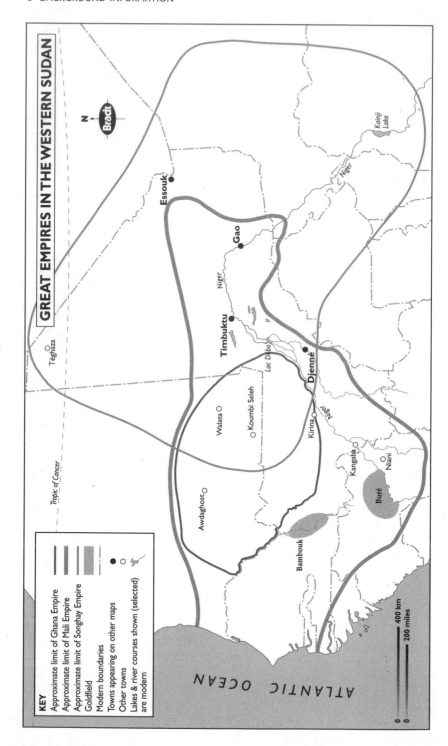

GREAT EMPIRES IN THE WESTERN SUDAN

KEY
Approximate limit of Ghana Empire
Approximate limit of Mali Empire
Approximate limit of Songhay Empire
Goldfield
Modern boundaries
Towns appearing on other maps
Other towns
Lakes & river courses shown (selected) are modern

N

Bradt

Tropic of Cancer

Teghaza

Essouk

Gao

Niger

Niger

Timbuktu

Lac Débo

Dienné

Walata

Koumbi Saleh

Kirina

Niger

Kangaba

Niani

Awdaghost

Buré

Bambouk

Kainji Lake

ATLANTIC OCEAN

0   200 miles
0   400 km

the fringes of the empire and formed separate states, the most important of which was Sosso to the southeast of Ghana. In 1087 Abu Bakr Ibn 'Umar was killed trying to suppress a revolt, and a short time afterwards Ghana regained its independence. The old empire, however, was in terminal decline and had been replaced by Sosso and other newly formed states as the region's true power brokers. In the 12th century Sosso successfully invaded Ghana, definitively ending the hegemony of the first great empire in the western Sudan. Another was soon to follow.

The Mali Empire

Around 1230 a young man named Soundiata Keita became the ruler of a small Malinké state in the Manding Mountains called Mali, which at this time was a vassal of Sosso, whose leader, Soumangourou Kanté, frequently used force to compel Malinké allegiance. After the failure of his brother to repel Sosso aggression, expectations were high when Soundiata took over. His early years certainly suggested that here was a legend in the making. A witch-doctor had predicted that Soundiata's mother, an extraordinarily ugly princess named Sogolan, would give birth to the greatest king in the world – a prophesy which seemed ludicrous when she produced a boy with paralysis in both legs. However, when he was nine years old Soundiata miraculously gained the use of his legs and he quickly developed into a prodigiously strong young man, who excelled in the arts of hunting and witchcraft. Soundiata's legendary status was secured in 1235 when he confronted and defeated Kanté at Kirina (near modern-day Koulikoro) and assumed the title *Mansa* or King of Kings. Having conquered Sosso, Soundiata set about transforming Mali from an alliance of independent Malinké chiefs into an empire, and, by the time he died in 1255, Mali encompassed most of the western part of modern-day Mali, including the all-important gold field at Buré. The empire's apogee, however, was still to come.

The Niger Inland Delta, Timbuktu and Gao were all conquered between 1285 and 1300, and during the reign of Kankan Moussa (1317–37) the Mali Empire extended from the Atlantic Ocean in the west to Gao in the east and from the desert town of Tadmekka (or Tadamat) in the north to the Fouta Djallon Highlands in the south. Kankan (or Mansa) Moussa was, along with Soundiata, Mali's most colourful and successful ruler. Islam had been established as the court religion after years of contact with Muslim traders from the north and Kankan was keen to display the magnitude of his own faith. In May 1324 he set off on a pilgrimage to Mecca with an entourage of over 60,000 – each one carrying a bar of gold. He stopped off in Cairo and visited the sultan, giving away so much gold in the city that the Egyptian money market crashed. Although it would take another ten years for the price of gold to recover, Kankan's visit had instantly put Mali on the map and his pilgrimage helped to foster political, cultural and intellectual links between the western Sudan and the Arab world. Trans-Saharan trade, meanwhile, continued to prosper in the secure and stable conditions provided by Mali's strong rulers, who received tribute from the many different clans stretching across the empire. In the second half of the 14th century, however, a series of weak rulers encouraged internal power struggles which, in turn, damaged the strong leadership upon which Mali's success had been based. Revolts broke out far from the Malinké heartland in the centre and west of the empire, and by the end of the 14th century Mali had started to decline.

The Songhay Empire

The most rebellious part of the Mali Empire was in the Sahelian and desert regions in the east. As Mali gradually lost control of these outlying provinces, a small vassal state along the banks of the Niger called Songhay grew in strength and began to fill the power vacuum. Songhay also benefited from a general west-to-east shift in the focus of trans-Saharan trade. The Akan gold fields (in modern-day northern Ghana) began to supersede Bambouk and Buré, while Timbuktu and Gao (the Songhay capital) became important trading posts between the gold fields in the south and the salt mines of Téghaza in the north. The first of Songhay's two ruling dynasties, the Sonni dynasty, was responsible for transforming this small chiefdom into the western Sudan's leading power for the next 100 years or so. Sonni Ali Ber (1465–92), a great warrior and ruthless leader, greatly expanded Songhay territory and enhanced its political hegemony, capturing Timbuktu in 1468 and freeing Songhay from Mali rule. Sonni Ali Ber's son, who succeeded his father in 1492, was overthrown by a lieutenant in Ber's army named Mohamed Touré. Touré took the title 'Askia', marking the end of the Sonni dynasty. Askia Mohamed (or Askia the Great) was also a great warrior, but, unlike Sonni Ali Ber, he was a devout – and practising – Muslim. He went on a pilgrimage to Mecca in 1496 and under his rule Islamic learning and scholarship flourished at Timbuktu. Askia Mohamed was himself overthrown in 1529 by his son, Askia Daoud, and for the next 50 years or so the Songhay Empire was at its zenith, stretching from the headwaters of the River Senegal in the west to what is now Niger and Nigeria in the east, and controlling the lucrative gold trade which passed through Djenné and Timbuktu. However, just as internal power struggles had weakened the Mali Empire at the end of the 14th century, when Askia Daoud died in 1583 dynastic rivalries brought to an end years of strong leadership and made the Songhay Empire vulnerable to external threats.

The Moroccans

Ahmed el Mansur, the Sultan of Morocco, had been waiting for an opportunity to invade Songhay and take control of the gold trade. Internal divisions after the death of Askia Daoud presented this opportunity, and in October 1590 he sent a force of 4,000 men armed with muskets, gunpowder and mortars across the Sahara to confront 40,000 Songhay warriors, with spears and bows and arrows, north of Gao along the banks of the River Niger. The two armies met at Tondibi in 1591 and the Songhay fled when they heard the sound of the muskets. Although military engagements between the two sides would continue for the next two years, Songhay was finished as a major power and the torch was passed to the Moroccans, who now controlled Djenné and Timbuktu.

The Moroccans, however, never managed to dominate the region in the same way that the empires of Mali, Songhay and, to a lesser extent, Ghana had done. Apart from having a strong presence in Timbuktu and around the central stretch of the River Niger, much of the rest of the former Songhay lands remained in a state of anarchy, allowing new states to develop and marking the emergence of Tuareg influence in the region. Among the new states to appear during this period were the Bambara kingdom of Ségou (see page 129); the Bambara kingdom of Kaarta (see page 260); a Peul kingdom which emerged in the Niger Inland Delta as early as the 15th century and was eventually replaced by the theocratic state of Amadou Sekou (see page 153); the Kénédougou kingdom (see page 246); Samory Touré's domains (see page 246); and several smaller states, such as Khasso and Logo in western Mali (see page 259). Meanwhile, the Moroccans had established Timbuktu as their headquarters. In the early years after the invasion *pashas* were sent directly from Fez to govern on behalf of the sultan, but after 1604 they were locally elected and, along with the Moroccan soldiery or *Arma*, gradually became a law unto themselves. Seventy years or so after the invasion, the sultan's authority had disappeared and the descendants of the invaders – who had intermarried with Africans – governed their own affairs. The Tuareg had become the Arma's most immediate threat, with their constant raids in the area of the Niger Bend. In 1737 the Tuareg won a decisive victory, forcing the Arma to retreat to Timbuktu, where they remained a major force until overrun by the Peul in 1883.

The Tukulor Empire

None of the states which emerged in the vacuum left after the decline of the Songhay Empire managed to dominate the region completely. Some were more powerful than others and expanded beyond their traditional heartland, but the days of the western Sudan's great empires had passed. During the second half of the 19th century, the Tukulor Empire created by El Hadj Omar Tall became, along with the French, the most influential force in the region.

El Hadj Omar Tall was a Tukulor Muslim cleric of the *Tijaniya* order of Islam. In 1852 he received his divine revelation and launched a *jihad* from his base in the Fouta Djallon highlands to convert the populations of the western Sudan to the *Tijaniya* brotherhood (at this time the rival *Quadiriya* order was influential in Macina). By 1862, El Hadj Omar's forces had swept through the western part of Mali, conquering the Bambara kingdoms of Kaarta (1854) and Ségou (1862) before finally overcoming Macina and taking control of its capital, Hamdallaye. In response, the Peul and Arabs of the *Quadiriya* brotherhood joined forces and drove the Tukulor army to the Bandiagara plateau, where El Hadj Omar was killed in 1864. Amadou Tall, El Hadj Omar's son, had already been installed as the Tukulor leader at Ségou, and now he assumed control of

DISCOVERING MALI

Pride-of-place in tourist brochures, pamphlets and web sites about Mali is often reserved for Timbuktu and the River Niger. These two attractions remain as potent today in enticing travellers to Mali as they were hundreds of years ago when explorers dreamed of reaching a city where the streets were said to be paved with gold and discovering the source and flow of a river which many thought was the main tributary of the Nile.

During the 11th century, various Arab geographers and chroniclers were writing about the ancient Ghana Empire and its capital at Koumbi Saleh. One of the earliest accounts of Koumbi – and the important trading centre of Awdaghust (in modern-day Mauritania) – was provided by the Mesopotamian traveller, **Ibn Hawkal**, who wrote in his travelogue, *On the Shape of the Earth*, about a land of fabulous wealth and a great river which flowed to the east and, therefore, was surely the upper course of the Nile. The famous Moroccan explorer, **Ibn Battuta**, was another early pioneer of travel to Mali. In 1325, after 25 years spent exploring Arabia, Persia, India, China, Sumatra and Africa, he crossed the Sahara with a camel caravan and arrived in Timbuktu, where he wrote a detailed record of the city's early growth.

These forays into Mali by early explorers and their written accounts of a land of untold riches, as well as stories heard at trading posts on the west coast of Africa about a mysterious river and a fabled city of gold, had caught the imagination of the Europeans. In 1788 a group of English gentlemen formed the Association for Promoting the Discovery of the Interior Parts of Africa, which became known as the Africa Association: two of its main priorities were to discover the source and flow of the River Niger and the city of Timbuktu.

After two abortive attempts, the Africa Association sent **Daniel Houghton**, a bankrupt Irishman who needed a job, to West Africa with instructions 'to ascertain the course and, if possible, the rise and termination of that mysterious river'. Houghton set off up the River Gambia in July 1790, only to be robbed and left to die by Muslim tribesmen in what is now eastern Senegal. Although he never reached Mali and the River Niger, his last letter spoke of a navigable river flowing eastward through a country where opportunities for trade in gold, ivory and slaves were great. This information was enough to persuade the Africa Association to fund another expedition, led this time by a Scottish doctor from Foulshiels, near Selkirk, with a passion for travel and a desire to break out of his humdrum life in the Borders.

Mungo Park's first expedition started as inauspiciously as Houghton's failed attempt to discover the Niger five years earlier. He set off up the River Gambia in December 1795, reaching Ségou in July 1796 after having been deserted by his companions and robbed and tortured by local Muslim kings. His reward was to be the first European to set eyes on the River Niger, 'glittering to the morning sun, as broad as the Thames at Westminster, and flowing slowly to the eastward'. Park wanted to continue down the Niger to Timbuktu, but only got as far as Sansanding before sickness forced him to abandon the journey. His second expedition, sponsored by the British government, was on a much grander scale than the first. A force of 40 Europeans set off in May 1805, but by the time it reached Bamako in August 1805 dysentery and malaria had reduced its number to seven. At Sansanding, the King of Ségou gave Park two canoes, which were joined together to make a raft, *His Majesty's Schooner Joliba* ('joliba' being the Bambara word for the River Niger). Park's team – four soldiers, three servants and a new guide by the name of Fatouma – left Sansanding in November 1805. Five years later the British government tracked down Fatouma, who explained what had happened to Park and his friends. They had continued down the Niger, passing Kabara (where they were refused permission to visit Timbuktu) and Gao before entering the small Hausa state of Yauri (in modern-day Nigeria) in March or April 1806. They received a hostile reception from the local king, who attacked the raft, forcing Park and his men to jump into the river where they eventually drowned in the Bussa rapids.

While Park's travels had taught Europeans much about the River Niger, Timbuktu was still a mystery; the race was now on to be the first European to visit the fabled city. **Major Alexander Gordon Laing** was another Scotsman, who had been stationed in Sierra Leone as a member of the British army. In July 1825 he led an expedition across the Sahara, ostensibly to discover the source of the River Niger. He joined a camel caravan heading south and, after a close encounter with the Tuareg in the desert, became the first European to set foot in Timbuktu on August 18 1826. He stayed in the city for about six weeks before joining another caravan heading north. Two days out of Timbuktu he was stopped by the Tuareg and killed with a spear through the heart. Meanwhile, the French Geographical Society had offered a 10,000-franc reward to the first European who could travel to Timbuktu.

One of the contenders was **René Caillié**, the son of a poor Parisian baker. Fearing the hostile reception that he would receive as a Christian in an Islamic land, Caillié spent nine months living with a Muslim tribe on the banks of the River Senegal in preparation for his trip. He learnt Arabic and studied the Koran so that he would be able to pass himself off as a Muslim. This tactic paid dividends as he travelled through Mali in 1828, visiting Djenné in March and arriving at Timbuktu by boat in April. The following month he joined a caravan heading north and travelled safely through Tuareg country, thus becoming the first European to visit Timbuktu and return home to tell the tale. Of the explorers who followed Laing and Caillié to Timbuktu, **Heinrich Barth** was the most noteworthy. A German by nationality, Barth was employed by the British government and is best known for his five-year expedition across the Sahara to Lake Chad. In September 1853 he arrived at Timbuktu, having travelled overland from Say (in modern-day Niger) disguised as a Tuareg. The houses in Timbuktu where Laing, Caillié and Barth stayed – along with those of later explorers who reached the city – can still be seen today.

the Ségou Tukulor Empire. Meanwhile, his cousin, Tijani Tall, became head of Macina after the Tukulor had gained the upper hand against the Peul and Arab forces of the *Quadiriya* brotherhood. Amadou never managed to exercise the authority enjoyed by his father and was constantly contending with internal rivals and the rebellious Bambara, who had never accepted Tukulor control of their lands. Thus deprived of the allegiance of much of his empire, Amadou was no match for the French when they finally arrived at Ségou in 1890.

The French

Prior to 1890, the French had tried to regulate their relations with the Ségou Tukulor Empire – the most powerful of the indigenous African states in Mali during the second half of the 19th century – through treaties and trade agreements. After the abolition of slavery, French commercial interests in the area were concentrated on gum arabic (a resin found in some acacia trees and used for fixing textile dyes and starching clothes). To protect this trade, forts were built along the River Senegal and agreements were discussed with Amadou Tall so that the trade based in and around Senegal could be linked to that in Algeria via Tukulor lands in Mali. This was all part of a policy inspired by the French governor in Senegal in the 1850s and 60s, Louis Léon César Faidherbe, to extend French influence in Africa from the Atlantic Ocean to the Red Sea. Amadou Tall was in no doubt as to the long-term French objective in the western Sudan and stubbornly refused to co-operate, stalling negotiations despite the ultimate inevitability of the French conquest. Finally, in 1887, Amadou signed the Treaty of Gouri, which made the Ségou Tukulor Empire a French protectorate and allowed traders access to the River Niger. It was now only a matter of time before the French annexed the Tukulor lands in Mali and joined them to what had become known as French West Africa. To this end, Lieutenant-Colonel Louis Archinard led a series of military campaigns in the late 1880s and early 1890s. In 1890 he entered Ségou, forcing Amadou Tall to flee to Nigeria where he died in 1898; in 1893 Macina, Bandiagara and Timbuktu fell to the French; the Kénédougou kingdom in the south was conquered when the French entered Sikasso in 1898; and Samory Touré was captured in the same year and exiled to Gabon. By the turn of the century, all of what is now Mali was under French control.

The French adhered to the time-honoured recipe for successful government in the western Sudan by adopting a highly centralised system of administration. The territory was divided into *cercles*, each one headed by a French commandant who reported to the governor of the colony, who, in turn, reported to the governor-general of French West Africa in Dakar. The name of the colony which, after independence, became known as Mali changed several times during the period of colonial rule.

Before the French conquests further east, the western part of Mali was renamed Upper Senegal in September 1880, with Kayes as its capital. In August 1890 French Sudan was created, comprising territory which would later be reapportioned to Senegal, Guinea, Côte d'Ivoire and Dahomey. In October 1899 Upper Senegal and Middle Niger came into existence, surviving for a short while before the colony was renamed Senegambia and Niger in 1902. During these changes, from 1890 to 1904, the eastern part of Mali was divided into three military districts. In October 1904 Upper Senegal and Niger replaced Senegambia and Niger, and four years later the capital was transferred from Kayes to Bamako. The three military districts were incorporated into the colony and Niger and Upper Volta (later Burkina Faso) were created in 1911 and 1919 respectively, from territory formerly belonging to Upper Senegal and Niger. In December 1920 the name French Sudan was restored, and would remain until the dissolution of the federation of French West Africa in October 1958.

The nature of colonial rule in French West Africa was initially dominated by a policy of 'assimilation' – educating Africans so that they could absorb French culture – but this was later abandoned for an approach based on 'association', encouraging Africans to associate their culture with French culture so that they could evolve towards the European idea of civilised society.

Independence
Open opposition to colonial rule came primarily from the Tuareg in the east, the Bambara in the Bélédougou region north of Bamako, and a Muslim sect known as the Hamallists (after its leader, Shaykh Mohamed al Tishiti Hamallah) in the west of the country. Otherwise, political opposition came from the African elite, who, by the late 1930s, had organised themselves into a number of voluntary organisations. These were not political parties, but rather cultural and sporting associations where the elite could meet with French approval, providing a forum within which politics – and eventual independence – could be discussed. Around the same time, in 1937, trade unions started to be formed, one of the first being the teachers' union founded by Mamadou Konaté. It is important to note that neither the voluntary organisations nor the trade unions united people along ideological or ethnic lines. The former simply facilitated communication between the elite, while the latter facilitated communication between the elite leaders and urban masses where social and economic concerns were paramount.

The formation of political parties in Mali can be dated to August 1945, when Africans were invited to participate in elections for the First Constituent Assembly of the Fourth Republic as part of a French policy to expand local involvement in the government of its overseas colonies. In response to the election of the pro-colonial candidate, Fily Dabo Sissoko, a number of political parties were formed. The Parti Progressiste Soudanais (PPS) was created by Sissoko's supporters and backed by the colonial administration, while the Union Soudanaise (US) led by Mamadou Konaté was affiliated with the Pan-African Rassemblement Démocratique Africain (RDA), which, in turn, was affiliated with the French Communist Party. By the time of National Assembly elections in 1956, universal suffrage had been introduced and the overwhelming popularity of the US-RDA was reflected in the election result.

Following its defeat, the PPS joined the US-RDA, whose leader, Mamadou Konaté, was now established as the country's leading political figure. Then, in the same year as his party's election victory, Konaté died of liver cancer. The co-founder of the Union Soudanaise, Modibo Keita, took over as head of the party – and would eventually be the man to lead his country to independence.

In October 1958 the federation of French West Africa was dissolved and replaced by the French Community, within which states could enjoy either political autonomy or complete independence from France as they saw fit. Only Guinea opted for immediate independence. Modibo Keita, who was now the leader of the Sudanese Republic (the new name for French Sudan), entered into talks with Léopold Sédar Senghor, the Senegalese leader, to unite their two countries in an independent federation. These talks eventually led to the creation of the Mali Federation, which declared its independence from France on June 20 1960 with Keita as its president. This unlikely alliance was to last just over three months. After independence, the thorny issue of presidential elections had to be addressed. This highlighted and exacerbated major policy differences between the two countries over vital issues such as the Federation's relationship with France and the command of the armed forces. Tension mounted, forces on both sides were mobilised, the border was closed and Modibo Keita returned to Bamako in a sealed train from Dakar where he had been campaigning for the elections. On September 22 1960 the US-RDA declared the independence of the Republic of Mali.

Modibo Keita

Modibo Keita had enjoyed a long association with the French communists and the first years of Mali's history as an independent state were to follow Marxist lines: a one-party state with a state-run economy modelled on the Soviet Union. One of Keita's first – and most drastic – actions was to withdraw Mali from the West African Monetary Union in July 1962 and introduce a national, unconvertible currency called the Mali Franc. This move upset Mali's regional merchants (numerous in a landlocked country with seven international borders), whose trade was badly hit by the introduction of an unconvertible currency. The riots which followed provided Keita with the ideal opportunity to strengthen his grip on power, and once the army had restored order several of the president's potential opponents, including Fily Dabo Sissoko, were rounded up, charged with treason and attempting a coup and sent to the desert prison in Kidal. In 1964 Sissoko and other prisoners were killed by a Tuareg ambush – although many believe that the government had ordered their deaths. The Keita regime was similarly uncompromising when it ruthlessly put down an armed revolt by the Tuareg (supported by Algeria and Morocco) in northeastern Mali in 1963. Meanwhile, Keita's economic policies were not having their desired effect. The unconvertible currency was largely responsible for the country's lack of hard currency, a scarcity of consumer products and, ultimately, food shortages. Eventually, in 1967, Keita was forced to swallow his pride and sign monetary accords with France which provided for a 50%

devaluation of the Mali Franc. The radicals in the party were outraged by this loss of dignity and demanded some tough national policies to restore the authority of the regime. Keita responded by announcing a cultural revolution. The Comité National de Défense de la Révolution assumed control of the government and had the objective of restoring Mali's Marxist policies and philosophy. The Popular Militia fulfilled the same role as the Red Guard in Mao's China, rooting out corruption and purifying the party using tactics based on harassment, intimidation and torture. They soon became hated by the people and resented by the army, whose younger officers were not spared their harassment. The military opposition rather than a great groundswell of popular dissent proved to be the catalyst for the *coup d'état* which would topple the Keita regime in 1968. On November 19 1968, while Keita was attending a conference in Mopti, there were rumours in the capital that the president was preparing to arrest a number of army officers on his return. Rather than test the truth of these rumours the army, led by a young lieutenant named Moussa Traoré, carried out a bloodless and successful coup. Keita was arrested on his way back to Bamako, bringing to an end independent Mali's First Republic.

Moussa Traoré

In the aftermath of the coup a provisional government, the Comité Militaire de Libération Nationale (CMLN), was established with the stated intention of solving the country's economic ills before returning it to civilian rule. The sensitive issue of the former government's socialist philosophy was not criticised by the new regime, which realised that many urban dwellers had benefited from secure employment during the Keita years and would not react well if they felt that their livelihoods were now under threat. Captain Yoro Diakité was placed at the head of the provisional government, although the real power lay in the hands of one of Diakité's inferior officers at military school, Lieutenant Moussa Traoré.

Moussa Traoré had always been a military man. Born in the region of Kayes, he received his military training in France before returning to Mali in 1960 and becoming an instructor at a military school in Kati. On November 19 1968 he led the group of 14 other officers in the coup d'état which toppled the Keita regime, and afterwards he was charged with the responsibility of returning the country to civilian rule. Not surprisingly, perhaps, Mali remained under military government for the next 11 years.

In the same way that Keita had used his first years as president to strengthen his grip on power, Traoré used the early 1970s to consolidate his own position and that of the CMLN. In April 1971 Yoro Diakité, Traoré's greatest political threat, was expelled from the CMLN on charges of conspiring to overthrow the government; he died two years later in prison. In the same year as Diakité's expulsion Traoré was promoted to colonel, and in June 1974 a referendum result gave overwhelming support to a new constitution which gave the CMLN a further five years to prepare the country for civilian rule. Arguably, Traoré's greatest challenge in the early 1970s – a period during which greater individual freedoms and the encouragement of private enterprise had brought about a short-term economic improvement – was drought in the Sahel between 1970 and 1974. International criticism of the Malian government's apathetic response to the plight of the nomadic Tuareg and Maure people most affected by the drought was widespread and vocal, and external pressure finally forced Traoré to establish refugee centres in the north – but not before a good deal of the assistance intended for the refugees had been embezzled by the elite in Bamako. Internal pressure, meanwhile, came mainly from Keita's supporters and trade unionists active under the Keita regime (Keita himself had died suddenly of lung cancer in May 1977 after having been moved from prison in Kidal to Bamako – although many believe that he was murdered by lethal injection). As the transition to civilian rule drew nearer, military hard-liners in the CMLN became increasingly anxious. In 1976 a political party, the Union Démocratique du Peuple Malien (UDPM), was formed in preparation for the transition, and the following year Traoré was elected as its secretary-general. Several members of the CMLN, along with many other army officers, attempted to bolster the military status quo by planning a coup d'état in 1978. The plot was discovered, the culprits were removed from the CMLN, and Traoré was left virtually unopposed by the time general elections were held on June 19 1979. All of the UDPM candidates were elected to the new National Assembly and the CMLN was disbanded, although the military still dominated the government, and Traoré took over as president of Mali's new civilian government.

The second half of the Traoré regime was characterised by growing economic hardship and increasingly outspoken opposition. The short-term economic improvements brought about after the Keita years were, by the beginning of the 1980s, negated by an inflated bureaucracy and widespread government corruption. Pressure from external organisations such as the IMF and World Bank forced Traoré to make economic reforms. Mali abandoned the Mali Franc and was readmitted to the West African Monetary Union in 1984 and privatisation programmes and a (half-hearted) war against corruption and embezzlement were initiated. To make matters worse, low levels of rainfall in 1984 caused drought across most of the country. Human rights and civil liberties were also pushed on to the agenda when President Mitterand linked foreign aid to democratisation in 1990. Until now, protests against the Traoré regime had been due largely to economic grievances brought about by the government's austerity measures (its failure to pay employees was a common gripe). By mid-1990, however, pro-democracy movements were starting to form. At the beginning of 1991, students, trade unionists and other pro-democracy campaigners took to the streets, and for the next three months protests were more or less ongoing. Finally, between March 22 and 24 Traoré used military force to suppress a demonstration in Bamako, killing 106 protestors and injuring many more. A day later, on the night of March 25, Traoré was overthrown in a *coup d'état* led by Lieutenant Colonel Amadou Toumani Touré.

Amadou Toumani Touré

The strength and momentum of the pro-democracy movement dispelled any thoughts that Touré and his supporters might have had of replacing the Traoré regime with yet another military government. Threatened with continued violent protests and the suspension of Western aid if democracy was not restored, the Comité de Transition Pour le Salut du Peuple (CTSP) was established in March 1991 to prepare for the transition to a democratically elected civilian government. In the meantime, Touré served as the country's third president.

Other than the call for democracy, the most pressing political issue inherited by the provisional government was a **Tuareg revolt** which had broken out in the north in 1990. Economic difficulties in Algeria and Libya had resulted in the repatriation of thousands of Malian Tuareg, who had taken refuge in these countries during the 1970–4 drought. In the late 1980s they returned to Mali, many of the younger men now possessing military skills and arms provided by the Libyans. Tuareg and Maure groups began attacking the Malian army along the Mali–Mauritania border in early 1990, organising themselves into various freedom movements calling for the independence of the Azaouâd, a large area of desert north of Timbuktu. A peace accord was negotiated by President Traoré at the Algerian town of Tamanrasset in January 1991 which, amongst other concessions, included the creation of the autonomous region of Kidal, but attacks by Tuareg splinter groups continued despite the accord. President Touré worked hard to bring the revolt to an end, involving other countries such as Algeria, Mauritania and France in the peace negotiations. Finally, the National Pact was signed in April 1992 between the government and the Mouvement des Fronts Unis de l'Azaouad (MFUA), an umbrella organisation containing four smaller groups all fighting for the independence of Azaouâd. However, although the National Pact would eventually provide the basis for a lasting peace, violence and banditry continued throughout 1992 and 1993. In response, sedentary populations in the north started to group themselves into ethnically-based self-defence militias to combat the Tuareg threat and protect their own interests. The most important of these militias was the Songhay-dominated *Ganda Koy* (Masters of the Land), which enjoyed the sympathy of the Malian army. At this stage, the situation could have escalated into a full-scale civil war. However, dialogue continued, and by 1995 all sides were working to find a peaceful solution. A process of disarmament was gradually set in motion, while at the same time the Tuareg – and other ethnic groups in the north – started to be integrated into the civilian and military arms of the government, according to the provisions of the 1992 National Pact. The end of the revolt was celebrated by the symbolic burning of weapons in the Flame of Peace at Timbuktu on March 27 1996 (see page 238).

Alpha Oumar Konaré

The Tuareg problem was still far from being resolved when presidential elections were held in April 1992 and Alpha Oumar Konaré became the country's first democratically elected president in over 30 years. Meanwhile, the outgoing President Touré had won widespread popularity and respect for handing over power to a civilian government and for his efforts in resolving the Tuareg problem. Konaré himself was formerly a teacher, with degrees in history and archaeology; his party, the Alliance pour la

Démocratie au Mali (ADEMA), was born out of the pro-democracy forces which had toppled the Traoré regime.

The problems facing Konaré at the start of his presidency were nothing new: a bloated bureaucracy, protests by civil servants, trade unionists and students for better pay, conditions and guaranteed state employment after graduation, a large foreign debt and a weak private sector. There was also the spectre of Moussa Traoré to deal with. The former dictator's trial began in November 1992, and in February 1993 he was condemned to death for his role in the deaths of the 106 protesters in Bamako nearly two years earlier. Konaré commuted this sentence to life imprisonment in November 1997, but a second trial – this time for embezzlement – resulted in a second death sentence in January 1999. As a last gesture, only days before stepping down from his presidential seat in June 2002, Konaré pardoned and liberated Traoré, which was very much in line with general opinion.

The Association des Elèves et des Etudiants du Mali (AEEM) had become the most powerful and intransigent of the student interest groups which were demanding increased grants and improved conditions, and rioting in 1993 and 1994 brought down Konaré's first two prime ministers, Younoussi Touré and Abdoulaye Sékou Sow (a 50% devaluation of the CFA franc in January 1994 also contributed to Sow's departure). In February 1994 Ibrahim Boubacar Keita was appointed to the post and quickly gained a reputation as a 'hawk', arresting all of AEEM's leaders and initiating rigorous post-devaluation austerity measures.

Presidential and legislative elections in 1997 secured Konaré a second five-year presidential term and confirmed ADEMA as Mali's dominant political party. However, these elections were poorly organised and widely boycotted by opposition parties, marking the beginning of a political stalemate between ADEMA and the radical opposition, who organised themselves into the Collectif des Partis de l'Opposition (COPPO) in November 1997 and boycotted subsequent municipal elections in June 1998 and May and June 1999.

Despite Konaré's internal problems – which were relatively trivial in the greater scheme of African politics – his government enjoyed a significant amount of goodwill from Western countries. Konaré proved to be a generally co-operative leader, who made an effort to reform the economy and was, after all, one of Africa's very few democratically elected rulers.

ATT: soldier for democracy

During the 2002 presidential elections, Mali showed the world that it understands the meaning of democracy. For one, Konaré never disputed the constitutionally determined limit of two full terms; he stepped down peacefully in May 2002. In the meantime, no less than 24 candidates had stepped forward as presidential candidates – one of whom was a woman. Eventually the field narrowed down to two candidates: Soumaïla Cissé – member of the ruling ADEMA party and considered favourite – and a surprising opposition candidate, former transitional president General Amadou Toumani Touré. The latter, affectionately called 'ATT' by the Malians, had spent the ten years of Konaré's presidency working as a benefactor in the humanitarian sector, and he was highly appreciated for his integrity. His return to politics came as a surprise, especially since ATT refused to side with any political party, although there were many to choose from. When it came down to the last poll, most of the opposition candidates, support groups and even incumbent president Konaré – despite belonging to the ADEMA party – supported ATT. The popular outsider, whose lack of personal ambition had gained him the other nickname of 'soldier for democracy', won 68% of the votes.

ATT started his term with powerful promises; he pledged to improve the economy and to promote social housing, education and jobs for the young. At the same time he moved carefully, leaving most of Konaré's government intact and aiming to unite the Malians in a politically stable environment. It was ATT's decision to implement strict IMF-supported reforming programmes that caused a first ripple in the calm waters of the political system. However, two years down the road with ATT, the Malian economy is performing surprisingly well, despite difficult circumstances. And even though unemployment is still soaring, about 35,000 jobs for the young have actually been created, while the housing programme is also yielding success with new residential areas popping up around Bamako and other towns.

Outsiders claimed that ATT would soon lose the popularity he had gained during Konaré's presidency. So far they have been proved wrong, as ATT continues to enjoy the support of the majority of Malians. Internationally, in September 2003 he earned a high standing for the Malian contribution to the liberation of 14 European hostages who had been held captive by terrorists in Algeria. The IMF, meanwhile, continues to praise and support Mali's achievements. It seems that ATT will continue to gently lead Mali through social and economic reforms.

ECONOMY

Mali's economy is heavily based on **agriculture**, which accounts for 43% of the country's GDP and occupies the lives of more than 80% of the population. Most people are engaged in subsistence agriculture, cultivating millet, sorghum, rice, corn (maize) and, to a lesser extent, potatoes, yams and cassava, to meet their own needs. Until the mid-1960s Mali was self-sufficient in these crops, but a combination of restrictive agricultural policies and drought made the country increasingly dependent on food imports and handouts. A return to food self-sufficiency was made a government priority in the 1970s and, thanks to agricultural reforms and adequate rainfall, the production of subsistence crops gradually recovered during the late 1980s and, by 1990, food self-sufficiency had been restored. The main export crops are cotton, rice, groundnuts and, to a lesser extent, sugarcane, tobacco and tea. The most productive agricultural area is along the banks of the River Niger between Bamako and Mopti and extends south into the region of Sikasso. The Office du Niger (see page 131), where most of the country's rice is produced, is in the region of Ségou. **Livestock** is also of great commercial importance and, with the exception of Nigeria, no other country in West Africa raises as many goats, sheep and cattle. Mali is also one of West Africa's largest producers of fish.

Industry is considerably less important than agriculture to Mali's economy, accounting for only 14% of the country's GDP. Food processing and the refining of agricultural products such as cotton and sugarcane are probably the most important industrial concerns. Mining is also growing in importance, although it remains marginal. Gold accounts for about 80% of mining activity (the largest mine is at Sadiola in the region of Kayes), while other resources such as salt (at Taoudenni), marble and kaolin (at Bafoulabé), and limestone (at Diamou) are exploited in relatively small quantities. Although iron ore is also widespread, it is not exploited due to Mali's limited infrastructure. Meanwhile, the construction of dams at Markala, Sotuba, Sélingué, Félou and Manantali have led to an increase in the role played by hydro-electric power.

Malian **trade** is dominated by the export of cotton and gold, which together account for 80% of the country's export revenue; livestock, dried and smoked fish and groundnuts are the other main exports. Much of this trade is with neighbouring West African countries, Italy and Thailand. However, despite being the largest producer of cotton in West Africa (West Africa itself is the third largest cotton producer in the world), Mali has always suffered large trade deficits as it imports food, textiles, machinery and petrol, mainly from Côte d'Ivoire and France.

Despite the fact that ATT's reform programme puts an emphasis on improving the economy, the conditions are not favourable. He may have started his term with figures that were on the rise – some sources estimate that the GDP went up by hundreds of US$ per capita in 2002 – but they soon plummeted again to where they came from: around a pitiful US$300. Two major causes can be pinpointed, and the first one is no stranger to Mali. As the economy is largely based on agriculture, one season of drought can make all the difference between a good harvest and a famine. In this respect, 2003 was not a good year. A second cause for concern is the lasting crisis in Côte d'Ivoire, which means that Mali has no access to the ecomically important port of Abidjan. With no obvious alternative, international trade has been hit hard. To a certain degree it could be said that the optimistic 2002 figures were also positively affected by a one-off event: the CAN2002.

Mali after CAN2002

In 2002, Mali hosted the pan-African soccer tournament called the *Coupe Africaine des Nations* (CAN2002) or African Cup of Nations. In preparation for the arrival of the continent's finest soccer teams and thousands of supporters, new stadiums were built in Bamako, Ségou, Mopti, Sikasso and Kayes. However, building the sportsgrounds where the Malian Eagles would defend the honour of their country was only the beginning. More facilities were needed to accommodate all the participants and visitors, and obviously Mali wanted to look its best in every possible way, so the five towns that hosted CAN2002 have largely benefited from being a soccer battleground. All five towns have a *Village CAN*, which – like the Olympic village – served as a secluded shelter in the vicinity of the soccer stadium, where participants could relax or prepare for the next game undisturbed. After the tournament, the soccer players left and Malian citizens moved into these newly built villages, which now serve as residential areas for the better off. Also, in these towns the structure and quality of the road system has been greatly improved. Ségou, for example, used to have only one paved road before 2002, but that has changed dramatically. Even some airports have seen considerable improvements, with extended runways or a new terminal building. In Kayes, the airport has been rebuilt altogether. Then there were existing projects which were simply speeded up because of the international attention Mali would get from the tournament. Some monuments were hastily finished and inaugurated, and new out-of-centre bus stations were built so that access to public transport would become easier and the traffic situation within the towns would improve.

While these changes are long-lasting, CAN2002 boosted the economy for only a short period of time, but then life returned to normal. In combination with the negative impact from the crisis in Côte d'Ivoire and the inadequate rainfall in 2003, it was the last straw for some. Many people of enterprise, who had seized the opportunity to set up a business in advantageous economic circumstances, are now struggling to stay afloat, while some of the new hotels and restaurants that mushroomed during CAN2002 have already had to close down .

PEOPLE AND SOCIETY

The many ethnic groups in what is now Mali have all played their part in the country's history, and as such they share a strong Malian identity which, with the exception of the Tuareg, generally takes precedence over their ethnic one. Indeed, although the potential for ethnic rivalries and violence in Mali is great, apart from the Tuareg problem (see page 17) and occasional disputes between sedentary and nomadic people (see page 96) – problems which are ultimately solved by peaceful negotiation – the people get on remarkably well together. This ethnic harmony is often attributed to Mali's most precious asset: **social capital**. This concept is almost the opposite of financial capital and cannot be neatly defined in terms of GNP, GDP or national debt. Instead, social capital relates to cultural, spiritual and human values, where interaction between people is more important than individual wealth. In this way, we can talk about 'rich countries with poor people' and 'poor countries with rich people'; Mali falls into the latter category. Due in part to strong historical ties, but also because of the harsh environment and difficult living conditions, relationships between different sets of neighbours in Mali are based on mutual respect and interdependence. There is a strong sense of both family and community, which transcends clan and ethnic affiliations and, despite depressing economic statistics, makes Mali one of the world's richest countries in human terms.

A crude distinction can be made between ethnic groups where agriculture is the main occupation and those people who are primarily pastoralists. The sedentary people can be divided into three sub-groups: Manding (including Bambara, Malinké, Dioula and Kassonké), Sudanese (including Songhay,

ALI FARKA TOURE: THE AFRICAN BLUESMAN

Ali Farka Touré was born in 1939, his mother's tenth child and the first to survive infancy. Named Ali Ibrahim, he was given the nickname Farka (Donkey) in commemoration of his dead brothers and his own stubborn refusal to die. In 1946 the family moved to the Sahelian town of Niafounké, where Touré still lives today.

Although his family were of noble lineage far removed from the caste of musicians, Touré was drawn to music at an early age and started to play the monocorde (traditional single-string guitar) for fun. He took the decision to make music his life when he saw a performance by the great Guinean guitarist, Keita Fodeba, in 1956. After this, Touré was 'an absolute fool for the guitar', making the transition from the traditional guitar to the Western instrument in no time at all.

Touré made his name in the regional orchestras and troupes which thrived in the post-independence climate of cultural awareness and promotion. In 1968 he made his first trip outside Africa to represent Mali at an international festival of the arts in Sofia, Bulgaria. It was here that he bought his first guitar. In the same year he heard the music of the Mississippi bluesman, John Lee Hooker, for the first time. He was struck by the similarity of Hooker's music to his own. ' I thought he was Malian because of what I heard,' said Touré, who has been dubbed 'the John Lee Hooker of Africa' by European critics. In 1970 Touré took a job as an engineer for National Radio Mali, where he also performed in Radio Mali's orchestra. His international career began in 1975 when, on the advice of a journalist friend, he sent a number of recordings of his radio broadcasts to a record company in Paris. In a matter of months the first Ali Farka Touré album was released.

Touré's most acclaimed work has been produced in collaboration with the UK record label, World Circuit. Look out for titles such as *Ali Farka Touré* (1987), *The River* (1987), *The Source* (1989), the Grammy Award-winning *Talking Timbuktu* (1994) with Ry Cooder, and his latest, *Niafounké* (1999), which was recorded in his home town.

Soninké and Dogon) and Voltaic (including Sénufo, Minianka, Bobo and Mossi). The main nomadic people are the Tuareg and Maures. Meanwhile, the Peul – one of Mali's largest ethnic groups – are nomadic cattle herders in some parts and sedentary farmers in others. To confuse matters further, the Bozo and Somono are neither agriculturists nor pastoralists, but fishermen.

The **Bambara** constitute about 30% of the country's population and dominate socio-political life. As was the case during the time of the old Bambara kingdoms of Ségou and Kaarta (see pages 129 and 260), the modern-day Bambara population stretches from Nioro du Sahel in the west to Nara in the east and extends south towards the Côte d'Ivoire border. The other principal Manding people, the **Malinké**, are the descendants of the Mali Empire whose heartland still lies between Bamako and the Guinean border. The **Songhay** live along the Niger Bend, the **Dogon** on the Dogon Plateau and along the Bandiagara escarpment, while the **Sénufo** and other Voltaic people are found in the southern part of the country.

Arguably, the two proudest ethnic groups – and the ones most easily identifiable for visitors – are the Peul and the Tuareg. The **Peul** are Mali's second largest minority and are found all over the country – but especially in and around the Niger Inland Delta. Noted for their ornate jewellery, the Peul are also physically distinct from other tribes, being tall, thin, light-skinned and often possessing Caucasian rather than negroid facial features. As descendants of the Berbers, the **Tuareg** of northern Mali are also lighter-skinned than the majority of their compatriots and are referred to as 'whites' by them; the Tuareg, however, call themselves *Tamasheq*, after the language they speak. Spread across five different African countries – Algeria, Libya, Mali, Niger and Burkina Faso – there might be as many as 500,000 Tuareg in Mali itself. Until the disruptive influences of the droughts of the 1970s and 80s, Tuareg society was highly organised and run along feudal lines. Woman had – and still have – an important role in the decision-making process, while, historically, black captives have been used as slaves – one of the reasons, perhaps, for the animosity between Mali's Negro majority and the Tuareg (for more about this animosity and its effects, see page 17).

Women in Mali

'Behind every beard you can see the point of a plait'

Manding proverb

Not having the space to launch into an in-depth analysis of the position of women in West African society, I must restrict myself to one or two subjective comments about the remarkable women of Mali. I am on safe ground when I say that Mali's women bear the brunt of the daily workload. Apart from during the wet season when the men tend the fields, the division of labour between the sexes in the country's rural areas seems to be grossly disproportionate. In addition to their childbearing and rearing responsibilities, the daily chores of an average Malian woman might include collecting wood and water, pounding millet, carrying produce to market and selling it. Meanwhile, the men try to earn a living the best way they can, but jobs are in short supply and their days are often spent sitting in the shade, watching and waiting for something to happen. I might be selling the men short, but the capacity, resolve and unflagging good humour of the women are self-evident.

The fact that women are overworked in Mali – as in most other West African societies – is a result of poverty rather than their social status (before the invention of electricity, running water and washing machines, Western women were overworked). Actually, the position of women in Malian families and society as a whole is, in the words of Amadou Hampaté Bâ (see page 28), 'almost divine'. They symbolise peace and harmony, communal decisions are never taken without prior consultation with the mothers of the families and, while children can disobey their fathers, a mother's word is final.

The traditional, symbolic importance of Mali's women is gradually being given political recognition. For example, in September 1997 the new government contained six female ministers, which was apparently a record in Africa. Moreover, in urban areas women are starting to be employed in non-manual jobs as secretaries, clerks and health workers, even if their salaries are often given to husbands and fathers. In rural areas, however, traditional gender roles remain largely intact and women continue to act as the country's 'engine-room'.

LANGUAGE

French is the official language of Mali and is spoken and understood – at least by someone – almost everywhere you go. This can act as either a blessing or a hindrance to travellers. On the one hand, non-francophone Western visitors are more likely to be able to get by in French than in any of the other indigenous African languages spoken in Mali. Conversely, travellers who don't speak any French at all will be at a disadvantage because French is spoken as an *alternative* to English rather than in conjunction with English. Therefore, brush up on your French before coming to Mali – and don't expect people to speak or even understand English.

There are over 30 other spoken languages in Mali. The lingua franca of trade and administration is Bambara or *Bamana*, with about 80% of the population speaking either *Bamana* (standard Bambara) or a Bambara dialect such as *Dyangirte*, *Kalongo*, *Masasi*, *Nyamasa* or *Somono*. Of the other significant languages, the most widely spoken are *Fulfulde* (Peul) – the lingua franca of the Niger Inland Delta – Malinké, Soninké, Songhay and *Tamasheq* (Tuareg).

See *Appendix 1* for a list of useful expressions and words in French and Bambara.

RELIGION

Islam is the dominant religion in Mali, and even the smallest villages possess a mosque. However, although most people are devout and practising Muslims – in other words, they pray regularly and observe Ramadan and other Islamic holidays – Mali is not a slave to its religion and is by no means a 'dry' state (a state where alcohol is prohibited). The infidel visitor should accept and respect religious practices – buses stopping mid-journey so that passengers can pray to Allah at the correct time of day is one which directly affects travellers – but should not be restricted, embarrassed or otherwise inconvenienced by the Malian brand of Islam (not that it is any of our business!).

Islam arrived in West Africa during the first millennium, having been brought across the Sahara by traders from North Africa. Subsequent conversions – either voluntary or imposed by *jihads* (holy wars) – have continued throughout the second millennium, and today about 80% of Malians are Muslim. The majority of these belong to one of the two main Sufi brotherhoods: *Quadiriya* (originating in Baghdad in the 11th century and brought to West Africa in the 15th century) and *Tijaniya* (founded in Fez in the 18th century and popularised by the Tukulor cleric, El Hadj Omar Tall, in the 19th century). While other smaller – and invariably radical – brotherhoods such as the *Hamallists* (see page 13) and the *Wahabiya* have come and gone during the course of the 20th century, attracting clearly-defined sections of society with a particular point to make, the *Quadiriya* and *Tijaniya* have remained the principal groups, the former being strong in the eastern part of the country and the latter popular in the centre and the west.

Before Islam began to filter across the Sahara, the people of the western Sudan were animist. Today, **animism** is still practised by the Bambara, Malinké, Bobo, Songhay, Sénufo, Dogon and other ethnic groups. One of the many consequences of this religious diversity is a bewildering number of names for God, including *Maa* (Bambara), *Irké* (Songhay), *Koulouikière* (Sénufo) and *Amma* (Dogon). It should be mentioned, however, that while animism still exists, Islam is gaining a foothold among animists and conversion rates are high.

Although **Christianity** has also made its mark in Mali, with converts amongst the Bobo and Dogon, for example, it remains a relatively minor religion. This might not seem the case given that most sizeable towns possess a *Mission Catholique* and, in a more restricted area, some form of Protestant representation. These missions, however, are far more important for their social and economic influence than their doctrinal clout.

THE ARTS
Music
Traditional music
The Mande people of Mali, Guinea, Senegal and the Gambia have a rich musical heritage. In Mali this tradition can be traced back to the days of Soundiata Keita and the Mali Empire, where *griots* or *jalis* (also spelt '*dyeli*') sang the praises of the kings and noblemen to whom they were attached. Nowadays, *jalis* sing the praises of their *jatiguis*, the wealthy politicians and businessmen who support them with money and gifts, while still performing old songs about Soundiata and other notable figures of Mali's past. In Mande society *jalis* form a caste rather like the minstrels of medieval Europe – not high on the social scale, but respected for their skills as entertainers. They are praise singers and the traditional keepers of oral tradition, which is often conveyed through song and dance. There are two basic styles of **Mande** music in Mali: the **Malinké** and **Bambara** styles. The former is noted for its medium tempo, attractive melodies and engaging vocals, while the latter has a slower tempo with starker and more haunting melodies and vocals. **Wassoulou** music, which has become popular in recent years, has a lot in common with the Bambara style.

In traditional Mande music the men are the musicians, while the women or *jalimusolu* are the singers – and the stars. In the years after independence several praise singers established their reputations. Fanta Sacko was one of the first, with her light, rhythmic melodies and trend-setting songs about love. Her most famous and only recorded song was *Jarabi*, which appeared on the *Anthology of*

Malian Music produced by the Ministry of Information in 1970. She was never paid for this work and retired in the mid-1980s following an overdose of mercury-based skin bleach (many *jalimusolu* associate a pale skin with fame and fortune). Fanta Damba started recording in the 1960s and, unlike Sacko, had a degree of international success, being the first *jalimuso* (singular of *jalimusolu*) to tour Europe. The Ségou-born Damba sang in the Bambara style and was noted for her stark, powerful voice. She retired in 1985. The late Siry Mory Diabaté was another highly-respected *jalimuso* of the earlier generation. More moralistic than praising, she was popular during the Modibo Keita years, but fell out of favour when she failed to sing songs in praise of Moussa Traoré. Many of the newer generation of *jalimusolu* – those who rose to prominence during the 1980s – have now become international stars. Ami Koita broke on to the scene with her 1988 album *Tata Sira* and has subsequently established herself as one of Mali's most successful musical exports. Tata Bambo Kouyaté and Kandia Kouyaté both sing for one of the richest men in Mali, Baba Cissoko, whose hotel lies half-finished on the banks of the River Niger in Bamako. Tata Bambo's most famous song, sung in her characteristically hot, gritty and passionate voice, is *Hommage à Baba Cissoko*, while Kandia's first international release, *Kita Kan*, was in 1999, after years spent as one of Mali's top *jalimuso*.

There are three traditional instruments in Mande music in Mali. The **kora**, a cross between a harp and a lute, is arguably the most recognisable, with its 21 strings (in Senegal and the Gambia there can be up to 25) and large gourd or calabash resonator. Although many of the greatest *kora* players are Gambian or Senegalese in origin, Mali boasts some of its finest exponents in Sidiki Diabaté, his son, Toumani Diabaté, and Batourou Sékou Kouyaté. The **ngoni** is a cross between a guitar and a lute and a forerunner to the banjo. It has three to five strings and, despite being a notoriously difficult instrument to master, is extremely popular in Mali. Tidiane Koné, founder of the Rail Band (see page 27), is one of the country's finest *ngoni* players. The **balafon** is an 18–21-key xylophone with a gourd resonator and is often played by two people – one performing the basic tune while the other improvises. Keletigui Diabaté is arguably Mali's seminal *balafon* player. There are three traditional Mande drums: the **tama** (popular in Senegal and Gambia), the **doundoun** (a large, double-headed drum played with a stick) and the **djembe** (single-headed, goblet-shaped, high-pitched and played with the hands). If you understand French, the website www.djembe.com will tell you everything you ever wanted to know about the *djembe* and its greatest exponents. Non-traditional instruments such as the saxophone, trombone and horn have also been introduced, and the **electric guitar** has become the instrument par excellence of modern Mande music. Mali's great guitarists include the late Bassoumana Cissoko, Zani Diabaté, Baboucar Traoré and Ali Farka Touré (see *Ali Farka Touré: the African Bluesman* on page 22).

Dance bands

The development of Malian music and the international reputation enjoyed by some of its stars today are thanks largely to the dance bands and state-sponsored orchestras which flourished after independence.

Before independence, orchestras in towns such as Kita and Ségou played music strongly influenced by jazz and by Latin and Afro-Cuban sounds. This trend continued after independence, when a number of state-subsidised, regional orchestras and Mali's first national electric dance band, the Orchestre National, were formed. Keletigui Diabaté, the *balafon* virtuoso, was head of the Orchestre National, and under his influence traditional Mande material began to be introduced into the repertoire of the modern electric band – although Cuban dance music remained the biggest influence on Malian music during the 1960s. At the end of the decade Mali's new leader, Moussa Traoré, was keen to promote a return to a more indigenous style of music and several new bands, incorporating traditional Mande music with the popular jazz and Afro-Cuban sounds, were formed. Among the first were Super Biton de Ségou, Super Djata and Kené Star of Sikasso. Meanwhile, National Badema became the official state orchestra, using a mixture of traditional and modern electric instruments. However, the two dominant Malian bands of the 1970s were the Rail Band – formed in 1970, state-sponsored and playing largely Mande songs at their permanent venue in Bamako, the Buffet Hotel de la Gare – and Les Ambassadeurs, formed in 1971, privately-funded and playing many foreign-style pop songs, rumbas, foxtrots and Cuban dance numbers. These two bands were to be the training ground for a number of Mali's biggest stars including Salif Keita (see below) and the Guinean-born Mory Kanté. Sadly, by the end of the 1970s Mali's big bands were in decline. Their best singers had left to pursue solo careers and their funding had been adversely affected by government austerity measures. Although the Rail Band (renamed the Super Rail Band) and Les Ambassadeurs (renamed the Ambassadeurs Internationaux) survived longer than most – indeed, the Super Rail Band is still playing today – Mali's big band era had petered out by the beginning of the 1980s.

Solo artists

Salif Keita is the biggest name in Malian music. His rise to fame is remarkable, not least because he broke down barriers of caste and attitude which would normally have barred the way to a career as a musician. Firstly, he was not born into the caste of *jalis*, but was instead of a higher lineage considered 'above' singing and playing musical instruments. Secondly, as an albino he had to contend with discrimination and fear – Keita trained as a schoolteacher, but bad eyesight and the fact that his appearance frightened the children prevented him from teaching for a living. So he turned to music and was asked to join the Rail Band when it was formed in 1970. He left in 1972 when the Guinean musician, Mory Kanté, supplanted him as lead singer, joining rival group Les Ambassadeurs. Keita remained with Les Ambassadeurs until 1982 when a dispute with another of the group's leading musicians, Kanté Manfila, persuaded him to leave and move to Paris. In 1987 *Soro* was released, putting Salif Keita and Mande music on the world map and becoming one of the biggest-selling African records ever. Meanwhile, musicians who had played with Keita in the past were establishing themselves as solo artists in their own right. **Kasse Mady**, for example, was the lead singer of National Badema before going solo in 1983 and finding great success with the release of *Fode* in 1989.

By the late 1980s, the Mande praise singers faced stiff competition from practitioners of the Wassoulou style of music from southern Mali. Unlike other Mande musicians, the singers of Wassoulou (over 90% of whom are women) are not *jalimusolu* and do not sing songs in praise of patrons. Instead, their subjects are life, love, jealousy, tradition and the position of women in modern-day Malian society. The most successful contemporary Wassoulou singers are **Nahawa Doumbia**, **Sali Sidibé** and **Oumou Sangaré**, whose 1989 release of *Moussoulou* (Women) sold over 200,000 copies.

Cinema

Despite the prevalence of kung-fu movies in cinemas all over the country, Malian film-making enjoys one of the finest reputations in Africa, and **Souleymane Cissé**, born in Bamako in 1940, is one of the leading figures of contemporary African cinema. Trained in the Soviet Union, he returned to Mali in 1969 and started to make films noted for their realism (Cissé prefers to use non-professional actors, who come from the same socio-cultural background as the characters they portray) and social themes emphasising the customs, problems and aspirations of his society. Cissé's films are invariably acknowledged at film festivals around the world, and in 1987 *Yeelen* (The Light) won the Jury's Prize at the Cannes Film Festival. Other Cissé films to look out for include *Den Muso* (The Young Girl), *Baara* (Work) and *Finyé* (The Wind), which depicts student opposition to the Moussa Traoré regime and was, at the time (1983), the most popular Black African film ever shown on French movie screens. Other notable Malian film-makers, some of whom also received their training in the Soviet Union, include Djibril Kouyate, Kalifa Dienta, Cheikh Oumar Sissoko and the former professional footballer, Mahamadou Cissé.

Although **Abderrahmane Sissako** is from Mauritania, his father is Malian and his film, *La vie sur terre* (Life on Earth, 1998), is set in Sokolo in the region of Ségou. The recipient of wide international acclaim, *La vie sur terre* is about the director's return to the town where his father still lives – and his subsequent readjustment to the pace and rhythms of African life (Sissako himself lives in Paris). Nothing much happens during the film, but the images and tableaux of day-to-day life in the Sahel are enchanting and beautiful. If you cannot get to Sokolo – and towns like it – yourself, this film is the next best thing.

Literature

The greatest storytellers in Mali are the *griots* or *jalis*, the keepers of oral history and tradition, who speak or sing their stories – but never write them down. This led the famous historian, diplomat and writer, Amadou Hampaté Bâ (1901–91), who devoted much of his life to translating oral tradition and attempting to put it down on paper, to invent the phrase: '*Un*

THE CAPITAINE'S TABLE

Order fish at a Malian restaurant and it will most likely be *capitaine*. However, this is just the first step, for then you must decide how you want your *capitaine* prepared. You might like to have it fried in breadcrumbs as *croquette de capitaine* or, provided that a banana is added to the dish, *capitaine à la bamakoise*. Grilled or barbecued is another option, with a simple *brochette de capitaine* consisting of huge chunks of fish speared on to a skewer and cooked over an open fire being a popular choice. A variety of sauces await the more discriminating palate. *Capitaine au beurre blanc* and *capitaine à la sauce moutarde* should both be self-explanatory: butter and mustard-based sauces respectively. *Capitaine à l'Africaine* is the more ambiguous name for a tomato sauce, while *capitaine à la sauce aurore* or 'daybreak sauce' is a tomato sauce with a splash of crème fraîche. For something even more exotic, try *capitaine papillot* (the French verb 'papilloter' means 'to twinkle'), which involves cooking the fish in vegetable soup before wrapping it in aluminium foil and roasting it on a fire.

vieillard qui meurt, c'est une bibliothèque qui brûle' ('When an old man dies, it is as if a library burns down'). This has not prevented many authors writing about Mali and giving their own versions of what went on in days gone by. (Almost all of the literature is in French rather than Bambara and other indigenous languages.) The most famous novel written by a Malian is *Le devoir de violence* (Bound to Violence) by Yambo Ouologuem. Covering the centuries since the Mali Empire, Ouologuem describes in every detail the crimes of violence and debauchery committed, not by Europeans and other foreign invaders as is the normal position of many African novelists, but by the Africans themselves. *Le devoir de violence* won the coveted French literary award, the Prix Renaudot, in 1968, but subsequent studies of the book have revealed close similarities between some of its passages and those of other works written by different authors – including Graham Greene's *It's a Battlefield*. Published a few years earlier, another well-known book, *Les bouts de bois de dieu* (God's Bits of Wood) by Ousmane Sembene, presented the railwaymen of the Dakar–Bamako railway in the more conventional role of good and virtuous Africans struggling to preserve and protect their culture from the onslaught of Western imperialism.

The other eminent writers of Mali are a mixture of novelists, poets, historians, anthropologists, politicians etc. There is Maryse Condé, for instance, whose historical novel *Segu* (1987) is about the social forces and conflicts at work during the apogee of the Bambara kingdom of Ségou, which is considered to be in the same league as Ouologuem and Sembene's efforts. There is also Massa Makan Diabaté, with his satirical tales about daily life in the small village of Kouta; Moussa Konaté, the highly regarded author of *Le prix de l'âme* (1981); and the politician-poet, Fily Dabo Sissoko, with his *Poèmes d'Afrique noire* (1963). Malian literature might not be as famous as the country's music, but it is certainly worth a look (there are English translations of *Le devoir de violence*, *Les bouts de bois de dieu* and *Segu*).

FOOD AND DRINK
Traditional dishes
'Do you have any Malian specialities?'
'Yes, rice.'
The manager of Hotel Lac Débo in Bamako was neither overstating nor underselling his nation's cuisine. Alimentation in Mali is heavily based on cereals – not only rice, but also millet and *fonio*. In most families rice is eaten at lunchtimes, and couscous or *tô* is served in the evenings. Couscous in Mali is made from millet rather than semolina, as is common in North Africa, while *tô* is moist, millet-based dough with a consistency similar to plasticine. *Fonio* is a variety of millet with very fine grains. Travelling around Mali, your diet will consist mainly of rice (Senegalese-style *riz au gras* or fried rice is popular and tasty), couscous, spaghetti, macaroni and bread; *fonio* and *tô* are less commonly served in restaurants.

If you want meat with your meal, it will probably be chicken (stringy and chewy) or mutton. Goat and beef are also eaten, while frog's legs are sometimes available in Bamako and the odd camel dish sporadically crops up on restaurant menus in the desert areas. *Capitaine* is the most common freshwater fish and is prepared in a variety of styles (see *The Capitaine's Table*, page 29).

The sauce is what makes – or breaks! – a traditional Malian meal. *Sauce d'arachide* (peanut sauce) is arguably the most typical. Served with rice, this sauce is made from a peanut butter-like paste which is dissolved in water and cooked with oil, a few tomatoes and onions. Results can vary, but it is usually pretty tasty and rarely inedible. The same is not necessarily true for *gumbo*, a thick, green sauce made with okra pods, which is commonly served with *tô*, a rather solid porridge made from pounded millet. Popular in Dogon country, the colour and consistency of this meal – which should be eaten with your fingers – may be as significant as its musty taste in deterring a second try. On the other hand, you might love it. Experiment! *Saga-saga* is another typical sauce which is made with manioc or cassava leaves. In Songhay country there is *fakoye* (lamb with herbs) and *algafta* – a Songhay Scotch egg – while the Tuareg speciality is *alabadja* – white rice mixed with minced meat and soaked in a butter sauce. These regional dishes – and others like them – might be available in one or two restaurants specialising in African cuisine, but are by no means as widespread as *riz au gras*, *sauce d'arachide* and couscous.

International cuisine
'International cuisine' can mean different things depending on where you are in the country. In Bamako there are restaurants serving food from all over the world: French, Italian, Chinese, Indian, Lebanese etc. In other towns, however, where restaurants tend to be less sophisticated, 'international cuisine' may

involve no more than a pile of spaghetti and a scrawny chicken leg. In Bamako there are also several excellent *pâtisseries* serving cakes, pastries and croissants. The French influence is equally apparent in the quality of the bread, which, although it varies from town to town, is consistently high. In Timbuktu the bread is baked in distinctive clay furnaces and has a sandy texture. Finally, a wide range of imported food products is available in the larger supermarkets in Bamako. These are mainly from France and are expensive.

Fruits and vegetables

It stands to reason that exotic fruits and vegetables do not exactly thrive in a dry, land-locked country such as Mali. Having said this, however, a surprising range of produce grows along the banks of the River Niger, and the Malians have become adept at getting the most out of semi-arid land. Moreover, thanks to the railway and paved road linking the remote western and eastern parts of the country to Bamako and the fertile south, fruit and vegetables are available almost everywhere – although in places such as Timbuktu the choice is often limited to sour oranges and withering tomatoes.

The fruits on offer are either grown locally or imported from nearby Côte d'Ivoire. The aforementioned oranges are widely available, while bananas, papayas, pineapples and mangoes are found in many of the larger markets. The mangoes are grown in Sikasso and deserve special mention – if only for their remarkable size.

Many of the riverside gardens produce potatoes, onions, carrots, tomatoes, cucumbers, aubergines, beetroots, cauliflowers and lettuce. If you don't see vegetables in their own right in a Malian dish, it is possible that they have been used to make the accompanying sauce.

Drinks

The globally ubiquitous soft drinks such as Coca Cola, Fanta and Sprite are widely available in Mali. The local brand, D'jino, comes in several flavours and, despite being described as 'juice', is as fizzy and sweet as its foreign counterparts. Freshly squeezed juices are not as common nor as exotic as you might expect. Orange juice is probably the most widespread, although other flavours such as lime and pineapple are not unheard of. Cold milk sold in sachets is also popular. Bottled water can be found all over the country, Diago and Tombouctou being two of several brands. Opt for water sold in sealed bottles rather than the stuff sold on the streets in polythene bags, the origins of which are dubious.

One of the most thirst-quenching of the local specialities on offer is *djablani*, sold on virtually every street corner in the country. Often flavoured with *bissap* (the red variety of *djablani*, made from hibiscus), ginger, or the fruit of the baobab tree, these small polythene bagfuls of juice are boiled before being frozen and are therefore generally safe to drink. Moreover, at CFA25 a time, there is no cheaper way to take the edge off your thirst. Served mainly in restaurants and homes, *jijimbere* and *crème de miel* are two other popular drinks:

the former is made with water, crushed ginger, lemon juice, sugar and mint leaves, while the latter contains ginger, lemon and honey and slightly resembles a milkshake. Tea, especially in Tuareg country, is an institution. It is served sweet and strong (one cupful of sugar for one cupful of tea), and the pot is filled three times. The first cup is said to be '*fort comme la mort*' ('strong as death'), the second is '*doux comme la vie*' ('mild as life') and the third is '*sucré comme l'amour*' ('sweet as love'). If you are served a fourth cup from the same pot, it means that you are not welcome.

Despite Mali being an Islamic country, alcohol is not prohibited. The locally-produced, bottled beer, Castle, is perfectly drinkable, while *dolo* (the Dogon name), *tchapulo* (the Bambara name) or *bière de mil* (millet beer) is the preferred tipple of the country's rural population. Mali also produces whisky, sold in Kleenex-sized sachets in selected bars around the country, and imported beer, wine and spirits are available in the larger supermarkets in Bamako.

Silk-cotton trees flowers

Natural History and the Environment

TOPOGRAPHY
Plateaux and plains

Despite being generally flat, Mali is better known for its highland areas of sandstone mountains and plateaux limited by steep escarpments. The most famous is the **Dogon Plateau** which rises eastwards from the Niger Valley and ends abruptly in cliffs known as the **Bandiagara escarpment**. These cliffs run southwest to northeast, cutting a 200km swath through central Mali and reaching heights of about 350m. Continuing east, some of the country's most dramatic landscape – including unusual rock formations and Mali's highest point, Hombori Tondo (1,155m) – is found in the **Hombori Mountains**. Other highland areas tend to be extensions of larger mountain ranges to the south and east. For instance, the **Manding Mountains** are an extension of the Fouta Djallon highlands in Guinea and stretch from the Guinean border to within a few kilometres east of Bamako, while the series of small, broken hills in the region of Sikasso are the remnants of the Guinea Highlands to the south. The Bambouk Mountains reach their westward limit below the town of Kayes, where the **Tambaoura escarpment** runs parallel to the Senegalese border. In the desert, the heavily eroded sandstone plateau called **Adrar des Ifôghas** is part of the Hoggar mountain system and has a valley called **Tîlemsi** running along its western edge for some 275km.

The rest of Mali is flat – sometimes very flat. Put a tennis ball on the **Tanezrouft**, a vast plain of bare rock stretching across the Malian and Algerian Sahara, and often it will be the only object visible on the horizon. South of the Tanezrouft and north of Timbuktu the **Azaouâd** and **Timétrine** arc sandy plains which are drier than the Sahel, but not as arid as the desert. In contrast to the north, much of central Mali is covered by the fertile **floodplains** of the River Niger.

Rivers

The **River Niger** rises in the Fouta Djallon highlands in Guinea and flows for 4,200km through four West African countries before emptying into the Gulf of Guinea on the Nigerian coast. The river traverses Mali for about 1,700km, literally bringing life to a country with no coastline and a negligible amount of rainfall. All along its banks fruit and vegetables are grown, in certain areas rice is cultivated, and the 20,000km^2 Niger Inland Delta is the largest reservoir of freshwater fish in West Africa. The river

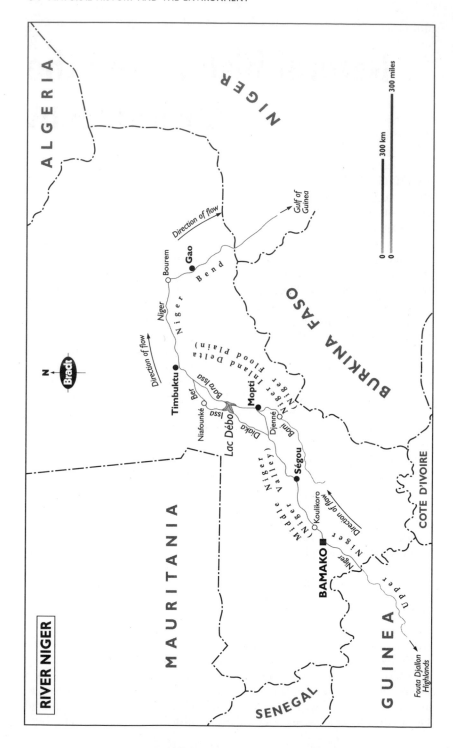

also provides a vital means of communication, linking remote desert towns such as Timbuktu to the rest of the country. Perhaps this is why the name 'Niger' is derived from the Berber word, '*gber-n-igheren*', meaning 'river of rivers'. Other names for the Niger, depending on whom you ask, include: *Djoliba* (Bambara), *Mayo* (Peul) and *Issa Ber* (Songhay). Entering Mali near the town of Kangaba, the Niger flows northeast across the Manding Mountains and passes Bamako before spreading out in a wide valley just beyond the town of Koulikoro. Continuing northeast, after Ségou the Niger forms a vast **inland delta** of channels, streams and lakes – the combined effect of the extremely flat land and the river's almost non-existent descent. The Niger then receives its main tributary, the **River Bani**, at Mopti. Beyond Timbuktu, the river's course changes from a northeasterly to an easterly direction and then bends dramatically to the southeast at the town of Bourem. It continues to flow in this direction and passes Gao on its way to the Niger border at Labézanga. The River Niger is navigable for larger craft during its high-water period between about July and January. The upper Niger is the first to rise (July–October), then the inland delta (September–November) and finally the Niger Bend (December–January).

Mali's other great river, the **River Senegal**, is formed by the confluence of the rivers **Bafing** and **Bakoye** at the town of Bafoulabé. It flows in a northwesterly direction for 900km, following the border between Senegal and Mauritania before emptying into the Atlantic Ocean at the Senegalese town of St-Louis. The river is at its highest between about July and October.

Sahara, Sahel and savanna

The majority of the surface area of Mali is taken up by desert and semi-arid land known as the Sahel, while in the southern areas there are subtropical savanna grasslands.

The Sahara is the world's largest desert. Roughly speaking, it extends from the Atlantic Ocean to the Red Sea and the Mediterranean Sea to the River Niger, occupying a total area of some seven million km^2. The Malian Sahara extends north from the latitude of the Niger Bend and is characterised by extensive plains and *ergs* or shifting 'seas' of sand which make up about 28% of the total area of the Sahara. This is one of the hottest regions in the world and, despite the presence of a small nomadic population, one of the most inhospitable. The Sahel occupies an area between the Niger Bend and a line linking the towns of Bandiagara and Kayes – although recent desertification (see page 44) has blurred this boundary. The Sahel is a transitional zone of semi-arid desert and thorny scrub: hot and dry – the well-watered floodplain of the River Niger notwithstanding – and susceptible to periods of drought. The further south of the Bandiagara–Kayes line you go, the less Sahelian the landscape becomes. These are Mali's savanna lands, where the climate is more humid, the landscape greener and one or two things can actually grow.

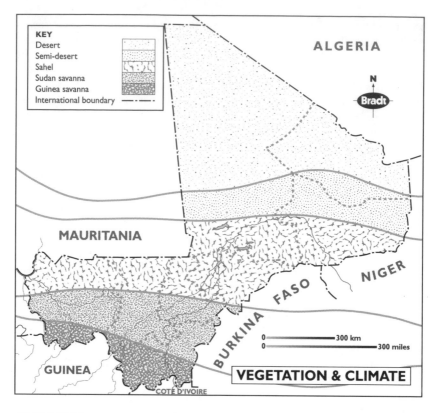

CLIMATE

with Lyn Mair

Hot, dry and dusty are the three words that accurately sum up the weather for most of Mali for most of the year. This weather pattern is governed by the Inter-Tropical Convergence Zone, ITCZ, which affects the weather of the entire tropical zone of Africa. The ICTZ, a low pressure zone, oscillates north and south annually following the sun but lagging behind by about five weeks. Warm and moist winds from the Atlantic are drawn in to the low pressure area when the ICTZ lies over the Tropic of Cancer around the northern summer solstice. Mali receives its rainfall from this wind between June and October, the **rainy season**. The southwestern part of the country has an annual rainfall of over 1,000mm accompanied by high temperatures and humidity. The effect of this weather system diminishes eastwards, and the further east, the less precipitation (rainfall) there is. Timbuktu has an average annual rainfall of only 200mm. During this period Mali is at its greenest; the rivers are high, the lakes full and the country as lush as it ever is.

During the months of November to June, the **dry season**, when the ICTZ moves south, the first wind to blow is the alize from the northeast. From December to February this wind brings a relatively cool spell, dropping temperatures to around a comfortable 25°C. For this reason the traditional

tourist season is between these months – in other words, the European winter. From about March to June the hot, dry, dusty Harmattan blows in from the east drawing in the dust of the Sahara, raising temperatures, eliminating humidity and turning much of the country into a dust bowl. Indeed, dust is a major inconvenience when travelling in Mali. The Sahara generates an estimated 300 million tonnes of dust a year (60% of the total global production), and much of it is blanketed across West Africa by the Harmattan. Bear this in mind when you choose your travel dates as dust can cause health problems, irritate contact-lens wearers and reduce the quality of photographs.

Temperatures in Bamako are usually at their coolest in August (21–31°C). The same is generally true for everywhere else in the country. The town of Kayes is considered to be the hottest in Africa, with temperatures occasionally rising to a sticky 50°C. The desert can be unbearable during the hotter months, although during the cooler months temperatures at night can fall dramatically (5°C is not unheard of in Timbuktu). Meanwhile, the coolest part of the country is in the south, in the region of Sikasso, where the maximum temperatures rarely exceed the high 30s.

BIODIVERSITY
Lyn Mair
Vegetation
So much of Mali's natural vegetation has been lost to agriculture of one sort or another, but odd patches of woodland and some fine old trees can still be found here and there. Much of the grassland is fast vanishing to the herds of grazing cattle and goats. Increased desertification is also playing a role in this respect.

In the extensive desert regions of northern Mali, the true Sahara, plant life is extremely sparse, if not non-existent except around oases. However, as one approaches the Sahel with its scant rainfall, scrubby bushes and tough, hardy drought-resistant palms and trees can be seen.

Many plants growing in such harsh conditions develop clever mechanisms to prevent loss of water and to retain whatever small amount comes along. Leaves are generally very small and will sometimes turn the thin edge to face the sun to avoid excess moisture loss; fine hairs act as an insulating layer as they cover the leaf surface.

Most of the trees do not have common names but I will mention a few that can be found in specific areas.

The **Doum palm**, *Hyphaene thebaica*, the only palm with a branching trunk, is common around Djenne and other dry areas. The long straight trunks are often used in the construction of mud buildings, and can be seen poking out of the walls.

Within the **Caesalpiniaceae** family, *Bauhinia rufescens*, with its tiny bilobed leaves and blackish twisted seed pods that remain on the tree for ages, is commonly seen in the Bandiagara region. Both Alexandrian and Italian senna, *Cassia senna* and *C. italica*, are to be found in the Timbuktu region. The

KARITÉ BUTTER
Lyn Mair

Karité butter, also known as shea butter, is produced from the karité tree. It was formerly known as *Butyospermum paradoxum parkii* but with the latest taxonomical divisions it is now called *Vitellaria paradoxa*. The trees can be seen growing along the road between Bamako and Segou and are especially common around the small village of Zantiguila. Karité trees have a dense crown of dark-green foliage and if it looks as though the trees have been trimmed in a neat line a metre and a half from the ground, this is in fact the goat and cattle browse line, as the animals like eating the leaves. The trees produce dark-brown, oil-rich nuts, which are gathered and processed by women and children. In fact this is often an important part of a woman's livelihood.

The nuts are stored in pits to preserve them and to prevent animals from eating them. When a sufficient amount has accumulated, a fire is lit at the base of a mud oven and the nuts are placed on top where they slowly roast. These ovens or kilns are often seen along the roadsides. Then the process of extracting the oil begins as the nuts are pounded with a little water and placed in enormous cauldrons and cooked over an open fire. They have to be stirred and watched carefully to prevent burning. The dark chocolatey-looking mixture soon begins to ooze a rich oil, which is ladled out and re-boiled to remove impurities. When cool it is a soft creamy colour and has the consistency of butter, and is known as either karité (pronounced *karitee*) or shea butter.

In many of the markets butter-balls the size of small tennis balls are piled up in enamel basins for sale, but the majority of the butter is collected and exported to France to be used in the cosmetic industry in lotions and soap. Locally, the karité butter is used for cooking, as well as being used as a skin cream and for keeping the Fulani girls' hair smooth and supple, especially when decorated with those lovely flat amber beads. There is a soap factory in Koulikoro, and the luxurious soap produced there can be found in some upmarket shops in Bamako.

Alexandrian senna is an undershrub with zigzag branchlets and upright spikes of bright yellow flowers.

Within the **Mimosaceae** family, **acacias**, with tiny leaves and thorns or prickles to protect them against browsing animals, are one of the most widespread plant families found in the Sahelian region. *Acacia senegal*, found around Timbuktu, is a small tree up to 7m tall, with a grey fissured bole, yellow peeling twigs and fragrant spikes of fluffy cream flowers.

In the Bandiagara region you may notice *Acacia pennata*, a scrambling and prickly shrub with little balls of white flowers.

Albizia species are also part of this family and the tallish, flat-crowned tree is distinctive and widespread. Like the other mimosas the leaves are composed of many tiny leaflets. *A. chevalieri* with its crimson flowers can be seen around Djenne.

Still with the Mimosaceae, there is a historically interesting tree that belongs to this family named after Mungo Park, the great 18th-century explorer. One of the most common savanna trees in Mali is the locust bean *Parkia biglobosa*; it has a spreading crown with orangey red flowers, and animals love the nutritious seeds that look like little balls on the end of a string.

There is also the Karité tree with many names; it produces Karité or Shea butter. The old name *Butyospermum paradoxum parkii* has been changed to *Vitellaria paradoxa* (see box opposite).

Bombacaceae family members are usually very large and distinctive trees with showy flowers. One of the most characteristic trees of the drier areas is the **baobab**, *Adansonia digitata*; the name comes from the Arabic 'bu-hibab' meaning the fruit with many seeds. The huge wide trunk is a purplish coppery colour with branches, usually bare of leaves, haphazardly reaching up to the sky. In optimum conditions the girth can reach monstrous proportions of up to 28m in circumference, although it will only grow to between 15 and 18m in height, making it a tree of squat proportions. It is very soft and fibrous and quite useless for furniture making. The bark is pounded to make rope and coarse fabric for floor mats. The large white waxy flowers, which turn brown when they drop, are thought to be pollinated by bats.

The velvety-looking seed pods are at least 12cm long and the seeds are embedded in white powdery pulp containing large quantities of tartaric acid. They are refreshing to suck and make a palatable drink, and when dry they make lovely baby rattles. It is said that many of the larger baobabs have reached an incredibly old age. Original carbon dating estimated that the oldest tree was about three thousand years old. More recent estimates put some of the older trees at a mere 800 years. Whatever, they do live for a very long time, which is perhaps why baobabs are thought to be tightly connected to the spirit world, and there are many folkloric tales throughout Africa about the importance of these strange and magnificent trees. In fact, as you travel through the drier areas you may find most of the natural vegetation removed except for a baobab standing as a lone representative of what was once a more wooded region.

Still within the general family is the red silk cotton, *Bombax ceiba*, also known as *Bombax malabaricum*. This is a tree native to tropical Asia, which has been extensively grown all over the drier parts of west Africa. It is a lovely tree with big red to orange flowers, which appear when there are no leaves; it reaches a height of about 15m and is found in the Koulikoro district.

One of the most spectacular trees in all of western Africa is the silk cotton or kapok tree, *Ceiba pentandra* (*fromager* in French), which can be found in the slightly moister regions of Guinea savanna in the southern part of Mali. This magnificent tree can reach the lofty heights of over 60m and has enormous sprawling buttress roots for extra support. The young trees have sharp prickles on the trunk, which diminish with age; the large flowers are white and appear on the leafless branches. The elliptical fruits are full of silken floss, which blows on the wind.

Another distinctive family is the **Papilonaceae** or pea family, and included in this group are the 75 species and 200 subspecies of **indigofera** or indigo plants. They are mostly low, shrubby little trees or bushes with red or pink pea-shaped flowers, and they grow in the sub-arid zones. Indigo dye, which comes from the *Indigofera tinctoria* species, is used extensively in the Bandiagara region and in Djenne, where cloth is woven and made into clothes and blankets. In the same large family are the lovely **erythrina** trees, sometimes known as lucky bean or coral trees. There are many species of this tall tree of the drier savanna, the two most common being *E. vogelii* and *E. senegalensis*. In November and December the scarlet cones of flowers make a strong contrast to the generally brown countryside between Bamako and Segou, in the patches of dry deciduous forest. The trees are in flower when there are no leaves present and later in the season the twisted seed pods are full of small, shiny, hard, red and black beans. The trees grow rapidly from cuttings and are very important in folkloric beliefs and traditions.

The **Moraceae**, or fig and mulberry, family contains large numbers of fruiting trees, the figs in particular. There are over 60 **ficus** species in West Africa and it is sometimes very difficult to separate them. They are usually large and sprawling with dark green, leathery leaves and a pale, smooth bark. The flowers form directly on the bark and therefore the fruits hang on the trunk of the trees. They are much loved by birds and insects, and often the figs, which are edible, are infested with worms and wasps – extra bird food. There are some amazing ficus species on the banks of the Bani River at the Djenne crossing; how they survive with so many exposed roots is a mystery. *Ficus platyphylla* can be found between Mopti and Djenne; the bark is rusty or pinkish and the figs are often pink tinged. *F. abutifolia* is a smaller tree of up to 7m and can be found on the rocky hillsides of the Bandiagara escarpment.

F. sycamorus is a savanna tree with a very large spreading crown growing near rivers. It has a pale yellow bark with yellowish to red figs.

The **Meliaceae** family harbours some of Africa's finest hardwoods and the West African mahogany *Khaya senegalensis* falls into this group. It is a beautiful tree up to 30m tall, with a wide dense crown of shining foliage. An avenue of them lines the Bani River outside the Kanaga Hotel in Mopti.

The arboretum behind the museum in Bamako has a wide selection of trees from all over the country. Sadly the names have worn off most of the labels, but you might be able to guess some of the trees, and it is a great place for a spot of birding as most of the trees are old and well established.

On the road between Bamako and Segou, stands of trees can be seen in close proximity to the villages. These are fast-growing exotic trees from Asia, Gmelina species, and were planted as a source of firewood by the first president after independence.

Termites

Evidence of these amazing little creatures can be seen in many patches of uncleared land. Termites have the most sophisticated systems in place for living, reproducing, feeding themselves and keeping cool! The alates or flying ants that hatch out just after the rain provide food for innumerable birds, animals and even people. The termite mounds are often found in association with specific trees and other plants, and many creatures use the empty holes as homes; snakes, lizards, mongooses, porcupines and even warthogs. After a heavy downpour of rain, the mounds can be worn down to resemble giant mushrooms. Eugene Marais wrote most eloquently about the *Soul of the White Ant* and Joan and Alan Root made a stunning documentary film, *Termites: Castles of Clay*.

Fish

Although Mali is so far inland, many people depend on fish for their protein intake. The great rivers, the Niger and Bani, have an abundant supply of edible and delicious fish, but with the ever-increasing population it remains to be seen how long the fishing industry can be sustained.

The choice fish is the *capitaine* (see box page 29), which can be found in many restaurants and which makes very good eating.

Birds

While Mali is not the region to rush to on a specific birding trip, because of its lack of infrastructure as well as its huge size and inhospitable climate, there are some interesting and important birds among the 655 species recorded here. Mali boasts one endemic bird.

There are six important areas for birding:

- Adrar des Ifôghas on the Algerian border
- Lac Faguibine north of the Niger delta
- Central Niger Delta
- Bandiagara escarpment
- Boucle du Baoule National Park, north of Bamako
- Mandigues Mountains, west of Bamako

Many birds that breed in Europe in the northern summer will migrate to or from more southerly parts of Africa and will stop over in Mali or may even spend the northern winter there. The waterways of the great rivers host huge numbers of Palearctic passage migrants at the end of the European summer and again as they return to the northern hemisphere to breed in spring, as well as all the resident birds. During the southern winter, some species of birds will migrate internally within Africa and spend time in Mali before returning south to breed in the austral spring.

Large concentrations of **waterbirds** move in response to conducive conditions, and sometimes enormous flocks of white-faced whistling duck, *Dendrocygna viduata*, congregate in the central Niger delta together with visitors from Europe, including numerous northern pintail, *Anas acuta*, garganey, *A. querquedula*, and northern shoveller, *A. clypeata*. Hundreds of black kites, *Milvus migrans*, can be seen swirling around the built-up towns on the banks of rivers, brazenly scavenging whatever they can find to eat. Passage migrant raptors, harriers and buzzards also pass over the Sahelian and savanna regions.

The African endemic **Egyptian plover**, *Pluvialis aegyptius*, is a smart little bird that can be seen on the banks of the Bani River around the ferry crossing to Djenne, as well as on the sand banks at the Bani/Niger confluence at Mopti. Its striking grey, black and buff colouring is distinctive.

Another African endemic, the beautiful and small **grey pratincole**, *Glareola cinerea*, is an intra-African migrant and can occasionally be seen in small flocks on large sand banks on quieter parts of the large rivers. Some heron, egret and ibis species are part of the birdlife diversity around the waterways and together with the astonishing array of wading birds, inland gulls and terns make any visit to the rivers worthwhile. Gull-billed terns, *Gelochelidon nilotica*, whiskered terns, *Chlidonias hybridus*, and white-winged terns, *C. leucopterus*, can be seen hawking for insects over the water.

Bee-eaters are amongst the most colourful birds you are likely to see in Mali. The red-throated bee-eater, *Merops bulocki*, and the white-throated bee-eater, *Merops albicollis*, favour grasslands, whereas the little green bee-eater, *Merops orientalis*, is often found in the drier sahel. **Rollers**, too, are very colourful birds with deep blue and turquoise markings. Both the Abyssinian roller, *Coracias abyssinicus*, and the blue-bellied roller, *C. cyanogaster*, are often observed perching on power lines waiting to pounce on insects.

Barbets are chunky, medium-sized and often brightly coloured fruit-eating birds that are generally found in forests, but the yellow-breasted barbet, *Trachyphonus margaritatus*, frequents the dry acacia savanna and desert edge, and can be found in the Niger inland delta.

Larks and **sparrow larks**, typical of the dry, arid belt, are usually cryptically coloured and difficult to spot, though the male sparrow larks have bold black-and-white head markings and a black belly. Migrating and resident **swallows** and **martins** can be seen throughout Mali at certain times of the year. Look out for Preuss's cliff swallow, *Hirundo preusi*, along cliff faces near rivers, especially along the Bandiagara escarpment. **Wheatear** and **wagtail** species migrate through Mali, but the boldly marked African pied wagtail, *Motacilla aguimp*, is resident in southern Mali, and Heuglin's wheatear, *Oenanthe heuglini*, is the only resident or intra-African migrant wheatear in Mali. It has buffy, rufous underparts and frequents degraded savanna, burnt ground and farmland.

One of the most widespread birds in Mali is the **common bulbul**, *Pycnonotus barbatus*, found in every locality, cheerfully and noisily making its presence known. The **tawny flanked prinia**, *Prinia subflava*, a small and vociferous bird, is also widespread, but if you are on the banks of the Niger between Goa and Tillabéri, check the prinias carefully as you may see the very rare **river prinia**, *Prinia fluviatilis*. Another very noisy little bird, common throughout Africa, is the **grey-backed cameroptera**, *Cameroptera brachyura*, that skulks in any vegetation.

The **cricket warbler**, *Spiloptila clamans* (old name scaly-fronted warbler), is a gorgeous little bird with a streaky head and black-and-white markings on the wings. Look out for small parties of them in the dry scrubby vegetation around Djenné-Djeno.

Only two **sunbirds** are likely to be seen in the dry sahelian zones; the pygmy sunbird, *Hedydipna platura*, has a bright yellow belly with long tail streamers and the beautiful sunbird, *Cinnyris pulchellus*, is iridescent green with a red breast bordered with yellow, and long, dark tail streamers. The males are brightly coloured and only maintain the brilliant plumage in the breeding season while the females are much duller at all times. **Sparrows** are represented by the rather dull northern grey-headed sparrow, *Passer griseus*, and the brilliant, tiny Sudan golden sparrow, *Passer luteus*, which lives up to its name.

White-billed buffalo weavers, *Bubalornis albirostris*, build huge, scruffy, communal nests and forage mostly on dry open ground, whereas the **village weaver**, *Ploceus cucullatus*, constructs a very tidy woven nest that can be seen in dense colonies near villages with trees.

The only endemic bird to Mali is the **Kulikoro firefinch**, *Lagonostica virata* (old name Mali firefinch). Its taxonomic status is debatable; in some instances it is variously considered a species of either Jameson's firefinch or blue-billed firefinch. This very small, mostly red bird is found in rocky, grassy areas between Mopti and Bamako.

Accessible places to look for birds
with Philip Briggs

If you are in **Bamako**, go to the arboretum at the back of the museum in Avenue de la Liberté. Here you will find tall mature trees and all sorts of birds from woodpeckers to warblers. There is a fitness track in the arboretum so you are likely to be in the company of plenty of joggers. Many of the trees are labelled, but most of the writing has worn off so you are none the wiser about the identification of the trees. Another good, accessible birding spot is the otherwise dismal zoo in Bamako: the lush woodland between the cages is full of avian life, most vociferously and visibly flocks of cackling Western plantain-eaters.

When in **Timbuktu**, look for blue-naped mousebirds, *Urocolius macrourus*, in the courtyard of the Djingareiber Mosque.

The **Bandiagara escarpment** is really good for birding as there are several habitat types, including cliff faces, some small rivers, grassland and even some woodland. Stop near any bit of natural habitat and you are likely to find something of interest. Yellow-billed shrikes, *Corvinella corvine*, abound, and you are likely to hear the ringing calls of the yellow-crowned gonolek, *Laniarius barbarus* (old name Barbary shrike). Pitch black, fork-tailed drongos, *Dicrurus modestus*, are always seen.

While Djenné cannot be described as a birding spot, the gardens around the **Campement de Djenné** are replete with indigo birds, sunbirds, weavers and even the occasional Kulikoro firefinch.

If you are seriously into birdwatching, *Birds of Western Africa*, a Helm identification guide by Nick Borrow and Ron Demey, is indispensable, although it is rather a heavy book to carry around.

Mammals

With encroaching desertification, increasing herds of cattle and goats, and ever-expanding agriculture, the wildlife of Mali is not doing too well. There are parks and reserves, but hunting is still permitted in certain areas of them. Yet, looking at the folklore of Mali, it is not hard to realise that in years gone by there must have been a fairly rich wildlife here.

There may still be a few **chimpanzees** in southernmost forests while several species of monkey inhabit the Parc National de la Boucle du Baoulé.

Common or golden **jackals** favour the drier regions and can even be found in the vicinity of villages. Jackals are very important in the divination rituals of the Dogon people and they are fairly common in the Bandiagara region; side-striped jackals are more commonly found in wetter areas.

What are left of Mali's lions take refuge in the extreme western *cercle* of Kéniéba around the River Falémé. Cheetahs are extremely rare.

The **elephants** of the Gourma region are justifiably famous. Constituting one of the last remaining Sahelian herds, each year it is estimated that between 360 and 630 elephants undergo a seasonal migration of some 800km (round trip) as they walk north from Burkino Faso in search of water and return south from the lakes and ponds of Gourma after the first rains in June. A visit to the Réserve de Douentza – where most of the elephants are concentrated – is as close as you'll get to a safari in Mali (see *Gourma*, page 201).

Hippos can still be found in certain parts of the Niger, particularly between Gao and Ansongo. Arguably the most dangerous of all African animals, they claim many lives, so it is important to watch out and to give them a wide berth between dusk and dawn when they leave the safety of the water to consume vast quantities of grass.

Antelope are becoming more scarce. In the drier Sahelian zone, the Dorcas gazelle is very patchily distributed. In slightly moister areas the red-fronted gazelle, a subspecies of Thomson's gazelle, may be found in suitable habitats.

ENVIRONMENTAL CONCERNS

The widespread famine in the countries of the Sahel in the late 1960s and early 1970s was, like the Vietnam War, a televised event. The global community was shocked by what it saw and promised to take action. Momentum gathered, until finally in 1977 the United Nations Conference on Desertification (UNCOD) was convened in Nairobi, Kenya. Drought, it was decided, was not the sole cause of the Sahel's problems; **desertification** was also a major contributing factor. It was now official: Mali's chief environmental concern was 'the encroaching Sahara'.

In an African context, desertification is often defined in terms of the Sahara and its gradual southern advance. 'The Sahara continues to creep forward,' announces one commentator, 'claiming an area the size of New York State every decade'. While the encroachment of sand-dunes can be locally significant – in Timbuktu, for example – Mali is not really being swallowed by the desert. I prefer the less emotive and more scientific definition of desertification given by UNCOD: 'the diminution or destruction of the biological potential of the land that can lead ultimately to desert-like conditions'. This is what is happening in Mali. In a nutshell, **soil erosion** is the main problem. This, in turn, is the result of a number of largely man-made causes.

Deforestation is arguably public enemy number one. Fuel wood is the leading energy source in Mali, providing more than 90% of the country's energy needs, with Bamako alone requiring about 400,000 tonnes of wood a year to keep going. At one time, fuel wood was always gathered from dead wood on farms and common lands, but, due to the rapidly increasing human population, live trees are now being felled to meet the demand. Population pressures also contribute to the problem of **overgrazing**, which destroys vegetation cover and tramples soil surfaces. In recent years periods of drought have forced nomadic herders such as the Tuareg, who have traditionally inhabited the edges of the desert, to move south to the outskirts of Sahelian towns. The subsequent concentration of grazing has also led to land degradation. Elsewhere, overcultivation, overirrigation, inadequate drainage and the inappropriate use of agricultural machinery have further damaged the soil. Once stripped of its plant cover by deforestation, overgrazing, or any of the other means mentioned above, the topsoil has no protection from **wind erosion**, and each year, as the harmattan and other desert winds blow across the Sahel, they take a piece of Mali's environmental future with them.

Responsible Tourism

'Responsible tourism' is a wonderful expression. It defines all of our obligations as tourists without really describing any. The ambiguity of the word 'responsible' is perfect. Picking up your rubbish and taking off your shoes before entering a mosque is, of course, responsible behaviour; but so is speaking a little of the local language and paying a fair price for things at the market. Responsible tourism means more than just obeying rules of social etiquette and being on your best behaviour. You must be proactive as well as reactive. In a nutshell, try to *give something back* to the country you are visiting. Speaking a little French, Bambara, or any of the other local languages – even just 'hello' and 'thank you' – is respectful and demonstrates a willingness to adapt to the local culture, which might in turn help you to make some friends. Remember that Mali is a developing country where life can be hard and very little is taken for granted. Think twice before haggling for an hour over the price of a T-shirt or a bunch of bananas. Paying a tourist price is not necessarily a bad thing if it is for the benefit of the local economy – in other words, the street vendors and hawkers in the market, who are normally the last to see the financial rewards of mass tourism. As an independent traveller, you are in the privileged position of being able to give something back directly to the people because you are in constant contact with them. Our ultimate responsibility, then, is to make sure that this opportunity is not wasted.

CULTURAL SENSITIVITY

A responsible tourist is a culturally aware tourist – or one who is willing to adapt to and respect local customs and traditions. I have already mentioned learning a bit of the language, which, I think, is an easy and enjoyable thing to do. The point about bargaining is as much about respecting the local way of life as not taking advantage of other people's poverty. In a similar vein, ask before you take photographs of people and places of worship; and be aware of the fact that your camera probably costs more than your subject's yearly wage. I am not saying don't do it – just be humble about the way you do it.

A responsible tourist will also adhere to the concept of **low-impact tourism**. This is another term which can mean different things to different people – although much of it is really just common sense. It hardly needs saying that you should refrain from uprooting plants and flowers and use energy resources such as water and electricity – so precious in Mali – efficiently. Less obvious, but equally important, aspects of low-impact tourism include not washing in lakes or rivers (regardless of local practices) or getting too close to the wildlife, all of which act to the detriment of the natural world in some form or another. Pollution of the environment by waste – polythene bags mainly – is a sensitive issue in Mali, as there is no elaborate waste-disposal system worth mentioning. Moreover, Malians show little awareness of the growing problem. Considering this, your best attitude is probably not to add to the existing amount of waste. Survival (see below) recommends the following:

- All human waste should be buried and toilet paper burned or buried.
- Rubbish should be disposed of as follows. Paper should be burnt, biodegradable waste should be buried and containers given away.
- Rather than using plastic bags for shopping, use longer lasting bags.
- It is better to buy drinks in returnable glass bottles than in cans or plastic bottles.

The need for low-impact tourism is arguably at its greatest when tribal peoples are involved (see *Responsible Tourism in Dogon Country* on page 184). Visiting communities with alien cultures and where there has been only minimal contact with the outside world is a minefield for tourists, and blunders – often quite unintentional – are easily made (for example, apparently innocuous diseases such as colds and influenza might prove to be killers amongst people with no immunity). **Survival** is a worldwide organisation based in London which supports tribal peoples and is currently campaigning on behalf of the Tuareg. In its own words, Survival stands for their (tribal people's) right to decide their own future and helps them protect their lives, lands and human rights'. **Tourism Concern** is another London-based charity devoted to promoting responsible tourism throughout the world. Contact details are as follows:

Survival 6 Charterhouse Buildings, London EC1M 7ET; tel: 020 7687 8700; fax: 020 7687 8701; email: survival@gn.apc.org; web: www.survival-international.org
Tourism Concern Stapleton House, 277–281 Holloway Rd, London N7 8HN; tel: 020 7133 3330; fax: 020 7133 3331; email: info@tourismconcern.org.uk; web: www.tourismconcern.org.uk

CHARITIES AND NGOS IN MALI
International charities and NGOs
Many of the largest international charities and NGOs (non-governmental organisations), along with high-profile United Nations organisations such as UNESCO and UNICEF, are currently active in Mali. The main British NGOs with operations in Mali are as follows:

ACORD Tel: 221 09 48
Action on Disability and Development Tel: 223 91 50
Christian Aid Tel: 221 59 49
Islamic Relief UK Tel: 221 44 41
Oxfam Tel: 222 27 77
PLAN International Tel: 223 05 83
Save the Children Fund Tel: 221 30 16

Sight Savers Tel: 224 91 22
SOS Sahel Tel: 221 02 85
SPANA and **UNAIS** Tel: 221 24 03

There is obviously not enough space here to describe each of these charities' work in great detail. Suffice it to say that most of them are concerned with basic needs such as improving health care and ensuring that the population is properly nourished, while some have additional, more clearly defined tasks – **Save the Children Fund**, for example, has been campaigning for children's rights for the past two years. Although the means employed to provide these basic needs may vary, it seems to be universally agreed that sustainable development is every bit as important as giving handouts. For instance, most international NGOs in Mali operate credit schemes in conjunction with local partners. These schemes are normally aimed at the country's indefatigable women (see page 23), who borrow – and repay – money to invest in making food products, arts and crafts and other small businesses. These modest money-making projects generally prosper, enabling the women to care properly for their children and giving them a degree of independence and self-esteem. In the words of a Malian woman who took part in one of the more successful schemes sponsored by the American charity, **Freedom from Hunger** (tel: 24 39 78; email: ffh@malinet.ml): 'With the three loans I have taken out, I have been able to triple my production of *bogolon* (mudcloth) and triple my earnings. When I had the capital to buy a lot of materials at once, I increased my production. Now when buyers come, I have a selection to show them and sometimes I can sell everything at once.'

Sponsoring a child through **PLAN International** is another variation on the development theme. You make an annual donation and follow it up with letters and gifts to your 'adopted' child. In return, you receive regular progress reports and letters from the child's guardians, which gives you the opportunity to see at first hand the difference that your contribution is making to someone's life and that of their community. Incidentally, PLAN's one-millionth sponsored child was a nine-year-old girl from Mali. The work of **SPANA** (Society for the Protection of Animals Abroad) is focused on improving the plight of Mali's donkeys, especially the unfortunate animals working in Bamako pulling the city's rubbish carts. SPANA's small veterinary team treats wounds caused by ill-fitting harnesses and saddles, which, in extreme cases, can cause a trauma known as fistulous withers. Concentrating on animals in a country where the human population is confronted with so many problems might seem slightly perverse. In reality, however, the interdependence between man and donkey in Mali is so great that the fortunes of one are often inextricably linked to the well-being of the other.

Local charities and NGOs

Making a donation to a local charity is one of the more obvious ways in which you can give something back to the country you are visiting. There are more than 600 national charities and NGOs in Mali and most are listed in the

FOREIGN AID: EVERY LITTLE HELPS
Jolijn Geels

The Malian economy is IMF-controlled to a large degree. Despite the negative impact of the economic crises in neighbouring countries like Côte d'Ivoire, the structural adjustment programme implemented by the IMF is considered to be beneficial overall. Nevertheless, according to statistics, the gross domestic product (GDP) per capita rose to an 'astonishing' US$900 before plummeting again to no more than a few hundred US dollars: a tell-tale figure. In the real world, this means that, while some Malians have it all, over 60% of the Malian population still lives below the poverty line, the majority in rural areas. Illiteracy is very common, since schools may be few and far between, and many parents cannot afford the expense of education anyway. By the same token, access to medical facilities is sometimes extremely limited – again, especially in rural areas. The statistics for infant mortality and HIV are shocking, while outbreaks of cholera claim most victims amongst the poorest of all. Indeed, Mali is rated one of the poorest countries in the world, and is heavily dependent on foreign aid. Some widely known international charities and NGOs are represented in Mali, and often very visibly so, with signposts and 4WDs adorned with their logos. Apart from these giants in foreign aid, numerous anonymous benefactors are devoted to supporting well-demarcated projects.

One example – both touching and impressive – is that of the Dutch architect Joop van Stigt and his wife Gonny van Stigt-Amesz. In the 1960s, Joop was invited to participate in the extensive expedition led by Herman Haan to study the Tellem – and so he travelled to the Dogon country for the first time. He was impressed, shocked and inspired by all that he saw, and returned on several occasions. Unwittingly, the restoration of a number of ginnas and binous (see page 183), and the construction of two dams in 1988, were only the initial impetus of a long chain of projects. On

Annuaire des ONGs, a directory of NGOs currently active in the country. You should be able to get hold of a copy at the headquarters of most international development agencies in Bamako, or the **Comité de Coordination des Actions des ONG**s. There will obviously be one or two bad apples in the barrel – the NGO privilege of having a duty-free vehicle is open to abuse by unscrupulous opportunists – but the majority are worthwhile and deserving of your support. On your travels you are bound to come across good causes which merit a small donation or help in some other form. In the meantime, here are a couple of my own discoveries:

AGVF (Association des Groupements Villageois Féminins), BP 37, Bandiagara (see the map on page 189). This is one of many national organisations devoted to the promotion of women. In this case, the focus is on rural women in the *cercle* of Bandiagara. As with many international NGOs, there is a strong emphasis on credit schemes which allow his visits to the Dogon country, Monsieur Joop – as he became known – always provided some soccer balls for local schools. One day, the response of one of the teachers must have hit him like a bombshell: 'You are a professor and an architect, you teach at a university. Instead of giving us soccer balls, you should build us a new school.'

It marked a turning point. In 1995 the first school – fully equipped and with ablution blocks, solar panels and a well – was built, and Mr Joop has not stopped building since. In 1996, during a serious drought and famine, he financed the purchase and transport of 530 sacks of wheat to feed several villages. Until then, all of the funds for the dams, the school and the food support had been drawn from the van Stigt's personal accounts, but in 1998 Mr Joop and his wife Gonny set up a foundation to meet the growing demand for schools and wells. Donations came trickling in only after a number of years, but by now the couple were fully dedicated and unstoppable. The foundation has completed the construction of many schools – with a total of 50 classrooms – more dams, a library and a hospital, and the installation of tens of solar-powered pumps and wells. The latest project-in-progress is the construction of a school for technical education in Mopti.

Mr Joop recently turned 70, but he and his wife still regularly visit Dogon country to initiate, support and follow up the various projects. When visiting the part of the *falaise* that is described in *Chapter 9* (see page 198) you will pass schools built by Mr Joop in Kani Kombolé and Amani. In Sanga, you could actually meet the couple in Hotel Campement La Guina if they happen to be there on one of their many visits. Should you like to know more about the foundation, contact Joop and Gonny van Stigt by email (see *Charities and NGOs* on page 48). Newsletters in Dutch, French and English are available and a website is under construction. Donations are welcome, of course, as every little helps.

women to develop their own small businesses and, in turn, a degree of self-sufficiency and independence. General education in matters such as family planning and the protection of the environment is also promoted. The AGVF office is conveniently located in the centre of Bandiagara and it is no hassle to pop in and find out more about the work they do. They should also be able to give you the addresses of other women's organisations around the country – or at least in the region of Mopti.

Les amis de Gossi or **La Retraite Gossi**, s/c *Mission Catholique*, BP 32, Gao. Sister Anne-Marie Saloman is in her 12th year at Gossi. She has run the local hospital since it opened in 1992, continuing her work during the dangerous and unpredictable years of the Tuareg rebellion. Well-known in these parts, Anne-Marie is a woman of the cloth by vocation, who began her medical studies when aged 45. The hospital on the edge of Gossi was originally established for Tuareg nomads displaced during the war. Nowadays, it treats all-comers – between 70 and 100 patients a day – for a variety of diseases, including tuberculosis, cholera and AIDS. All types of donations are welcome, although money (to pay salaries and purchase medication) is by far the most useful form of assistance. If you are intending to visit Gossi – to see the elephants, for example – be sure to say hello to Sister Anne-Marie.

BACK AT HOME

When Mali is not being confused with Bali, it is synonymous with poverty and drought. Simply by talking about the many other, positive aspects of the country will help to dispel preconceived – and often erroneous – stereotypes. You might also consider joining groups through which you can continue to contribute to the country you have just visited. Along with Survival and Tourism Concern, there are many other international charities, environmental organisations and conservation projects worth investigating. Below is a list of some of the charities and NGOs with programmes in Mali. There are, of course, many others from all over the world, especially France, Germany and Scandinavia.

Charities and NGOs
UK
Joliba Trust 108 Egerton Rd, Bristol BS7 8HP; tel: 0117 989 2599; email: jolibatrust@hotmail.com; web: www.jolibatrust.org.uk. Works for sustainable development with rural communities in Mali.

Oxfam 274 Banbury Rd, Oxford OX2 7DZ; tel: 0870 333 2700; email: oxfam@oxfam.org.uk; web: www.oxfam.org.uk

PLAN International 5–6 Underhill St, London NW1 7HS; tel: 020 7485 6612; fax: 020 7485 2107; email: mail@plan-international.org.uk; web: www.plan-international.org

Save the Children Fund 17 Grove Lane, London SE5 8RD; tel: 020 7703 5400; fax: 020 7703 2278; web: www.oneworld.org/scf

SPANA 14 John St, London WC1N 2EB; tel: 020 7831 3999; fax: 020 7831 5999; email: hg@spana.org; web: www.spana.org

US
Freedom from Hunger 1644 DaVinci Court, Davis, CA 95616; tel: 1 800 708 2555; fax: 530 758 6241; email: info@freefromhunger.org; web: www.freefromhunger.org

CARE 151 Ellis St NE, Atlanta, GA 30303; tel: 1 800 521 2273 ext 999; email: info@care.org; web: www.care.org

Peace Corps 1111 20th St NW, Washington DC, 20526; tel: 1 800 424 8580; web: www.peacecorps.gov

PLAN International US 155 Plan Way, Warwick, RI 02886–1099; tel: 401 738 5600; fax: 401 738 5608; web: www.plannsa.org/index.php

Save the Children US 54, Wilton Rd, Westport, CT 06880; tel: 203 221 4000; fax: 203 227 5667; email: info@savechildren.org; web: www.savethechildren.org

Netherlands
Stichting Dogon Onderwijs (Dogon Education Foundation, see box on page 50) Herengracht 408, 1017BX Amsterdam; email: j.gvanstigt@burovanstigt.nl

Previous page Masked dancer at the Dama festival in Ireli
Above Abandoned cliff dwellings above Teli village, Dogon Country
Below Sanga market, with flat-topped houses in the background

Before You Go

RED TAPE AND IMMIGRATION
Entry requirements
In general, the following documents are required to enter Mali:

- A passport with at least six months left to run
- A visa
- An International Certificate of Vaccination or Revaccination Against Yellow Fever

Visas
Unless you are a national of a selection of North and West African countries, or the Principalities of Monaco and Andorra, you will need a visa to visit Mali. Visas are issued without much fuss in countries with Malian representation; the problem is finding these countries. There is currently no embassy or consulate in London, so residents of the UK are obliged to send their passports to either Paris or Brussels. The Consulat Général du Mali in **France** is quick and efficient at issuing visas. Write to them – or the Centre d'Information et de Documentation at the embassy in Paris – for an application form, and return it with two photographs, €30, your passport and, most importantly, a stamped addressed envelope (or addressed envelope plus international reply coupons). The visa itself takes four days to issue, but you must allow at least another ten days while your application is held up in the post. Visas at the consulate in **Brussels** takes three working days to issue. Although you can send in your passport by post, the consulate will not post it back to you; you must either collect it in person or use a courier service such as DHL or APS. Alternatively, you could pay a **visa service** to do the work – which will be expensive, because they must also deal with consulates abroad. Another option is to stop in Paris en route to Mali and submit your application in person (see *The Paris option* on page 54). The visa issued permits a single entry and is valid for one month after the date of arrival. If you intend to leave Mali and return at a later date, you must obtain a new visa. For American citizens, the application procedure is similar and the visa issued is valid for three months. The Malian Embassy in Washington asks for five working days to process applications and charges US$80 for a three-month visa plus postage. Visit their website for more details (see page 55).

If obtaining a visa before travelling to Mali is not an option and if your point of arrival is the airport in Bamako, there is always the possibility of getting a *visa d'entrée*. This visa costs CFA15,000 and is valid for five days only, so you will have to have the visa validated and extended within a matter of days. The *visa d'entrée* is payable in local currency only, but you should be able to change cash euros or US dollars at the exchange office before going through customs. If the exchange office happens to be closed – which does occur – officials will refer you to unofficial ways to obtain the necessary CFAs. At some border posts – like Diboli at the Senegal border – a *visa d'entrée* may be issued under the same conditions.

When you are travelling overland, you may be able to get a visa in one of the neighbouring countries. In Dakar (Sénégal) a visa costs CFA23,000 and takes 24 hours to issue. In Ouagadougou (Burkina Faso) a visa (single-entry, one month validity) costs less and takes only 15 minutes to issue. For more details of embassies and consulates see page 55.

Once you are in Mali, visa extensions can be obtained at the Direction Générale de la Police Nationale in Bamako. Stamps for an additional month cost CFA5,000, regardless of whether or not you intend to be in Mali for the whole month. Extending your visa in Bamako can usually be done in 24 hours and requires one photograph. Compared with many other countries in West Africa, the Malians are not big on bureaucracy, so, provided that your papers are in order, red tape should not be too much of a problem.

There have been reports, though, about the Direction Générale de la Police Nationale in Bamako being foul-tempered at times. If you have the choice, get your visa extended in Mopti instead. Service is much quicker and always friendly, so the whole procedure should take no more than the time it takes to fill out the necessary forms, and stamp and sign your passport. In Mopti you need two photographs, and wherever you get your visa extension, remember that one empty page in your passport is required.

The Paris option

Whether by choice or necessity, stopping in Paris en route to Mali has a number of advantages and is worth considering.

Firstly, flights to Bamako from Paris are cheaper and more numerous than from other European capitals. There is also a Malian Consulate in Paris (nearest metro: Chemin Vert) which issues visas quickly and efficiently; and at the embassy (nearest metro: Vaneau) the Centre d'Information et de Documentation (open Mon–Fri 09.00–13.00 and 14.00–17.00) has a lot of relevant reading material, including telephone directories and Malian newspapers. Other information and travel aids, such as the excellent map of Mali produced by the Institut Géographique National de France and numerous books about the country and its attractions, are also more readily available in Paris than, for example, London or New York. Finally, if you need any last-minute vaccinations or medical advice, the Dispensaire Edison (nearest metro: Place d'Italie) is run by the Mairie de Paris (Paris town council) and is cheaper than the private clinics – although the service is slower (see page 62).

Embassies and consulates abroad

The extent of Mali's representation abroad is not vast. The more important embassies and consulates are as follows:

Belgium 487 Av Molière, 1060 Brussels; tel: 02 345 74 32; fax: 02 344 57 00

Burkina Faso Ouagadougou; tel: 38 19 22; fax: 38 19 23

Canada 50 Goulburn Av, Ottawa, Ontario, K1N 8C8; tel: 613 232 1501; fax: 613 232 7429; email: ambassademali@bellnet.ca

Côte d'Ivoire Maison du Mali, 46 Boulevard Lagunaire, BP 2746, Abidjan; tel: 20 32 31 47; fax: 20 21 55 14

France *Paris* Embassy: 89 rue du Cherche Midi, 75006 Paris; tel: 01 45 48 58 43; fax: 01 45 48 55 34; Consulate: 43 rue Chemin Vert, 75011 Paris; tel: 01 48 07 85 85; *Marseille* Consulate: 47 rue de la Paix, 13001 Marseille; tel: 91 54 90 09

Ghana Liberia Rd, Ministeries Area, Accra, BP GP 1121; tel: 21 663 276; fax: 21 774 395

Guinée Coleach Corniche, BP 299, Conakry; tel: 461 418/443 303

Germany Basteistrasse 86, D-53713 Bonn; tel: 0228 35 70 48; fax: 0228 36 19 22

Italy (consulate) Viale Parioli 56, I-00197 Rome; tel: 06 8543 537, 06 8070 4437, 06 8085 062

Maroc Rabat; tel: 37 759 125; fax: 37 754 742

Mauritania BP 184, Nouakchott

Niger Bd de la Liberté, BP 10115, Niamey; tel: 722 883/732 342; fax: 733 346; email: consmali@intnet.ne; web: www.gsi-niger.com/consulat-mali

Senegal 48 St Maginot, BP 478, Dakar; tel: 823 48 93; fax: 823 48 94

Switzerland (Consulate) St. Jakobs-Strasse 30, case postale, CH-4002, Basel; tel: 061 295 38 88; fax: 061 295 38 89; email: info@maliconsulat.ch; web: www.maliconsulat.ch

Togo (Consulate) Quartier Ablogame, Rue de la Paix, BP 821, Lomé; tel: 213 458

USA 2130 K St NW, Washington DC 20008; tel: 202 332 2249; fax: 202 332 6603; email: infos@maliembassy-us; web: www.maliembassy-usa.org

HEALTH

With Dr Jane Wilson-Howarth and Dr Felicity Nicholson

Inoculations

Yellow fever is only a risk in Mali south of 15°N, but a certificate proving that you have been vaccinated against the disease is an entry requirement whichever part of the country is being visited. The International Certificate of Vaccination against Yellow Fever is not valid until ten days after the date of the vaccination, and then lasts for ten years.

Most people are immunised against **polio**, **tetanus** and **diphtheria** in infancy. This protection, however, must be renewed every ten years with booster vaccinations.

Typhoid is caught through the consumption of food or water contaminated with *Salmonella typhi*. Once ingested, this bacterium multiplies quickly, and even if you recover from typhoid fever, it may remain in your bloodstream. A high, sustained fever is the usual symptom, although typhoid sufferers can also experience stomach pains, headaches, a pin-point red rash and a loss of appetite. Vaccination against the disease is advised and is best taken in the injectable form (eg: Typhim Vi). This vaccine is about 80% effective and will last for three years. Ideally it should be taken at least seven days in advance of travel, but is still worth giving even at the last minute, providing the trip is longer than a week. An oral form of the vaccine exists, but studies have shown that there is an inconsistent response and in the UK it is considered second choice.

Hepatitis A is a viral disease which attacks the liver and usually causes jaundice. Whilst it is rarely fatal it can cause serious illness. It is spread most commonly from faecally contaminated food and water. It can be spread from person-to-person when poor personal hygiene exists. Simply washing hands carefully after visiting a public lavatory can help to reduce the risk. Travellers are advised to be immunised against hepatitis A with hepatitis A vaccine (eg: Havrix Monodose, Avaxim). One dose of vaccine lasts for one year and can be boosted to give protection for up to ten years. The course of two injections costs about £100. Ideally it should be taken at least two weeks prior to travel although it is now accepted that it can be used even closer to the time of departure (since the disease itself takes at least two weeks to incubate). Gamma globulin was taken off the market in the UK in 1998 and should no longer be used for protection against hepatitis A.

Hepatitis B is another serious viral disease which is present in the blood and body fluids of an infected individual. It attacks the liver and can sometimes be fatal. Transmission is by unprotected sexual intercourse, unsterilised needles and through unscreened blood or blood products. This makes it less of an immediate threat to the average traveller than the more freely transmitted hepatitis A. However, the vaccine is recommended for travellers who will be working in medical environments, and for those who may be spending six weeks or more in the country. Ideally three doses of vaccine should be taken, and there are a variety of schedules available, from as little as three weeks (Engerix is the only vaccine licensed for this schedule) up to 6 months. The vaccine provides good protection against hepatitis B, although the precautions recommended to combat AIDS (see page 59) also help to minimise the risks of catching hepatitis B and hepatitis C.

Rabies is carried by all mammals – dogs are the commonest carriers – and is passed on to humans through a bite, a scratch or a lick of an open wound. You must always assume that any animal is rabid (unless personally known to you) and medical help should be sought as soon as is practicably possible. In the interim, scrub the wound thoroughly with soap and bottled/boiled water for several minutes, then pour on a strong iodine or alcohol solution. This can help to prevent the rabies virus from entering the body and will guard against wound infection and the very real risk of catching tetanus. The decision whether or not to have the highly effective rabies vaccine will depend on the nature of your trip. If you intend to have a lot of contact with animals, it is definitely worthwhile. It is also advised if you are likely to be more than 24 hours away from medical help. Ideally, three pre-exposure doses should be taken over a minimum of twenty-one days. If you are bitten by any animal, treatment should be given as soon as possible. At least two post-bite rabies injections are needed, even in immunised people. Those who have not been immunised will need a full course of injections together with rabies immunoglobulin (RIG), which is expensive (around US$800) and may be hard to come by – another reason why pre-exposure vaccination should be encouraged for travellers who are planning to visit more remote areas! It is never too late to seek help as the incubation period for rabies can be very long. Bites closer to the brain are always more serious. Remember that if you contract rabies, mortality is 100%.

Meningitis (the inflammation and infection of the membranes surrounding the brain) can be caused by a viral or bacterial infection. Viral meningitis is the less serious of the two and normally clears up in about ten days. Bacterial meningitis, however, can be fatal. Several different varieties of bacteria can cause this type of meningitis which, in severe cases, can result in brain damage, paralysis and death. Common symptoms include a high fever, thumping headaches and, most classically, a stiff neck and sensitivity to light. The worrying thing about this disease is the relatively easy way in which it is transmitted and the speed at which symptoms may develop. One of the most contagious forms of meningitis is caused by the *Neisseria meningitidis* bacterium, also known as meningococcal meningitis, which is spread through respiratory and oral secretions such as coughing, sneezing and kissing. Due to periodic epidemics of meningococcal meningitis in Mali, the tetravalent meningococcal vaccine (ACWY) is recommended. It gives protection for three years and ideally should be taken at least one week before departure.

Malaria

The risk of malaria in Mali is high in all parts of the country all the year round. The risk is greatest in the savanna regions of the south and decreases as you travel north through the Sahel towards the desert. Transmitted by an infected mosquito, malaria can cause anaemia, jaundice and, in its most serious *falciparum* form, kidney failure, coma and death. Symptoms can develop from seven days to as much as one year after the initial infection, and may be any one or all of the following: general aches and pains, fever, chills, diarrhoea and headaches. However, the only consistent feature is a fever of 38°C or more. To conclude this rather gloomy paragraph, even if you stringently follow the preventative measures outlined below, you can still catch malaria.

Taking some form of prophylactic medication is recommended for all visits to Mali. The antimalarial drugs prescribed will depend on where in the world you come from, so check with your GP or a specialist doctor at a travel clinic. In the UK and US, the once weekly tablet **mefloquine** (Lariam) is considered the most effective agent for this region. If this is recommended, start taking it two to three weeks before departure to check that it suits you; stop immediately if it seems to cause mood swings or other changes in the way you feel, visual or hearing disturbances, fits, severe headaches or changes in heart rhythm. Anyone who is pregnant, who has suffered fits in the past, has been treated for depression or psychiatric problems, or who is epileptic or has a close blood relative who is epileptic should avoid mefloquine. A newer drug, Malarone, is almost as effective as mefloquine, but has far fewer side effects. It need only be started two days before arrival in a malarial area, continued whilst there and then taken for seven days after leaving. The down side is that it is expensive, but it is ideal for shorter trips. At the time of writing, it is licensed for use for up to three months in the UK. A paediatric form of Malarone is also available and is prescribed on a weight basis. If you are travelling with children it is helpful to know their weight in kilograms before you visit the doctor.

Another useful alternative is the antibiotic **doxycycline** (100mg daily). Like Malarone it need only be started two days before arrival in a malarial region, but like mefloquine it must be continued for four weeks after leaving. Like Malarone, it may also be used by travellers with epilepsy. There is a possibility of allergic skin reactions developing in sunlight in approximately 1–3% of people. If this happens the drug must be stopped and advice sought from a doctor as soon as possible. Women using the oral contraceptive should use an additional method of protection for the first four weeks when taking this antimalarial prophylactic agent.

Elsewhere in Europe (France, for example), a drug called Savarine, once again taken daily, is popular. The instructions for taking these drugs should be read, understood and followed. Chlorquine (Nivaquine, Avloclor) and proguanil (Paludrine) are no longer considered effective for this area, and should only ever be used as a last resort, and on the advice of a doctor. Whichever prophylactic agent is prescribed, it should be completed, unless unwarranted side effects occur. All malaria tablets are best taken midway through your main meal.

Travellers to remote parts may wish to consider carrying a course of treatment to cure malaria. There are a variety of treatments available, and the most appropriate will depend on which prophylactic agent you are taking. Presently quinine and doxycycline together, or Malarone alone, are the favoured regimes, but it is always best to take up-to-date advice since recommendations can change. Self-treatment is not without risks and generally people over-treat themselves. If at all possible, consult a doctor as soon as you can if you have a fever, whether or not this is accompanied by other symptoms, since diagnosing malaria is difficult without laboratory facilities.

Preventing insect bites

Don't let your malaria pills lull you into a false sense of security. You must also take measures to avoid being bitten by mosquitoes. The malaria-carrying *Anopheles* mosquito comes out from dusk till dawn and often targets feet and ankles. At this time, cover up your arms and legs and wear socks. You should also use a good insect repellent, preferably one containing **diethylmethyltoluamide** or DEET; a concentration of 55% DEET is recommended for adults. Consider using 100% DEET (eg: Repel 100) if you are prone to being bitten, or if you are not taking the most effective prophylactic regime. Some hotels in Mali have mosquito nets, while most others can provide either mosquito coils or insect spray; air conditioning also keeps mosquitoes away. Check that the nets are not damaged and that they're freshly impregnated with permethrin. If in doubt, buy your own before you leave. Nets give good protection whilst you're asleep; coils and spray reduce the amount you are bitten.

With a combination of prophylactics, insect repellent, mosquito nets, coils, protective clothing and common sense, you should have nothing to worry about on the malaria front. Nevertheless, the onset of headaches, aches, pains, fevers and chills should be treated with extreme suspicion and warrants a prompt visit to the doctor.

Dengue fever

This mosquito-borne disease may mimic malaria, but there is no prophylactic medication available to deal with it. The mosquitoes that carry this virus bite during the daytime, so it is worth applying repellent if you see any mosquitoes around. Symptoms include strong headaches, rashes, excruciating joint and muscle pains, and high fever. Dengue fever lasts only for a week or so and is not usually fatal. Complete rest and paracetamol are the usual treatment; plenty of fluids also help. Some patients are given an intravenous drip to prevent dehydration. It is especially important to protect yourself if you have had dengue fever before, since a second infection with a different strain can result in the potentially fatal dengue haemorrhagic fever.

AIDS

According to the World Health Organisation approximately 80% of all HIV positive and AIDS sufferers come from sub-Saharan Africa and India. A particular feature of the AIDS epidemic in sub-Saharan Africa is that, since it first started in the late 1970s and early 1980s, it has mostly been spread through heterosexual intercourse, as opposed to homosexual intercourse and drug-taking. Consequently, four out of five of the world's HIV-positive women live in Africa. This should drive home the importance of practising safe sex, which means wearing a condom – or perhaps a femidom – especially if you have sex with a prostitute. The same rule applies if you want to reduce the risk of catching other sexually transmitted diseases, such as hepatitis B (see page 56).

Other diseases

Extremely severe diarrhoea, sometimes accompanied by vomiting, is a symptom of **cholera**. This food- and water-borne disease, which in acute cases can kill within hours, occurs in epidemics. In Africa, however, there has been a cholera epidemic for the past 20 years, so to be forewarned is to be forearmed. The current cholera vaccine (UK) is no longer considered sufficiently effective to be administered. Cholera vaccination is not required by the Malian authorities even if you are coming from a cholera-infected country. The best way, therefore, to prevent cholera is to be careful about what you eat and drink (see page 30).

Bilharzia or **schistosomiasis** is a disease caused by parasites found in fresh water – which in Mali effectively means its two great rivers, the Niger and the Senegal. These parasites penetrate human skin and worms grow inside the blood vessels of the body, producing eggs, which can, in severe and rare cases, damage the liver, intestines, lungs and bladder. Initial symptoms might include a rash or itchy skin; fevers, chills and muscle aches can follow one or two months later. Preventing bilharzia is simple enough: avoid swimming and bathing in rivers, lakes and ponds and, obviously, drinking the water. If you do bathe in danger areas, try not to spend longer than ten minutes in the water and dry off thoroughly with a towel. Covering yourself with DEET insect repellent will also provide some protection.

Diarrhoea

Diarrhoea is the body's way of flushing out noxious bugs, and few visitors to Africa escape without experiencing at least a mild dose of it. Even if you take great care to eat and drink sensibly, the simple fact that your normal diet and way of life have changed is often enough to bring on the 'runs'. Rest, relaxation and a little abstinence is the best way to combat diarrhoea. When you feel hungry, opt for bland foods such as bread, rice and *fonio* (see page 30). Most importantly, drink plenty of fluids to avoid dehydration, the most serious complication of diarrhoea and a particular danger in hot countries. In addition to the fluid streaming from your bottom end you will also be sweating constantly, although due to the low humidity and the drying effect of the wind, you might not always realise it. Try to drink after each bowel movement: two glasses of water with a four-finger scoop of sugar and a three-finger pinch of salt added to each glass (to one litre of safe water, add eight level teaspoons of sugar and one level teaspoon of salt).

If the diarrhoea is particularly bad and accompanied by a fever and/or blood and slime, you will probably need antibiotics in addition to fluid replacement. Ideally seek medical advice as soon as you can. If this is not practicably possible then you may need to consider self-treatment. A two tablet course of ciprofloxacin (500mg taken immediately followed by a second dose 6–12 hours later) or norfloxacin 500mg twice a day for three days should treat most cases of bad diarrhoea and dysentery. However, you should always seek medical attention as soon as possible, as there are many other causes which may not respond to those treatments. Diarrhoea tablets or 'blockers', such as Imodium and Lomotil, keep the poisons in the body, causing the diarrhoea to last longer than it would if left to run its natural course. Only use them if you have to – on a long bus or river journey, for example.

Prevention is best. Given that the majority of travellers succumb to diarrhoea after eating contaminated food or drinking dirty water, and because Mali is a developing country competing with a climate in which bacteria love to breed, you should take *sensible* precautions when choosing what to eat and drink. Ironically, street food served fresh and hot is safer than the reheated buffet food found in many of the more expensive restaurants. Other things to avoid, or at least be wary of, are salads, unpeeled fruit, ice and ice-cream – all of which are potential carriers of bacteria. The only way to be sure that water is completely clean is to bring it to the boil, something which is not always very practical. Since bottled water is so readily available in Mali, you should not risk tap water. If there is no other choice, purify it first. Iodine drops or tablets are the favoured method for most travellers, but are not advised for pregnant women. Water filter bottles, such as Aquipur, are also excellent. Chlorine-based water purification tablets are also popular, but are less effective than the other measures. A bout of diarrhoea, unpleasant as it is, should not last more than about 24 hours. If it persists, see a doctor as soon as possible.

Sunburn and heatstroke

Of all the potential health risks in Mali, the sun is arguably the most dangerous. The increased chances of developing skin cancer after constant over-exposure to its ultraviolet rays are well documented. Heatstroke, meanwhile, is when the body severely overheats, much like a car engine, and is the more immediate – and sometimes fatal – consequence of getting too much sun.

The sun, therefore, should be treated with the same suspicion as mosquitoes and unprotected sex, and measures to protect yourself from its ultraviolet rays are just as important as malaria pills and condoms. Wear a good sunblock and a pair of sunglasses. If travelling in an open-backed vehicle or on a motorbike, wear a shirt. Use a wide-brimmed hat, cover up as much as is possible and practical in the heat and avoid being out in the midday sun from 12.00 to 15.00. Finally, don't be suckered into thinking that there is no risk when it is cool – in the desert during winter, for example – and hazy, which is often the case due to high levels of dust in the atmosphere, because even on these days 80% of the ultraviolet radiation can still be present.

Respiratory problems

Mali is a dusty country at the best of times. When the desert winds start to blow, however, dust particles are swept off the ground and into the atmosphere, where it becomes impossible not to breathe them in. Long-term exposure to dust can cause serious respiratory problems, especially if it enters the lungs. Even relatively brief stays in this sort of environment can be uncomfortable, and respiratory infections such as colds and bronchitis are common. The discomfort is most pronounced in the desert regions, which, of course, is why the Tuareg, Songhay and other people of the desert wear turbans. Consider following their example.

Note also that dust and wind are a lethal combination for contact-lens wearers.

Medical kit

Many of the items in my recommended medical kit should have been packed already as a matter of course. The remainder are designed to give you peace of mind rather than save your life. Remember that pharmacies are common in Mali, and in cases of emergency a medical kit should never replace on-the-spot medical advice. With this in mind, a traveller's medical kit could include the following:

- Malaria pills (and possibly a malaria treatment kit)
- Clean syringes and needles
- Plasters (Band Aids)
- Scissors or a knife and a pair of fine-pointed tweezers
- A good drying antiseptic such as iodine or potassium permanganate (not antiseptic cream)
- Antifungal cream (eg: Canesten)
- Calamine lotion to ease the discomfort of sunburn and over-scratched mosquito bites
- A good sunblock lotion
- Mosquito repellent
- Aspirin or paracetamol
- Antibiotics, such as ciprofloxacin or norfloxacin for severe diarrhoea
- Another broad-spectrum antibiotic such as amoxycillin for chest, urine and skin infections
- Condoms (or femidoms)

Travel clinics and health information

A full list of current travel clinic websites worldwide is available on www.istm.org/. For other journey preparation information, consult ftp://ftp.shoreland.com/pub/shorecg.rtf or www.tripprep.com. Information about various medications may be found on www.emedicine.com/wild/topiclist.htm.

UK

Berkeley Travel Clinic 32 Berkeley St, London W1J 8EL (near Green Park tube station); tel: 020 7629 6233

British Airways Travel Clinic and Immunisation Service There are two BA clinics in London, both on tel: 0845 600 2236; web: www.britishairways.com/travelclinics. Appointments only at 111 Cheapside; or walk-in service Mon–Sat at 156 Regent St. Apart from providing inoculations and malaria prevention, they sell a variety of health-related goods.

The Travel Clinic, Cambridge 48a Mill Rd, Cambridge CB1 2AS; tel: 01223 367362; fax: 01223 368021; email: enquiries@travelcliniccambridge.co.uk; web: www.travelcliniccambridge.co.uk. Open 12.00–19.00 Tue–Fri, 10.00–16.00 Sat.

Edinburgh Travel Clinic Regional Infectious Diseases Unit, Ward 41 OPD, Western General Hospital, Crewe Rd South, Edinburgh EH4 2UX; tel: 0131 537 2822. Travel helpline open 09.00–12.00 weekdays. Provides inoculations and anti-malarial prophylaxis and advises on travel-related health risks.

Fleet Street Travel Clinic 29 Fleet St, London EC4Y 1AA; tel: 020 7353 5678; web: www.fleetstreet.com. Injections, travel products and latest advice.

Hospital for Tropical Diseases Travel Clinic Mortimer Market Centre, 2nd Floor, Capper St (off Tottenham Ct Rd), London WC1E 6AU; tel: 020 7388 9600;

web: www.uclh.org/services/htd/index.shtml. Offers consultations and advice, and is able to provide all necessary drugs and vaccines for travellers. Runs a healthline (09061 337733) for country-specific information and health hazards. Also stocks nets, water purification equipment and personal protection measures.

MASTA (Medical Advisory Service for Travellers Abroad), at the London School of Hygiene and Tropical Medicine, Keppel St, London WC1 7HT; tel: 09068 224100. This is a premium-line number, charged at 60p per minute. For a fee, they will provide an individually tailored health brief, with up-to-date information on how to stay healthy, inoculations and what to take.

MASTA pre-travel clinics Tel: 01276 685040. Call for the nearest; there are currently 30 in Britain. They also sell malaria prophylaxis memory cards, treatment kits, bednets, net treatment kits, etc.

NHS travel website, www.fitfortravel.scot.nhs.uk, provides country-by-country advice on immunisation and malaria prevention, plus details of recent developments, and a list of relevant health organisations.

Nomad Travel Store 3–4 Wellington Terrace, Turnpike Lane, London N8 0PX; tel: 020 8889 7014; fax: 020 8889 9528; email: sales@nomadtravel.co.uk; web: www.nomadtravel.co.uk. Also at 40 Bernard St, London WC1N 1LJ; tel: 020 7833 4114; fax: 020 7833 4470 and 43 Queens Rd, Bristol BS8 1QH; tel: 0117 922 6567; fax: 0117 922 7789. As well as dispensing health advice, Nomad stocks mosquito nets and other anti-bug devices, and an excellent range of adventure travel gear.

Thames Medical 157 Waterloo Rd, London SE1 8US; tel: 020 7902 9000. Competitively priced, one-stop travel health service. All profits go to their affiliated company, InterHealth, which provides health care for overseas workers on Christian projects.

Trailfinders Immunisation Centre 194 Kensington High St, London W8 7RG; tel: 020 7938 3999

Travelpharm The Travelpharm website, www.travelpharm.com, offers up-to-date guidance on travel-related health and has a range of medications available through their online mini-pharmacy.

Irish Republic

Tropical Medical Bureau Grafton Street Medical Centre, Grafton Buildings, 34 Grafton St, Dublin 2; tel: 1 671 9200. Has a useful website specific to tropical destinations: www.tmb.ie.

USA

Centers for Disease Control 1600 Clifton Rd, Atlanta, GA 30333; tel: 888 232 3228 (toll free and available 24 hours) or 1 800 311 3435; fax: 877 FYI TRIP; web: www.cdc.gov/travel. The central source of travel information in the USA. Each summer they publish the invaluable *Health Information for International Travel*, available from the Division of Quarantine at the above address.

Connaught Laboratories PO Box 187, Swiftwater, PA 18370; tel: 800 822 2463. They will send a free list of specialist tropical-medicine physicians in your state.

IAMAT (International Association for Medical Assistance to Travelers) 417 Center St, Lewiston, NY 14092; tel: 716 754 4883; email: info@iamat.org; web:

www.iamat.org. A non-profit organisation that provides lists of English-speaking doctors abroad.

Canada
IAMAT (International Association for Medical Assistance to Travellers) Suite 1, 1287 St Clair Av W, Toronto, Ontario M6E 1B8; tel: 416 652 0137; web: www.iamat.org
TMVC (Travel Doctors Group) Sulphur Springs Rd, Ancaster, Ontario; tel: 905 648 1112; web: www.tmvc.com.au

Australia, New Zealand, Thailand
TMVC Tel: 1300 65 88 44; web: www.tmvc.com.au. Twenty-two clinics in Australia, New Zealand and Thailand, including:
Auckland Canterbury Arcade, 170 Queen St, Auckland; tel: 9 373 3531
Brisbane Dr Deborah Mills, Qantas Domestic Building, 6th floor, 247 Adelaide St, Brisbane, QLD 4000; tel: 7 3221 9066; fax: 7 3321 7076
Melbourne Dr Sonny Lau, 393 Little Bourke St, 2nd floor, Melbourne, VIC 3000; tel: 3 9602 5788; fax: 3 9670 8394
Sydney Dr Mandy Hu, Dymocks Building, 7th Floor, 428 George St, Sydney, NSW 2000; tel: 2 221 7133; fax: 2 221 8401
IAMAT PO Box 5049, Christchurch 5, New Zealand; web: www.iamat.org

South Africa
SAA-Netcare Travel Clinics PO Box 786692, Sandton 2146; fax: 011 883 6152; web: www.travelclinic.co.za or www.malaria.co.za. Clinics throughout South Africa.
TMVC 113 DF Malan Drive, Roosevelt Park, Johannesburg; tel: 011 888 7488; web: www.tmvc.com.au. Consult the website for details of clinics in South Africa.

Switzerland
IAMAT 57 Voirets, 1212 Grand Lancy, Geneva; web: www.iamat.org

TRAVEL INSURANCE
With a bit of luck, money spent on travel insurance will be money down the drain. This, of course, is not much of an incentive to buy it in the first place, but you should never leave home without it.

Buying travel insurance is really no different to buying a pair of shoes: shop around and opt for the policy which best fits your needs. Avoid being pressured into buying the comprehensive insurance offered by most travel agents when you purchase your ticket. Compensation of £2,000 for the inconvenience of being hijacked might sound impressive, but do you really need it?

Some degree of health cover is obviously essential. Most policies offer at least £1 million in emergency medical expenses and repatriation to your home country – which should be sufficient to cover most disasters. Note that in most cases the first £50 or so of any claim is payable by the policy holder.

Your most difficult decision will probably be whether or not to insure your baggage and personal belongings. This really bumps up the cost of travel insurance, so calculate if the amount of cover offered would reimburse the amount you stand to lose. It rarely does, in which case you would be better off saving your money – or leaving your camera at home. If you have other personal or household policies, they may cover some belongings: check the small print.

The standard travel policy covers you for a single trip and is priced according to your destination and the length of your stay. Most travel insurance companies these days also offer 'multi-trip' policies designed for travellers who make a number of journeys during the year. The premium is often very good value, but the length of each trip abroad is normally restricted to about four weeks. Most of the travel agencies specialising in independent travel (see page 70) also sell travel insurance, which is tailored to the needs of the independent traveller and often slightly cheaper than the norm. You can also buy your insurance quickly, cheaply and painlessly over the telephone. In the UK I particularly like the friendly and efficient service provided by **Club Direct** (tel: 0800 083 2466; web: www.clubdirect.com), which has several policies to suit various needs. You pay by credit card and your policy schedule is dispatched within a couple of days. **Columbus Direct** (tel: 0845 330 8518; web: www.columbusdirect.co.uk) is one of several other companies working along the same lines.

WHAT TO TAKE

The golden rule is to travel light. By definition, independent travel involves using public transport, finding your own accommodation and being on the move a good deal of the time. A heavy and cumbersome bag – or bags – will metaphorically and literally drag you down. Moreover, quite apart from the hassle and discomfort, there are sound financial reasons for keeping your baggage to a minimum, as bus companies, *bâchées* and *pinasses* invariably charge extra for large bags and backpacks. So, bearing this golden rule in mind, what should you take?

Baggage

Backpacks have become synonymous with independent travellers – and not without good reason. As long as it is well packed and worn properly, even a heavy backpack can be carried for hours with little discomfort. Meanwhile, your hands are left free to consult this guide. Try to centre most of the pack's weight on the hip belt and minimise the pressure on your shoulders – otherwise it will drag you down.

Durability is also important in a country where luggage is rarely handled with care. These days, most backpackers opt for internal frames which tend to be better for active travel and keep the load closer to your own centre of gravity. However, for hiking in hot weather – in Dogon country, for example – and carrying large loads, you might consider an external frame which is stronger and allows air to circulate between your body and back. The purchase of a new backpack can eat up a lot of your holiday money, so make sure that you choose one to last. Check the material, the stitching, the zips and the straps before you hand over your hard-earned cash.

You could, of course, elect to carry your worldly possessions in something other than a backpack – a **suitcase**, for example. Personally, I carry a small,

PHOTOGRAPHIC TIPS
Ariadne Van Zandbergen

Mali doesn't offer the possibilities for wildlife photography that exist in many other parts of Africa, but the people and scenery are exceptionally photogenic, and it takes only a small amount of forethought and care to come home with good pictures.

Equipment The simpler the camera, the less there is to go wrong, since complex electronic gadgetry can be sensitive to rain, dust and heat. For landscapes and portraits, a solidly built manual-focus camera will be adequate and can be bought cheaply secondhand. An autofocus camera will, however, focus with greater precision than any person can hope to on a regular basis, and is particularly useful for capturing moving objects. If you carry only one lens in Mali, a 28–70 or similar zoom should be ideal. For a second lens, a lightweight 80–200 or 70–300 or similar will be excellent for candid shots and varying your composition.

Film Print film is the preference of most casual photographers, slide film of professionals and some serious amateurs. You should definitely use slide film if you hope to have anything published. Slide film is more expensive than print film, but this is broadly compensated for by cheaper development costs.

Most serious photographers working outdoors in Africa favour Fujichrome slide film, in particular Sensia 100, Provia 100 (the professional equivalent to Sensia) or Velvia 50. Slow films (ie: those with a low ASA (ISO) rating) produce less grainy and sharper images than fast films, but can be tricky without a tripod in low light. Velvia 50 is extremely fine-grained and shows stunning colour saturation; it is the film I normally use in soft, even light or overcast weather. Sensia or Provia may be preferable in low light, since 100 ASA – or ISO – allows you to work at a faster shutter speed than 50 ASA. Because 100 ASA is more tolerant of contrast, it is also preferable in harsh light.

For print photography, a combination of 100 or 200 ASA film should be ideal. For the best results it is advisable to stick to recognised brands. Fujicolor produces excellent print films, with the Superia 100 and 200 recommended.

Some basics The automatic programmes provided with many cameras are limited in the sense that the camera cannot think, but only make calculations. A better investment than any amount of electronic wizardry would be to buy or borrow a photographic manual for beginners and get to grips with such basics as the relationship between aperture and shutter speed.

Beginners should also note that a low shutter speed can result in camera shake and therefore a blurred image. For hand-held photographs of static subjects using a low magnification lens (eg: 28–70), select a shutter speed of at least 1/60th of a second. For lenses of higher magnification, the rule of thumb is that the shutter speed should be at least the inverse of the magnification (for instance, a speed of 1/300 or faster on a 300 magnification lens). You can use lower shutter speeds with a tripod.

Most modern cameras include a built-in light meter, and give users the choice of three types of metering: matrix, centre weighted or spot metering. You will need to understand how these different sytems work to make proper use of them. Built-in light meters are reliable in most circumstances, but in uneven light, or where there is a lot of sky, you may want to take your metering selectively, for instance by taking a spot reading on the main subject. The meter will tend to under- or overexpose when pointed at an almost white or black subject. This can be countered by taking a reading against an 18% grey card, or a substitute such as grass or light grey rocks – basically anything that isn't almost black, almost white or highly reflective.

Autofocus is more reliable than manual focus, but can instil a tendency to place the subject at the centre of the frame. A more interesting image will normally be obtained if the subject is at least slightly off-centre; this can be achieved by focussing on the main subject, then holding the focus button down while moving the camera to adjust the framing.

Dust and heat Dust and heat are a constant problem in Mali. Keep your equipment in a sealed bag, stow films in an airtight container (such as a small cooler bag), leave used films in your hotel room, and avoid changing film in dusty conditions. On rough roads, I always carry my camera equipment on my lap to protect against vibration and bumps. Never stow camera equipment or film in a car boot (it will bake), or let it stand in direct sunlight.

Light The light in Africa is much harsher than in Europe or North America, for which reason the most striking outdoor photographs are often taken during the hour or two of 'golden light' after dawn and before sunset. Shooting in low light may enforce the use of very low shutter speeds, in which case a tripod (ideally) or monopod (lighter) will be required to avoid camera shake. Be alert to the long shadows cast by a low sun; these show up more on photographs than to the naked eye.

With careful handling, sidelighting and backlighting can produce stunning effects, especially in soft light and at sunrise or sunset. Generally, however, it is best to shoot with the sun behind you. Because of this, most buildings and landscapes are essentially a 'morning shot' or 'afternoon shot', depending on the direction in which they face. When you spend a couple of nights in one place, you'll improve your results by planning the best time to take pictures of static subjects (a compass can come in handy for this).

When photographing people or animals in the harsh midday sun, images taken in light but even shade are likely to look nicer than those taken in direct sunlight or patchy shade, since the latter conditions create too much contrast. But do avoid photographing a shaded subject against a sunlit background, which creates severe contrast. Fill-in flash is almost essential if you want to capture facial detail of dark-skinned people in harsh or contrasty light.

Protocol Except in general street or market scenes, it is unacceptable to photograph Malians without permission. Many traditionally dressed people will refuse to be photographed, others will agree for a small payment. Local guides generally have more success than tourists in negotiating paid photographs. The most willing subject will often pose stiffly when a camera is pointed at them; relax them by making a joke, and take a few shots in quick succession to improve the odds of capturing a natural pose.

black attaché case when I travel. Rather formal, I admit, but with one compartment for my clothes and another for my notes it suits me very well. Provided that you travel light, this type of bag can actually be more convenient to carry than a bulky backpack, slipping nicely between the legs on crowded *bâchées* and fitting easily into aircraft overhead lockers. Backpacks, I must say, make me feel very conspicuous. This is entirely subjective, but carrying an attaché case gives me confidence when I travel. This, in turn, has a knock-on effect when it comes to interacting and communicating with the local people. Choose your bag for its practical suitability, but also think whether it could benefit you psychologically.

Clothing

Selecting your wardrobe for a trip to a hot country such as Mali should be an exercise in common sense. Cool, light clothing is good for the days, while trousers and a long-sleeved shirt will help fend off mosquitoes in the evenings. A comfortable pair of shoes is obviously very important.

Don't forget that during the cool season it can be very cold – even freezing – in the desert areas at night. Hotels are often quite stingy when it comes to providing blankets, so consider bringing a sleeping bag if you plan to spend a lot of time in the desert between about November and February. Turbans can also be a good investment in the desert, where even the slightest wind kicks up the sand – which gets everywhere. (Accordingly, **contact lenses** are not recommended – not just in the desert, but all over this dusty country. Note that if you do bring them, cleaning fluids and replacements are almost impossible to find in Mali.)

Maps

Thanks to the recent – and continuous – roadworks all over the country, you would be lucky to find a map that matches reality. A good, if rather outdated, map is produced by the **Institut Géographique National de France (IGN)**. It is one of the few to deal with the country on its own, and is widely available (scale 1:2,000,000). A new Mali map by **ITMB Publishing** shows a huge number of smaller villages rather than the overall road system. It doesn't appear to be highly accurate, with erroneous degrees of latitude and plenty of inaccurate place names. In the 2004 edition (scale 1:2,400,000), the source of the information was clearly a lot older than that. Nevertheless, the map may prove to be useful for hikers and cyclists. At the **Institut Géographique du Mali** (or **IGM**: Mali's counterpart of the IGN) in Bamako, more updated road maps are available. At the time of writing, the latest version dated from November 2002 (scale 1:3,500,000). It shows little detail, but is fairly adequate where the condition of the main roads is concerned. The map can be printed out while you wait and costs CFA8,500. Detailed Ordnance Survey maps are also available at the IGN. Mali is also included on the various regional maps of West Africa which are good if you are planning to visit other countries in the area. In the UK, a good source of maps is Stanfords in Long Acre, London; tel: 020 7836 1321; web: www.stanfords.co.uk.

Money

Ideally, you should take a combination of cash and travellers' cheques, along with a Visa card for emergencies. All over Mali, but by no means in every town, it is possible to draw local currency on a **Visa** card– and Visa alone – while in the more expensive establishments, Visa is occasionally accepted as a means of payment. There is just one automatic dispenser – again for Visa card only – in Bamako. Otherwise, plastic is of little use. Since there have been many problems with stolen or counterfeit **travellers' cheques**, many banks no longer deal with them. As with Visa cards, planning when and where to exchange travellers' cheques for local currency is crucial. Travellers' cheques in euros are more widely accepted than cheques in US$. Note that many banks require to see the receipt, and that a hefty commission charge is incurred. Taking all this into account, it is tempting to carry most of your money in **cash**, preferably euros, with US$ as a second choice. Always have a good supply of cash in small denominations, so that you can avoid buying more CFA than you need at one time. Bring other currencies only if you have no alternative and when you do not mind changing a significant quantity at once while there is a bank that will take your currency.

Necessities and luxuries

Many of the items mentioned below as 'necessities' are downright patronising and as obvious as your nose. Treat this section as a checklist, ticking off the items you should not leave home without (the 'necessities') and pondering whether or not to take one or two articles to make your life more comfortable (the 'luxuries').

Necessities
- Passport
- Airline ticket
- Insurance policy
- Photocopies of passport, airline ticket and insurance policy
- Travellers' cheques and credit card
- Money belt to store the above. You should always wear it underneath your clothing.
- Medical kit (see page 62)
- Spare glasses (avoid contact lenses if possible; see page 68)

Luxuries
- Penknife
- Torch (flashlight) and batteries (power cuts are common)
- Matches to light gas lamps and mosquito coils
- Washing powder to wash your clothes as you dirty them. (A 'wash-and-wear' approach means that you can reduce the number of clothes you pack in the first place. Also remember that the more powder you use, the lighter your bag becomes.)
- Lipsalve to protect against chapped lips caused by the sun and wind

- Map – detailed and recent (see page 68)
- Calculator for currency conversion
- Camera with some spare film

TOUR OPERATORS

The list below represents a small fraction of the travel agencies and tour operators around at the moment. They are all well established and most tend to specialise in independent travel – some offering tailor-made tours to Mali. In many cases these agencies also sell travel insurance and have health clinics for vaccinations and other medical advice.

UK

Bridge The World 45–47 Chalk Farm Rd, Camden Town, London NW1 8AJ; tel: 087 0443 2399; email: info@bridgetheworld.com; web: www.b-t-w.co.uk
British Airways Travel Shop 156 Regent St, London W1R 6LB; tel: 084 5606 0747
Explore Worldwide 1 Frederick St, Aldershot, Hants GU11 1LQ; tel: 012 5276 0000; fax: 012 5276 0001; email: info@exploreworldwide.com; web: www.explore.co.uk
Nomadic Expeditions 26 Matthews Green Rd, Wokingham, Berks RG41 1JU; tel: 0870 220 1718; fax: 0870 220 1719; email: info@nomadic.co.uk; web: www.nomadic.co.uk
STA Travel 6 Wrights Lane, London W8 6TA; tel: 020 7361 6099; fax: 020 7938 4755; email: enquiries@statravel.co.uk; web: www.statravel.co.uk. STA has 12 branches in London and 25 or so around the country and at different university cities.
Tim Best Travel 68 Old Brompton Rd, London SW7 3LQ; tel: 020 7591 0300; fax: 020 7591 0301; email: info@timbesttravel.com; web: www.timbesttravel.com
Trailfinders 194 Kensington High St, London, W8 7RG; tel: 020 7938 3939; web: www.trailfinders.com
Travel Cuts 295a Regent St, London, W1R 7YA; tel: 020 7255 2191
Truck Africa 37 Ranelagh Gardens Mansions, Fulham, London SW6 3PA; tel: 020 7731 6142; fax: 020 7371 7445

USA

Council Travel The New York office is at 205 East 42nd St, New York, NY 10017-5706; tel: 212 822 2700; web: www.counciltravel.com. 60 offices around the US; tel: 1 800 226 8624; web: www.ciee.org
Mountain Travel–Sobek 1266 66th St, Emeryville, CA 94608; tel: 1 800 687 6235; email: info@mtsobek.com; web: www.mtsobek.com
STA Travel 6560 Scottsdale Rd, F100, Scottsdale, AZ 85253; tel: 1 800 781 4040; web: www.sta-travel.com
Turtle Tours PO Box 1147, Carefree, AZ 85377; tel: 480 488 3688; email: turtletours@earthlink.net; web: www.turtletours.com

RESEARCH

Before travelling to Timbuktu, the French explorer, René Caillié (see page 11), prepared for his trip by spending nine months studying the Koran and learning

Arabic with a Muslim tribe on the banks of the River Senegal. Caillié knew that Christians were not welcome at that time in the fabled city, so he had to pass himself off as a Muslim. These days a trip to Mali requires less meticulous preparation, but Caillié's spirit of research is no bad thing to emulate.

It pays dividends to know something about the country you are about to visit. Not only does research whet the appetite before departure, it can also help to break the ice and establish contact with the local people if you know something – anything! – about their country and way of life. I hope that the background sections of this book are informative and interesting. In *Appendix 2* I have suggested some further reading and a selection of websites to visit, so that you can become an 'armchair expert' before hitting the road and seeing it all for yourself. If you are from the UK, consider contacting **Friends of Mali** (see *Appendix 2*), a London-based organisation that seeks to promote Mali and the Malian culture through a variety of activities. Caillié never had it so good!

Baobab trees

Practicalities

GETTING THERE AND AWAY
By air
Europe

There are no direct flights to Mali from the UK. However, travel agents in London can route you through Casablanca (Royal Air Maroc), Addis Ababa (Ethiopian Airlines) or Paris (Air France). Paris is the main European gateway for flights to Bamako: Air France has daily direct flights to the capital of Mali, but their flights are amongst the more expensive ones. There are, however, less pricey options to choose from.

Since December 1995, a French organisation called Point Afrique (see *Airline offices in Bamako* on page 74) has been operating flights between Paris and Marseille (in the south of France) to Bamako, Mopti and Gao in Mali. Their ethos is to provide access to the more isolated parts of West Africa – they also fly to Mauritania and Niger – and, although you have to get to Marseille or Paris first, there is no cheaper way of travelling to Mali from Europe. Most flights operate during the high season only (mid-December to March). Trans African Airlines (STA) also have relatively inexpensive flights from Paris to Bamako and Kayes. It is well worth checking out the websites of Point Afrique and STA, as they sometimes have special offers. Obviously these flights do fill up rather quickly.

Without exception, choosing another airline implies flying via another African country – often one of Mali's neighbouring countries. Also listed below (with their respective IATA codes) are most airline companies operating regular services to and from Bamako, with flights to and from West African capitals like Ouagadougou, Nouakchott, Cotonou, Accra, Dakar and Niamey. As a matter of fact, you could even opt for a flight to one of these destinations, then travel to Mali overland. Depending on where in Mali you would like to start your trip, this may well be an easy way to cut down your expenses.

North America

Residents of the USA, like their British counterparts, will have to make at least one connection before arriving in Mali. This could be in Europe (Paris or Marseille) or several destinations in Africa, depending on your choice of airline (see *Airline offices in Bamako* on page 74).

Africa

Several of the airlines mentioned below are regional carriers, flying to Bamako from around Africa. STA goes to various countries in the region, as well as to Brazzaville and Pointe Noir in the Congo. Not represented in Bamako is South African Airways, with flights from South Africa via Abidjan or Accra to Bamako. The other companies, their names incorporating the country they are based in, operate at least between Bamako and their respective capitals – but more often than not their flight schedule includes more African destinations. In short, continental air travel to and from Mali is not a problem.

Arriving at Bamako-Sénou International Airport

Arriving in a new country is exciting and, at the same time, a little daunting. After a long, tiring flight, the last thing you want to do is grapple with awkward immigration officials and persistent taxi drivers. Fortunately, Bamako-Sénou Airport (tel: 220 2701) is as informal and relaxed as a West African airport can be.

Planes stop a short distance from the terminal buildings. Walk across the tarmac, enter the terminal, change some money and buy a temporary visa if applicable, complete a simple landing card, get your passport stamped, show your Yellow Fever Certificate to a man in a white coat, and collect your baggage – all of which should not take more than 30 minutes. Remember to retain your boarding pass with the luggage barcode or number; you may have to present it on leaving the terminal to prove that your luggage is really yours. Porters are available – and sometimes even hard to avoid – and taxis will be waiting outside in the car park.

If you are arriving from Paris, you can buy some CFA at the bureau de change in the departure lounge at Charles de Gaulle Airport. It is a good idea to have some local currency before you arrive, just in case the exchange office at Bamako-Sénou is closed – as it often is.

See *Bamako: Getting there and away* on page 104 for information about other facilities available at Bamako-Sénou Airport, as well as transportation from the airport to Bamako.

Airport tax

The international departure tax of CFA19,000 should be included in your air fare, unless you are flying Air Guinée. The airport tax for domestic flights is CFA2,750, payable before checking in.

Airline offices in Bamako

Afriqiyah Airways 8U (Libya) ACI 2000; tel: 229 77 63
Air Algérie AH Av Modibo Keita, Immeuble Sylla, BP 172; tel: 222 31 59; fax: 222 84 05
Air Burkina 2J Immeuble Sonavie; tel: 221 01 78
Air France AF Square Patrice Lumumba, BP 204; tel: 222 22 12; fax: 222 47 34; web: www.airfrance.com

Air Gabon GN Av Mamadou Konaté; tel: 223 52 07
Air Guinée GI Av de la Nation, BP 2414; tel: 221 31 50
Air Ivoire VU BP 2445; tel: 223 95 59; fax: 223 95 75
Air Mauritanie MR Square Patrice Lumumba, Immeuble SCIF, BP 2651; tel: 223 87 38
Air Sénégal V7 555 Av Modibo Keita, BP 1551; tel: 223 9811; email: bamako@airsenegalinternational.sn
Cameroon Airlines UY Quartier du Fleuve, Immeuble Babemba; tel: 223 82 85
Ethiopian Airlines ET Square Patrice Lumumba, BP 1841; tel: 221 60 36; fax: 222 60 36; web: www.flyethiopian.com
Ghana Airways GH Square Patrice Lumumba, Immeuble SCIF, BP 932; tel: 221 92 10 ·
Point Afrique BIE France Le Village, 07 700 Bidon; tel: 04 75 97 20 40; fax: 04 75 04 16 56; Bamako Av de L'Yser, Immeuble ex USAID, BP E762; tel: 223 54 70; fax: 223 57 76; email: bamako@point-afrique.com; web: www.point-afrique.com
Royal Air Maroc AT Av de la Marne, Hôtel de l'Amitié, BP 3260; tel: 221 61 05; fax 221 43 02; web: www.royalairmaroc.co.uk
SAE Airlines Domestic flights only – Route du Sotuba, Bamako, BP 324; tel: 223 14 65/674 68 08; fax: 223 14 66
STA Trans African Airlines T8 Avenue de l'Yser, Immeuble ex USAID; tel: 222 33 33/222 44 44; email: reservez@sta-airlines.com; web: www.sta-airlines.com
Tunis Air TU Avenue de la Marne, Hôtel de l'Amitié; tel: 675 91 92
West African Airlines WZ (Benin) Avenue de l'Yser, Immeuble ex USAID, BP E2949; tel: 223 43 83; email: fakeita@cefib.com

By river

The River Niger rises in Guinea and flows through Mali before bending south towards Niger. The country's other great waterway, the River Senegal, starts in the eastern region of Kayes and flows along the border between Senegal and Mauritania. Therefore, in theory, it is possible to travel to Mali by river from four neighbouring countries. In practice, however, it is rarely done. All international river travel is a question of finding a boat going in your direction, fixing an acceptable price and hoping that the river is navigable. Travelling to and from Mali by this means is for real adventurers, and the River Senegal might be more practicable than the Niger (see *Kayes: Getting there and away* on page 261).

By train

The Dakar–Bamako railway was completed in 1923 and, although it has certainly seen better days, it remains of great economic importance and one of the favourite ways for travellers to get to Mali. 'Favourite' is perhaps an ill-chosen word, for the overcrowded and habitually late Dakar–Bamako train is no Orient Express. Even so, it does provide a link between the two capitals which ensures its continued popularity for the foreseeable future. Trains leave Bamako on Wednesdays to arrive in Dakar the following day, while trains leave Dakar on Saturdays, with a stop at Kayes on Sunday mornings.

By road

What with Mali being a landlocked country with seven different international borders, many of its visitors arrive by road. As far as independent travellers are concerned, the routes to and from Senegal and Burkina Faso are arguably the most popular. There is public transport from Senegal to Kayes, and Burkina to several Malian towns, including Bamako, Ségou, Mopti and Sikasso. Public transport is also available to Niger (from Gao). Fewer people choose to travel to Guinea and the war-torn countries of this corner of West Africa, although *bâchées* do run from Bamako to the Guinean border and from Sikasso to Côte d'Ivoire. The desert routes to Mauritania and Algeria are not served by public transport, although *locations* and *camions* (see page 84 for an explanation of these terms) can be found. A steady stream of tourists with their own 4WD vehicles cross into Mali from Mauritania, but, due to the security situation in Algeria and Tuareg banditry in the desert, the so-called Route de Tanezrouft is seldom used. The road linking Mali to Burkina Faso is paved and in a generally good state; elsewhere, there are only tracks. (For more information about road travel between Mali and neighbouring countries, see the *Getting there and away* sections for relevant towns.)

Border crossings

The most commonly used border crossings between Mali and its neighbours are as follows:

Algeria Via Gao and Tessalit (which is not actually on the border itself, but the last settlement before you cross into Algeria)
Burkina Faso Via Koutiala and Kouri (although a substantial number of visitors with their own vehicles go via Bankass and Koro, stopping in Dogon country en route)
Côte d'Ivoire Via Sikasso and Zégoua
Guinea Kourémalé (about 100km from Bamako)
Mauritania Via Nioro du Sahel or, more rarely, Nara
Niger Via Gao, Ansongo and Labézanga
Senegal Via Kayes and Diboli

GETTING AROUND
By air

Given the immense size of Mali, the isolation of some of its main towns, and the shortcomings of ground transportation, getting around by air is an option worth considering. From the tourist's point of view, flying to places such as Timbuktu, Gao and Kayes will save time and avoid arduous journeys. On the other hand, flying is a rather sterile and unrewarding experience which minimises contact with the realities of life in one of the world's poorest countries. Therefore, fly to save time – not to see Mali. At the time of writing, however, the situation with regard to domestic flights was by no means clear. In 2003, after a long struggle trying to beat the odds, Air Mali has ceased to exist. Since they were responsible for the majority of the domestic flights – well, at least in theory – this has left a void which is still to be filled. Two airlines had already stepped in before Air Mali's final exit, but their services are limited and rather erratic thus far. And so, but for the domestic flight schedule which has become strikingly restricted, nothing has changed really. Should you wish to travel by air, remember two things: book your flight well in advance (since most planes have no more than 17 seats) and check if it is actually going shortly beforehand.

For what it is worth, these were the flight schedules and fares at the beginning of 2004:

Société Avion Express (SAE)

Day	Destination	dep1	dep2
Monday	BKO–Kayes–BKO	07.00	10.30
	BKO–Yélimané–BKO	07.30	11.00
Tuesday	BKO–Mopti–Timbuktu	08.00	11.00
Wednesday	Timbuktu–Mopti–BKO	08.00	10.30
Thursday	BKO–Kayes–Yélimané–BKO	07.00	10.30
	BKO–Yélimané–Nioro–BKO	07.30	10.30
Friday	–	–	–
Saturday	BKO–Mopti–Timbuktu	08.00	11.00
Sunday	Timbuktu–Mopti–BKO	08.00	11.00

One-way fares	CFA
BKO–Kayes	65,050
BKO–Yélimané	78,150
BKO–Mopti	53,700
BKO–Timbuktu	103,050
BKO–Nioro	70,400
Mopti–Timbuktu	78,350
Kayes–Yélimané	32,250
Yélimané–Nioro	29,650

Trans African Airlines (STA)

Flights from Bamako to Kayes and vice versa are on Monday, Tuesday, Thursday, Saturday and Sunday, departing from Bamako at 05.45 and returning at 08.00.

Fare: CFA67,000 (one way) and CFA107,500 (return, valid for one week). Note: all SAE and STA fares exclude CFA2,750 airport tax.

By river

Quite apart from its romantic past and dramatic presence today, the River Niger is a vital means of communication, especially for the isolated

ALONG THE NIGER RIVER
Peter Udell

My journey along the Niger ended in chaos at three on a Sunday morning, after two days and – almost – three nights on board an old, steel-built river steamer. Its sailors shouted raucously to each other as it docked at Korioumé, the nearest port to Timbuktu. The passengers surged in disarray down the gangplank, carrying, dragging and pushing their possessions.

The journey had begun in similar chaos at eight on the previous Thursday evening, just a few hours after I'd booked my berth in a first-class cabin for two, rather than in a cabin for four or more, at a quayside office in the river port of Mopti. Crowds of men and women – some carrying their babies on their backs – struggled on board. They climbed up the gangplank with baskets of fruit and vegetables, with bulging sacks, with pots and pans and food for the journey. They settled down on the open decks where they lived, cooked, ate and slept.

There had, too, been chaos at each of the larger villages where the steamer made its scheduled stops. As we approached them, villagers dressed brightly in all the colours of the rainbow – and more besides – appeared as if from nowhere. Women from the villages came to sell their chickens and fish, sometimes piled in baskets on their heads. Women from the steamer rushed ashore to sell their fruit and vegetables. Some of us passengers followed, and were surrounded by the smiles and greetings of the instant crowd.

A different chaos came at the many more unscheduled stops our steamer made; with a huge barge strapped to its side – and, I was disconcerted to discover, filled with petrol – it ran aground again and again. Sometimes it was pushed into the riverbank by strong winds. At others it ran on to mud banks where the Niger had, by the very last days of November, become too shallow. Whatever the cause, the crew made frantic and often ineffective attempts to refloat it.

But for most of my time on board, what was most memorable – and extraordinarily enjoyable – was the calm and peace. The fish market smells and flies of Mopti were forgotten. The extreme dry midday heat of Timbuktu was still to come.

towns of the Niger Inland Delta and the Sahara. Travelling along the Niger can be slow and uncomfortable, but is rarely dull or forgettable.

When the level of the water is high enough – roughly from the end of July to the end of December – the River Niger can be navigated by large steamers run by COMANAV (Compagnie Malienne de Navigation) between Koulikoro, 57km from Bamako, and Gao. The total voyage takes just under a week, although most passengers get on and off at various ports en route, including Ségou, Mopti and Kabara (for Timbuktu). There

At our leisurely meals we – the tiny band of first-class passengers who included two nurses and an airline pilot from Luxembourg, and a Greek artist with his Italian wife – talked at length in a mixture of French, German and English. Over river fish and sometimes meat, and rice with almost everything – in no way haute cuisine but perfectly edible – we spoke about the adventures we'd already had in Burkina Faso, Senegal, Mali, and about the goal that had by chance brought us all together: Timbuktu.

Between meals, sitting for hours on the steamer's windswept top deck or leaning on the rail outside our tiny bunk-bed cabins and along from our showers and lavatories – primitive but mostly in working order! – we watched the world pass slowly by.

Although it was sailing downstream, the steamer moved only at a snail's pace past the long, narrow wooden boats of the river's fishermen. It slid past their little villages, each a line of huts with mud walls and thatched roofs and water lapping almost up to their doors. It slid past thick reedbeds that stretched as far as I could see, an enormous expanse of dry green framed by the pale grey blue of the sky and by the darker grey blue of the Niger. It slid past the half-desert of the Sahel. Past dark green trees, low and scattered. Past scrubland whose bushes and grasses seemed at best only partly living, and in danger of being overwhelmed by the sand. Past near desert where the pale sand was interrupted only by occasional plants.

But most dramatic, memorable and magnificent were the sunrises and sunsets. Before dawn, the sky in the east and the high, thin clouds were set on fire, until the sun burst up from behind the horizon and the flaming orange faded away.

At dusk, the sky behind us, and the waters of the Niger with it, became orange again, until the stars, so brilliant and so close, filled the sky and, from being part of the magic of a Mali sunset, I became part of the magic of an African night.

These nightfalls on the Niger were, quite simply, unforgettable – as unforgettable as the next when, from a Tuareg camp on the very edge of the desert that I'd reached on camelback, I watched the sun setting behind the sand dunes and, soon after, the stars beginning to appear over the Sahara and over the crumbling walls and decaying buildings of the legendary city of Timbuktu.

are currently three COMANAV boats in service: the *Kankou Moussa*, the *Général Soumare* and the *Tombouctou*. The *Kankou Moussa* is the largest of the three, although they all have similar facilities. There are five classes in total: the *cabines de luxe* have large double beds, air conditioning and bathrooms and are on the upper deck; first-class cabins with two beds and a basin are on the upper or middle deck; second-class cabins sleeping four people are on the middle deck; third-class cabins with bunk beds for at least 12 people are on the lower deck; while fourth-class is the lower deck itself. Do not delude yourself with wordings like *cabines de luxe*; these characterisations are merely meant to describe the level of luxury – or the lack of it – as compared to the other classes. There are communal showers and toilets for those not in luxury cabins and, although the dining room and bar are intended for first-class passengers, you should be able to use them regardless of your status. Fares range from very expensive to dirt cheap, depending on the level of comfort required. The following is a selection of prices in CFA to some of the more popular ports for tourists:

	Cabine de luxe	First class	Second class	Third class	Fourth class
Koulikoro-Gao	282,915	147,640	107,080	63,090	14,010
Koulikoro-Kabara	194,730	101,680	73,805	43,555	9,815
Koulikoro-Mopti	109,380	57,165	41,475	24,660	5,625
Mopti-Gao	174,290	90,955	65,920	38,910	8,825
Mopti-Kabara	85,915	44,110	32,805	19,535	4,525

The beginning and end of the season – when navigation is restricted – are characterised by a limited service between Mopti and Kabara only. Roughly between mid-August and mid-December, a regular departure schedule becomes operational for journeys from Koulikoro to Gao. Though departure times are more or less respected at the start of the trip, the COMANAV boats rarely cover the distance without delays. There is one weekly departure on Tuesdays, with the three boats alternating. The *Tombouctou* and the *Général Soumaré* go all the way to Gao in five to six days, returning on Mondays. The *Kankou*, meanwhile, arrives at its final destination Kabara after four to five days, to return to Koulikoro on Sundays.

Downstream

	departure	time	from	to	arrival
Tombouctou	Tuesday	22.00	Koulikoro	Gao	Sunday
Général Soumaré	Tuesday	22.00	Koulikoro	Gao	Sunday
Kankou	Tuesday	22.00	Koulikoro	Kabara	Saturday

Upstream

	departure	time	from	to	arrival
Tombouctou	Monday	20.00	Gao	Koulikoro	Sunday
Général Soumaré	Monday	20.00	Gao	Koulikoro	Sunday
Kankou	Sunday	14.00	Kabara	Koulikoro	Thursday

When the river is too low for the COMANAV steamers, travel is still possible – although extremely unpredictable – by *pinasse* and pirogue. Roughly speaking, a *pinasse* is a large pirogue with a motor used to transport goods and people along the river. Even though there is space for passengers on *pinasses* transporting goods, it is often severely restricted – which is tolerable during the day but uncomfortable at night. By contrast, the smaller – and much more expensive – *pinasses* run by tour operators (primarily to

Timbuktu) have mattresses, tents and other creature comforts. The *Getting there and away* sections for towns along the river have more information about this form of travel. Note, however, that much depends on the level of the water at the time, and most voyages will take longer than you think. The River Senegal and the River Bani are also navigable, although they are less travelled than the Niger.

By train

For years, it was a policy decision not to build a road between Bamako and Kayes for fear that it would compete with the railway, which links these two towns and passes through other regional centres such as Kati, Kita and Bafoulabé. Daily trains used to be hopelessly overcrowded and overworked. However, in recent years the road system in the region of Kayes has been significantly improved, and for the first time in history road transport can compete with the railway for efficiency and comfort. With bus-fares matching the fare for a second-class train ticket, many Malians now prefer to travel by road, which results in the decline of the number of people travelling by rail. The railway track is now mainly used for freight transport, and there are only four passenger trains running in either direction. One of them is the famous Bamako–Dakar express. The railway has been privatised since October 2003, changing its name from *Chemin de Fer du Mali* (CFM) to **Trans Rail SA**. Even though the heyday of the famous railway may be over, the new Canadian owners intend to upgrade the track, locomotives and carriages over time and keep the trains running.

All trains have first and second class, and are usually in a poor condition. In first class, seats are reserved and the carriages are slightly more spacious, although by no means luxurious, with sagged seats and torn upholstery. In second class, seats are claimed on a first-come-first-served basis (despite what your ticket might say) and the carriages are a lot more crowded. Two trains have a luxury class with couchettes and a bit more space. Only the Bamako–Dakar express has a restaurant carriage where you may get basic meals and a chilled drink at best. Seats in the restaurant are often taken by jolly drinkers for the duration of the journey. At every stop, vendors will sell some food, fruit and chilled – but untreated – water.

When travelling by train in Mali, bear in mind the following pieces of advice:

- Always try to buy your ticket the day before you intend to travel
- Although delays are habitual, turn up at the station at the scheduled time of departure
- Beware of theft, especially during the rush to board the train and during stops along the way.

Though the following is the official timetable, departure times may change without prior notice. Check the blackboard in the hall or on the platform for modified departure times. Delays are frequent. For more information, call the Service Commercial (tel: 222 19 63).

Train	Day	Bamako	Kita	Kayes	Dakar
Express2	Wed	09.15	12.40	22.25	13.20★
14	Fri	19.30	22.40	06.30★	–
12	Sun	07.15	10.40	18.20	–
12	Mon	07.15	10.40	18.20	–

Train	Day	Dakar	Kayes	Kita	Bamako
Express1	Sat	10.45	05.30★	12.45	16.15
15	Sun	–	20.15	03.25★	07.05
13	Tue	–	07.15	14.15	18.05
13	Fri	–	07.15	14.15	18.05

★ The following day (note that Express1 from Dakar arrives in Kayes on Sundays)

The following fares are those for the more expensive Bamako–Dakar express. Trains 14 and 15 also have couchettes – unlike trains 12 and 13.

Bamako to	Couchette	First Class	Second Class
Kita		6,370	4,595
Mahina		13,570	9,955
Kayes	22,565	16,190	11,480
Dakar	53,520	34,620	25,480

Theoretically it is still possible to have your vehicle transported by train. With the construction of the paved road linking Bamako to Kayes, the need for this service is no longer obvious. Nevertheless, for a handsome sum of money cars can still be hoisted on and off freight trains (not passenger trains) in Dakar, Kayes and Korofina – the latter being the freight train station in Bamako, along the Route de Sotuba.

By road

While the proportion of *goudron* or tarred road in Mali is not as high as in neighbouring countries such as Senegal, Côte d'Ivoire and Burkina Faso, most of the main tourist attractions (with the notable exception of Timbuktu) are on – or not far from – the principal highway, which stretches for over 1,000km from Bamako to Gao on the edge of the Sahara. The country's other main road does a loop in the southern region, linking the capital to Sikasso and, in better times, Abidjan, Mali's closest port. Until only a few years ago, apart from one or two other stretches of paved road, that was it; the rest of the country had to make do with dusty, sandy tracks. Financed by both the Malian governement and foreign funds, however, ambitious plans have been put into effect, turning existing road maps into historical documents. And more road construction works are in progress.

The biggest achievement so far must be the construction of a paved road linking Bamako to Kayes, opening up a region that was almost totally bereft of good roads – and even of good tracks. But also the smooth tar to Bandiagara turns an expedition to this major stepping stone to Dogon country almost into a picnic. The improved piste to Timbuktu, meanwhile, certainly reduces the time needed to drive from Douentza to Korioumé – the ferry across the Niger at 19km from Timbuktu – but the going is still tough. However, with all that has been achieved in just a few years, one may even be tempted to believe that the rumours of a Bamako–Timbuktu highway may materialise one day. Indeed, road construction workers from various European countries have moved in already, taking on the challenge to improve the section from Timbuktu to Goundam and Niafunké for a start.

By no means does all this mean that the whole of Mali has been – or will be – opened up; it has just become somewhat easier to reach the more inaccessible parts of the country in a fairly comfortable way.

Hiring a vehicle

Having a 4WD vehicle at your disposal is a definite luxury, permitting you to forget the hassles of public transport and navigate the more difficult tracks to out-of-the way places. It saves time and is the most comfortable way to see Mali by land. However, for all this you pay a small fortune. A 4WD with driver – and you should not consider anything else unless you are sticking to the paved roads – rarely costs under CFA50,000 a day, and quite often considerably more. This price, of course, does not include petrol and the driver's meals and accommodation. The larger hotels and most tour operators can arrange car-hire. Be wary of individuals offering a similar service for considerably less money, as there is usually a catch.

Buses, bâchées and bush taxis

For travel along the main highways and tracks where 4WD is not absolutely essential, a combination of buses, *bâchées* and bush taxis are at the travellers' disposal. You will find them at certain departure points and bus yards or – in French – *gares routières*.

There are several bus companies in Mali. Some run along the Bamako–Gao highway, while others serve the region of Sikasso. Examples of the former include Bani Transport, Somatra, Binké Transport and Diakité Transport, while Kénédougou Voyages and Somatrie are examples of the latter. These buses leave at fixed times and stop only at the larger towns. Buy your ticket from the company's representative (often sitting at a desk beside the bus) and wait for your name to be announced before boarding. It all seems rather chaotic, but in fact seats are rarely overbooked. Whether or not the bus departs on time, however, is another matter.

Bâchées and bush taxis (*taxi brousse* in French) ply the routes along the paved highways and also serve the smaller towns and villages. A *bâchée* can be anything from a small van or minibus to a Peugeot 504 or 505 converted into something resembling a pick-up truck. Bush taxis, meanwhile, are these same Peugeots, kept in their original state, but used to carry at least twice their intended load. Travelling by *bâchée* and bush taxi, therefore, is not particularly comfortable, especially if the road is dusty and the weather hot. This type of transport invariably leaves when there are enough passengers to justify the trip – which means that if you are the first to buy your ticket, be prepared to wait several hours before the others are sold. The net result is that travel is often as slow as it is uncomfortable and, although the road might be in a good state, going just a few kilometres can take a big chunk out of your day.

Some roads – in the desert and the region of Kayes, for instance – are too rough for buses, *bâchées* and bush taxis. In these cases, the traveller must either look for a ride on a *camion* (the French word meaning 'lorry' or 'truck') or find a *location* (from the French word meaning 'hire'). A *location* is often a Land Rover – preferred for their renowned resilience – with enough space in the back for about 16 people. They are most common in Timbuktu and other desert towns where 4WD is necessary. The price of a *location* or a *camion* is usually fixed, but is sometimes a matter for discussion between the passenger and driver.

Hitchhiking

If – or when – the buses and *bâchées* start to get you down, hitchhiking is a feasible option. Along the main highway, especially between Bamako and Mopti, there is a fair amount of NGO and tourist traffic – your best bets for free rides. The section of the highway between Mopti and Gao is considerably quieter, while on some other routes – in the desert, for example – there can be nothing at all. The best place to wait for rides is at the police checkpoints a few kilometres out of the towns. Tell the police where you want to go and they will sometimes stop vehicles on your behalf.

Around town

Though Bamako is best seen by walking the streets, some attractions and hotels are quite far from the centre. The capital has an extensive system of organised transport, which makes travelling around the city easy and efficient. Bamako is famous for its green minibuses and *bâchées*, known as **sotramas** and **dou dourenis** respectively. They are cheap and plentiful, with often less than minutes between vehicles plying the same routes. Taxis for private hire are called **locations** (not to be confused with the *locations* mentioned above), while **shared taxis** provide the same service, but pick up and drop off passengers along the way.

Mali's other towns are easily covered on foot, and sometimes the only alternative is the relatively expensive *location* or private taxi. Some expansive towns, on the other hand, may have a limited system of public transport, using the same, easily recognisable green sotramas and *bâchées*, and yellow taxis.

ACCOMMODATION

Trying to categorise hotels in Mali is a dangerous business; and labelling accommodation 'expensive', 'moderate' or 'budget' according to its price is often misleading. Just because you pay CFA15,000 for a room – a price I consider to be above average – does not necessarily mean that you will end up with good or even moderate accommodation. Travellers often complain that you pay a lot for a little in Mali and, on the whole, I agree. This is why I have tried to avoid pigeon-holing hotels, preferring to give an opinion as to whether or not I think they are good value for money.

Above Yellow-crowned gonolek (*Laniarius barbarus*)
Below Village weaver (*Ploceus cucullatus*)

Above Nile monitor
(*Varanus niloticus*)

Right Green monkey
(*Cercopithecus aethiops*)

Luxury hotels, as westerners understand the term, are rare in Mali. There are, however, many comfortable hotels designed for tourists or people visiting the country on business, most of which are found in Bamako. If you pay more than CFA30,000 for a place to stay, you can normally expect all mod-cons: air conditioning, television, telephone, en-suite toilet and sometimes even a bath. The frills disappear as you start to economise, and you should not take it for granted that a CFA15,000 room, for example, has luxuries such as air conditioning and an en-suite toilet. The more frugal you become, the less you can expect. The cheapest places in Mali are around CFA2,000, which buys you a mud box or a place on the roof under the stars.

If a town does not have a hotel, it will often have a *campement*. While at many you can bring your own tent and pitch it in the garden, most people stay in the functional – but not luxurious – rooms. However, you can stumble across a *campement* which is every bit as good as, if not better than, an expensive hotel. This will not be the case, however, in **Dogon country**, where *campements* are now available in most of the popular villages. Almost without exception, these places are very basic and without running water; but at the same time, very welcoming and often quite charming.

If you arrive in a town where there seems to be nowhere to stay, what are your options? In places where there is a *Mission Catholique* (Catholic mission), you might be able to stay in accommodation reserved for visiting clerics and their families. In fact, in Bamako the religious missions have become favourites with backpackers and other budget travellers. *Maison de passage* is an ambiguous French expression which can embrace many types of lodgings, but typically refers to the ad hoc accommodation one finds in family homes, restaurants, bars and NGO houses. For these opportunities, however, you have to ask around and be willing to make friends. Always offer to pay. Occasionally you may find a *chambre de passage* with an hourly rate. Though theoretically these could be used to freshen up and rest for a while, more often than not these rooms are a cover for prostitution.

Taxes
There is a tourist tax on hotel rooms of CFA500 per night. This may be included in the total price or added on to the basic room rate. The prices quoted in this book usually include the tourist tax.

TOURIST INFORMATION
L'OMATHO and the Mission Culturelle
Formal **tourist offices** are a rarity in Mali. The Office Malien du Tourisme et de l'Hôtellerie (or OMATHO) is a governmental institution working under the Ministère de l'Artisanat et du Tourisme. Its objectives include charting and streamlining potential tourist destinations and events, promoting and increasing tourism in Mali, and implementing a compulsory training for professional guides. OMATHO also seeks to improve the quality of various services, such as dispensing information to visitors; a kind of tourist office, one could say, and sometimes even signposted as such. Though staff are very

friendly and ready to help, in real terms it is mainly a place to pick up some brochures and not much else. Having said that, you may encounter the chef or a member of staff who is passionate about his profession, and find yourself discussing local history and culture in depth – at times even in English! In short: the OMATHO has not yet come to full bloom, but can no longer be ignored, so give it a try. Apart from the main office in Bamako (rue Mohamed V, BP 191; tel: 222 56 73; fax: 222 55 41), there are representations in Kayes, Sikasso, Ségou, Mopti, Timbuktu, Gao and Kidal. A regional office in Bamako represents Bamako and Koulikoro. For more information visit: www.le-mali.com or email: omatho@le-mali.com.

Look for the **Mission Culturelle** at Djenné, Bandiagara and Timbuktu. Established to protect, restore and promote Mali's World Heritage Sites, the tasks of the Mission Culturelle sometimes overlap with those of a conventional tourist office. However, while all three offices are run by leading authorities on the history of Djenné, Dogon country and Timbuktu, they should not be treated as tourist offices. Ask them for advice and recommendations by all means; but also understand – and take an interest in – their struggle to protect the country's patrimony from a multitude of sins (see *Responsible tourism in Dogon country* on page 184 for more about these 'sins').

TOUR OPERATORS IN MALI

Tour operators in Mali – and there is no shortage of them – fulfil a number of functions. The larger ones, most of which are based in Bamako, sell airline tickets, arrange vehicle hire and offer a number of *circuits* or tours in Mali and neighbouring countries. Others specialise in certain regions (Dogon country, the desert etc) and may be based outside Bamako. As far as the tours in Mali are concerned, the majority of tour operators are sent groups of tourists by travel agencies acting as their partners in Europe. Independent travellers are quite welcome to turn up and book a tour, but it is often expensive, especially if you are not travelling in a group yourself. There are, however, advantages to taking a tour. Provided that you choose a reputable operator, you should be guaranteed a decent guide who knows what he's talking about. Transportation problems are also negated by 4WD vehicles and, for river trips, comfortable *pinasses*. The downside, of course, is the expense and the minimal contact with the realities of Malian life.

Almost all tour operators organise trips to places such as Ségou, Djenné, Mopti, Dogon country and Timbuktu (by river or road). Gao is a good place to join organised trips into the desert, but, unfortunately, Mali's national parks and reserves do not interest tour operators eager to cash in on the country's better-known attractions. The list below contains one or two of the major tour operators in Bamako – all of them reputable enough, but perhaps lacking the personal touch found at some of the out-of-town options. If you want to avoid the larger agencies in Bamako, try the meticulous **Tara Africa Tours**, a Dutch-Dogon partnership that provides tailor-made tours throughout the country. For obvious reasons, Tara Africa Tours is particularly good for trips to Dogon country. Another agency that combines expertise with a personal touch, is the American-Dogon run **Toguna Adventure Tours**. Based in Ségou, **Balanzan Tours** is arguably the largest tour operator outside Bamako, and the best for trips to the various attractions in and around Ségou. **Affala Voyages Initiatives** in Kidal is a solid choice for ventures deep into the desert. The agency is run by the same respectable Tuareg who is the president of the committee which organises Takoubelt – the Tuareg festival in the Kidal region (see page 220). Be persistent; at times Affala Voyages are difficult to contact.

Affala Voyages Initiatives (tel Bamako: 221 02 70) BP 09, Kidal; tel: 285 00 92; cellphone: 672 91 56; fax: 285 00 90; email: cagbaye@aol.com; web: www.affala.com

Ashraf Voyages BP 63, Mopti; tel: 243 02 79; fax: 243 00 66; email: ashraf@dds.nl; web: www.xs4all.nl/~ilja/mali/camel-f/htm

Balanzan Tours BP 402, Ségou; tel/fax: 232 02 57; email: balanzan-tours@nomade.fr; web: perso.wanadoo.fr/soubigou

Bani Voyages BP E1290, Bamako; tel: 223 26 03; fax: 223 44 74; email: bani@malinet.ml

Mali Voyages BP 148, Mopti; tel: 243 08 02/672 67 89; email: youssoufditgole@hotmail.com

Point Afrique web: www.point-afrique.com

Sahara Passion BP 44, Gao; tel/fax: 282 01 87; email: spassion@malinet.ml; web: www.sahara-passion.com

Tara Africa Tours BP E5661, Bamako; tel/fax: 228 70 91; email: tara@afribone.net.ml; web: www.tara-africatours.com

Timbuctours BP 222, Bamako; tel: 223 55 64; fax: 222 53 15; email: TBT@cefib.com; web: www.resume.fr/timbuctours

Toguna Adventure Tours BP E5096, Bamako; tel/fax: 229 53 66/69; email: togunaadventure@afribone.net.ml; web: www.geocities.com/toguna_adventure_tours

This is far from being an exhaustive list of Mali's tour operators and, particularly in Bamako, there are many more to choose from.

Guides

OMATHO and the Mission Culturelle are working together to improve the quality of the tourist guides in Mali. This is just as well, because as things stand there is very little regulation. The result has been a proliferation of *petits guides* – young men and boys who may know how to get from A to B, but not necessarily be able to explain what A and B mean. Lack of knowledge, although disappointing for inquisitive tourists and potentially damaging from a cultural point of view (see *Responsible tourism in Dogon country* on page 184), can be forgivable, provided that guides are friendly and obviously trying their best. In this case, you are paying for their company rather than expertise. However, in too many towns – Bamako, Mopti and Djenné are amongst the worst – good nature has been replaced by an uncharacteristic aggressive streak. Some blame this on drug addiction, the alienating effects of unemployment and other social ills but, whatever the cause, the effect on the visitor – especially in a small place such as Djenné where there is no escaping the guides – is tiring and frustrating.

The Minister of Culture is aware of the problem and since 2005 tourist guides are required to register for a *carte professionelle*. OMATHO and Mission Culturelle are in the process of establishing an infrastructure involving exams and diplomas. Even so, for every guide worth his salt, there will be ten who are not.

PUBLIC HOLIDAYS

Being a country where Islam and Christianity dominate, Mali's public holidays are largely based on these two religions. The dates for the various Islamic holidays (Ramadan, Tabaski, Maouloud...) vary from year to year, so check a current diary. The other public holidays in Mali are:

January 1	New Year's Day
January 20	Army Day
March 26	Martyrs' Day
March/April	Easter
May 1	Labour Day
May 25	Africa Day
September 22	Independence Day
December 25	Christmas Day

FESTIVALS

Throughout Mali and throughout the year there are numerous festivals and traditional festivities. Many of these events are open to the public and some events have in fact been designed or reshaped for the benefit of tourists. In other cases, festivities are first of all local celebrations or rituals, but visitors are welcome. In certain regions, the OMATHO (see page 85) are urging communities to facilitate access to a wider public, for example by having the event take place in the cooler months. Obviously, certain events are strictly seasonal by nature, but some festivals have indeed been rescheduled. Even though there is a growing tendency to invite the public in to participate, some rituals and festivities are sacred and intended for a select group of the population only. Your only chance of attending such a ceremony or festivity is by personal invitation.

The list below is by no means complete, but some of the more popular festivals and celebrations – all open to the public – are listed. For more information, contact the OMATHO or check the websites mentioned below.

District of Bamako
Festival des Masques de Koulouba
A popular Bambara celebration during which traditional masks are exhibited in the villages of Koulouba and Sogonafing. No fixed date.

Region of Ségou
Fesmamas
The yearly Festival des Masques et Marionettes (Festival of Masks and Puppets) is grafted on to two traditional rituals during which the gods are invoked for a successful harvest. For this occasion, however, the masks and puppets provide a profane but spectacular display. Malian groups as well as international groups take part in competitive and vivid choreographies, staged in two quarters of Markala. Fesmamas takes place in March – on a 'favourable' date according to the lunar calendar – though OMATHO is trying to bring the festival forward.

Sankémon
An animist ritual involving sacrifices, incantations and 'collective fishing' in the Mare de San. See also page 144.

Region of Mopti
Diafarabé
Every year in November or December, as the grasslands of the northern Sahel dry out, the semi-nomadic Peul return with their cattle to the River Niger. New pastures await on the other side, but the cattle have to swim across. There are other cattle-crossing places, but Diafarabé is the scene of the biggest and most important crossing. Families stay reunited for a few days only, before the herders move on, which makes this short gathering both exuberant and emotional.

Crépissage de la Mosquée
The ends of wood sticking out of the façade of Djenné's famous mosque do actually serve a purpose. Each year before the start of the rainy season, the people of Djenné volunteer to resurface the mosque with a new layer of *banco* by hand. Huge quantities of *banco* are hauled up to the Djennenké, whose feet seek support on the wooden protrusions. Not so much a festival but a huge event all the same, the crépissage usually takes place in April.

Festival des Danses des Masques
This festival is held in one of the villages along the *falaise* de Bandiagara. Different groups of masked dancers from all over Dogon country compete for the honour of being the best group of all. Like a performance for tourists in any village, these dances are grafted on to their sacred counterparts, but without the ritual denotation. However, it's the element of competition that makes all the difference, as all dancers give it their best shot to impress the international audience and their kinsmen alike. The festival takes place every year at the end of December or the beginning of January. See also page 187.

Region of Gao
Takoubelt: Festival de Kidal
Traditionally a gathering of Tuareg, this three-day festival is opening up to visitors from around the world. It serves as a stage for Tuareg music, poetry

and dance, while more serious matters like archaeological digs and forum-discussions are also scheduled. In 2004, the festival took place in Essouk in the beginning of January, but each year a different location is chosen. For more information, see pages 220–1 or go to www.kidal.info/FETE/Essouk.

Tamadacht: Festival de Andéramboukane
The Tamadacht Festival is a celebration of Tuareg arts and culture, with many participants – including other ethnic groups such as the Woodabe – from both Mali and Niger. Its basic principles are similar to those of the Kidal festival. The location is always Andéramboukane, a speck on the map situated on the border between the two countries. Rumour has it that the dates will be fixed on 26 to 28 January.

Timbuktu Region
Festival in the Desert
Essakane has been chosen as the fixed setting for the Festival in the Desert which takes place in mid-January. Of the three desert festivals, the one in Essakane receives the highest number of visitors. Some favour the idea to merge the three events into one big happening, but that would be a loss. Already the festival in Essakane seems to be straying from its original blueprint, with many non-Tuareg elements creeping in. The quality is no less, but a merging of the three seems like a final blow to the principal ideas. For more information see pages 238–9 or go to www.festival-au-desert.org.

Traversé des troupeaux du Gourma
When the water level of the Niger starts dropping, in the Gourma area troops will also swim across the river. As in Diafarabé, this event goes hand in hand with frolic festivities.

WHAT TO BUY
A guidebook probably goes too far when it starts telling you what to buy when you visit Mali. Many of your souvenirs will – and should – be spontaneous purchases made at the market. In provincial towns and villages the main market usually takes place on a certain day of the week; in Bamako it is a daily event. Haggle for the best deal, but always pay a fair price.

Mali is well-known for its arts and crafts, which vary from region to region. **Wood-carvings** and *bogolans* are two of the most popular souvenirs. The former are sold all over Dogon country, along with wooden **masks** and enough **jewellery** to sink the *Titanic* (see *Responsible tourism in Dogon country* on page 184 for advice on souvenir-hunting there). *Bogolans* can be blankets, or items of clothing, decorated with a dye made from mud, tree-bark and various other ingredients, and are of particularly good quality in Mopti, Ségou, and some Dogon villages like Endé. **Pottery**, meanwhile, is a speciality in Ségou, and Tuareg **metalwork** – especially daggers and swords – is certainly worth a look. The standard of **basketwork** and **leatherwork** in Mali can be quite high; **musical instruments**, such as *djembes*, *koras* and *balafons* (see page 26), are original – and often expensive – souvenirs; and few people leave without having invested in some form of **headwear** – be it a turban (five metres is a good length), a pointed Peul hat, or a rather comical (to our eyes at least) Dogon bonnet.

COMMUNICATIONS AND MEDIA
Post
Most towns in Mali have a post office. They are normally open from Monday to Friday (about 08.00–16.00, sometimes interupted by a lunch-break) and on Saturday morning (08.00–12.00), although precise opening times differ from town to town. **Sending mail** is generally safe and reliable. Letters and postcards to France seem to arrive quickest, while post to elsewhere in Europe and the Americas takes longer. The price of postage for a postcard/letter under 100g is CFA385/CFA445 to France, CFA395/CFA465 to the rest of Europe and CFA405/CFA485 to the USA, Canada, Australia etc.

As for **receiving mail**, the larger offices around the country have poste restante facilities. An alternative is to have your post, faxes and emails sent to the American Express Travel Service (AMEX) in Bamako: Avenue Kasse Keita, Immeuble Babemba, BP 2917; tel: 222 44 35/222 78 92; fax: 222 94 50; email: agence@ats.com.ml (AMEX share an office with the travel agency Afric Trans Services). Whether using poste restante or AMEX, ask your correspondent to write your surname clearly in capital letters and to underline it to avoid your letter being filed under the wrong name.

Telephone
Much of the 'action' of the Malian film *La vie sur terre* (see page 28) takes place at the post office around the one telephone in Sokolo. At one point in the film, the phlegmatic telephone operator states that 'la communication est une question de chance' (communication is a matter of luck). This still applies to certain towns (like Djenné and Kidal) and in remoter areas, where sometimes there is a dialling tone, sometimes not. However, with a growing demand for a reliable network for both telephone and access to the internet, times are a-changing. The existing network is improving as installations are being upgraded, while a mobile network is rapidly developing simultaneously.

The Société de la Télécommunication Malienne (Sotelma) is responsible for Mali's landline network, as well as the public telephone boxes in the major towns throughout the country. You can buy telephone cards to use in these boxes. However, although they work out slightly cheaper than calling from a *cabine téléphonique*, they are not as reliable. *Cabines téléphoniques* are privately-run call shops which sometimes also have fax and photocopy machines. The cost of your call depends on the number of units used. A short local call normally consumes one unit, which is priced at around CFA150, while a ten-minute call I made from Sévaré to Bamako needed 85 units or CFA12,750! International calls are even more expensive.

The two major mobile network providers are Malitel and Ikatel. With little variation between the two, the receiving range is approximately 30km around most major towns. It can be expected that before too long all towns of some importance will be incorporated in the mobile network. SIM-cards are available in Bamako from CFA15,000, and scratch-cards to feed your credit are widely available all over the country. Note that mobile calls are expensive.

Email and internet

As in most countries in the world, the internet is becoming increasingly popular. Telephone lines permitting, most bigger towns now have cybercafé's where the public have access to the internet and email services. The charge varies from CFA1,000 to CFA2,000 per hour. See the *Practical information* sections of *Chapters 6 to 14*.

Media

The press in Mali is in French. *L'Essor*, founded in 1949, is the oldest and the best newspaper, with plenty of national coverage as well as international news and sports stories. *Les Echos* and *Nouvel Horizon* are other daily newspapers, while *L'Observateur*, *Le Républican* and *L'Indépendant*, amongst several others, are published weekly. In general, English-language newspapers and magazines are hard to find. If you do come across them, they will probably be in Bamako and something like the *International Herald Tribune*, *Time* or *Newsweek*.

Malian television is restricted to one channel which plays a lot of music and shows Brazilian soap operas dubbed into French. Many hotels, however, have a selection of channels beamed in by satellite from France. Any town worth its salt seems to have its own radio station; and if you have a short-wave radio, try tuning in to the BBC World Service (MHz 17.83 – 15.40 – 11.76 – 9.605) or Voice of America (MHz 21.49 – 15.60 – 9.525 – 6.035). (Note that these frequencies are subject to change.)

MONEY

Mali, along with six other French-speaking countries in West Africa, is a member of the West African Monetary Union. There is a central bank, the Banque Centrale des Etats d'Afrique de l'Ouest (BCEAO), with its headquarters in Dakar, Senegal, and the member states share a common currency, the CFA (Communauté Financière Africaine) franc. Mali was admitted to this union in 1984, at which time the CFA franc (here abbreviated as CFA, although you may also see CFAF and CFAFr) replaced the Malian franc.

The exchange rate is fixed at CFA655.597 (often rounded up to CFA656) for €1. Other currencies are bought and sold, although the fluctuating rates are usually less advantageous; US$1 is worth about CFA540 while £1 buys you around CFA980 (March 2004). The CFA franc comes in old notes of 10,000, 5,000, 1,000 and 500, and in new, smaller notes of 10,000, 5,000, 2,000 and 1.000. Old coins are of CFA250, 100, 50, 25, 10 and 5, while there are new coins of CFA500 and 200.

Some older editions of the old notes will lose their value in the first half of

2004, and this applies to certain notes from all members of the West African Monetary Union. Those notes that have not been handed in at the bank will eventually lose their value. Care should be taken to avoid becoming the dumping ground for the worthless notes that were not returned to the bank in time. Familiarise yourself with the notes that were handed out to you by the bank and look out for posters at the bank with images of the notes concerned.

Exchanging money

The preferred foreign currency in Mali is, for obvious reasons, the euro. Euro notes are easily exchanged for CFA all over the country, and preferably travellers should carry at least some of their money in this way. Smaller notes, such as 10s and 20s, will permit you to change only as much as you need at any one time. US$ come only second in popularity with banks, but are still widely accepted at a fluctuating rate. The same applies to travellers' cheques: euros are more widely accepted than US$, and other currencies are not recommended. Retain your purchase receipt, as some banks require to see it. As for plastic money, American Express can be used at the AMEX office in Bamako and in top end hotels and restaurants only. Otherwise, since certain banks will give cash advances on a Visa card, this card is of some – but limited – use.

Banking hours in Mali vary according to the bank and its location. Generally speaking, they are open until the early afternoon (not usually later than 15.00) from Mondays to Thursdays, while on Fridays they are normally closed by midday. Some banks are open on Saturday mornings, and a few branches of certain banks open on Sunday mornings as well. Do not count on it, though, and plan ahead when and where to exchange cash or travellers' cheques, or draw local currency with your Visa card. Changing travellers' cheques can be a long and arduous procedure, involving a mountain of paperwork, a commission payable to the government and another commission payable to the bank.

Mali's national bank is the Banque Centrale des Etats de l'Afrique de l'Ouest (BCEAO). Other main banks include: Banque de Développement du Mali (BDM), Banque Internationale pour le Mali (BIM), Banque Nationale de Développement Agricole (BNDA), Banque of Africa (BOA) and Banque de l'Habitat du Mali (BHM). In general, the BIM and BHM are of little use to travellers, as they do not deal with foreign currency (though the BHM sometimes exchanges euros). The more useful banks are the BDM and BNDA, since they are widely represented all over Mali and usually accept Visa card (BDM) or cash and travellers' cheques (BNDA). Many banks – and post offices – have a Western Union office for international money transfers. Many Western Union branches usually have longer opening hours than banks, and are often also open on Saturdays and Sundays. Practical though they are in case of a precarious cash flow situation, their services do not come cheap.

There is a black market, especially in Bamako. However, the usual warnings apply: changing money or travellers' cheques on the black market is illegal, the rates vary and may or may not be beneficial (but are sometimes negotiable), and there is always the risk of running into the wrong person at the wrong time, which could be both nasty and costly.

HEALTH AND SAFETY
Hospitals, doctors and pharmacies
There are two large **hospitals** in Bamako and one in each of the country's regional centres which deal with emergency cases. Otherwise, doctors, pharmacies and your own medical kit will normally suffice to treat most travellers' maladies. Although the quality of the medical care should be of the same standard in clinics and hospitals alike, **private clinics** are generally better equipped for care and comfort than general hospitals. English-speaking doctors are available in Bamako, and you should contact the American Embassy or the embassy or consulate of your country for recommendations. In case of a serious medical situation, the **African Trans Services** or **ATS** (tel: 222 44 35/22 78 92) in Immeuble Babemba can offer assistance. Outside the capital, however, you might have to get by in French. **Traditional medicine** is very popular in Mali. Apart from the dubious cures derived from the diverse range of West African fauna sold behind the main mosque in Bamako (see page 125), traditional medicine also includes herbal remedies which have proved so effective that the hospitals in Bamako have departments dedicated to researching this form of medicine.

Meanwhile, **pharmacies** in Mali are generally well equipped and normally stock most of the component parts of a good medical kit. They can be found all over the country. For further information on health see *Before you go* on page 53.

Security
On his way to Timbuktu in 1825, Gordon Laing (see page 11) wrote that the Tuareg were so feared 'that I shall consider myself as fortunate if I get through their territories with the loss of half my baggage'. Mali has been politically stable since the end of the Tuareg rebellion in 1995. However, although the war has ended, Tuareg attacks do still occur in the desert regions and occasionally along the main highway on the approach to Gao. These attacks are no longer politically motivated, but rather a reversion to good old-fashioned Tuareg banditry. Expensive 4WD vehicles are particular targets and victims have included politicians and the French military. In the past, incidents have occurred on the road between Gao and Timbuktu and in the desert around the Algerian and Niger borders. The risk, however, should not be exaggerated. National and local authorities are very much aware of the impact insecurity has had on the lives of the northern communities and on tourism. While the problem is being addressed at different levels, the region as a whole is being promoted as a tourist destination. Indeed, the desert regions of Mali have seen growing numbers of visitors, while the number of incidents is declining. That is no guarantee, but the statistics are encouraging. Nevertheless, authorities in towns that could be labelled as gateways to the desert – like Timbuktu, Gao and Kidal – still encourage tourists who intend to travel further north with their own vehicles to take a few safety precautions: seek local advice and register before heading out to remote destinations. Travellers using public

THE BLACK TRAVELLER IN MALI

Bola Fatimilehin

As a black woman travelling in Mali, I had many exhilarating and thought-provoking adventures. The red dust, which for me is a mark of true African soil, will be forever ingrained on my mind – thanks to long arduous bus journeys taken in 40° heat with windows shut tight.

Visiting out-of-the-way places brought me into contact with genuinely warm and friendly people. Most memorably, when travelling along the escarpment where the Dogon people live, the chief of one of the villages took a particular shine to me and my white partner. It emerged that the Dogon creation story involves twins, one of whom is black, the other white; under the influence of millet beer, we had become mythology in the flesh.

Often in Mali, local people would assume I knew far more about what was going on than I actually did. This had definite advantages in that I could pay less for things and avoid insincere banter aimed at parting me from my money. On one occasion, I was even bribed to keep my mouth shut by a guide! He had secured a week's work with a single American tourist for about ten times the amount I was paying. He did not want to lose his prime fee so gave me a brass necklace as 'hush money'.

For the black traveller, feelings of isolation may come as a surprise. In general, the most common image of 'the tourist' is of a white person – black tourists are still considered a rarity. Local black men and women were often bemused and suspicious of me, assuming I was there for some sort of economic gain. It is understandable that both Malians and white tourists – for similar and different reasons – do not have a ready image of the black person as a tourist. However, the isolation which may descend as a result of this dubious privilege can be overcome by creating opportunities to talk to people. Getting my hair done was one way of meeting and talking to women in Mali – rusty and rudimentary though my French is! The quality of hair braiding was incredibly high and, at only CFA300 (about US$2), excellent value for money. The other tactic I found very useful was to show people photographs of family and friends at home. This worked well, both to stimulate conversation and to allay some suspicion, as Malians are always interested in family connections.

Travelling on a budget meant sleeping in cheap hotels – but at the risk of being mistaken for a prostitute. Staying in more expensive hotels might have avoided this situation, but my budget would not allow for it. Bamako felt like a relatively safe city and there were advantages in staying at the centre of things: being able to mingle with the market traders, street sellers, beggars, bus touts and ordinary citizens, and generally absorb *l'ambiance*.

SAFETY FOR WOMEN TRAVELLERS
Janice Booth

When attention becomes intrusive, it can help if you are wearing a wedding ring and have photos of 'your' husband and children, even if they are someone else's. A good reason to give for not being with them is that you have to travel in connection with your job – biology, zoology, geography, or whatever. (But not journalism – that's risky.)

Pay attention to local etiquette, and to speaking, dressing and moving reasonably decorously. Look at how the local women dress, and try not to expose parts of yourself that they keep covered. Think about body language. Direct eye-contact with a man may be seen as a 'come-on'; sunglasses are helpful here.

Don't be afraid to explain clearly – but pleasantly rather than as a put-down – that you aren't in the market for whatever distractions are on offer. Remember that you are probably as much of a novelty to the local people as they are to you, and the fact that you are travelling abroad alone gives them the message that you are free and adventurous. But don't imagine that a Lothario lurks under every bush: many approaches stem from genuine friendliness or curiosity, and a brush-off in such cases doesn't do much for the image of travellers in general.

Take sensible precautions against theft and attack – try to cover all the risks before you encounter them – and then relax and enjoy your trip. You'll meet far more kindness than villainy.

transport – in other words, vehicles not worth stealing – are obviously at less risk than those with their own transport.

A decade ago the areas around Nioro du Sahel and Nara along the Mauritanian border were sensitive due to conflict between sedentary farmers (largely Bambara and Soninké) and nomadic cattle-herders (Peul). These days, the situation is a lot calmer.

Elsewhere, travelling in Mali is as safe as it can be in Africa. Common-sense precautions, such as watching your belongings – particularly at bus and railway stations – and avoiding dodgy areas at night, should be taken as a matter of course. Confidence-tricksters operate in Mali, as anywhere else in the world, but incidents involving violence are rare. There is a strong police presence all over the country, all traffic passes security checkpoints when entering and leaving major towns and you are never very far from a *commissariat de police* – for what it's worth! **Emergency telephone numbers** are 15 for health services, 17 for the police and 18 for the fire brigade.

Part Two

The Guide

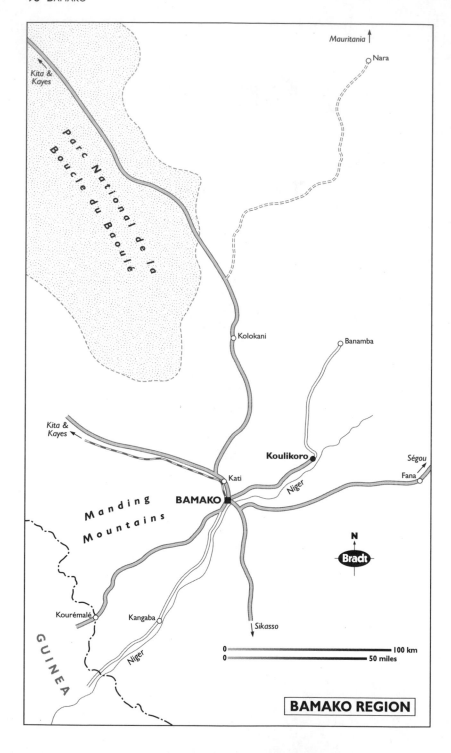

BAMAKO REGION

Bamako

Far too many guidebooks delight in describing Bamako, Mali's capital, as 'the most African of all African cities'. Should we take this to mean that Bamako is the most dirty and overcrowded place on the continent – for these are certainly characteristics shared by many African cities – or a city of mud houses without a single skyscraper in sight? It is, of course, neither one nor the other – but a bit of both: a rather typical African city, in fact, facing the same contemporary problems as most other metropolises in the developing world.

Overcrowding is one of these problems. In a country with a population of over 11 million, around one million live in Bamako. In recent years the perimeters of the city have expanded eastwards, westwards and, most dramatically, south of the River Niger, so that now Bamako occupies an area of 40km². However, there are not enough jobs and the urban infrastructure is inadequate to support these growing numbers. This is the Bamako of littered streets and impossible traffic jams; an oppressive city of noise, pollution, dust and unbearable heat. Fortunately, however, there is more to this place than meets the eye. You need to stay a while before you start to feel it, but Bamako's true heartbeat has more to do with the gentle ebb and flow of the river than rush-hour traffic and its chorus of beeping horns. For this is a relaxed city – and can also be a relaxing city. People are busy, but not so busy that they no longer want to communicate with one another. Simple things, such as smiling at passers-by, throw-away 'bonjours' and 'ça vas' and shaking hands are still important in Bamako. Could we say the same thing for London, Paris and New York – or, for that matter, Dakar, Abidjan and Lagos? In this way, I suppose, Bamako has remained typically African.

HISTORY

The general consensus is that Bamako was founded some time during the 16th century. Precise details of the town's creation, however, are contested by the conflicting oral traditions upon which the hapless historian has no choice but to rely. The most common version of events is that Niakaté, a hunter from Lamidou near Nioro du Sahel in the Kaarta region, travelled down to the Niger Valley to look for new hunting grounds, and met another hunter, Samalé Bamba, who granted him an area of land upon which Niakaté founded Bamako. Niakaté was gradually shortened to Niaré – the town's first ruling dynasty – after which Bamako's first quarter, Niaréla, was named. This tidy explanation of Bamako's beginnings is disrupted by the Malian historian, Dominique Traoré, who claims that, before Niakaté arrived, another hunter, this time from the town of Kong in northeastern Côte d'Ivoire, had already established the town on the banks of the river. Bamba Sanogo, having killed an elephant while hunting, sought and was granted permission from the local Bambara ruler to create a town in the place where the elephant had fallen. It was initially called Bamba Kong after its founder and his town of origin, but was later shortened to Bamako, meaning 'the posterity of Bamba'. If all this seems a little too dry, you might prefer the story according to which Bamako owes its name to the crocodile-infested stretch of river beside which it was created – *bama* meaning 'crocodile' and *ko* meaning 'river'. These are just some of the stories explaining the origins of Bamako. There are variations on each theme and probably several other versions of events.

Whatever you choose to believe, by the time Mungo Park (see page 10) arrived in 1805, Bamako was a small trading centre of about 6,000 people – most of them Bozo fishermen. Between then and 1883, however, when the town was captured for the French by Lieutenant Colonel Borgnis-Désbordes, its population had dwindled to under 1,000.

The coming of the railway proved to be the making of Bamako. Work was started in 1904 on a line between Bamako and the western town of Kayes which, along with the former's better location, was the main reason why the capital of Upper Senegal and Niger was moved from Kayes to Bamako in 1908. When the railway reached Dakar and the Atlantic coast in 1923, Bamako also replaced Kayes as the country's commercial centre – a title it has never renounced.

ORIENTATION
In all likelihood, your first arrival in Bamako will be by air, road or train. Bamako-Sénou International Airport is about 15km south of the city near the village of Sénou on the road to Sikasso; the main bus station or *gare routière* is in the quarter of Sogoniko, 5km south of the River Niger; and the railway station is in the downtown area.

Metropolitan Bamako
Tourist brochures avoid describing Bamako as a 'dust bowl', although during the dry season dust and bluish clouds of exhaust fumes seem to hang over the capital like a vindictive blanket. This is because Bamako lies in a depression, with the foothills of the Manding Mountains rising to nearly 500m in the north, the smaller hills of Badalabougou and Magnambougou in the south, and the River Niger flowing through the middle.

Originally, Bamako was confined to a modest area on the left bank of the Niger – that is to say, north of the river. Nowadays, the city has sprawled to the east, west and, most notably, south of the river. The District of Bamako consists of six *communes* which stretch as far south as the airport, but do not include the administrative district of Koulouba and Point G in the north. Each *commune* is divided into several *quartiers* or quarters. From the visitor's point of view, the oldest quarters (those in Communes II and III) are the most interesting. Commune II consists of the following quarters: Bozolo, Niaréla, Bagadadji, Quinzambougou, Cité du Niger, Zone Industrielle, Médina Koura, Missira and Hippodrome. This is arguably the oldest part of Bamako, characterised these days by foreign embassies and consulates, hotels, restaurants and nightclubs. Commune III, meanwhile, is essentially what I have treated as downtown Bamako.

Most of Bamako's recent development has taken place south of the river, where largely residential neighbourhoods have almost doubled the size of the city. Two bridges link the northern and southern parts of town. Pont des Martyrs – also known as 'ancien pont' (old bridge) – serves traffic coming from the heart of downtown and is always crowded. For this reason, a new bridge – Pont du Roi Fahd – was built by the Saudis half a kilometre or so east of the old one to divert traffic away from the centre, thus improving access to Bamako and the airport.

There are two main roads leading out of Bamako. Cross Pont des Martyrs and continue along the same road for several kilometres – passing the *gare routière* after about five – and you reach the main highway for towns in the east and south of the country. Back in the downtown area, Avenue Al Quds becomes Route de Koulikoro after a few kilometres – the trunk road to the port of Koulikoro. Another short stretch of paved road leads up to Koulouba and on to the nearby town of Kati, after which it becomes a track and continues as such in the direction of Kayes.

Downtown Bamako

For the purposes of this chapter, downtown Bamako includes the quarters of Commune III – Centre Commercial, Dravéla, Bamako Koura and Quartier du Fleuve – as well as the western edges of Bozola and Bagadadji. In more visual terms, the heart of Bamako lies more or less between the minarets of the *Grande Mosquée* (great mosque) in the north and the giant buildings of Hotel de l'Amitié and the Banque Centrale des Etats de l'Afrique de l'Ouest (BCEAO) in the south. These three landmarks, visible from almost anywhere in the city, should be your main points of reference.

That's about as much help as Bamako is prepared to give the first-time visitor, as the roads, traffic circulation and street signs are all totally user-unfriendly. Start off by grasping the basics, and then add to your knowledge as you become accustomed to the layout of the capital. The main thoroughfare is Boulevard du Peuple, which runs from south to north through the heart of Bamako. It is crowded, dirty and chaotic, but hard to avoid. Avenue du Fleuve – renamed Avenue Modibo Keita, but still widely known by its old name – is for the north-to-south cross-town traffic. Both of these roads emanate from Square Lumumba, where several airline offices and the French Embassy can be found. Most of the main tourist attractions, however, are in the northern part of the downtown area, as is Bamako's railway station and Le Grand Hotel. One other road you should try to remember is Avenue de la Liberté, which continues north

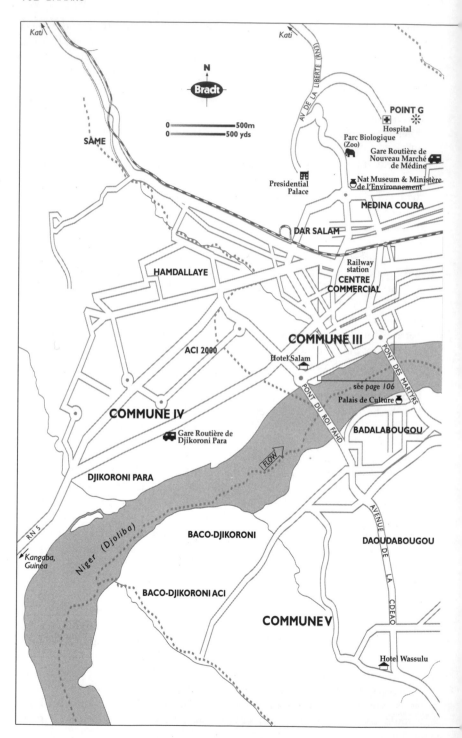

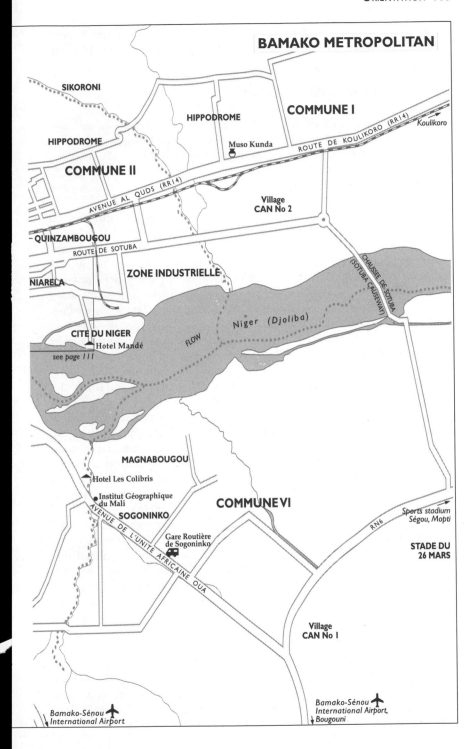

BAMAKO METROPOLITAN

SIKORONI

HIPPODROME

COMMUNE I

HIPPODROME

Muso Kunda

ROUTE DE KOULIKORO (RR14)

Koulikoro

COMMUNE II

AVENUE AL QUDS (RR14)

Village
CAN No 2

QUINZAMBOUGOU

ROUTE DE SOTUBA

NIARELA

ZONE INDUSTRIELLE

CHAUSSÉE DE SOTUBA
(SOTUBA CAUSEWAY)

Niger (Djoliba)

FLOW

CITÉ DU NIGER

Hotel Mandé

see page 111

MAGNABOUGOU

Hotel Les Colibris

Institut Géographique
du Mali

COMMUNE VI

SOGONINKO

AVENUE DE L'UNITÉ AFRICAINE OUA

Gare Routière
de Sogoninko

RN6

Sports stadium
Ségou, Mopti

STADE DU
26 MARS

Village
CAN No 1

Bamako-Sénou
International Airport

Bamako-Sénou
International Airport,
Bougouni

when Avenue du Fleuve stops more or less at the railway track. Avenue de la Liberté winds up to Koulouba and Point G, passing the National Museum and the zoo en route.

GETTING THERE AND AWAY
By air
For international arrivals and departures see *Practicalities: Getting there and away* on page 73. Similarly, for the schedule and fares for domestic flights to some of Mali's provincial towns, see page 77. Note that these schedules – the latter one in particular – are liable to change.

Bamako-Sénou International Airport
Bamako-Sénou International Airport (tel: 220 27 01; for information on flights: 222 32 04) is small, informal and occasionally chaotic – but it works. Airport facilities are limited to an exchange office which opens at erratic hours, public telephones, one or two gift shops, a small bookshop, an upstairs restaurant overlooking the runway, and an information kiosk which dispenses airport information only. Outside, across the car park, is the restaurant Cordon Blue – basic, but convenient to have a drink and a bite while waiting.

The airport is several kilometres from Bamako, so forget walking into town. There is no inexpensive public transport shuttling between the airport and Bamako. From the nearby village of Sénou it would be possible to take a *sotrama* into town; however, walking to Sénou is not recommended. In any case, if you arrive in the evening or at night, as many international flights do, the *sotramas* will have stopped running. So, unless you manage to get a ride on one of the airport buses provided by the bigger hotels, taking a taxi is probably going to be your best, if not only, bet. Try to find other travellers to share the cost, and note that, at the instigation of the airport authorities, taxi drivers have reluctantly fixed and signposted their rates. While this reduces the space for outrageous fares and negotiation tremendously, it also turns out to be a semi-legal way to inflate the fares for unsuspecting tourists. Rates are fixed according to the various communes, exceeding CFA6,000 (per ride) only for the two most distant communes. However, a separate signpost fixes the uniform rate for the bigger hotels – all well within the CFA6,000 zone – at CFA7,500, for no obvious reason. Until the authorities have handled this scheme, the only way around it is to double check that the hotel of your choice is indeed within the CFA6,000 range (see *Orientation: Metropolitan Bamako* on page 100), then have the exact amount ready, and stay firm while your driver argues why you should pay more than the local client who got off just around the corner.

By river
COMANAV (tel: 222 38 02) occupies a building not far from the railway station. Although you can get information and buy tickets here, boats actually leave from Koulikoro, 57km down river (see page 126). COMANAV's fares and timetable are listed in *Practicalities: Getting around* on page 76.

Bear in mind that if you want to go to Djenné or Bobo-Dioulasso, for example, you can always do the trip in stages. Note that departures for Abidjan (Côte d'Ivoire) have been suspended. You may find occasional buses leaving for Bouaké, but otherwise travel to Sikasso first to find onward transport to Côte d'Ivoire.

A motley collection of vehicles (buses of all sizes, and *camions*) depart from the **Gare Routière de Ngolonina**, not far from Niaréla. It is located within walking distance to the east of Hotel l'Amitié, and is chaotic in a pleasant sort of way. Though there seem to be official departure times, nobody was quite sure where to get these. However, these are the fares for destinations – to the four winds of the compass – in clockwise order:

Ségou CFA2,500
Niono CFA4,000
Djenné mostly on Sundays to meet the Monday market, CFA7,000
Koro (via Somodougou) CFA10,500
Sikasso (via Koutiala) CFA5,500 (CFA4,500); (via Bougouni) CFA4,000 (CFA2,000)
Kouri (bordering Burkina Faso) CFA6,500
Zégoua (bordering Côte d'Ivoire) CFA6,500
Kita CFA3,000
Diéma CFA5,500 (trucks) or CFA11,000
Nioro du Sahel CFA13,750
Kolokani CFA3,100
Nara CFA6,500
Koulikoro CFA900

The **Gare Routière du Nouveau Marché de Médine** – not far from Stade Modibo Keita – is the place to look for transport to the west and north of Bamako, and for the occasional *camion* to Timbuktu. Apart from *bâchées* and minibuses to **Kati** (CFA300) and **Koulikoro** (CFA900), look for Diéma Transport, who have converted trucks leaving for:

Diéma 07.00, Mon & Thu, CFA7,500
Nioro du Sahel 07.00, Mon & Thu, CFA10,000
Yélimané 07.00, Mon & Thu, CFA12,500
Kayes 07.00, daily except Sun & Wed, CFA12,500

Mandé Transport leaves for:

Kita 10.00, 16.00, daily, CFA2,500
Nioro du Sahel and **Touroungoumbé** Saturday afternoon, CFA6,500 or CFA10,000, depending on the type of vehicle

Faguibine Transport has one weekly departure for **Niafounké** and **Tonka** on Thursdays (to return on Sundays), CFA11,000 and CFA12,000.

Tikambo Travel has its unique 'Navette du Nord', travelling to **Timbuktu** via **Niono** and **Goundam** on Friday around noon, CFA17,500.

Bani Transport and Bram leave for **Diré** at 16.00 on Thursday and Friday; CFA13,000. The odd one out is Somatra, leaving for **Bandiagara** on Wednesday and Saturday; CFA7,000

The bus station for the Manding Mountains and Guinea is the **Gare Routière de Djikoroni Para** in the far western quarter of Djikoroni. To get there from downtown, take a *sotrama* from the Monument de l'Indépendance. Vehicles vary from smaller buses to bush taxis.

Kourémalé (and **Sibi**) daily when full, 2–3 hours, CFA2,500
Kangaba daily when full, 2–3 hours, CFA1,750
Conakry (Guinea) daily when full, CFA20,000

For more transport to Kangaba (Manding Mountains) and Koulikoro, Gana du Nord have a departure point between the National Museum and the Stade Modibo Keita. The only public transport to leave from behind the Grand Mosque and the unpaved nearby streets are some *grands cars* with daily departures at 16.00 for Mopti (CFA6,000), and sometimes *petits cars* to Nara and Niono.

GETTING AROUND

Bamako is a sprawling city. While most of the main attractions are within walking distance of each other in the downtown area, many other facilities, such as hotels and restaurants, are some way from the centre. This means that at some point you might contemplate using public transport to get around.

The yellow taxis in Bamako are generally shared. They will take you where you want, picking up and dropping off passengers along the way. A typical fare for a journey varies from CFA700 to CFA2,000 (eg: when crossing the river and during rush hour), but the price will go up for a group or if you prefer to be taken from A to B without stopping for other passengers. In that case you should specify that you want a *location*.

Minibuses and converted Peugeot 504s and 505s – all painted bright green – represent the cut and thrust of Bamako's public transport. The standard fare is CFA100–150 and they go virtually everywhere. The minibuses are known locally as *sotramas*, after the Société de Transport Malienne, the first company to operate them. The smaller vehicles – often Peugeot estates converted into something resembling a pick-up truck – are called *dou dourenis*, which is Bambara for '25 francs', their original fare.

Three of the main departure points for *sotramas* and *dou dourenis* are Square Lumumba (for destinations south of the river, including the *gare routière*), at the intersection of Boulevard du Peuple and Avenue Al Quds (for Hippodrome and Route de Koulikoro) and Rue Baba Diarra in front of the railway station (for various destinations in all directions).

Note that from Monday to Friday the Pont des Martyrs is closed in one direction during rush hours. From 07.00 to 09.00 it is open only to traffic going into town, while from 16.00 to 18.30 outgoing traffic can make use of the full width of the bridge. All transport in the opposite direction has to make the detour using the other bridge.

WHERE TO STAY
Accommodation in Bamako is not cheap. Apart from one or two notable and often unappealing exceptions, rooms for under CFA15,000 are hard to find. The cheapest – and the most expensive – accommodation is in the centre of town. Elsewhere, mid-range and expensive hotels mingle with the foreign embassies in Niaréla and Hippodrome, while other options exist south of the river in districts such as Badalabougou.

Downtown
Top end
Hotel de l'Amitié (tel: 22 43 21), along with the mosque and the BCEAO building, dominates the Bamako skyline, although on closer inspection it is no more attractive than a high-rise block on a gloomy south London housing estate. At the time of writing, the hotel had closed for major renovations, so no new information was available. However, it will open during 2004 and, assuming that the renovations will boost the rates rather than the opposite, you can expect to pay at least CFA50,000 for a single or double. In return, you get to enjoy a room with a view of the hotel's golf course and the River Niger. As well as the golf course, there was, and probably still is, a heart-shaped swimming pool, a casino and a lobby, with boutiques and a motley collection of tour operators, car-rental agencies and money-changers. Bamako's other top hotel, **Le Grand Hotel** (tel: 222 24 92) had also nearly finished its renovations at the time of writing. It is more intimate than the Amitié, catering especially for people visiting Bamako on business. Facilities are similar (swimming pool, tennis courts, shops etc), while all rooms are completely renovated and have direct access to the internet. The rate is CFA60,000 for a single/double, but this is likely to increase.

For many years, these top-end hotels were considered the best and the most expensive alike. However, the new **Hotel Salam** (tel: 222 12 00) exceeds both of them and offers all that one could wish for in terms of service, glamour and luxury. The price is set accordingly, at CFA75,000 for a single/double or CFA125,000 (or CFA165,000) for a junior (or presidential) suite.

Mid-range
The rest of the options in the centre of town are some way down the scale in terms of price and comfort. The next best is **Hotel Yamey** (tel: 223 86 88) – formerly known as Hotel Le Fleuve – on rue 311 in Quartier du Fleuve, a quiet, shady part of town not far from the river. Rooms start at CFA18,000 and, as there are only 12 of them, they fill up quickly – often with Italian tourists. The venerable **Hotel Lac Débo** (tel: 222 96 35) is friendly, very central and relatively cheap. The building, which is more than 50 years old, is quite beautiful despite its lack of maintenance, and the rooms, although suffering from the same neglect, are OK. Singles with a fan are CFA12,000, doubles CFA16,000 and triples CFA25,000. Romantics might be drawn to **Hotel Buffet de la Gare** (tel: 223 19 10), a dapper establishment during colonial times and the long-time home of the famous

Super Rail Band (see page 27), but should be sufficiently put off by the dingy, showerless rooms, overpriced at CFA10,500 for a single.

Budget

The best budget accommodation in town is provided by the religious missions. A word of warning, however, before you approach them looking for a bed for the night: remember that these foyers are intended for visiting clerics and their parents, and tourists will only be put up if space permits. You should neither demand a room as of right nor overstay your welcome. The **Foyer des Soeurs** is open 07.00–13.00 and 16.00–22.00, with dormitory beds costing around CFA4,000. The **Mission Libanaise** (tel: 223 50 94), which seems more set up for tourism than the Foyer des Sœurs, charges CFA2,500 for dormitory accommodation, as well as having a selection of rooms starting at CFA6,000. Camping is CFA2,500 per person. The **Paroisse Sacré Coeur** (tel: 222 58 42) opposite the cathedral has rooms at CFA6,500 per person. The **Carrefour Des Jeunes** (tel: 222 43 11), opposite the Musée de Bamako along Avenue Kasse Keita, has basic rooms at CFA3,000 (single or double) without a fan, and CFA5,000 with a fan. **Auberge Lafia** is behind a photo studio near the Centre Culturel Français, and has dorm beds at CFA4,000. A few blocks away, a real backpackers' place and charging the same for a bed, is **Mohamed De La Casa**. **Restaurant De La Paix** has at least one room at CFA3,000. The **Maison des Jeunes de Bamako** (tel: 222 23 20), next to the Pont des Martyrs, is the nearest Mali has to a youth hostel. There is a one-week maximum stay; dorms cost CFA2,000, single rooms CFA3,000, and double rooms CFA4,000. It is also possible to camp in the garden. A small house near the Foyer des Sœurs, universally known as **Chez Fanta**, is a popular hangout for backpackers. Fanta charges CFA4,000 for a bed on the ground floor, double that for a room on the first floor. **Bar Mali**, the one other budget option in the centre of town, is an insalubrious dump. The rooms are cheap and nasty, but less off-putting than the staff and clientele, who seem to be perpetually drunk and aggressive.

Niaréla

For all the good accommodation in Niaréla itself, the best hotel in this area is actually in a new district east of Niaréla called Cité du Niger. When Bobby Charlton, the famous English soccer player, visited Bamako on a mission to win Mali's World Cup vote (England want to host the finals in 2006), he stayed at the **Mandé Hotel** (tel: 221 19 93). With an unrivalled location on the banks of the River Niger, the Mandé also has a soccer connection, being owned by the greatest of all Malian players, Salif Keita. When you stay at the Mandé, you swap easy access to downtown Bamako for the peace, tranquillity and mosquitoes of the river. Rates compare favourably with those of other hotels in Niaréla which have less to offer, with singles costing CFA42,500 and doubles CFA43,000. There is also a large swimming pool and two restaurants.

Niaréla is a district full of foreign embassies and consulates and most of its hotels are a stone's throw from one of the largest embassies in Bamako. North

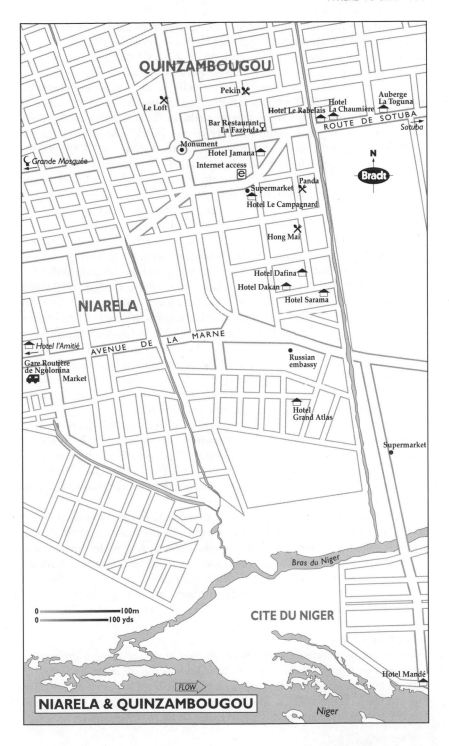

QUINZAMBOUGOU

Pekin

Le Loft

Bar Restaurant
La Fazenda

Hotel Le Rabelais

Hotel
La Chaumière

Auberge
La Toguna

ROUTE DE SOTUBA

Sotuba

Monument
Hotel Jamana

Internet access

N

Bradt

Grande Mosquée

Supermarket

Panda

Hotel Le Campagnard

Hong Mai

Hotel Dafina

Hotel Dakan

Hotel Sarama

NIARELA

Hotel l'Amitié

AVENUE DE LA MARNE

Gare Routière
de Ngolonina

Market

Russian
embassy

Hotel
Grand Atlas

Supermarket

Bras du Niger

0 ▬▬▬ 100m
0 ▬▬▬ 100 yds

CITE DU NIGER

Hotel Mandé

FLOW

NIARELA & QUINZAMBOUGOU

Niger

of the Russian Embassy, at least seven hotels are within about 200m of each other. **Hotel Le Campagnard** (tel: 221 92 96) is a comfortable hotel, where air-conditioned rooms with TV and fridge cost CFA32,500 (single) and CFA38,000 (double). The adjacent annexe has a small garden with a swimming pool. Continue walking north until you reach Route du Sotuba, and **Hotel Le Rabelais** (tel: 221 52 98) is on your right. 'Le Rabelais' is, in fact, the name of the newly constructed building in striking white and blue, which is hidden from view by the older, more intimate part of the hotel. Officially called 'Le Touraine', few people make the distinction. All new rooms – at CFA41,000 for a single or double – are individually designed and attractive. The whole establishment is immaculately kept and the amenities include a hairdresser, a nurse and a pharmacy, a gym, mudbath, sauna and beauty parlour, as well as a library. Non-guests also have access to most of these facilities, including the swimming pool (CFA3,500). Next door is **Hotel La Chaumière** (tel: 221 76 60), open since October 2003. Though by comparison there is nothing wrong with the well-equipped rooms at CFA30,000 (double) or CFA37,500 (twin), the quiet 'Chaumière' will have a hard time competing with the buzzing 'Rabelais'. **Hotel Jamana** (tel: 221 34 56) has renovated rooms at CFA21,000/24,000/27,500 for a single/double/triple, while rates at **Hotel Dafina** (tel: 221 03 04) start at CFA29,000/35,000 for a single/double. Non-residents pay CFA2,000 for access to the swimming pool. **Hotel Sarama** (tel: 221 05 63) is rather expensive at CFA39,500/46,000 for a double/twin, but offers many extras – like a swimming pool and internet – in a tastefully decorated and welcoming setting. Just around the corner, **Hotel Dakan** (tel: 221 91 96) is cheaper and better value with rooms starting at CFA20,000, including breakfast. It also has a pleasant garden with plenty of shade, where camping is allowed.

Behind the Russian Embassy there are more hotels, most of which offer the comfortable but uninspiring brand of accommodation for which Bamako has gained a reputation. **Hotel Le Grand Atlas** (tel: 221 48 17) which caters more for businessmen than tourists has a slightly sterile feel and charges CFA33,000 for a single and CFA36,000 for a double. The nearby **Hotel Oasis** (tel: 221 46 07) is similar in price and quality.

Of a different style and budget altogether is the **Auberge Toguna** (tel: 221 16 93), from Hotel La Chaumière a little further east along the Route du Sotuba. Friendly and straightforward, this is good value if you prefer inexpensive accommodation in a quiet location well away from hectic downtown Bamako. Rooms range from CFA10,000 for a single with a fan and shared facilities, to CFA18,500 for a self-contained double with air conditioning. Sleeping on the roof is also an option.

Hippodrome

Hippodrome is another district with its fair share of foreign embassies, consulates and hotels, although it is best known for its restaurants. About 200m west of the Hippodrome itself, actually in the district of Missira, **Le Djenné** (tel: 221 30 82) is a *maison des hôtes* (guest house) run by the former outspoken Minister of Culture and Tourism. Predictably, this small and pleasant hotel is a veritable showcase of Malian culture. The rooms, each of them different, are like small museums, full of local handicrafts and colourful *bogolans* (see page 90). At CFA21,000 for a single and CFA30,000 for a double, you pay for the character of the place rather than its extraordinary comfort.

Tamana (tel: 221 3715) is another *maison des hôtes*, this time east of the Hippodrome. Run by a French couple who try, with some success, to create a family atmosphere, the six rooms are not unattractive – art-deco with an African twist, perhaps! CFA25,000 buys you a room (single or double), although you pay slightly less if you choose to share the immaculately clean communal bathroom. Nearby, on rue 224 behind the Canadian Embassy, **Hotel Le Maxim** (tel: 221 98 56) is around the CFA25,000 mark. The rooms have air conditioning, but you pay an extra CFA3,500 if you use it during the day. There is a pool, and breakfast is included in the price. **Hotel P'tit Ballon** (tel: 221 77 91) on Boulevard Nelson Mandela enjoys a good reputation. Well-run and quite friendly, the main drawback is its location – on a noisy road far from the centre of town. Rooms cost CFA20,000 for a single, and CFA25,000 for a double. Extra beds are CFA5,000.

South of the river

Of all the hotels south of the river in Bamako's newer districts – and there are quite a few – only a handful are practical in terms of access to downtown. Choosing a hotel in Bako Djikoroni, for example, will involve travelling for maybe half an hour to reach the tourist attractions on the other side of the river. With this in mind, try to stick to the places not far from the main road leading out of Bamako towards the *gare routière*, where *sotramas* to the centre of town are plentiful. **Hotel Les Colibris** (tel: 222 6637), opposite the Saudi Arabian Embassy, is cosy, quiet and better value. Prices for bungalows range from CFA20,000 to CFA30,000, and all of them are well above average in terms of quality and comfort. **Olympe Hotel International** (tel:223 46 63) is a fairly new hotel, with singles at CFA35,500 and doubles at CFA40,500. If you like to bathe in luxury, why not take the presidential suite at CFA150,000? For those who prefer to stray not too far from the airport, **Hotel Wassulu** (tel: 228 74 74) provides comfort and quality in a convenient location. The hotel is owned by the famous vedette Oumou Sangaré (see page 28), and when she is not on a tour, she occasionally treats her guests to a concert in the garden by the swimming pool. Rooms are a hefty CFA36,500 for a single and CFA46,500 for a double. **Hotel L'Aquarius** (tel: 226 18 31), just after Pont du Roi Fahd, is another option within a reasonable distance of downtown. Rooms are CFA23,000 for a single and CFA28,500 for a double, breakfast included.

There is also a religious mission, *Mission Catholique* **'Paroisse'**, in Badalabougou, although the same reservations apply here as they do in the missions in the downtown area (see page 109). Walk across Pont des Martyrs, turn right at the second set of traffic lights, and the mission is near the police station of the 4th *arrondissement*.

WHERE TO EAT

Most restaurants in Bamako serve international cuisine of varying standards. There are some very good French restaurants and some very bad ones. Chinese, Indian and Lebanese food is also available, and some of the town's *pâtisseries* are excellent. African food, meanwhile, is a hit-and-miss affair. In addition to the places mentioned below, bear in mind that almost all of the hotels have restaurants or are willing to prepare you a meal if you give them enough notice.

Downtown

Restaurant Le Casino at the casino next to Hotel de l'Amitié is considered by many expats to be the best in Bamako. The menu is largely French and the ambience more Caesar's Palace than McDonald's – so dress appropriately. The Amitié's other place to eat is **Restaurant Oasis**, which has a Sunday lunch buffet by the pool for CFA8,000. A similar buffet is cheaper at Le Grand's **Restaurant Azalaï**, but the poolside ambience is less agreeable. **Restaurant L'Olympien**, just off Square Lumumba near the BDM, is another popular expat hangout. This is by virtue of the excellent bar as much as the cooking, most of which is provençal (the restaurant is named after Marseille's soccer team, Olympique Marseille). Reasonable pizzas are also served in the restaurant or home-delivered (tel: 23 87 93). Next door, **Restaurant Bol de Jade** has been serving Vietnamese food under the supervision of Madame Cat since the 1960s. Her son, meanwhile, prepares the oriental food at Hotel Débo in Sevaré (see page 170).

In the downtown area of Bamako the choice of restaurants is probably better at the cheaper and considerably less pretentious end of the market. **Les Délices de Bamako** in Immeuble Nimagala at the intersection of rue Mohamed V and Famolo Coulibaly, and **Phoenicia Pâtisserie**, around the corner on rue Mohamed V, are two popular *pâtisseries*. While the décor is still attractive, it seems that at the newer and once highly recommended *Les Délices de Bamako* outstanding standards have slipped dramatically within a matter of years. Decide for yourself which display has the most – or least – appetising selection of cakes and pastry.

Not far from the railway station is the Chinese **Restaurant La Muraille**, for cheap beer and decent meals with a different flavour – a good hide-out from the busy streets! Another friendly place to retreat for a break from the city is **Restaurant Bafoulabé**, also in the vicinity of the railway station. Meals usually come in the form of good helpings of rice and something. **Restaurant Central** has daily menus as well as a variety of Lebanese food. **Restaurant Le Gourmet** is a good place for lunch and take-away meals. This small, clean restaurant has daily menus including *sauce arachide*, *fonio*, *tô*, *ris gras* and, occasionally, something specifically Malian like *saga saga* or *fakoye*. **Restaurant de la Paix** is another small restaurant on rue Ousmane Bagayogo which specialises in Senegalese cooking and is popular with the backpacking crowd. On Avenue Moussa Travele, **Restaurant le Tempo** serves the usual variety of meals on the patio.

Niaréla

Some of the best restaurants in Bamako are to be found at the hotels of Niaréla and the quarters nearby. The two restaurants at the Mandé Hotel enjoy an unrivalled location on the banks of the River Niger. **Restaurant Le Toît de Bamako** is on the top floor of the hotel, with a French menu, fully-fledged European prices and a more formal atmosphere than **Restaurant Le Pilotis**, which is built on stilts in the river. **Restaurant Le Campagnard** is the finest in Bamako, while next to Le Campagnard, **Restaurant Kaïssa** is another smart, French restaurant, which sometimes has live music in the evenings. Meanwhile, **Restaurant Le Loft**, just to the north of Route du Sotuba, specialises in the *cuisine du Périgord*, which includes duck and fowl *à la Française*. Until **Le Rabelais** has constructed another extension on the premises, the small crêperie doubles as a restaurant. The menu is limited but very select and will be appreciated by connoisseurs. The same can be said of **Restaurant La Chaumière**, with its refined menu and pleasant service. Three Chinese restaurants – **Restaurant Pekin**, the **Panda Bar Restaurant** and **Restaurant Hong Mai** – may appeal to those with a tighter budget. **Bar Restaurant La Fazenda**, next to the Rabelais, is more like a beergarden but also serves basic meals.

Hippodrome

Avenue Al Quds is just another busy, oppressive road in Bamako until you reach the turning for the Hippodrome, after which it becomes a hot spot for some of the most popular places to eat in the capital. On the corner of Avenue Al Quds and the Hippodrome road, **Restaurant Le San Toro** is, like Le Djenné (see page 152), run by the former Minister of Culture and Tourism. The style of the hotel is mirrored by the restaurant, with its arts and crafts shop, Malian décor, live kora music and a menu featuring many excellent national dishes. Further along Al Quds, past the two large supermarkets, two restaurants with *pâtisseries* are virtually carbon copies of one another. Both owned by Lebanese families, they serve burgers-and-fries type food, spiced up by the odd *kafta* and kebab dish. **Le Relax** is perhaps the most popular, especially with travellers, and is open until late for the custom brought in by the nightclub next door. **L'Express** is further along the road and is of a similar style, quality and price. The cakes and pastries at both are good. Turn left just past L'Express and **Restaurant Akwaba** (meaning 'welcome' in some Ghanaian and Ivoirian languages) is not far down rue 235. Try to dine here in the evenings on Tuesdays, Fridays or Saturdays, when there should be some live music. Otherwise, this is a pleasant place to eat and is another favourite of the expat crowd. Back on Avenue Al Quds, past the duo of Lebanese places but before the Canadian Embassy, there is the Chinese **Restaurant Piano**, where the evenings are adorned with live piano music. Still further along Al Quds – which has now become Route de Koulikoro – past the Canadian embassy, the **Montécristo Restaurant** is another posh French restaurant, more typical of the Niaréla area than the Hippodrome.

Towards Koulikoro

Continuing along Route de Koulikoro, one or two other places are worth a mention. **La Sanza Bar Restaurant** is in the quarter of Korofina Nord on rue 110. While the menu is small and the quality of the food unpredictable, a great deal of effort has been put into making this new restaurant a little different from the competition. On most evenings films in their original languages are shown while you eat; there is also live music at the weekends, a small library, and even plans for a cybercafé. The tables are in a quiet garden and the service is good. Nearby, **Restaurant Gwa Kunda** at Muso Kunda (see page 123) has as good a selection of Malian dishes as you'll find in Bamako. There are daily menus and the staff are both friendly and knowledgeable about the food they serve – something you cannot always take for granted. Finally, **Restaurant Le Lagoon** is about 10km further along Route de Koulikoro in an idyllic spot on the banks of the River Niger. Despite the limited choice – essentially *brochettes de capitaine* or roast chicken – which can take ages to arrive if you come for lunch at the weekends, you can spend hours under the trees enjoying the light river breeze and a peacefulness not easily found in the capital itself.

South of the river

Restaurant Pâtisserie Amandine, along the Avenue de l'OUA not far from the Pont des Martyrs, is arguably the best *pâtisserie* in town. It has an excellent choice of pastries and serves tasteful food (like pizzas, salads and *capitaine* dishes) as well, which makes it a popular place for *toubabous* (white people) to hang out. Meanwhile, **Restaurant Le Kandjo** at Hotel les Colibris is in a garden next to the hotel, while Hotel Le Beauregard has **Restaurant Le Vieux Fusil**, a pizzeria and a terrace with partial views of the river. Just past the Gare Routière de Sogoninko is **Pâtisserie de l'Étoile**, which is quite acceptable if you have to wait a few hours for a bus. Somehow, though, it lacks the refinement and appeal of the Amandine. **Restaurant Wassulu** has a decent choice of meals at sensible prices.

Supermarkets

Several large supermarkets in Bamako service the needs of the city's expat community. Most of the produce, therefore, is imported from France and is very expensive. Opened in February 2004, the **Azar Libre Service** on Avenue de l'OUA in Badalabougou Est is easily the best supermarket in town. This is *the* place to spend a fortune on camembert and Italian salami, vintage wines and energy drinks, crunchy muesli and chilled hazelnut chocolate bars. Open on Monday–Saturday 08.00–13.00 and 15.30–20.00, Sundays 09.00–13.00. **Le Fourmis** and a smaller **Azar** branch, both on Avenue Al Quds between Restaurant Le San Toro and Le Relax, are lesser gods but nonetheless well stocked. In Niaréla, underneath Hotel Le Campagnard, **Le Metro** is convenient if you are staying at one of the many hotels in this part of town.

ENTERTAINMENT AND NIGHTLIFE

The state of the arts in Mali has never been better. Malian music enjoys worldwide acclaim, its cinema is starting to receive international recognition, and in December 2003 Bamako hosted an African festival of theatre.

The **Centre Culturel Français de Bamako** (tel: 222 40 19; web: www.ccfbko.org.ml) is the best place to go to sample some of this art and culture. Concerts – not just by Malian performers, but by musicians and dance troupes from all over Africa and the world – are staged in the CCF's large theatre, where Malian favourites, such as Ali Farka Touré and Amy Koita (see page 26), rub shoulders with drummers from Burundi and Canadian jazz bands. Ticket prices range from CFA3,000 to CFA10,000, and you should pick up a monthly programme of events to see what's going on. The **Musée Nationale** (tel: 222 34 86) on the Route de Koulouba towards Point G, has weekly concerts and other events on Thursday afternoons at 16.30, and sometimes on Friday mornings. Every day but Mondays at 10.00 and 14.00, the museum screens films about the history and the culture of Mali. Admission is CFA500. On the other side of the river, the large, pink building to the right of Pont des Martyrs is the **Palais de la Culture** (tel: 222 33 70), which also holds concerts and other cultural events (CFA2,500–3,500). This is the home of the Théâtre National du Mali, which rehearses there most mornings from about 10.00. If you ask nicely, you should be allowed to watch. Similarly, you can catch evening rehearsals of traditional dance and music at **Carrefour des Jeunes** in the centre of town – another cultural centre showcasing young, local talent. The **Buffet de la Gare** next to the railway station occasionally still enjoys live music played by the Super Rail Band of Bamako (see page 27). Live music can also often be heard at several restaurants around Bamako, notably the **Akwaba** on Tuesdays, Fridays and Saturdays, and **La Sanza** on Fridays.

Nightclubs in Bamako basically fall into two categories. King of the glitzy, western-style discotheques, playing international music for a largely expat crowd, is **Le Byblos**, next to Le Relax (see page 115) and owned by the same Lebanese family. Even on Saturday nights when this place is invariably packed, there is an easygoing, seductive atmosphere. A word of warning, though: gorgeous Malian ladies, dressed to kill and with a smile to match, who approach men – particularly older men – asking to dance, are not necessarily doing it for the pleasure of their company. The cover charge at Le Byblos is expensive at CFA5,000, but includes a free drink. There is another nightclub further down the road at **L'Express**, which is also Lebanese-run and not dissimilar to Le Byblos. **Le Spot** is on the Route de Koulikoro in Korofina, but its dance floor remains uncluttered while Le Byblos enjoys the lion's share of the expat market. The fairly new but already popular **Platinium** is in Immeuble Babemba on Avenue Kasse Keita, while Atlantis and the Bla Bla Club are next to the Centre Culturel Americaine in Badalabougou Est. Malian nightclubs – those playing mostly African music – are not hard to find in Bamako. Try **Night Club Calao** on rue Fankélé Diarra near Carrefour des

Jeunes, which plays salsa on Tuesday nights (CFA3,000); **Le Tempo** in Quartier du Fleuve; or **Le Metropolis** – arguably the most popular – on Route de Sotuba. The one **casino** in town is operated by Hotel de l'Amitié.

The biggest **cinema** in Bamako is also at Hotel de l'Amitié, where commercial American films dubbed into French are shown on a big screen for CFA2,000. French – and sometimes Malian – films are screened at the Centre Cultural Français on Wednesdays, Saturdays and Sundays. A fairly new cinema showing top of the bill films – all dubbed into French – is Cinema Babemba, located in Immeuble Babemba, which is on the corner of Avenue Kasse Keita and the Boulevard de l'Indépendance. Two films are shown every evening except Mondays (tel: 223 95 77 for information on their weekly programme). And for senseless karate films, Cinema Vox, almost opposite the cathedral, is going to be your best bet. Meanwhile, films in their original languages are shown – power-cuts permitting – on a small screen most nights at La Sanza Bar Restaurant. A monthly programme of events is available on request. There is no charge, but presumably you are expected to eat at the restaurant.

For information on the various cultural events in Bamako, pick up the monthly programme from the Centre Culturel Français and the monthly edition of *Le Dourouni*, an interesting booklet aimed at expats. It is distributed rather randomly and they are sometimes hard to find. Try the Centre Culturel Français, the embassies, the bigger hotels or the CODI (see page 119).

On the same premises as Restaurant Bafoulabé are two shops: **Faso Dambé** sells quality *bogolans* (see *What to buy*, page 90) and other textiles, and **Dambéso** sells musical instruments. On request, classes in African dance and djembé can be organised at CFA3,500/hour.

ACTIVITIES

The sporting options for visitors to Bamako are somewhat limited. There are **tennis** courts at Hotel de l'Amitié, Le Grand Hotel and Carrefour des Jeunes; large **swimming** pools at l'Amitié, Le Grand, the Mandé Hotel, Hotel Les Colibris and Le Rabelais, to name a few; and a nine-hole, par-three **golf** course behind l'Amitié, where a round of golf, including club rental and a caddy, will cost about CFA15,000 (there's no charge if you are staying at the hotel).

Bamako's **horse-riding** club is next to the Hippodrome, a large, open space of sand (and the occasional blade of grass) where informal football matches are played. To see professional **football matches**, go to the Stade Omnisport at the foot of the hill leading up to Point G, and the Stade du 26 Mars along the road to Ségou.

PRACTICAL INFORMATION
Tourist office

The main **Office Malien du Tourisme et de l'Hôtellerie** (tel: 222 56 73) is on rue Mohamed V near Square Lumumba. They have several, dated leaflets on the country's main tourist attractions (Bamako, Mopti, Djenné etc), but not a great deal else. They are, however, extremely willing to help plan itineraries and give advice. Unfortunately, few, if any, of the staff speak English. A new office – the **Bureau Régional du Tourisme** – representing OMATHO for Bamako and Koulikoro opened in February 2004; it is located in ACI2,000 near Hotel Résidence Bouna.

Communications and media

The **post office** occupies an impressive building on rue Karamoko Diabi. All services, including poste restante, are available; opening hours are 07.30–17.30 Monday to Friday, 08.00–12.30 on Saturday.

Making **telephone** calls – local, national or international – is a simple procedure from the numerous *cabines téléphoniques* around Bamako, many of which also have **fax** and **photocopy** machines. Alternatively, use your Sotelma card in the public phone boxes. There are several **Ikatel** and **Malitel** branches selling cellphones and SIM cards. The main branches, meanwhile, are in Hamdallaye just past the Centre Culturelle Islamique for Ikatel, and on Avenue Kasse Keita behind the Musée de Bamako for Malitel.

Within the past few years, Bamako has seen a true proliferation of the number of establishments with **internet** access. In some areas whole clusters of cybercafés seem to happily coexist, though at the same time some may suddenly abandon business while new ones keep popping up. A few addresses are marked on the map (see page 106), but without any doubt you will stumble upon plenty of others.

If you are expecting to receive mail at the American Express office in Bamako (see *Practicalities: communications and media* on page 91), you can find it at the travel agency called Afric Trans Service in Immeuble Babemba, at the corner of Avenue Kasse Keita and the Boulevard de l'Indépendance.

The best **library** in Bamako is at the **Centre Culturel Français**; while the Centre Culturel Français has more flexible opening hours – depending on activities – the following opening hours apply for the library only: Tuesday 09.30–18.00, Wednesday, Friday and Saturday 09.30–17.00 and Thursday 13.00–18.00. They have books on Mali, as well as a wide selection of newspapers and magazines – all in French. A small stand with books and maps on Mali is in the open air bar area. For newspapers and magazines in English, go to the **Centre Culturel Americain** (tel: 223 65 85) in Badalabougou Est. Do not expect to find books about Mali, as the centre is mainly focused on providing information on the United States to Malians. Opening hours are: Monday and Wednesday 08.30–16.30, Thursday 13.30–16.30 and Friday 08.30–11.00. The **Centre d'Orientation et de Documentation et d'Information** (or **CODI**, tel: 223 68 13) is located on Avenue Kasse Keita, behind the Musée de Bamako. Theoretically, this is where you can learn just about everything you ever wanted to know about Bamako's past and present. Access to the information, though, depends very much on who is around to help you. However, the notice boards, with a selection of articles and useful addresses, are always there, and so is the reading table with a selection of newspapers in French.

There are **bookshops** at the Hotel de l'Amitié and Le Grand Hotel, where the odd book or magazine in English is sold. Ankakalan Bookstore in Niaréla sells books in French and maps. The area between the Mission Libanaise and Avenue de la Nation is littered with book stalls that sell a colourful amalgam of both new and second hand books. Almost everything here, however, is in French. You can usually pick up a recent copy of *Time* or *Newsweek* from the **magazine vendors** around Square Lumumba. Haggle over the price.

For fairly updated and detailed maps, contact the **Institut Géographique du Mali or IGM** (tel: 220 28 40) nearby Hotel Les Colibris in Badalabougou Est. You can pick and choose from many maps and have a copy printed out while you wait. The SAE office (tel: 223 14 65) – for domestic flights, see page 77 – is on Avenue da la Nation near the Centre Culturel Français. The STA office (tel: 222 33 33) – for more domestic flights – meanwhile, is not far from Square Lumumba next to Point Afrique.

Money

There are two BDM **banks** on the Avenue du Fleuve: on the corner of Square Lumumba and opposite the cathedral (to change euros, US$ and sometimes other currencies, and for Visa cash advances). The BIM branches near the railway station and the Centre Culturel Français have a **Western Union** office (as do many other banks), but do not deal with foreign currency. The only bank in the whole of Mali with a **cash dispenser** (Visa cards only), is BICIM on the Boulevard du Peuple. The nearby Ecobank changes cash, but their main branch near the Monument de l'Indépendance also changes travellers' cheques (euros and US$). The Bank of Africa, on Avenue de la Marne next to Hotel de l'Amitié, changes both cash and travellers' cheques in most currencies. The BHM bank on Avenue Kwamé N'Krumah, opposite the Direction Générale de la Police Nationale, changes euros only.

There are a number of **exchange offices** – one of them is marked on the map, see page 106 – where you can change cash at the official exchange rate, but travellers' cheques are exchanged at an adverse rate. However, you can actually negotiate for a better deal. The same applies for exchanging cash or even travellers' cheques on the black market, but beware of conmen who may end up having it all, while you are left empty handed.

Health and safety

There are two main hospitals in Bamako. **Hôpital Gabriel Touré** (tel: 222 27 12) on Avenue Van Vollenhoven near Le Grand Hotel is the more central, while **Hôpital du Point G** (tel: 222 50 02) is on a hill overlooking the city.

While these hospitals are adequate for outpatient treatment and analysis, they are not places where you will find a lot of comfort and compassion. In case you should be admitted, a private hospital like **Clinique Pasteur** is the better option.

Pharmacies are thick on the ground and normally stock the main creams, pills and lotions. Contact-lens fluid, however, is almost impossible to find, and you'll be wasting your time in a pharmacy. If you are in desperate need, contact the eye hospital behind Hôpital Gabriel Touré or any other eye specialist. One optician (tel: 223 62 08) near Hotel Mirabeau has fluid for hard contact-lenses only.

Each *arrondissement* in Bamako has a **police** station, so you will rarely be very far from the law. The **Direction Générale de la Police Nationale** – where you should go for visa extensions (see *Before you go: Red tape and immigration* on page 53) – is just off Avenue Kwamé N'Krumah in the quarter of ACI-2,000, not far from the Pont du Roi Fahd.

Foreign representation in Bamako

The following is a selection of some of the more useful embassies and consulates in Bamako:

Belgium (Consulate) Hippodrome, Route de Koulikoro (opposite the Dutch embassy); BP 187; tel: 221 96 22; fax: 222 98 81; email: ambelba@cefib.com

Burkina Faso ACI 2000, near the Police Nationale; tel: 221 31 71; fax: 221 9266; email: ambfaso@datatech.toolnet.org

Canada Hippodrome, Route de Koulikoro, opposite the Luna Parc; tel: 221 22 36; fax: 221 4362; email: nassoun.sylla@dfait-maeci.gc.ca

Côte d' Ivoire Plaçe Patrice Lumumba, Immeuble Tam Voyages, opposite Air France, BP 3644; tel: 221 22 89; fax: 222 13 76

Denmark Immeuble Sima, BP 3259; tel: 222 06 91; fax: 222 86 28

France Square Patrice Lumumba, BP 17; tel: 221 29 51; fax: 222 31 36; email: ambassade@france-mali.org.ml

Germany Badalabougou-Est, Av de l'OUA (one block after the Pont des Martyrs), BP 100; tel: 222 37 15; fax: 222 96 50; email: allemagne.presse@afribone.net.ml

Ghana ACI 2000, near Hotel Bouna; tel: 229 60 83; fax: 229 60 84

Guinea Immeuble Saïbou Maïga, Quartier du Fleuve, BP 118; tel: 222 29 75/221 08 06

Italy Quinzambougou, BP 2386; tel: 221 73 10

Mauritania Hippodrome (just before the Fort premises to the left); tel: 221 48 15

Netherlands Hippodrome, Route de Koulikoro, BP 2220; tel: 221 56 11; fax: 221 36 17; email: bam@minbuza.nl

Niger Represented by Côte d'Ivoire in Mali

Norway (Consulate) Badalabougou Ouest; tel: 222 38 84; fax: 222 62 74

Senegal Hippodrome, BP 42; tel: 221 82 74; fax: 221 17 80

Spain (Vice-consulate) rue Lyantey, BP 1823; tel/fax: 224 64 52

Sweden Immeuble Babemba; tel: 222 32 40; fax: 222 45 66; email: anders.ostman@sida.se

Switzerland (Consulate) Route de Sotuba, BP 2386; tel: 224 45 49; fax: 221 32 05; email: coop.suisse@afribone.net.ml

UK (British Embassy Liaison Office – BELO – located in the Canadian Embassy) Hippodrome, Route de Koulikoro, BP 2069; tel: 277 46 37; fax: 221 83 77; email: belo@afribone.net.ml

USA Rue Rochester and Mohamed V, BP 34; tel: 222 56 63; tel: 222 77 68

WHAT TO SEE
Views of Bamako

Before doing anything else, go to **Hotel de l'Amitié**, take the lift to the 14th and top floor, and enjoy the semi-panoramic view of the northern part of Bamako, dominated by the twin minarets of the Grande Mosquée and the foothills of the Manding Mountains. While you are up here ask to have a look at the rooms, each of which has a balcony with unobstructed views of the River Niger. This is the quickest, simplest and cheapest way to see Bamako.

For truly panoramic views, go up into the hills overlooking the city. After the zoo, Avenue de la Liberté starts to wind up to **Koulouba**, the hill on top of which perches the Presidential Palace, government ministries and several decaying colonial houses. Before you reach the top, signposts indicate a *piste touristique* – one for Koulouba and another for **Point G**, the hill next to Koulouba where Bamako's largest hospital is situated. These *pistes*, or tracks, wind around the sides of each of these hills, affording spectacular views of Bamako and, when the dust is not too thick in the air, the River Niger and beyond. There are also some **grottoes** at the foot of Point G, with rock paintings depicting hunting scenes, men, tools and animals, which date back to perhaps as early as the Palaeolithic period some three million years ago.

The River Niger

The River Niger is not at its most picturesque as it flows past Bamako, but it is a focal point of activity and as such is interesting to see. Although nowadays two proper bridges link the left and right banks of the river – **Pont des Martyrs** and **Pont du Roi Fahd** or the 'old' and 'new' bridges respectively – at one time the only way for vehicles to cross the Niger was by the **Chaussée de Sotuba** (Sotuba Causeway). Situated about 8km east of the centre of Bamako, this causeway is cut into rocks which line the river bed and are submerged, along with the road itself, when the water is high. A couple of kilometres upstream, the **Barrage des Aigrettes** is a dam dedicated to providing the capital with hydro-electric power.

Mention of the River Niger often conjures up images of women washing clothes and children splashing about in its murky waters. This type of activity seems to be most popular on the right bank or south of the river next to Pont des Martyrs. On the same side, between the old and new bridges, **flower and vegetable gardens** are common. These are found all along the river (even in desert towns such as Gao), but in Bamako they seem to be greener and more colourful than elsewhere, and the number and variety of plants and vegetables grown is greater. Bougainvillea, poinciana, mango trees and Chinese trees with their distinctive yellow flowers are grown (and sold) in the gardens close to the British Consulate, while potatoes, onions, carrots, tomatoes, cucumbers, aubergines, beetroot, cauliflower, lettuce and other vegetables are cultivated in the small plots of land beside the river. Back on the left bank opposite the BCEAO building, women can be seen pounding and sifting *fonio*, one of Mali's staple foods (see page 30).

Musée National

Open 09.00–18.00 (closed Mondays). Admission CFA2,500.
Reopened to the public in 2003 after some major renovations, Mali's national museum on Route de Koulouba – just before the zoo – must be one of the most well-presented and informative museums in West Africa. The permanent exhibits include artefacts from almost every era of Malian history, accompanied by good written descriptions – for now all in French, though. Another permanent exhibition is an excellent display of a whole array of textiles, highlighting historical facts as well as details about the different materials and techniques used to make them. In addition, there is a temporary display dedicated to contemporary shows and performances. Guided tours in French are available. Every day but Mondays at 10.00 and 14.00, the museum screens films about the history and cultures of Mali. The programme is regularly available from the Centre Culturel Français. The admission fee for the films only is CFA500, but for visitors to the museum access to the auditorium is included in the admission fee. Also on the premises is a shop selling pricey books about Malian – and African – culture, and souvenirs. Enquire about the concerts and events, scheduled for every Thursday afternoon at 16.30 and sometimes on Friday mornings. These happenings generally attract a good number of visitors, many of them expats.

Musée de Bamako

Open 09.00–18.00 daily except Mondays. Admission free.
When compared to the mature National Museum, the Musée de Bamako is the younger stepsister that still has to get over her teething troubles. As the museum was inaugurated only in December 2003, it is forgivable that it may not yet be apparent to the public what the museum is about. Two small rooms with pictures and some artefacts are dedicated to Mali's colonial era, with the emphasis on the evolution of Bamako. Another room shows a number of ethnic artefacts, as well as reviews on saltmining and the life and culture of the Maures. To add to the confusion, the first floor is all about contemporary Malian art, with a mishmash of textiles and paintings of extremely diverse quality. It doesn't matter; this is a museum in the making, admission is free, and there is always the attractive garden – with some colourful, life-size animal sculptures – to be enjoyed.

Muso Kunda

Open 09.00–18.00 daily. Admission free.
Muso Kunda (also called Musée de la Femme) is in Korofina Nord on the same road as the Tunisian Embassy (rue 161) and not far from La Sanza Bar Restaurant. This museum, dedicated to the women of Mali, was opened by its founder, Adame Ba Konaré, the spouse of the former president, on March 8 1998 – International Women's Day (*muso kunda* means 'from the woman's side'). The very existence of a place like this in a country where the women do so much (see page 23) is perhaps more significant than its rather questionable

merits as a museum with interesting things to see. Apart from a few statues, masks and photographs, the main exhibit is a glass cabinet full of mannequins dressed in colourful regional costumes. The museum shop sells handicrafts made by women, and there is a good restaurant serving some of the best African food in Bamako (see page 116).

Parc Biologique
Open 07.00–18.30 daily. Admission CFA500.
As Avenue de la Liberté winds up to Koulouba and Point G, it passes Bamako's **zoo**. The selection of animals is limited and, while their living conditions are certainly not ideal, they could be worse. The gazelles and warthogs seem to have the best of it, wandering about in relatively large, open spaces, while the caged animals – the monkeys, birds etc – are worst off. A camel, a crocodile and a couple of mangy lions are the other main attractions. There is a restaurant which has cold drinks and a small menu.

Turn right just before you reach the Parc Biologique for the **Arboretum**, a park used by many of Bamako's keep-fit enthusiasts. This is quite a nice spot for a stroll, away from the dust and noise of the centre; and if you are contemplating a visit to Mali's largest national park, the Office du Parc National de la Boucle du Baoulé is situated here. See also page 272.

Grande Mosquée
The Grande Mosquée was built by the Saudis in a style more in keeping with Mecca than Mali. While this is not the most attractive mosque in the country, it is not as strict as others are about letting foreigners inside. You should not, of course, assume that you can enter as and when you like, but rather seek the necessary authorisation and then observe the appropriate etiquette once inside.

Cathedral
The sandstone cathedral is on Avenue du Fleuve, but will soon be usurped by a new church which is being built on the outskirts of town. Services are in the evening at 18.00, which is when you should turn up if you want to have a peek inside; at most other times it is shut. Every Sunday morning at 10.00 it is possible to attend mass, which is French-spoken in the cathedral, and English-spoken in the courtyard at the mission across the street.

Markets
Bamako's original Grand Marché (main market), affectionately known as the *marché rose* (pink market), burned down in 1993. A new one, built in neo-Sudanese style, bears a striking resemblance to the original. The area bounded by rue Mohamed V to the west and Boulevard du Peuple to the east is also almost entirely given over to commerce. It takes time and patience to walk around these streets and, while everything is probably available if you look for it, a monotonous procession of imitation brand-name clothing, shoes, bags, pots and pans is the reward for your efforts.

For arts and crafts, you should go to the **Artisanat** on Boulevard du Peuple next to the *Grande Mosquée*. A bit of everything is sold here – woodwork, leatherwork, ironwork, jewellery, musical instruments etc – much of it made by craftsmen who work on the premises and might have been taught at the Institut National des Arts which is over the road.

Behind the mosque in the Place de la République, a market specialising in **traditional medicine** has a morbid fascination. It is ultimately very sad to see animal skins, skulls of monkeys, crocodiles, warthogs and hyenas, dried chameleons and snakes and various other animals or parts of animals being sold to cure maladies or bring good luck, but it can be fascinating to see the sick and superstitious hand over a month's wages for these cures and charms, never doubting that they will work. Be warned that if you want to take photographs of the *marabouts* (witchdoctors) and their medicines, there will, in all likelihood, be a fee.

EXCURSIONS FROM BAMAKO
The Manding Mountains
The Manding Mountains are an extension of the Fouta Djallon highlands and stretch from the Guinean border to about 50km west of Bamako. Made up of eroded sandstone cliffs and well watered by various affluents of the country's two great rivers, the Senegal and the Niger, this is an area of striking rock formations, waterfalls and a fair amount of birdlife in the mountains and around the rivers and streams – although serious birders will prefer the Niger Inland Delta (see page 172). Furthermore, as the original home of the Malinké, whose Mali Empire was to become one of the greatest in the history of West Africa, the Manding Mountains are of considerable historical interest.

Access is obviously easiest with your own vehicle – although it's not impossible by public transport. The bus station for the Manding Mountains is the Gare Routière de Djikoroni Para. See *Getting there and away* on page 108. Gare Routière de Djikoroni Para is in the far western quarter of Djikoroni. Some of the most interesting things to see are along Route de Guinea, which leads to the border town of Kourémalé. For example, there is an archaeological site at **Woyowayanko**, where there was a battle between the forces of the last West African emperor, Samory Touré (see page 246), and the French colonialists; and at **Kourounkorokalé** there are ancient grottoes and rock paintings.

Kangaba
At the foot of the Manding Mountains, some 96km from Bamako, Kangaba is the spiritual home of the Manding people – a term used to cover a number of West African ethnic groups, including the Malinké and Bambara. It was here in 1235 that the Manding rulers signed a pact creating the Mali Empire in a clearing known as **Kouroukan-Fouga** at the town's northern entrance. However, it is the *casse sacré* (sacred house) of the Manding people, **Kamablo**, for which the town is famous. Only the *griots* (see *Traditional*

music, page 25) know exactly what is inside: fetishes belonging to the ancestors of the Mali Empire are most likely; ancient Islamic manuscripts from Mecca are a possibility; and, according to legend, the Kamablo also contains a sacred rock from Mecca. Every seven years, the all-knowing *griots* perform a ritual ceremony whereby the thatched roof of the sacred house is lifted on to the ground with the help of magic verse so that it can be cleaned and repaired.

Note that there are two roads to Guinea: one goes through the Manding Mountains, while the other runs parallel to the river. Kangaba is along the second of these two routes. For transport, see *Getting there and away* on page 104.

Kati

Kati is an important market town a few kilometres north of Bamako. The town itself is sprawling, unattractive and not much of a sight in itself. However, 10km further down the road in the direction of Kita, in a large, open space known as Le Drale, one of the largest **cattle markets** in the country takes place on Saturday mornings. Do not confuse this with the meat, fruit and vegetable market at Kati which takes place on Sundays.

The simplest way to get to Kati is by waiting for a *bâchée* or taxi on Avenue de la Liberté (next to the Musée National is a good place to stand). On Saturdays you should have no problem finding transport to and from Le Drale.

KOULIKORO

In 1977 Koulikoro became the second region of Mali. Geographically, it includes the areas of the former Bamako region such as Kangaba and Nara near the Mauritanian border, but not the city of Bamako itself. Its administrative centre is the town of Koulikoro, 57km east of the capital and, after Mopti, the country's most important river port. Indeed, the river is what brings most visitors to Koulikoro, for it is from here that the COMANAV boats leave for their weekly voyages downstream to Gao. Otherwise, Koulikoro is an industrial town dominated by Mali's largest factory, Huicoma, which processes cotton, oil and Koulikoro's famous soap. This town is more aesthetically pleasing than Mali's other factory towns, such as Koutiala and Bougouni and, as well as the river and its sandy beaches, there are some attractive colonial buildings – particularly the Commissariat de Cercle and the railway station – and a fair amount of greenery and hills to the north of the river. Indeed, the road between Bamako and Koulikoro is a good place for birdwatching. Look out for Egyptian plover, grey patincole, rock-loving cisticola and the endemic Mali firefinch.

Getting there and away
By river
The COMANAV building (tel: 226 20 95) is on the bank of the river, not far from the railway station. The voyage to Gao or Kabara starts every week on

Tuesday evenings at about 22.00. The scheduled return from Gao is two weeks later on Sundays, while the boat from Kabara returns on Thursdays. See *Practicalities: Getting around* on page 76 for more information and fares.

By road
Gana du Nord have a departure point for Koulikoro between the National Museum and the Stade Modibo Keita, where buses leave at 10.00 and 17.00, take about one hour and cost CFA1,000. Minibuses and *bâchées* leave from the nearby Gare Routière du Nouveau Marché de Médine and charge CFA900. In Koulikoro the terminus is in the eastern part of town known as Koulikoro Ba, although the more convenient stop is next to Café Club Amitié in Koulikoro Gare. (Koulikoro Gare is the commercial and administrative centre, while Koulikoro Ba is where the descendants of the town's original inhabitants live.) Buses leave for Bamako from Koulikoro Ba at 06.00 and 15.00 and stop at Café Club Amitié to pick up passengers. At other times, *bâchées* and bush taxis leave when full from opposite the railway station. Trains, meanwhile, carry goods but not passengers between Bamako and Koulikoro.

Where to stay and eat
Koulikoro is an ideal day-trip from Bamako. However, should you choose to stay overnight, there is one comfortable and pricey hotel in town, **Motel 'Le Saloon'** (tel: 226 20 24), which is owned and operated by Huicoma. It is next to the factory on the western edge of town, and clean, air-conditioned rooms cost CFA15,000 (single) and CFA18,500 (double). The **Centre d'Accueil** is the less luxurious and cheaper option on the eastern edge of town.

For meals, the restaurant at Motel 'Le Saloon' offers the widest choice. Other places, including **Café Club Amitié**, can be found in Koulikoro Gare, but the selection of restaurants is not overwhelming.

Practical information
Koulikoro has basic facilities, including a **post office** and a **bank** (BDM and Western Union).

KOLOKANI AND NARA
Few travellers choose to go all the way to Nara, but remote and little known places seem to have an irresistible appeal to the adventurous John Kupiec. He provided the following information.

Travelling from Bamako to Kolokani, just past the village of Tiorobougou, is the turning to Lac Ouénia (sometimes spelt Lac Wanga). From there, John walked the 17km towards the lake: 'You will come to a wide open space. On your left, look for a slanted, tin-covered corrugated roof. This is a chapel, part of a fenced compound and other buildings owned by the Catholic Mission.' Walk around the compound to find the lake, which John describes as 'a peaceful swimming place, tree-lined and with a few birds'.

Transport to Kolokani (CFA2,500 from Bamako) is best found on market day, which is Wednesday. There are two mosques in the market area.

Market day in Nara (CFA6,500 from Bamako) is usually on Friday and there is a mud-built mosque here. On the road leading to the market there are two places to stay: the Novotel and a *campement*.

Ségou

For many travellers starting their trip in Bamako, the region of Ségou will be their first taste of provincial Mali or, as the expatriate community like to say, '*la brousse*' (the bush). This is a gentle introduction, for Ségou is one of the country's richest regions and the countryside, whilst not exactly lush, is considerably more hospitable than the Sahelian and desert areas which begin in earnest further north and east. Much of the greenery in this area is provided by the *balanzan* or shea-tree, which is typical of the region and is the symbol of its principal town, Ségou.

HISTORY
The Bambara kingdom of Ségou

Much of the history of the region of Ségou is tied up with the history of the Bambara kingdom of Ségou and its two great dynasties: Coulibaly and Diarra. Before the first of these ruling families took control, however, the Bambara people, who had arrived in the region some time during the 16th century, lived in small districts under the control of the ruling Soninké aristocracy.

This remained the case until 1712, when all of the villages of the Niger Valley from Niamina (about 80km west of Ségou) to Sansanding were grouped together under the leadership of the first of the Bambara rulers of Ségou, Mamary or Biton Coulibaly, who established his court at Ségoukoro (see page 138). Biton was able to challenge and conquer the Soninké – and then gradually expand his kingdom – with the help of an extremely loyal army known as the *ton djon*. Rival Bambara clans were suppressed without mercy, and one – the Massassi – fled northwest to Kaarta, where they created a second Bambara kingdom (see page 260). By the time Biton died in 1755, a powerful kingdom under strong autocratic rule had been created to fill the void left by the decline of the Mali and Songhay empires. However, while the *ton djon* had given their allegiance to Biton, they were reluctant to accept the authority inherited by his sons, and for the next ten, generally anarchic, years the kingdom was ruled by a succession of *ton djon* chiefs, thus marking the end of the Coulibaly dynasty.

In 1766 N'Golo Diarra – a *ton djon* leader and husband of one of Biton's daughters – came to power, establishing the Diarra dynasty and restoring stability to the kingdom. N'Golo was a great warrior and an intelligent organiser, and under his leadership the Bambara kingdom continued to expand,

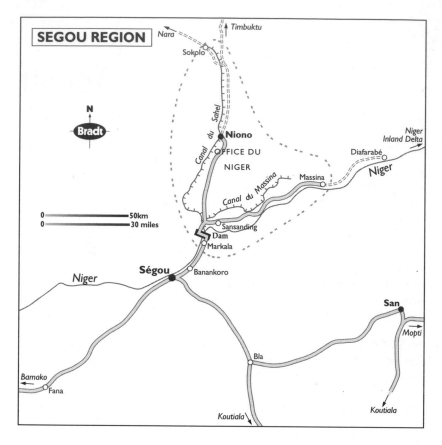

stretching from the desert in the north to Tengréla (Côte d'Ivoire) in the south, and from Kouroussa (Guinea) in the west to Lake Débo in the east. When N'Golo died in 1787, the Diarra dynasty was continued by his sons – first Nianankoro (1787–92), then Monzon (1792–1808) – and then by a succession of Monzon's sons, beginning with Da Monzon (1808–27). Despite enjoying great military victories and presiding over a renaissance of Bambara culture, Da Monzon and the seven brothers that were to succeed him as *fama* (king) of Ségou found it increasingly difficult to rule effectively. The kingdom had grown too large and unwieldy, making distant wars difficult and expensive to wage. There were also new enemies to fight, such as the theocratic Peul Empire of Macina to the east (see page 160) and the Tukulors from the Futa Djalon led by El Hadj Omar Tall (see page 9).

The declining Bambara kingdom finally fell to El Hadj Omar at the Battle of Wéta on March 11 1861, and Ségoukoro became the capital of the Ségou Tukulor Empire – part of a much larger Tukulor Empire founded in 1852. El Hadj Omar died in 1864 while fighting in Macina, leaving his son, Amadou, in charge. However, although the town of Ségou and its surroundings were under effective Tukulor control, elsewhere the Bambara remained unconquered and in rebellious mood right up until April 1890 when French colonial troops, led by Colonel Louis Archinard, took control of the region.

Office du Niger

The Office du Niger is the great legacy of colonialism in the region of Ségou. The vision of its first director-general, the French engineer Emile Bélime, was to turn deserts into farms by irrigating nearly one million hectares of a zone northeast of Ségou known as the *delta mort* (dead delta), which was once supposed to have been a major arm of the River Niger. After an initial experiment with irrigation in the form of the Sotuba Dam (completed in 1929), the Office du Niger was created in 1932 as a semi-autonomous government agency dedicated to the production of cotton and rice through extensive irrigation. To this end, a massive dam was built at Markala (see page 140) and two canals were dug to bring water to the *delta mort*. This construction work was performed by forced labour, as was the subsequent cultivation of the land. However, when forced labour in French West Africa was abolished in 1946, Office du Niger managers could no longer compel construction crews or farmers to work. Therefore, by 1946, a scheme originally intended to provide French industries with raw materials was only producing cotton for the domestic market. By 1960, a mere 60,000 of a possible 960,000 hectares of the *delta mort* had been irrigated; and in 1970 the Office du Niger formally abandoned its commitment to cotton, concentrating instead on the cultivation of rice and sugarcane. Two sugar refineries have been established, while experimental rice-cultivation is taking place under the supervision of Chinese experts. Only just over ten percent of the total capacity of the Office du Niger has been cultivated over the last few years, as farmers complain that the levy they have to pay for the use of the land – which is owned by the Office du Niger – makes it hardly worth their while. These days, the Office du Niger continues to operate, but faces the combined problems of rising production costs and an outdated infrastructure.

SEGOU TOWN

Ségou is the first main stop on the highway to Gao, 235km east of Bamako on the banks of the River Niger. After independence in 1960, Ségou became the capital of the country's fourth region and was widely recognised as Mali's second city. It was – and still is – a town of great economic potential, being the headquarters of the Office du Niger and several other important national industries such as Comatex (Compagnie Malienne de Textiles) and Ségou Lait (milk). However, this economic importance should not fool you into thinking that Ségou is an industrial black spot full of factories, foul smells and smoke – because it is not. Instead, spending time here can be more pleasant than in some of Mali's other larger towns and, while it does not quite deserve the label 'tranquil', Ségou is certainly one of the least stressful places on the tourist circuit in the eastern part of the country. There is no one outstanding attraction at Ségou – like the port at Mopti or mosque at Djenné – but rather a little bit of everything: the River Niger, historical villages, colonial architecture, arts and crafts etc. This makes Ségou a somewhat subtle and understated tourist town – which is precisely why it is worth visiting.

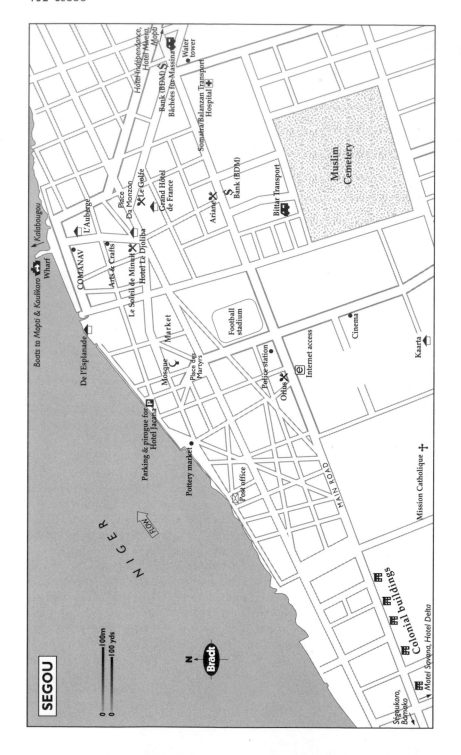

SEGOU

0 ____ 100m
0 ____ 100yds

Bradt

N

N I G E R

FLOW

Boats to Mopti & Koulikoro

Kalabougou

Wharf

De l'Esplanade

COMANAV

L'Auberge

Arts & Crafts

Le Soleil de Minuit

Hotel Le Djoliba

Place
Da Monzon

Le Golfe

Grand Hôtel
de France

Hotel Indépendance,
Hotel Mwena, Mopti

Bank (BDM)

Bâchées for Massina

Water
tower

Somatra/Balanzan Transport

Hospital

Ariane

Bank (BDM)

Bittar Transport

Muslim
Cemetery

Mosque

Market

Place des
Martyrs

Parking & pirogue for
Hotel Jacana

Pottery market

Post office

Police station

Ortus

Internet access

Football
stadium

Cinema

Kaarta

MAIN ROAD

Mission Catholique

Colonial buildings

Motel Savana, Hotel Delta

Ségoukoro,
Bamako

Trees – many of them *balanzans* – line either side of the main highway as it approaches Ségou from Bamako. According to legend, the town was built on a forest of *balanzans* by N'Golo Diarra, who himself used to sit under a great shea-tree (or *balanzan*) during his time as a customs officer before becoming king. The name of the town comes from Sikoro, which means 'at the foot of a *balanzan*'.

Orientation

Like many other towns in Mali, orientation in Ségou is a question of familiarising yourself with different quarters rather than street names, which are, in any case, largely non-existent. Visitors will spend most of their time in places like Office du Niger (where much of the colonial architecture is found), Balankoro and Sokalakono (the old quarters), and Centre Commercial (with the market and main hotels). The main drag is the highway from Bamako. The left bank of the River Niger and town centre are due north, while most of the residential quarters begin on the other side of the road. Although Ségou itself is not large, many of the interesting things to see are a few kilometres away. For example, Ségoukoro is 10km along the road to Bamako, and Kalabougou and other villages are on the right bank of the river.

Getting there and away

By river

The COMANAV building (tel: 232 02 04) is by the wharf near Hotel L'Auberge. Boats stop at Ségou on Wednesdays for Mopti, Timbuktu and Gao, and on certain Wednesdays or Saturdays for Koulikoro. See *Practicalities: Getting there and away* on page 73 for more information and fares. *Pinasses* ply the section of river between Ségou and Mopti, although the existence of a good road link makes the river of secondary importance as far as trade is concerned.

By road

The main bus companies, such as Somatra/Balanzan Transport and Bittar Transport, leave from stations just off the main road, respectively near the water tower and the Muslim cemetery. Both provide regular services throughout the day to Bamako (3–4 hours, CFA2,000). Somatra/Balanzan has departures for Mopti at 09.00 and around noon, while Bittar leaves for Mopti at 11.00, 14.00, 18.00 and 21.00 (CFA4,500). Bittar also has a direct service to Gao (Mondays and Thursdays at 11.00, CFA10,000), and regular transport to Niono and Koutiala, with several departures in the afternoon (CFA1,500 and CFA2,000 respectively). Other destinations with Somatra/Balanzan include Sikasso (daily at 09.00 and 12.00, CFA3,500), Bobo-Dioulasso (daily at 12.00, CFA6,000) and Lomé (Saturdays at noon, CFA17,500).

Kouma Transport and Binke Transport leave from the Marché de Sougou (past the Shell service station in the direction of Mopti). Kouma has departures for Koutiala and Sikasso twice daily (09.00 and 11.00) and an onward bus to Bobo-Dioulasso leaves at noon. Though services to Abidjan have been suspended, Kouma does provide some transport to Bouaké (CFA15,000).

TOUBAB, GIVE ME A PEN!
Jolijn Geels

Imagine you are driving in your car on the highway, it is rush hour, and all of a sudden you get caught in slow-moving traffic: who is driving in front of that lengthy chain of cars? Who caused the traffic jam?

Now think of Mali – or Africa for that matter – and think of the chains of children sticking out empty hands, asking for pens and sweets and money and what not. Who was the first tourist who came up with the brilliant idea to teach these kids to do so?

Of course that is not how it happened; no one person is responsible for a traffic jam during rush hour, and no one tourist can be singled out and accused of turning children into beggars. However, in a country where lengthy greetings are commonplace, children are somehow allowed to get down to business straight away, with phrases like: '*Toubab*, give me a pen!' or '*Ça va, le bonbon?*' This attitude evolved over time and it is not going to go away just like that. Unless perhaps – one can always dream – all white visitors to a country change their behaviour first and start preaching new ways for children to get a gift: earn it! Do something in return and do not naturally expect white people to carry bags full of pens! Such a new approach would take a while to sink in, but educating people has worked before. Have some former poachers not become rangers in countries where wildlife needed protecting? Did we ourselves (read: white folks from the 'first world') not need a lot of time to understand the importance of recycling waste or wearing seatbelts in a car, to name a few examples? So, theoretically, changing attitudes is possible.

Some kids – some adults, too – have become quite cunning at coaxing gifts and donations off tourists. In Ségou, for example, young boys regularly approach tourists with a convincing story of their new soccer team which is in desperate need of soccer balls, shirts and such. Could you please help the team? Any donation given is not likely to be invested in the team, though, so be cautious and try to check out similar schemes before handing over your money.

Binke Transport has a service all the way to Gao and Kidal (departure around noon, CFA10,000 and CFA20,000 respectively).

Along with those larger companies, smaller buses with destinations like Niono, Massina, San, Bla and Djenné (the latter only on Saturdays and Sundays) leave when full from the Marché de Sougou and from the unpaved roads across the street from the Somatra/Balanzan bus yard and water tower.

Where to stay

The hotel in favour with most visitors is **Hotel L'Auberge** (tel: 232 01 45). Along with the renovated **Hotel Indépendance** (tel: 232 04 62), which is some

While all of the above sounds rather discouraging, there is nothing wrong with giving as such. On the contrary: in a country like Mali, where there is no system of social security, the unfortunate, the crippled and the blind sometimes have no other option but to beg for food and money. As one of the pillars of Islam, giving alms is actually a matter of course. The young boys who are attending Koran-school are even dependent for food on begging; they roam the streets – a bucket or tin container in their hand – and recite Koran verses, hoping for something to fill their stomachs. In the Malian society, both these pupils and the unfortunate are genuine beggars with little choice. They rely on handouts from Malians and visitors alike: a coin, some food, or even fresh leftovers. Did you know that when you are eating out, it is totally acceptable to have your leftovers passed on to the needy? Ask for a doggy-bag (and remember that dogs in Europe or the US may well be better off than the poorest people in Mali) or empty your plate in the bucket or tin of a pupil. Though it may feel strange at first, this makes more sense than putting a pen or a sweet in the hand of an endearing nipper.

If you wish to contribute directly while you are travelling, the best way to go is through a local authority or an organised channel like a charity. A box of pens, excercisebooks and all the educational necessities you can think of will be of use for schools, while a women's association or a children's home will always highly appreciate a gift of kiddy's clothes and substantial amounts of rice, flour, sugar, cooking oil and soap. If you wish to donate something to a clinic, do not automatically assume that the leftovers from your medical kit are what is needed. In any case, local clinics should never be seen as a dumping ground for anything that is past the 'best before' date. Many clinics and hospitals, however, will gladly accept a gift of money – often they keep a record of donations – and will use it to purchase whatever meets the particular needs of the institution.

As for the chain of kids demanding a gift: I tend to ignore them most of the time, but occasionally – when I am in the right mood – I give them time and attention instead of sweets. That is hardly ever disappointing. Children may seem greedy when they take their chances as you are skimming past their lives, but spend some time with them and curiosity supersedes.

way from the centre on the road to Mopti, Hotel L'Auberge is run with characteristic efficiency by a couple of Lebanese brothers. Rooms with a fan start at CFA12,000 (single) and CFA15,000 (double), rooms with air conditioning start at CFA18,000 (single), and all rooms are invariably clean and sometimes quite large. On the last day of my stay I discovered that the hotel also has a swimming pool. It is well-hidden behind trees in the garden where meals are taken, so don't miss out on this small and rare luxury. **Hotel de l'Esplanade** (tel: 2320127) still has some economy accommodation at CFA10,000 (single) and CFA12,500 (double), but most rooms are self-contained, with a fan or air conditioning, and range from CFA17,000 to CFA24,000. Some rooms have river views, and a bar-restaurant is located on the river bank. For CFA2,000 non-residents can make use of the swimming pool in the secluded courtyard. Hotel L'Auberge and Hotel de l'Esplanade are comparable in price and quality. The former is popular with tourists, while the latter could be described as a business hotel. Consequently, the guides congregate around Hotel L'Auberge. Another hotel in Ségou with a central location is **Grand Hotel de France** (tel: 232 03 15), which is friendly and good value. CFA7,500 buys you a room with a fan and mosquito net and free transport to the bus station is also on offer – not that it is very far to walk. If you are lucky, you might meet the 'Grand Griot', the big, jovial owner who occasionally gives music concerts in the hotel courtyard. Also centrally located is the pleasant **Hotel le Djoliba** (tel: 232 15 72), with clean and comfortable air-conditioned rooms at CFA20,500 (single) and CFA23,500/26,000 (twin/double). If these rooms are too pricey, a dorm bed comes at CFA5,000, while a mattress and mosquito net on the terrace costs CFA4,000. Accommodation elsewhere is quite far from the centre. On the main road just before the Hotel de Ville (town hall), there is a turning for **Hotel Savana** (tel: 232 09 74) and **Hotel Delta** (also known as Campement de l'Office du Niger, tel: 232 02 72). The former has rooms ranging from CFA8,000 (single with a fan) to CFA22,000/27,000 (double/triple with air conditioning), and a dorm bed costs CFA5,000. Bikes are available at CFA1,500 per day. The latter has rooms for CFA10,000–12,000 and feels a bit like a youth hostel, in the spacious and colonial setting that is typical for the Office du Niger quarter. There is nothing wrong with **Motel Mivera** (tel: 232 03 41, rooms starting from CFA10,000) just before Hotel Indépendance at the crossroads for Niono, except that it is too far from the centre to be practical for those without their own transport. The same can be said for **Hotel Wawa** (tel: 232 18 85, CFA15,000 and up) and **Hotel Résidence Balanzan** (tel: 232 02 57, CFA20,000 for a room, CFA4,000 for a dorm bed) – both on the road to Bamako, and **Hotel Teriya** (tel: 232 10 75, CFA7,500 and CFA12,500), which is behind the Marché de Sougou. An interesting new place is **Hotel Jacana**, located on the opposite side of the Niger. To get there, report to the pickup point (between Hotel l'Esplanade and the pottery market) to have the *piroguier* called over from the other side. The boat ride is free and so is parking your car, but you have to get past the very moody guardian first to get a telephone number and hopefully the use of a telephone. That doesn't always work, so no information is available. The **Kaarta Hotel** is undergoing thorough renovations and will open again under new ownership and a different name.

Where to eat

Of all the hotel restaurants, the most pleasant is at **Hotel L'Auberge**. The food is well prepared and there are some Lebanese dishes on the menu; but the real draw is the lush garden, which is cool during the day and peaceful in the evenings. On Saturday evenings, enjoy some live music while you wait for your pizza to be baked in the furnace on the first floor terrace of the **Hotel le Djoliba**. The restaurant at **Hotel l'Esplanade** looks rather unappealing, but have your meal served at the terrace overlooking the river, and even fish 'n chips would taste like capitaine à la something. Bring mosquito repellent, though.

Outside the hotels, most of which have restaurants serving the usual range of international cuisine, the eating options are somewhat limited. **Restaurant Le Soleil de Minuit**, at the top of the road leading to the wharf, has plenty of *capitaine* dishes (see *The Capitaine's Table* on page 29), while **Restaurant Le Golfe**, by the roundabout in Place Da Monzon, is cheaper and has a more Malian feel, with *hamburgers à cheval* (a beef hamburger with an egg on top) and good breakfasts. The small **Restaurant Orlus** opposite Sotelma's cybercafé serves cheap, tasty meals. There are one or two other restaurants in Ségou around the bus yards and on the road to Mopti, but these are probably only worth a visit if you happen to be passing. The **market** and various small **grocery stores** sell basic foodstuffs and bottled water.

Entertainment and nightlife

Just off the main road, Ségou's **cinema** specialises in violent Indian and Oriental films and pornography (entrance: CFA300). If you are in Mali during the **football** season, matches are played at the weekends on real grass at the smart stadium in the centre of town.

For apéritifs, choose between the garden at **Hotel L'Auberge** or the bar beside the river at **Hotel de l'Esplanade**. The latter also has a nightclub called **Le Rivage** (entrance: CFA2,500). The **Mabaso** on the road linking Place Da Monzon to the main highway is another bar-cum-nightclub which sometimes has live music on Fridays, Saturdays and Sundays.

Practical information

Most of Ségou's public buildings are along the main highway. The notable exception is the **post office**, which is rather out of the way by the river at the western end of town. To send postcards and small letters, the post-box at Hotel L'Auberge is perhaps more convenient; they also sell stamps. There are three banks. BDM has a Western Union branch and does Visa cash advances. BNDA (at Carrefour Markala, the crossroads for Niono) takes cash and travellers' cheques in euros and US$. BHM takes no foreign currency at all. **Sotelma**, Sotelma's **internet** (CFA1,500 per hour) and the **police station** are all close to each other on the main highway. The **hospital** is opposite the Somatra/Balanzan bus yard.

Tucked away behind the Marché Sougou is the **Office Malien du Tourisme et de l'Hôtellerie** or OMATHO (tel: 232 24 94, see also page 85). The very helpful and knowledgeable Chef de Bureau will gladly inform you about guides, festivals in the region and local history. Feedback on local guides is most welcome (see below). Should you run into some serious kind of trouble with the authorities, guides or *transporteurs*, he may help to sort you out. The **Association des Guides** can be found at Hotel l'Auberge. Ask for one of the senior guides. All the associated guides should in fact have received some training from l'OMATHO on natural history. A schooling programme on Segou's history, cultures and traditions should be made available to the guides in the not too distant future.

What to see

Ségou's main attractions are a short distance from the town itself (see *Excursions from Ségou* below).

Since Ségou was the headquarters of the Office du Niger, the French spent a lot of time there during the colonial occupation. Today, government ministries occupy most of the **colonial buildings** along the main road in the western part of town. Nearby, at the *Mission Catholique*, there is a large church, while in the side streets behind the church you can watch millet beer being made. Ask for directions when you arrive at the church. In the same vicinity (ie: south of the main highway), there is a large **Muslim cemetery** where piles of stones define each grave.

Although the port at Ségou is not the hive of activity it is at Mopti, for example, a walk along the **River Niger** is a good way to while away the time. Working your way west from the port, you'll see a **pottery market**, **vegetable gardens** and **pirogue-makers**. In the evening – perhaps after dinner at Hotel L'Auberge – walk down to the **wharf** and enjoy the stars and the silence.

With the cotton-producing Office du Niger within a stone's throw, it is no wonder that various cotton-processing businesses have been established in Segou. Two eye-catching *galeries* opposite Hotel l'Auberge show some fine examples of *bogolans* that were manufactured in their respective workshops, both of which can be visited. **Soroble Centre** is in the Sokalakono quarter next to the Collège Moderne; the other one is just out of town past the Carrefour Markala. Impossible to overlook, the **Centre de Textile Ndomo** is built in the same style as the associated Galérie Kasobané.

The **Club des Mères de Bougoufiè** (Rue 210, no 579, not far off Avenue Biton Coulibaly, tel: 232 16 33) is their more idealistic counterpart. What started as a programme to combat illiteracy, gradually evolved into an association of women joining forces to improve their standard of living. Most of their activities include the processing of cotton fabric in some form or another, and their products (*bogolans*, clothes, soft toys and more) are sold directly from the workshop. These Mères de Bougoufiè are a jolly bunch of women who welcome visitors.

Excursions from Ségou
Ségoukoro

Today, Ségoukoro (old Ségou) is a small village 10km from Ségou along the road to Bamako. In the 18th century it was from here that the Bambara kings ruled a kingdom which stretched for thousands of kilometres across West Africa. The tomb of the founder of this kingdom, Biton Coulibaly (1712–55), is still in the village, along with three mosques, one built by Coulibaly for his Islamic mother, Ba Sounou Sacko – the king himself was animist. Guides will routinely show you the tomb and mosques, but also take time to explore the village itself – the Sudanese architecture, granaries and activity down by the river.

There are two ways to get to Ségoukoro: by river or by road. Pirogues can be arranged at **Balanzan Tours**, based at Hotel Résidence Balanzan (tel: 232 02 57) on the road to Bamako; through **Savana Tours** – based at Hotel Savana (tel: 232 09 74); or with the guides outside Hotel L'Auberge for about CFA25,000. *Bâchées* do not venture out of Ségou, so you must take a taxi or walk to Ségoukoro. Guides, it seems, are obligatory. Upon arrival, you will be taken to the chief – a descendent of King Coulibaly – who levies a CFA2,500 tax to visit the village. This permits you to ask him questions about the village and take photographs.

The government has embarked on a programme of restoration and development in Ségoukoro aimed at emulating the achievements of Songo in Dogon country (see page 198). In addition to the renovation of the village's historical monuments, there are plans to open places for tourists to spend the night and promote arts and crafts in the area.

Kalabougou
Kalabougou is on the other side of the river about 45 minutes by pirogue from Ségou, roughly northeast as the crow flies. This village produces much of the pottery for which Ségou is renowned. During the week, women are preoccupied with moulding and shaping the pottery, while at the weekends the furnaces are lit. Men traditionally forge iron, although they do not seem to work as regularly as the women do.

Privately arranged pirogues to Kalabougou cost around CFA20,000 – a little more if a guide is included. Find the village chief when you arrive and introduce yourself; be prepared to pay a visitors' tax.

Bozo fishing village
The village on the other side of the river visible from the wharf at Ségou is a small settlement of Bozo fishermen. This is a shorter excursion and, unlike at Ségoukoro and Kalabougou, there is a public pirogue costing CFA150 which leaves when full from beside the wharf.

BETWEEN SEGOU AND NIONO
Much of the land between Ségou and Niono is Office du Niger country, and the paved road between these two towns is testament to the area's economic importance. It also facilitates relatively quick and easy travel in the central part of the region. Continuing north from Niono, however, is rather more arduous.

Banankoro
Banankoro was the village administered by Da Monzon before he became the Bambara ruler in 1808: now it is his final resting-place. Apart from the king's tomb, Banankoro is no more spectacular or pretty than other villages around Ségou.

As the first settlement on the road to Niono, the best way to get to Banankoro is by taking a bus bound for Niono. The village is about 9km from Ségou. As always, introduce yourself to the village chief before wandering about.

Markala and Massina

About 40km from Ségou, a bridge crosses the River Niger at the town of Markala. This bridge and a 2,600m-long dam, the **Barrage de Markala**, were constructed between 1933 and 1949 as the central nervous system of the Office du Niger's hydrologic machinery. The idea was to raise the level of the water in the Niger to such a point that it would overflow into two man-made canals with raised dykes along their banks, thus irrigating but not flooding the *delta mort*. One of these canals, the **Canal du Sahel**, branches off towards Niono in the north, while the other, the **Canal du Massina**, passes Sansanding and continues eastward in the direction of Massina.

This impressive dam is not the only reason to visit Markala. The **Festival des Masques et des Marionettes (Fesmamas)** takes place in March and is one of the largest of its kind in Mali. Invented by the Bozo and traditionally performed by groups of young people, the *théâtre des marionettes* usually takes the form of dances in human or animal costumes endowed with some historic or symbolic meaning. Although the dancing at Markala is well-reputed, these festivals also take place in other Bozo areas.

There is accommodation at Markala. Try the **Centre d'Accueil 'Le Cacao'** (tel: 234 20 43) or **Hotel Campement Emile Bélime** just before the bridge.

Since the road is now tarred all the way, **Massina** is easily accessible by public transport (see *Getting there and away* on page 73). It is also possible, though, to travel to and from Massina by pirogue on the River Niger. On Independence Day (September 22), Massina stages masked dances and *concours de pirogues* (pirogue races) take place on the river. For more information on this event, contact the OMATHO office in Ségou. A *campement* provides basic accommodation in Massina.

While sailing to Mopti by pirogue – count on two days – you pass **Diafarabé**, which is the scene of the most important cattle crossing in Mali. It is said that hippos reside along this stretch of the river.

For more information on both Fesmamas in Markala and the cattle crossing in Diafarabé, see *Chapter 5: Practicalities* on page 73.

NIONO

The paved road becomes increasingly pot-hole-ridden as it approaches its terminus at Niono. Beyond here, there are only sandy tracks across the Sahel.

The town of Niono is well worth a visit. The bulk of the Office du Niger's rice cultivation takes place here, which makes it one of the most important economic centres in the region and, as a result, not an obvious port of call for tourists. However, there is a famous mosque and a canal in town, although descriptions of Niono as 'the Malian Venice' should be taken with a shovel-full of salt.

Getting there and away

Some bus companies have regular services linking Bamako and Niono (CFA3,500). Bittar Transport, for example, leaves daily at 08.00, 10.00, 12.00

and 16.00 from the *Gare Routière* in Sogoninko, Bamako (see *Bamako: Getting there and away* on page 104). It is quite feasible – and perhaps preferable – to visit Niono as a day trip from Segou. The journey takes about two hours and costs CFA1,500.

All buses leave Niono from the small yard which serves as the town's *gare routière*. As well as returning to Ségou, you might also be able to travel to Timbuktu from Niono via Léré, Niafounké and Goundam. No-one in town will commit themselves to stating a precise time, but vehicles seem to make the journey once a week when there is sufficient demand. The route north of Niono is a track, so journey times are subject to wide fluctuations according to the season and the condition of the road.

Where to stay and eat

Hotel Niono and Centre d'Accueil (tel: 235 21 58) is perfectly acceptable for a short stay. The simplest rooms have fans and mosquito nets and cost CFA5,000 for a single or double. You pay a little more for air conditioning. There is also a restaurant and bar – which is fortunate given the lack of similar facilities in town. Hotel Niono is about 1km from the mosque along the road leading out of town, opposite the police station. Another recommended place to stay goes by the abbreviated name of **CEFE**, about 3km from Hotel Niono not far off the road to Molodo. Dorm beds cost CFA2,500, while private rooms and food are also available.

Practical information

Between the mosque and *campement* are a **post office**, two **banks** and the aforementioned **police station**.

What to see

Use the bus yard as your main point of reference. Turn right out of the main entrance, walk along the paved road until you reach the Total service station, and on your left is Niono's main attraction, the **Mosquée du Vendredi** (Friday Mosque). In 1983 this structure won first prize in an international Islamic architecture competition, and it remains one of the most noteworthy mosques in Mali today. You should not enter without permission, but the building's design allows you to peer inside without actually going in. The **Canal du Sahel** is behind the bus yard. On the other side of this long stretch of water – which is the most pleasant place for a walk – are the **rice paddies** of the Office du Niger. 'I started to walk along the canal from Niono to Sokolo. It was a beautiful day and by walking on the dyke itself I was able to view the rice fields and activities on the other side; the canal itself; the road to my right, along with villages and mosques; and the layout of compounds of the villages and the people inside them.' (John Kupiec)

About 50km further north the canal peters out and the Sahel begins in earnest. This is where **Sokolo**, the town made famous by *La vie sur terre* (see page 28), is situated.

SAN

There is little else in the region to detain the visitor for very long. The main highway continues southeast from Ségou for about 80km to the town of **Bla**, which is one of the larger settlements in the region and a crossroads for traffic continuing south towards Koutiala and east towards Mopti.

A further 111km from Bla along the road to Mopti, San is possibly worth a short visit. Few tourists stop here for more than lunch, which makes it relatively free from the tourist-induced hassles of nearby Djenné, Mopti and, to a lesser extent, Ségou. On the other hand, San is not as attractive as its more illustrious neighbours and there is less to see and do. With many buildings under construction, the outskirts of San lack any sort of grace, and sadly the whole town is littered with waste and plastic bags. However, the centre of town is pleasantly lively, especially on market days (Mondays).

Getting there and away

All big bus companies running between Bamako and Mopti stop at San at their respective bus yards; and there are many. However, buses are usually full since San is not a major destination. Certain companies, like Bittar Transport, sometimes reserve a number of seats to be filled by passengers leaving from San. As they are sold on a first-come-first-served basis, you may be in for a long wait, even though buses will be passing through at regular intervals.

Reporting time for Bittar buses to Segou (CFA2,500) and Bamako (CFA5,000) are 10.00, 13.00 and 18.00, while the times for Mopti (CFA2,500) are 14.00, 16.30, 22.00 and 01.00. A regular Bittar service to Koutiala (CFA2,500) and Sikasso (CFA5,000) leaves from Restaurant Bon Coin. Like Bittar, Bani Transport also has buses driving all the way to Gao (CFA8,500), scheduled to leave at 14.00 and 17.00.

Bâchées and small buses with the same destinations leave when full from the bus yard in the centre of town next to the *campement*. For direct transport to Bobo-Dioulasso (CFA5,000), check with Satime at the same bus yard. On certain days of the week, especially on Mondays which is market day at both ends, you may find *bâchées* going directly to Djenné. Alternatively, take a *bâchée* bound for Mopti and get off at Carrefour Djenné, from where you should be able to find an ongoing *bâchée*.

Where to stay and eat

Just off the road to Mopti, **Hotel Campement Teriya** offers many clean and comfortable rooms with a fan for CFA7,500/9,000 (single/double), while rooms with air conditioning, TV and hot water are CFA15,000. Camping is allowed for CFA2,500 per person. Although the restaurant has an extensive menu, meals other than the ordinary have to be ordered well in advance. Too far out of town to be convenient, unless you have your own vehicle, **Hotel le Relax** offers spacious self-contained double rooms with a fan (CFA7,500) or air conditioning (CFA12,500). Meals are only available on request. Right in the

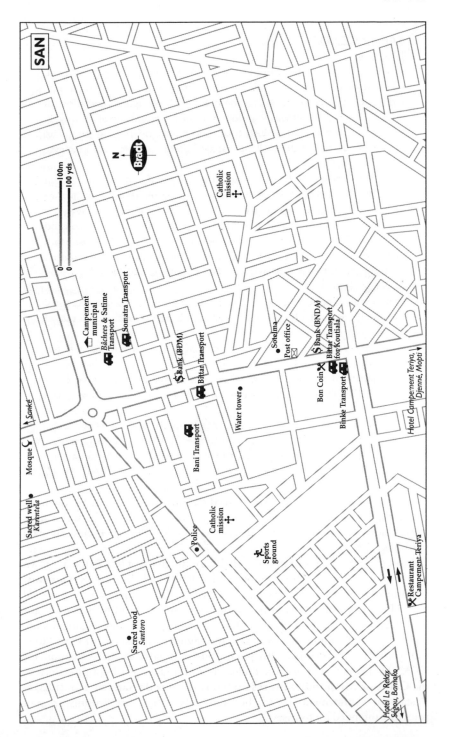

SAN

Sacred well
Karentela

Mosque

← *Sanké*

Sacred wood
Santoro

Police

Catholic
mission

Bani Transport

Water tower

Sports
ground

Campement municipal

Bâchees & Satime Transport

Somatra Transport

Bank (BDM)

Bittar Transport

Sotelma

Post office

Bon Coin

Bank (BNDA)

Bittar Transport
for Koutiala

Binke Transport

Catholic
mission

Bradt

N

0 100m
0 100 yds

Hotel Campement Teriya,
Djenné, Mopti →

Restaurant
Campement Teriya

Hotel Le Relax
Segou, Bamako →

SAN LEGENDS

Jolijn Geels

A hunter by the name of Marka and his dog came walking from Tion, when they got lost near what is now known as the town of San. Exhausted by hunger and thirst, the hunter fell asleep in the shadow of a tree. While the dog was wandering about, it stumbled upon a well, which was surrounded by lush trees and a fruit-bearing fig tree. The dog led its master to the well, nowadays known as Karentela (meaning 'out of danger').

To the northeast of the fig tree and the well, the two discovered a huge lake ('*mare*') where fish were abundant. The hunter decided to take to farming in the vicinity of this lake, and this is where his family at long last found him. Marka exclaimed: 'I will stay here during the rainy season and throughout the year!' The town became known as San from the Bambara word '*san*', meaning 'year'. The fig tree has since been known as 'Santoro', meaning 'the fig tree of San', and the lake has been named 'Sanké', with '*ké*' meaning 'here'.

Karentela, Santoro and Sanké are all sacred places to the inhabitants of San. Even though the fig tree has perished, the name lives on in a sacred wood – or rather a clump of trees – in the middle of town.

Another version that describes the naming of the town of San tells the story of a caravan of Manding merchants (Koïta and Sékiné) who came travelling from the south. They were one of many caravans who for centuries had traded kola nuts from the south for salt and dried fish from the north.

As it happened, this group of merchants camped on a small hillock to the south of Sanké, where they remained to see the end of the rainy season, then the end of the farming season, and finally the end of a full year, a '*san*'.

centre of town, **Campement Municipal de San** (tel: 237 21 15) is the most practical place to stay. Although the accommodation is basic, the welcome is warm and friendly; singles are CFA4,000, doubles CFA6,000, and an extra person is CFA1,500.

Most tourists who visit San stop only long enough to eat lunch, for this town is a convenient 'pit stop' between Bamako and Mopti. **Restaurant Campement Teriya** (owned by the same jovial owner, but not to be confused with Hotel Campement Teriya) is well placed on the road to Ségou to take advantage of transiting tourists. It has efficient service and a good menu, especially at lunchtimes. If necessary, the owner will take you to the Hotel Campement, but you may also pitch your tent next to the restaurant for CFA2,000 per person. For more budget accommodation, ask for directions to the **Catholic Mission Les Frères du Sacré-Coeur de San** (tel: 237 21 85) at Restaurant Campement Teriya, but remember that these rooms are not primarily intended for tourists.

Around lunchtime, buses often stop at **Restaurant Bon Coin**, which, to add to the confusion, is sometimes referred to as Restaurant Teriya (and indeed is owned by the same person). Meals are basic but tasty. Anywhere else, restaurants are of the soup-kitchen variety.

Practical information

The **post office** and BNDA **bank** are both near Restaurant Bon Coin. The BDM bank in the centre of town does not change foreign currency, but it has a **Western Union** branch. In the not too distant future, you may find **internet connections** at the Restaurant Campement Teriya.

What to see

A sacred well, a sacred wood and a sacred lake (see box opposite) are there to be seen to this day, though the well is now walled in. Ask the family across the road for the key. Suffice it to say that these are the main attractions in an otherwise rather ordinary town.

However, if you happen to be here in the seventh lunar month of the year, the Sanké-mon is a festival of celebration which takes place by the sacred lake and involves offerings, incantations and a lot of fishing.

The traders at the market in Bamako specialising in traditional medicine (see page 125) speak of a *marabout* in San who can prepare an irresistible **love potion** which, once administered, will induce its taker to fall in love with the first person she or he sees. Despite my best efforts, however, I failed to find him.

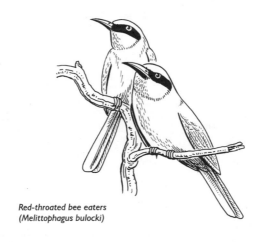

Red-throated bee eaters
(Melittophagus bulocki)

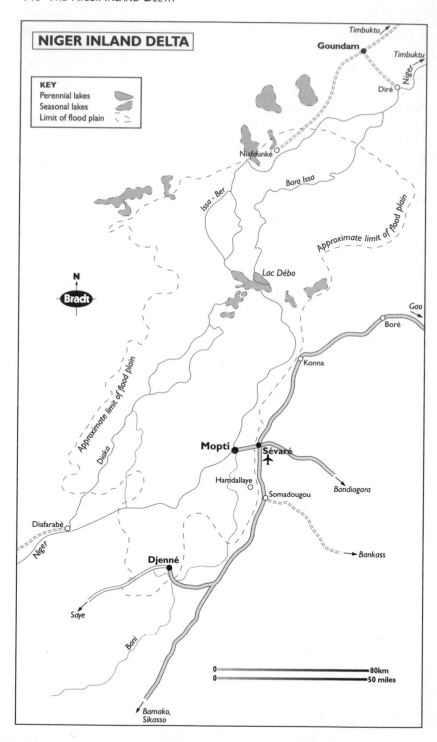

NIGER INLAND DELTA

KEY
Perennial lakes
Seasonal lakes
Limit of flood plain

Timbuktu
Goundam
Timbuktu
Niger
Diré

Niafounké

Bara Issa

Issa - Ber

Approximate limit of flood plain

N
Bradt

Lac Débo

Gao
Boré

Konna

Approximate limit of flood plain

Dioka

Mopti   Sévaré

Hamdallaye
Somadougou   Bandiagara

Diafarabé

Niger

Bankass

Djenné

Saye

Bani

0   80km
0   50 miles

Bamako,
Sikasso

The Niger Inland Delta

As the River Niger continues to flow in a northeasterly direction through the region of Ségou and into the region of Mopti – which also includes Dogon country and part of Gourma (see *Chapters 9* and *10*) – it forms a vast inland delta. Beyond the region's principal town, Mopti, the river splits into two main channels – the Issa-Ber and the Bara Issa – which, along with a network of smaller branches, spread out across a large, flat plain, flooding it during the rainy season and creating shallow lakes. The Niger floodplain stretches almost to the edge of the desert before the Issa-Ber and the Bara Issa are reunited and the River Niger flows past Timbuktu.

Most visitors come to see the towns of Mopti and Djenné, both of which are accessible by road and river: the main Bamako–Gao highway runs along the southeastern edge of the inland delta before veering eastwards after the town of Konna; the River Niger receives its main tributary, the River Bani, at Mopti, and Djenné is on the banks of the Bani at the southern edge of the floodplain. This is also the best place in Mali for birdwatching. Between November and March the numerous lakes and ponds of the floodplain are full of wintering Palaearctic waterfowl and shorebirds, as well as plenty of African species.

DJENNE

Historians allege that Djenné's best days are behind it. Competing at one time with Timbuktu as the western Sudan's pre-eminent centre of trans-Saharan trade and Islamic scholarship, nowadays Djenné is a moderately important agricultural town situated on an island in the Niger Inland Delta, with a population of around 10,000 people and a lively market on Mondays. However, perhaps Djenné's best days are yet to come – as Mali's pre-eminent tourist attraction. With its famous mosque and unique architecture, Djenné is already a firm fixture on the tourist circuit – a fact demonstrated by the emergence of hotels and restaurants to cater for the town's growing number of visitors. Unfortunately, the guides have also latched on to Djenné's potential and, perhaps because the town itself is so small, are omnipresent and, at times, aggressive. This is the downside of a visit to Djenné. On the other hand, you will not find a more beautiful or well-preserved town in Mali. Physically, at least, not much has changed here in the past few centuries, and walking around, particularly at the end of the day when the setting sun casts mysterious

POLLUTION IN DJENNÉ
Jolijn Geels

While you have every reason to wander around at leisure and admire the beautiful *banco* buildings in Djenné, you may find yourself watching where to put your feet much of the time. Many of the narrow streets are marred by open gutters, and sometimes one really has to be agile to avoid the wet and slippery ooze; in Djenné you should wear wellies rather than sandals. However, the danger can also come from above, from the pipes sticking out of the façades. Beware of sudden showers of waste water! As they routinely manoeuvre around the gutters, the *Djennenké* (as the local people are referred to) do not seem to find it too bothersome that their town is scarred and dirty. Do not be fooled by appearances, though; it hasn't always been like this and the Djennenké do not like it any more than visitors do.

In fact, less than a few decades ago, the gutters weren't even there. The Djennenké used to make use of the River Bani to bathe in, to do the laundry, clean cooking pots and so on. Only a limited amount of water, mostly from wells and used for drinking and cooking, found its way to the many households. Then – financed through foreign aid – numerous pumps, water pipes and taps were installed throughout Djenné. As more and more families benefited from this luxurious novelty, the problem of waste water gradually grew out of proportion. This consequence had simply been overlooked. Narrow trenches were dug to funnel off the murky water, and when the channels get clogged – as is often the case – the black, slimy substance is scooped out and deposited along the edges; not a pretty sight, and most of all, a serious health hazard. More foreign aid had to be found first to address this problem. But now there is reason for optimism: the first specially

shadows and shafts of light on the mud-brick skyline and winding alleys, is absolutely enchanting.

History

Much of the historical information about modern-day Djenné is contained in the *Tarikh es-Sudan*, a 17th-century chronicle of the western Sudan written by the Islamic scholar, Es-Sadi. (For details about Djenné's ancient predecessor, Djenné-Djeno, see page 158.)

According to Es-Sadi, the town was founded in the 13th century. Like Djenné-Djeno before it, Djenné became an important commercial centre, frequented by traders of the central and western Sudan and those of the Guinea's tropical forests. As in Timbuktu – which is often described as Djenné's 'twin city' – gold, slaves and kola nuts coming from the south were exchanged for Saharan salt, making the town one of the richest and most cosmopolitan in Africa. Indeed, the influence of Muslim traders from North Africa contributed to Djenné's conversion to Islam at the end of the 13th century by its 26th ruler, Koy Kounboro.

designed cesspools with filter systems have been installed in two quarters of Djenné. The year 2004 should see the end of a huge undertaking, where all individual households will get their own installation.

Watch out for vertical PVC and terracotta pipes – ideally concealed by a layer of *banco* – ending in a square, concrete tank and lid. Those square tanks aren't a textbook example of beauty, and less so in a town with so few square angles. Let's not be fussy, though: when the gutters stand dry and can be filled with earth again, the overall result will be a major improvement.

What about the other kind of pollution, such as the waste and plastic littering the big market square and the streets? Generally speaking, Mali is waking up to the problem of waste – plastic waste in particular. With no money to set up a sophisticated waste disposal programme, the government is trying to encourage the people to act themselves. This results in occasional and isolated cleaning frenzies, with groups of volunteers – mostly women – sweeping and picking up and burning rubbish. It is really no more than a drop in the ocean.

The solution that has been proposed for Djenné is quite interesting, since it is supposed to be a kind of structural solution: the Djennenké may be given the use of some 100 donkeys and carts. For five out of seven days these will be for private use, to try and lure people into this programme. The only condition is that on the two remaining days – Tuesdays after the weekly market being one of them – these donkey carts must be used to collect and remove garbage from town. Eventually, the collected waste will be burnt well away from Djenné. Whether or not this idea is viable, only time will tell. From a theoretical point of view, there is reason for mild optimism.

For much of the 14th and 15th centuries Djenné was part of the Mali Empire. In 1468 (or 1473) the city was captured by the ruler of the Songhay Empire, Sonni Ali, after a siege which, according to Es-Sadi, lasted for seven years, seven months and seven days. Djenné's best years were those spent under the stability and security of Mali and Songhay rule – a time when trade flourished and the city developed into a centre of Islamic scholarship. When the Moroccans took over in 1591, however, Djenné started its gradual and irreversible decline. The Moroccan period of control in the western Sudan was characterised by instability and anarchy (see page 8) which, along with the general shift of trade routes towards the coast where the Europeans had landed during the 16th century, had a detrimental effect on trans-Saharan trade – the key to Djenné's fortune. The arrival of Sékou Amadou in 1819 and his attempts to reform the practice of Islam in Djenné did nothing to restore stability, and the period of Tukulor control from 1862 to 1893 was equally unsuccessful. In fact, for nearly 300 years Djenné had been successively occupied and exploited by regimes lacking the authority and legitimacy of

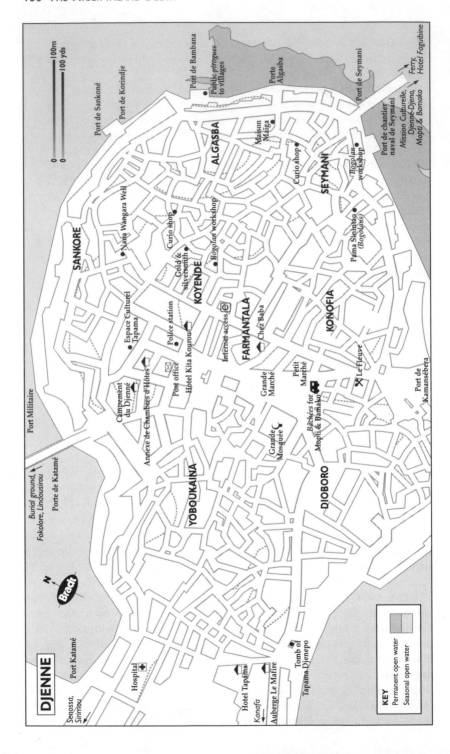

DJENNE

the Mali and Songhay empires, so that in April 1893, when Colonel Archinard marched into the town without opposition, he found only the remnants of one of the most important centres of trade and culture in Africa. The French preferred Mopti as the region's commercial centre, leaving Djenné to continue life as an agricultural town with a glorious past.

Getting there and away
By river
It is possible to travel to Mopti along the River Bani. Departure points vary according to the level of the water: when it is high enough, pirogues sometimes leave from the riverbank beside the town itself; however, the more common departure point is a stretch of water a few kilometres away, where vehicles arriving at and leaving Djenné are carried across the river by a ferry. Negotiate the fare for this trip and count on it taking at least five hours. If you want to stretch the duration of the trip, camping on the riverbank is a wonderful way to experience the desolation of the Delta. Do bring a tent or mosquito net and plenty of repellent, for the absence of people is amply made up for by the presence of mosquitoes.

By road
Buses and *bâchées* leave from the marketplace. The volume of traffic to and from Djenné is dictated by the town's Monday market. On Mondays and Thursdays there are buses to Bamako (CFA6,000), Ségou (CFA4,500) and Sikasso (CFA5,000). At other times, the only regular service is to Mopti (CFA1,750). Carrefour Djenné (the turn-off for Djenné on the main highway) is about 30km from town along a paved road. Buses running between Mopti and Bamako stop here to drop off and, if space permits, pick up passengers. *Bâchées* are waiting to ferry people into town for CFA1,250. A *Taxe Touristique* of CFA500 is payable at the Carrefour Djenné. Retain your ticket for the duration of your stay in Djenné.

When you are driving your own vehicle, note that the ferry crossing costs CFA2,500 for a car and CFA500 for a motorbike. Since at some point you will be leaving Djenné again, most likely by the same way, these rates include the return trip. A new road (exiting Djenné at the western end) is under construction though. Eventually, this road will link Djenné directly to Ségou, providing a slightly shorter connection between the two towns.

Where to stay
Competition in Djenné's hotel business is hotting up. For many years, the **Campement Du Djenné** (tel: 242 04 97) used to be the best place to stay by far. Its central location and friendly atmosphere ensure that it will remain very popular with travellers. The rooms certainly have seen better days, but are still all right, if overpriced at CFA8,500/10,000 for a single/double with a fan and shared facilities, and up to CFA17,500/20,000/22,500 for a self-contained and air-conditioned single/double/triple. Camping costs CFA3,000 per person. In recent years,

the *campement* has opened the **Annexe de Chambres d'Hôtes** across the road. The rates are the same, but since the rooms are new, they provide slightly better value.

The most upmarket option, and the only one in town with hot showers, is the immaculate **Auberge Le Maafir** (tel: 242 05 41). Centered around a quiet garden, the well-decorated rooms come at CFA18,000 for a single/double with a fan, and CFA23,000 for a single/double with air conditioning. Breakfast is included in the price. One dormitory-sized room may be particularly good value for a group of up to around eight people.

An imposing family residence has been converted into the friendly **Hotel Tapama** (tel: 242 05 27). The courtyard reflects some of the grandeur this household once must have had, but the rooms are rather unpretentious by comparison. As spacious as they are, more beds may be added to reduce the price per person. Rooms start at CFA10,000 for a double with shared facilities, ranging up to CFA25,000 for a five-bed self-contained room with a fan. Camping is allowed for CFA2,500 per person.

If a plain room (some with a fan) or a mattress on the floor is all you need, try **Hotel Kita Kourou** (tel: 242 01 38) for CFA4,000/3,000 per person. Baba is the friendly, fatherly character who owns and runs **Chez Baba** (tel: 242 05 98), where CFA2,250 buys you a mattress and mosquito net on the terrace, and for CFA3,250 you'll get the same in a room.

Just outside Djenné, not far from the police checkpoint on the main road leading into the old town, is **Hotel Faguibine** (tel: 242 00 90). Facilities are rudimentary, but then the price reflects this. Clean, double rooms are CFA4,000, and camping on the roof is also permitted.

Where to eat

The *campement* and all hotels have restaurants, serving hearty meals at reasonable prices, although the food is pretty similar wherever you go. Note that alcohol is not available everywhere. However, the **Campement du Djenné** not only serves cold beers, but has a choice of liquors too. The restaurant at **Hotel Le Maafir** offers a set menu, and any other choice of meal must be ordered in advance. A limited daily menu and cold beers are available at **Chez Baba**, where on Sundays and Mondays some youths will play the *djembé*, and sing and dance in the courtyard.

One point worth making is that if you choose to eat at one of the restaurants in town – **Restaurant Kita Kourou** or **Restaurant Le Fleuve**, for example – the children, guides and hassle are never too far away. Eating at the hotels where entry policies are stricter usually guarantees you more peace and quiet.

Nightlife

Formerly a much appreciated guide, a young man of enterprise – locally known by the name of Pygmée – has opened up the **Espace Culturel Tapama**, which doubles as a stage for live concerts and as a bar cum disco. Djenné's youth very much needed a place of entertainment like this, since there was virtually nowhere else for them to go. Abandoned most of the week, this place comes alive in the evenings during the weekend. Give it a try!

Arts and crafts

When you go on a guided tour around town, at some point your guide will propose taking you to one of the 'Maisons des Bogolans', where families specialise in this craft. Even if you are not buying, call in and see how *bogolans* are made. The *bogolans* (see page 90) sold by **Pama Sinintao** have an excellent reputation. Her shop is signposted on the road leading out of town, before you cross the bridge.

A visit to a gold- and silversmith's workshop is not a fixed element of a guided tour, but it is worth asking to be taken to one. Alternatively, ask for **Ali Kouyaté** to come and see you at your hotel with a selection of his work.

Practical information

Facilities in Djenné include a **post office** – which is between the mosque and the Campement du Djenné – but no bank. You can make **telephone calls** at the post office or at one of many *cabines téléphoniques*. Until the local telephone network is significantly improved, do not expect too much in the way of **internet** facilities in Djenné. Your best chances to get connected – at the *campement* or at Cyberplus, a *cabine téléphonique* just off the market place – are early morning and evening. The **Mission Culturelle** is just before the police checkpoint on the road leading out of town.

What to see
The Djenné Mosque

The mosque at Djenné is the largest mud structure in the world; it must also have a claim to be the most beautiful. It dominates Djenné's central square and is the town's *pièce de résistance*.

The Djenné Mosque is sometimes called the Konboro Mosque in deference to King Koy Konboro, the 26th ruler of Djenné, who converted to Islam in the 13th century and, intoxicated with new-found devotion, knocked down his royal palace and built a huge mosque in its place. This structure survived until the arrival of the Peul fundamentalist, Sékou Amadou, in the 19th century. As a student at Djenné, Amadou had been shocked by the liberality of the townsfolk and the practice of singing, dancing and drinking millet beer in front of the mosque. Therefore, when he captured the town in 1819, he abandoned the Konboro Mosque – which he considered to be 'contaminated' by evil practices – and let it go to ruin because the Koran forbids the actual destruction of a mosque by a *fidèle* (faithful Muslim). Meanwhile, a new, more sombre mosque was built on a site east of the old one and was inaugurated in 1834.

The present-day mosque dates from 1907 and is constructed on the foundations of Konboro's original structure – Amadou's effort was pulled down

sarafar fula

musi bumo

sarafar idye

funey

gaga

toron

sarafar woy

gum hu

sarafar har

tintin

Tukulor house

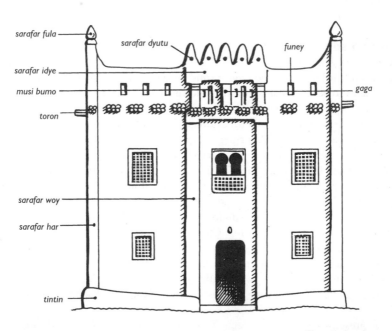

sarafar fula

sarafar dyutu

funey

sarafar idye

musi bumo

gaga

toron

sarafar woy

sarafar har

tintin

Moroccan house

and a *medersa* (Muslim college) built in its place. Viewed from the outside, the mosque's architecture is classically Sudanese. The three minarets are each more than 10m high and, along with the rest of the structure, are riddled with bunches of wooden sticks or *toron*, which are used for decoration and as scaffolding when repairs become necessary – after the rains, for example. There are two entrances: the one on the southern side (ie: facing away from the market place) is the more ornate, while the northern entrance is characterised by six steps leading up to it. The whole mosque is raised 3m above the level of the market place, and these six steps symbolise the transition from the profane to the sacred. Inside, the mosque is equally impressive. The prayer area is some 50m by 26m, and 90 pillars hold up the wooden roof. Unfortunately, infidels have not been allowed inside the mosque ever since a French fashion photographer used its interior as a surreal backdrop for his scantly-clad models in suggestive poses.

THE MASONS OF DJENNE

Building is an art form in Djenné and its builders are revered as great artists – and magicians. Their techniques are simple and have been practised since the foundation of the first caste of masons back in the 15th century. The *bareys*, as they are known, carry no tools, except for an iron trowel to cut and smooth clay walls. The mortar is mixed with the feet, the bricks moulded by hand, and façades as high as those of the Djenné Mosque are erected without the use of a plumb line. To reach this level of skill requires years of preparation. Potential *bareys* – young boys around seven years old – begin their apprenticeship under the guidance of an old mason, who acts not only as a teacher but also as the boy's second father. The apprentice learns about the tools and techniques of the trade – but not its innermost secrets – and by about 18 is skilled enough to graduate as a fully-fledged *barey*. However, at this stage he is still only on the second rung of the hierarchical ladder. Next up are the accomplished younger masons, who are experienced enough to work independently and as foremen on building sites. Then come two categories of *maîtres-maçons* or master masons: those who are still active and those who have retired. Both know their trade inside-out and the older ones hold the magic secrets handed down from generation to generation of Djenné masons. These magic spells – a mixture of Arabic and indigenous words – are cast to protect the building and its builder from harm and injury. For example, before work is started on a new construction a *maître-maçon* with occult powers recites a text invoking Abrahim or Ibrahim, who, according to the Koran, built the *Ka'bah* or the House of God at Mecca. This event marked the beginning of masonry and the *Ka'bah* is considered to be indestructible. Therefore, a spell invoking Abrahim brings bad luck to anyone who tries to destroy or modify the new building without the *barey*'s permission. In this way, customer loyalty is more or less guaranteed.

Monday market

Djenné may no longer be the commercial powerhouse it once was, but it can still boast one of the most colourful markets in West Africa. Every Monday, the town's population roughly triples as people from surrounding villages and as far afield as Bamako and Sikasso come to sell their wares. Although the range of items for sale is bewildering, the real attraction of the Monday market for the visitor is its colour, animation and imposing location in front of the famous mosque. Try to be in Djenné for market day; and if you are arriving in town on a Monday, it might be worth reserving a bed for the night in advance.

Architecture

Djenné was named a World Heritage Site in 1988 to preserve its unique architectural integrity. Despite the emergence of one or two modern-style, concrete buildings, the traditional Djenné houses have stood the test of time thanks to the continued presence of the town's expert masons (see *The Masons of Djenné* on page 155) and a seven-year project – financed by the Dutch government – to restore and rehabilitate traditional houses to their former glory (see box on page 157).

Houses in Djenné are basically rectangular in shape, with one floor and an inner courtyard. Interior planning is gender-based: the men occupy the front of the house and have windows and doors facing out on to the road; the women are at the back overlooking the courtyard and isolated from the outside world. The most distinctive thing about these houses, however, is their façades or *potiges*, which basically fall into two categories: Moroccan or Tukulor (see the drawings on page 154). The easiest way to distinguish between these two architectural styles is to look at the entrance. A Tukulor house – from the period of Tukulor occupation, 1862–93 – is characterised by a small canopy or *gum hu* over the front door. The most common explanation for the presence of the *gum hu* is that it offered protection against the Tukulor cavalry, preventing them from entering houses on horseback as they rode through town looking for slaves. Another equally feasible explanation is that these small roofs kept out torrential rain.

The most famous house in the Tukulor style is the **Maison Maïga** (Maïga House) situated in a quarter of town called Algasbah (turn right immediately after the bridge when entering town). Meanwhile, much of the Moroccan architecture is found in the nearby quarter of Sankoré or Maître Blanc.

Tomb of Tapama Djenepo

According to oral tradition, Djenné owes its existence to a young Bozo girl called Pama Kayamtao. As the town was being constructed, the presence of bad, malevolent spirits caused buildings to collapse as soon as they had been built. *Marabouts* turned to the good spirits for help and were told that the problem could only be solved if a young Bozo virgin was buried in the city wall. Pama Kayamtao was sacrificed so that Djenné could be built.

The tomb of Tapama (meaning 'our mother Pama') Djenepo (meaning 'corpse of Djenné) is behind the mosque near the banks of the river.

A MONUMENTAL CHALLENGE
Jolijn Geels

After Djenné was declared a World Heritage Site in 1988, it was time to evaluate the current state of the architecture. There was good news and bad news. The good news was that Djenné as a whole had hardly been affected by modernisation; amenities such as electricity were scarce and most parts of Djenné remained inaccessible to cars – hence there was little associated disfiguration from things like cables, wires, lampposts and cars. The bad news was that many traditional houses were in an appalling state, many had been abandoned, and a shocking number listed as historical monuments had been demolished and replaced.

One of the reasons why houses were either rebuilt or left to crumble was the fact that modern-day Djennenké have different demands for housing; the traditional lay-out simply wasn't considered adequate any longer. At the same time many Djennenké longed for a place to live that was low in maintenance. *Banco*, the fermented mixture of mud, chaff and water that is used to plaster the buildings, involves not just a lot of work, but also a lot of mud and water. After two consecutive years of drought – 1984 and 1985 – there just hadn't been enough raw material to keep the *banco* free from serious wear and tear. Before too long families decided to give up their traditional homes, and to build one that better suited their needs – sometimes using modern building materials such as cement and bricks.

The alarm was raised, a plan was drawn up, funds were made available. In 1996, phase one of the plan was put into effect. It took a while to convince the Djennenké of the importance and the integrity of the programme; there were many more hurdles to overcome and a lot of criticism to be swallowed. Nevertheless, the actual job of rehabilitating and restoring houses had begun. It took seven years to complete, or perhaps it is more appropriate to say that by then the money had run out and thus this particular project came to a close. Perhaps not all the objectives were met, but what has been achieved is still truly impressive: over a hundred houses have had a thorough make-over. The traditional façades have been restored to their former beauty, while the interior lay-out of the dwellings – invisible from the streets – has often been altered to meet the demands of modern Djennenké families. The project has been a learning process too, and since maintaining the architecture in Djenné is a never-ending story, future programmes to continue this hefty task will be able to lean heavily on past experience and expertise.

More information on the project and guided tours are available from the Mission Culturelle. During the tour you will have the opportunity to visit the interior of some of the restored houses. An excellent book – in French – about this project is available from the National Museum in Bamako (see *Appendix 2: Further Reading*).

Sacred well of Nana Wangara

The sacred well of Nana Wangara is another interesting relic of Djenné's magical past – this time, from the period of Moroccan occupation. Legend has it that the well was built as a gift from the Moroccan ruler of Djenné to his favourite wife, who resented having to collect water along with the other concubines. Apart from being a token of affection, the well was also the 'eye' of the ruler, enabling him to communicate directly with Fez and to see into the future. Meanwhile, on Thursdays and Fridays it could apparently cure illnesses.

Finding the well of Nana Wangara is no easy task, as it is hidden in a family courtyard in an intricate maze of winding streets and alleys. It is in the old Moroccan quarter, Sankoré or Maître Blanc ('White Master'), not far from the Maïga House.

Museum

There is a small museum at the Mission Culturelle with information about Djenné-Djeno and the serious problem of archaeological pillage at the site – scavengers go to Djenné-Djeno at night and steal precious artefacts which are then passed on to dealers and finally sold to collectors. There are also other exhibits and photographs relating to modern-day life in Djenné, and, unlike most museums in Mali, many of the explanations are in English.

The museum is just before the police checkpoint on the road leading out of town. It is usually open every day from 09.00 to 17.00 (these times are informal) and there is no entry fee. Introduce yourself to the curator of the museum, Amadou Camara, before visiting.

Excursions from Djenné

Djenné-Djeno

Djenné-Djeno, or ancient Djenné, is about 3km southeast of the town's modern-day location. Before exploring this historic site, you are strongly advised to visit the museum – which is on the way – to get an idea of what was once there. You may also arrange a guided visit to Djenné-Djeno through the museum.

Although archaeological research continues at Djenné-Djeno today, the most ground-breaking discoveries were made during excavations directed by the American anthropologists Susan and Roderick McIntosh, in 1977 and 1981. Thanks to radiocarbon dating and a number of important finds – including the foundations of round mud-brick houses, fragments of pottery, statuettes and the remains of the city wall – the McIntoshes were able to prove that Djenné-Djeno flourished many centuries before the Arabs first established trading posts in the Sahara, thus making it the oldest known city in West Africa. Dating from around 250BC, when it was a small settlement of round mud huts, by about AD800 Djenné-Djeno had grown into an important trading centre with thousands of inhabitants. The city continued to prosper until around AD1400 when it was suddenly and mysteriously abandoned, perhaps to appease the powerful Islamic elite who were offended by a city 'contaminated' by pagan practices. Whatever the reason for Djenné-Djeno's decline, in its heyday the city reaped the rewards of far-reaching trade – first by river and later by caravan – with the desert town of Timbuktu. Initially, Saharan iron, copper, stone and salt were probably bartered for food; later, salt and gold became the two principal trading commodities.

When you reach the site, you are left to imagine what it must once have looked like. A sign erected by the Mission Culturelle announces your arrival, but there is hardly anything to see. To get there, walk past the police checkpoint and turn right at the arch. Continue across country until you reach a teardrop-shaped mound, about 7m high and 2km in circumference, and see the sign.

Peul and Bozo villages

Despite the fact that Djenné's hinterland holds much beauty, it is still relatively unknown and unexplored. Depending on the water level, you need a pirogue, a donkey cart or bike – or sturdy hiking boots if you like – a guide, and plenty of time. Scattered all over the Inland Delta are small and picturesque Peul and Bozo villages and settlements, erected from *banco* on muddy mounds. The real hidden pearls are the numerous mosques that sometimes look like melting ice cakes. Inquire at the Mission Culturelle or Chez Baba about guides to accompany you on your explorations.

Two interesting villages within realistic walking – or boating – distance of Djenné are **Senossa** and **Sirimou**. The slightly closer one is Senossa, a Peul village of around 6,000 inhabitants some 4km north of Djenné. The Peul have always been nomadic people, but drought has forced them to become increasingly sedentary and settle in villages such as Senossa. The other village, Sirimou, is a Bozo settlement about 7km west of Djenné.

Whether or not you can reach the two villages as the crow flies depends on the level of the water and the state of the tracks cutting across the fields – if they have emerged again at all after the river retreated, that is. If so, ask a local to indicate which is the best way to go, as you may otherwise find yourself stuck in a maze of mud and water (and bear in mind that once outside Djenné very little French – and no English – is spoken). While you can walk around Senossa – having first introduced yourself to the village chief, of course – there is no easy way across the moat surrounding Sirimou most of the year. This Walt Disney-style village is on an island in the middle, with an imposing mosque and a very medieval appearance. You should be able to find a pirogue to take you across the moat.

When the water level is high, the obvious way to visit the villages is by pirogue. Public pirogues provide a shuttle service and cost very little, and there is always the option to rent a private pirogue. Even when the river has dropped tremendously, Sirimou can still be reached by pirogue, following a tributary of the Bani. Senossa, meanwhile, can usually be reached by following the causeway that begins behind the hospital and water tower. This is the first section of the new road that will eventually lead all the way to Ségou, but it is definitely no shortcut to Senossa.

HAMDALLAYE

The ruins of Hamdallaye, the political and intellectual capital of the Peul Empire of Macina, lie between Djenné and Mopti. Created in 1810 when the *jihad* (religious war) led by the Muslim cleric, Sékou Amadou, defeated the combined forces of the Peul and Bambara Kingdoms in Macina, the Peul Empire was a theocratic Islamic state which at one time exercised control as far away as Timbuktu. Hamdallaye was founded around 1815 and remained the empire's capital until it was overrun by the Tukulor forces of El Hadj Omar in 1862, at which point it became the Tukulor headquarters in Macina.

The modern-day remains of Hamdallaye warrant a visit to the site, although you should not expect spectacular, Athenian-style ruins and fantastic photo opportunities. The walls of what was once Sékou Amadou's palace are most in evidence. Inside, his tomb, along with that of Amadou Sékou, the son who succeeded him in 1844, can be found, while the outline of the site where the mosque once stood is next to the palace. Hamdallaye is about 5km past the picturesque village of **Somadougou** in the direction of Mopti. Stop when you see a small hamlet by the side of the road or, if you are coming from Mopti, the sign. The first house on the right of the main path leading through this hamlet belongs to the descendants of Sékou Amadou. Introduce yourself and ask their permission before proceeding to the site, which is about 1km from the main road. It is usually open from around 09.00 to 18.00 and, although there is no entrance fee, you should leave something for the attendant who will be happy to show you around.

MOPTI

Mopti began its transition from small Bozo fishing village to the commercial hub of central Mali and the capital of the country's fifth region at the start of the 19th century. The importance of Djenné had been gradually declining, and Mopti was seen as the ideal replacement – first by the Peul emperor, Sékou Amadou, who was keen to develop the town's potential, then by the French, who transferred the trading functions of Djenné to Mopti in 1893 when they arrived in the region. Initially, the town we now call Mopti was spread over several islands in marshland at the confluence of the rivers Niger and Bani. Over time, these islands were reduced to three interconnected pieces of terra firma by means of dykes and tonnes of landfill. A causeway was then constructed to connect Mopti to the main highway at Sévaré, making it easily accessible by road as well as by river. Since its completion – for this is a town constructed virtually from scratch – Mopti has never looked back. Nowadays, it is by far the most important urban centre in the Niger Inland Delta, performing a role once played by Djenné as a crossroads for trade between the north and south. The official population is made up of mainly Bozos and Peuls – but also includes Dogon, Tuareg, Songhay and Bambara communities – and stands at around 100,000; the itinerant population of travelling merchants, however, may be just as large.

Mopti lives in the present rather than the past. Its commercial importance and ideal river location mean that life is dominated by the daily activity around the busy port. This is just as well from the visitor's point of view because Mopti is of little historical interest and, despite its famous mosque, is no Djenné in terms of architecture and aesthetic beauty.

Orientation

There are two main roads leading into Mopti: one from Sévaré on the main highway, the other from the town's residential quarters. The commercial centre – the shops, restaurants, bus stations etc – are centred round the port, while the main thoroughfare, Avenue du Fleuve, runs north along the banks of the River Bani, which joins the Niger a little further downstream.

Getting there and away

By air

See *Sévaré: Getting there and away* on page 168.

By river

Boats operated by COMANAV (tel: 243 00 06) provide a service up and down the River Niger when the water is high enough, roughly between the end of July and the end of December. They leave Mopti bound for Timbuktu – and sometimes Gao – on Thursdays, and sail upstream to Koulikoro on certain Tuesdays or Fridays. See *Practicalities: Getting there and away* on page 73 for more information and fares.

When the water is low, *pinasses* and pirogues link Mopti to the towns of the Niger Inland Delta. The river provides the sole means by which food and merchandise can be transported to these isolated places, so the traffic is usually quite regular. Accurately predicting this regularity, however, is impossible, as everything depends on the level of the water at the time. Large *pinasses* can normally make it to Timbuktu, but if their cargo is too heavy, they can easily run aground. If this happens, the sacks of rice, slabs of salt and other produce must be unloaded before the boat can be refloated, recharged and set sail again. Sometimes this can occur several times during a single voyage, which makes it equally hard to predict travel times.

As a rough guide, count on at least two days and nights for the journey from Mopti to Timbuktu. When the water is low, larger boats are sometimes prevented from crossing Lake Débo after dark by fishing nets put in the lake at night. There is no comprehensive schedule of departures to Timbuktu, so the best advice is to ask around at the port. Tikambo Transport has two boats – both two-deckers – taking turns for the journey to Timbuktu. They leave every Friday at 13.00 from the departure point opposite the Catholic Mission. The smaller boat reaches its destination on Saturday evening, departing for Mopti on Sunday morning. The bigger Tikambo boat takes a little longer, arriving in Timbuktu on Sunday mornings, to depart for Mopti again on Monday morning. The upper decks are slightly more spacious,

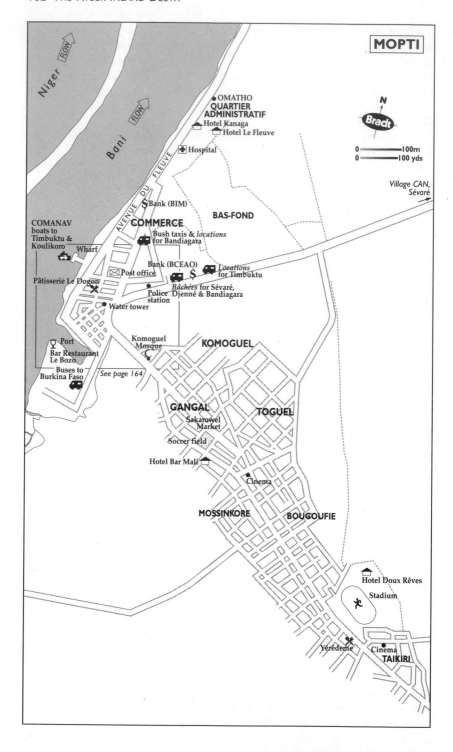

MOPTI

Niger *FLOW*

Bani *FLOW*

N

Bradt

0 ————— 100m
0 ————— 100 yds

Village CAN, Sévaré

• OMATHO
QUARTIER ADMINISTRATIF
▥ Hotel Kanaga
⌂ Hotel Le Fleuve

✚ Hospital

AVENUE DU FLEUVE

$ Bank (BIM)

COMANAV
boats to
Timbuktu &
Koulikoro
Wharf

COMMERCE

BAS-FOND

Bush taxis & *locations*
for Bandiagara

Pâtisserie Le Dogon

Bank (BCEAO)
✉ Post office
$ *Locations*
for Timbuktu

• *Bâchées* for Sévaré,
Police Djenné & Bandiagara
station

▽ Port
Bar Restaurant
Le Bozo

Water tower

Komoguel
Mosque
☪

Buses to
Burkina Faso

See page 164

KOMOGUEL

GANGAL

Sakarowel
Market

Soccer field

Hotel Bar Mali ⌂

TOGUEL

• Cinema

MOSSINKORE

BOUGOUFIE

⌂ Hotel Doux Rêves

🏃 Stadium

Vérédeme

• Cinema

TAIKIRI

since most of the freight that travels along with the passengers is stacked on the lower deck. Some drinks and basic meals are provided on board. The full fare to Timbuktu is CFA20,000 on the upper deck, and CFA17,500 on the lower deck. Mopti-Diré is CFA15,000 and CFA12,500 respectively. For some peculiar reason, the upstream prices for the return trip are lower, at CFA15,000 and CFA13,000 for Timbuktu-Mopti and CFA12,500 and CFA10,500 for Diré-Mopti.

Many smaller *pinasses* also seem to depart from Mopti on Fridays, and the following two are no exception. Ask around for the Lac Horo owned by Issa Maïga. He charges CFA10,000 for Mopti-Timbuktu, and the journey should take about 30 hours, with one night spent camping somewhere on the riverbank. The *Pagou-Manpagou* sails as far as Diré, charging CFA6,000 for Mopti-Diré and CFA5,000 for the return trip. There may be an extra charge for luggage.

The other interesting voyage for travellers is along the River Bani to Djenné. If all goes well, the journey takes about five hours. Once again, ask at the port for departure times.

Tour operators in Mopti (see page 87) offer boat-trips as far as Timbuktu, which take three days and two nights. *Pinasses* are equipped with mattresses and other creature comforts; you camp on the banks of the river and meals are provided. The price to Timbuktu can be anything from CFA100,000 to CFA300,000, depending on the number of people travelling.

By road

The major bus companies depart from various points around town. Many of these companies – like Bani Transport, Bittar Transport, Gana Transport, Binke Transport etc – are found along Avenue du Fleuve, while Somatra is located opposite the post office. They all have daily services for Bamako, some both in the mornings and afternoons, and the fare is either CFA6,000 or CFA7,000 for Bamako and CFA4,500 for Ségou.

Bani Transport leaves daily at 18.00 for Gao, while Touré Transport – opposite the Nouveau Marché Ottawa – leaves Tuesdays and Fridays at 08.00 (Douentza: CFA2,500, Hombori: CFA4,000, and Gao: CFA6,500).

The departure point for Burkina Faso is by the port. A bus leaves every day at 17.00 for Bobo-Dioulasso (CFA6,500) and Ouagadougou (CFA12,000).

A fair amount of public transport departs from various points not far from the Campement Hotel. At the *gare routière* just past the police station, *bâchées*, minibuses and bush taxis wait for enough passengers to justify journeys to Sevaré (CFA210), Djenné and Bandiagara (Bandiagara: CFA1,500, Bankas: CFA2,200 and Koro: CFA3,000). A little further down the road to Sevaré is a place called Bas Fond. It looks like a cross between a deserted market and a junk yard, but nevertheless this is where you should be looking for *locations* (usually Land Rovers) to Timbuktu. For CFA12,500 you must squeeze in the back, while CFA15,000 pays for a shared place on the front seat. Considering the fact that the journey will take at least 8-9 hours, paying the extra CFA2,500 is well worth it.

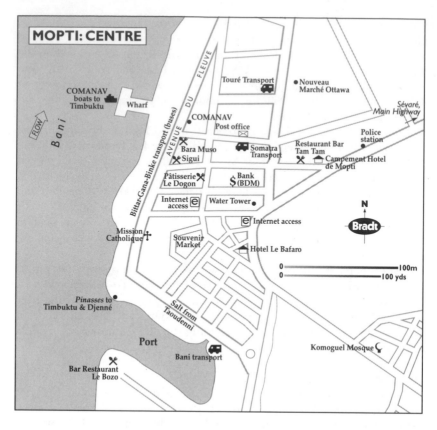

A ride in a shared taxi within the old or the new part of town should cost no more than CFA150 per person, while a private ride from door to door costs around CFA1,000–1,500.

For more transport by road, see the same section for Sévaré on page 168.

Where to stay

Hotel Kanaga (tel: 243 05 00) on the banks of the river is one of the best and largest hotels outside Bamako. It has 80 rooms, most of which are nicely decorated with *bogolans* and other Malian handicrafts. For CFA43,000 (single/double) you can expect rooms with remote-control air conditioning, TV and telephone. The hotel also has a swimming pool and internet service. A few streets behind the Kanaga Hotel is the friendly **Hotel le Fleuve** (tel: 647 15 77), with a dormitory and 14 rooms in many different price categories in two adjacent villas. The rooms are a bit barren, but airy and adequate considering the prices, ranging from CFA3,000 for a dorm bed up to CFA20,000 for an air-conditioned, self-contained double room with hot water. A supplementary bed costs an extra CFA2,500.

Right at the other side of town, in a new residential quarter behind the sports stadium, is **Hotel Doux Rêves** (tel: 243 04 90). There is nothing wrong with the rooms (CFA8,000/11,000 for a single/double with a fan, up to CFA16,000/19,000/22,000 for a self-contained and air-conditioned single/double/triple), and a dorm bed at CFA4,500 is fine. However, the best buy is a mattress on the rooftop for CFA4,000. What a superb view! On Tuesdays and Saturdays from 18.00 to 20.00, guests are treated to traditional live music in the courtyard.

Centrally located, painted in striking pink and silver, and of peculiar industrial design, is **Hotel Bafaro** (tel: 243 00 87). The rooms are no less clinical and spacious in every direction, and range from CFA9,000/13,500 (with a fan) to CFA15,000/19,500 (self-contained and air conditioned) for a single/double. The huge *grand salle* serves as a dormitory (CFA2,500 per person). Thank goodness for the pleasant garden, with – once the trees have reached maturity – 'free bananas for guests'. Another conveniently located place is the **Campement Hotel de Mopti** (tel: 243 00 32) with some spacious but rather gloomy air-conditioned rooms (CFA14,000/16,000 for a single/double) and small rooms with a fan (CFA12,000/14,000 for a single/double). All rooms are self-contained, a supplementary bed costs CFA3,000. Camping in the yard is allowed for CFA2,500 per person. One traveller I met described **Hotel Bar Mali** (tel: 243 01 70), which is beyond the mosque in a quarter called Gangal, as 'a real Fagin's house' – and, with its dark, labyrinthine corridors and a huge tree growing in the middle of the house, I can see what she meant. The rooms, which range from CFA4,000 to CFA6,00, are dirty and dingy – designed and used more for prostitution than holidaymaking. On the plus side, however, there is a roof where you can wash and dry clothes.

Where to eat

The restaurants at the hotels fall into three categories: good and expensive (Hotel Kanaga); moderate and satisfactory (Hotel le Fleuve, Hotel Bafaro and Campement Hotel de Mopti); and cheap and basic (Hotel Bar Mali). Apart from the usual dishes at Hotel Kanaga's **Restaurant le Niger**, there are several African specialities such as *fonio*, *tô* and *fakohoye* (a Songhay dish, see *Traditional dishes*, page 30). A three-course meal costs CFA7,000, the buffet is CFA8,000. Meals at the **Campement Hotel de Mopti** are actually very tasty, but between next door's music and the television the noise level can be quite intrusive. **Restaurant Yérédeme**, which forms a part of the Association Yeredeme (see *Arts and crafts* on page 166) has been recommended by other travellers, but note that the more interesting meals have to be ordered in advance. The menu will be presented to guests of the nearby **Hotel Doux Rêves** – which has no restaurant – as a matter of course.

The food served in the garden at **Restaurant Sigui** is fine, but also quite expensive at around CFA5,000 for a main course plus garnish. Guides and hawkers will try and get your attention though, and they are not easily discouraged. The absence of guides and the good choice of music makes **Restaurant Bar Tam Tam** a most pleasant place for a decent and affordable meal or a drink. With a prime location overlooking the busy port and good food served in copious quantities, **Bar Restaurant le Bozo** is also justifiably popular.

Not so much frequented by tourists, but usually busy at lunchtimes, is **Restaurant Bara Muso**, between the post office and the river. The menu is invariably something-or-other with rice or couscous. **Pâtisserie le Dogon** is popular with travellers for a cup of tea and a slice of cake or a croissant. The choice and quality of the pastries is bit of a disappointment though.

Entertainment and nightlife

Mopti has two cinemas, both in the old town. The one near the sports stadium features Hindu films mostly, while the one nearer to the port shows violent movies, all dubbed into French and run through very poor-quality film projectors. It is not so much the film you should be watching, though, since the real entertainment is provided by the highly empathic and expressive Malian audience.

For some serious nightclubbing, Sevaré has more to offer than Mopti. In fact, since the Tam Tam Africa Night Club burnt down a few years ago, nightlife in Mopti has pretty much come to a standstill. However, until the *boîte de nuit* has been restored, **Restaurant Bar Tam Tam** (same owner, same location) is a satisfactory substitute. The open-air *paillotte* serves as a dance floor, with a good selection of mostly local music being played every evening. Entrance is free, though an admission fee of CFA1,000 is required on special occasions. Live percussion music is played on Thursdays, Fridays and Saturdays between 17.00 and 21.00. If you like percussion, the Tam Tam organises *djembé* courses on request.

Arts and crafts

Because of its cosmopolitan population and trading importance, Mopti is a good place to buy souvenirs. You can find almost anything here, either in the side streets north of the port or at the port itself. The region of Mopti is well-known for its *bogolans*, patterned, woollen blankets (*kassa*), and pottery sold by the wharf where the COMANAV boats dock. Jewellery – especially Peul earrings and bracelets – and various arts and crafts from Dogon country can also be good buys.

Young single mothers have joined forces in the **Association Yérédeme**. As well as a restaurant, they run a shop selling home-made jams, dried fruit and fruit juices. Fabrics and clothes manufactured in their own workshop are also for sale.

Practical information

The **post office**, **Sotelma**, and one of the **banks** (BDM/Western Union: for Visa cash advances, also open on Saturdays 08.30–14.00) are all centrally located. The BCEAO bank past the police station exchanges cash euros only. A third bank (BIM/Western Union, also for exchanging cash euros only) is between Hotel Kanaga and the town centre, as is the town's **hospital**.

Opinions differ as to whether or not it is necessary to have your passport stamped at Mopti. It doesn't seem to be, though the official answer will always be that it is. As far as your own safety is concerned, it is certainly less important than in the desert towns of Gao and Timbuktu; on the other hand, it might be worth the hassle so as not to fall foul of Malian bureaucracy. Anyway, having your passport stamped is free of charge and takes little time. The **police station** is located next to the Campement Hotel du Mopti, and you need to bring a photograph. Incidentally, this is probably also the best place to get a **visa extension**, should you need one. While it takes at least a day in Bamako, having your visa extended in Mopti takes about five minutes and is done with a smile. Bring two photographs and make sure your passport has an empty page. The fee for a month's extension is CFA5,000, and is CFA10,000 for two months.

The **OMATHO** office (tel: 243 05 06, see also page 85) is located two blocks past Hotel du Kanaga. You may also be registered and have your passport stamped here 'for statistics on tourism', but since this is a random procedure it is not clear what these statistics reflect. Staff are very friendly though, and willing to give out information on guides and tourist points of interest.

Ashraf Voyages (tel: 243 02 79) is run by a Dutch woman and her Malian husband, and is good if you want to visit some of the river villages of the Niger Inland Delta. They are based in the centre of town next to Pâtisserie le Dogon, where you can rent **mountain bikes** for CFA1,000 an hour or CFA6,000 a day. One **internet** café is next to the Campement Hotel courtyard, two more are located in shops not far from the water tower, while a fourth is opposite Pâtisserie Le Dogon.

What to see

Although there is a weekly market on Thursdays, it is somewhat overshadowed by the continually busy **port** – the essence of Mopti. The main local industry is fishing and one side of the port is awash with dried and smoked fish – which is also exported abroad. One of the other principal commodities is salt, which is brought down the river in huge tablets from Timbuktu and the mines at Taoudenni. Salt comes in three categories: the top-grade stuff has a smooth, layered texture, while the other two varieties are rougher, the second quality being whiter than the third.

Wandering around the port you might also see dried onions from Dogon country, along with the millet and assorted spices typical of all West African trading centres. Next to Restaurant Le Bozo on the southern side of the port there are **pirogue-builders**, some of whom might be constructing the large *pinasses* which fan out around the harbour and can carry up to 150 tonnes of cargo. These are just some of the highlights of Mopti's port; there are plenty of others.

The small settlements on the other side of the river are **Bozo fishing villages**. They can be reached by pirogue from the port or various points along the Mopti side of the river. Remember to introduce yourself to the village chief before wandering about.

In the same way that Mopti inherited Djenné's trading functions, it also tried to emulate its neighbour's beautiful architecture. These attempts are best viewed in the quarter of **Komoguel**, which has retained many of the traditional *banco* houses typical of Djenné. The town's main **mosque** is also in Komoguel. It was built in 1935 in the same style as the mosque at Djenné and, although certainly not ugly, in this respect at least the new kid on the block has failed to surpass its elder sister.

SEVARE

Sévaré is a small but important town on the main highway between Bamako and Gao, through which all traffic to Mopti and Bandiagara must pass. This position at the major crossroads in the centre of Mali, along with its close proximity to Mopti airport, has made Sévaré a popular base for several of the largest NGOs operating in Mali. Amongst others, Save the Children UK, Plan International and the Peace Corps have offices here.

There is nothing to see in Sévaré – in fact, it is quite an ugly town. However, the accommodation and restaurants are plentiful and there is none of the tourist-related hassle for which Mopti is renowned. The distance between the two towns is only 12km and public transport is regular and inexpensive. Taking these factors into account, you might consider basing yourself in Sévaré instead of Mopti.

Getting there and away
By air
Mopti airport is less than 1km from the main highway, from where *bâchées* and bush taxis leave for Mopti and Bandiagara, passing through Sévaré en route. Apart from a small waiting-lounge and bar, the airport has no facilities. From mid-December to March, Point Afrique has one weekly flight from Paris to Mopti/Sevaré on Sundays, returning to Paris on Mondays, as well as a weekly flight from Marseille on Sundays, returning the same day. SAE (tel: 643 05 59) has flights from Mopti/Sevaré to Timbuktu on Tuesdays and Saturdays, while flights to Bamako leave on Wednesdays and Sundays. These schedules are liable to change (see *Practicalities: Getting around* on page 76).

By road
The crossroads at Sévaré is one of the busiest in the country. The enormous *gare routière* is 1km out of town on the road to Bandiagara. Since all the major bus companies are represented here, it is easy to shop around for a bus that suits your itinerary best. Names of the companies, their destinations and fares are clearly marked near the respective ticket offices. Departure times are to be taken with a pinch of salt, since many buses come from a distance and may have run into all sorts of delay. On the other hand, you as a passenger should always be on time, of course. Even if a bus is not due to leave within hours, a

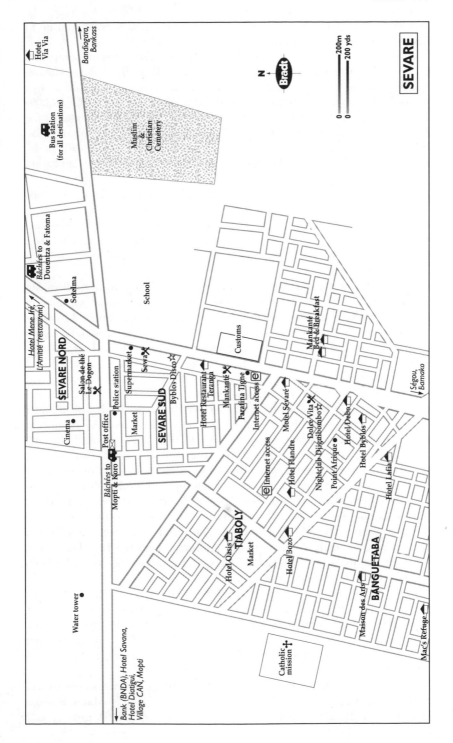

SEVARE

N

Bradt

0 ———— 200m
0 ———— 200 yds

→ Bandiagara, Bankass

Hotel Via Via

Bus station
(for all destinations)

Muslim
&
Christian
Cemetery

Báchées to
Douentza & Fatoma

Soteima

School

Hotel Mene Iré,
L'Amitié (restaurant) ↑

SEVARE NORD

Salon de thé
Le Dogon

Police station

Supermarket

Sewa ✗

Byblos Disco ☆

Customs

Mankanté
Bed & Breakfast

Cinema

Market

Post office

SEVARE SUD

Hotel Restaurant
Teranga

Mankanté ✗

Pacafina Tigne

Internet access ℮

℮ Internet access

Hotel Flandre

Dolce Vita ✗

Nightclub Digmibonbo ☆

Point Afrique ●

Motel Sévaré

Hotel Debo

Hotel Byblos

→ Ségou,
Bamako

Báchées to
Mopti & Koro

TIABOLY

Hotel Oasis

Market

Hotel Bozo

Hotel Lafia

BANGUETABA

Maison des Arts

Mac's Refuge

Water tower ●

← Bank (BNDA), Hotel Savana,
Hotel Diatigui,
Village CAN, Mopti

Catholic ✝
mission

vendeur des billets is never too far away, but you may need to wake him up to have your ticket written out for you.

To give just a few indications of destinations and fares: various companies have buses to San (CFA2,500), Ségou (CFA4,500) and Bamako (CFA6,000/7,000) in the mornings and afternoons. Somatrie has a daily service to Koutiala (CFA4,000), Sikasso (CFA5,000) and Bobo-Dioulasso (CFA7,000) in the afternoon. Yacouba Traoré (YT), amongst others, has departures for Douentza (CFA3,000), Hombori (CFA4,500), Gossi (CFA5,000) and Gao (CFA6,000). Somatra has buses leaving for Bandiagara (CFA1,500) early in the morning, though there are also *bâchées* and small buses leaving for Bandiagara just outside the gate of the bus station.

Another departure point for *bâchées* and small buses to nearby destinations is between the main crossroads and Sotelma, on the road to Gao. Look here for transport to Fatoma (CFA300), Kona (CFA1,250) and Douentza (CFA2,250). Walk towards the Shell station for transport to Mopti (CFA210).

Where to stay

Many hotels are located on – or just off – the main road to Bamako. **Motel Sévaré** (tel: 242 00 82) is good, friendly and popular. Groups on organised tours tend to stay here, so in high season it might be worth making a reservation. Prices start at CFA10,500 (single) and CFA15,000 (double) for a room with a fan, hot water and breakfast included. Prices at **Hotel Débo** (tel: 242 01 24) are a little dearer at CFA20,000 and CFA23,000 for single and double respectively. All rooms are self-contained and air conditioned, and breakfast is included. Of similar quality and price is **Hotel Byblos** (tel: 242 07 82), just off the main road with a quiet garden, especially since the nightclub has moved elsewhere. All rooms are CFA20,000 (single/double), though they are often fully booked through tour operators. The German-run **Mankanté Bed and Breakfast** (tel: 242 01 93) offers very peaceful accommodation in two villas just off the main road. Prices start at CFA15,500 for a single up to CFA24,000 for a room with four beds. An extra bed costs CFA5,000. Again off the main road is **Hotel Lafia** (tel: 601 01 98), a friendly, family hotel with rooms from CFA8,000 up to CFA16,000, and CFA5,000 for an extra bed. Though first of all a restaurant, the Senegalese-run **Auberge Teranga** (tel: 242 07 06) has four rooms with large beds, fans and shared facilities for CFA7,000 (single), CFA9,000/11,000 (double) or CFA13,500 (triple).

Less centrally located are the clean **Hotel Flandre** (tel: 242 08 29), with rooms ranging from CFA14,000 to CFA21,000, and the similarly priced **Hotel Bozo** (tel: 242 02 11), which has a more Malian feel to it. Equally clean but rather sober is **Hotel Oasis** (tel: 242 04 98), where rooms start at CFA10,000/11,000 (single/double). A mattress on the rooftop costs CFA2,500.

Two new kids on the block in the Banguetaba quarter are places to feel at home for a couple of days and meet other travellers. In **Mac's Refuge** (tel: 242 06 21) all rooms are named after Malian ethnic groups, and decorated accordingly. Original in style and very friendly, these rooms start at CFA10,000/15,000 (single/double) for a room with a fan and shared facilities. Camping is allowed for CFA4,000 (with your own gear) or CFA5,000 (gear included). A small swimming pool in a hidden corner may also be used by non-lodgers for CFA1,500. No less original in free-style *banco* design and run by a sympathetic mixed British-Dogon couple, is the **Maison des Arts** (tel: 242 08 53). Immaculate rooms – note the soft pillows! – start at CFA6,000/10,000 (single/double), the most expensive being a room that sleeps four at CFA18,000. A dorm bed with a mosquito net is CFA4,500, while sleeping on the terrace costs CFA3,000/4,000 (without or with mattress and mosquito net).

Unless they cut down their prices, there is no reason to check in at **Hotel Mene Iré** (tel: 242 00 94), located on the road to Gao. At CFA7,500 to CFA15,000, these rooms have no appeal whatsoever. **Hotel Via Via** (tel: 679 48 41) opened as recently as June 2003, and given its location next to the bus station, it may well serve those travellers who find themselves stranded there. Rooms are clean and comfortable and cost CFA15,000. Because of their location in Village CAN, **Hotel Savana** (tel: 678 11 82) and **Hotel Diatigui** (tel: 242 07 60) should officially be listed under Mopti. However, Village CAN is more of an extension to Sevaré than anything else, hence the listing under Sevaré. The latter feels more like a private villa converted into a pleasant and comfortable, if slightly overpriced, hotel. Rooms are CFA18,500 (single) and CFA22,000 (double). Hotel Savana, meanwhile, run by the helpful and energetic French lady Mme Jacqueline, is the better deal. Rooms are spotless, and start at CFA12,500 for a single and CFA17,500 for a double.

Where to eat

All of the hotels in Sévaré have restaurants. There is a nice garden at **Motel Sévaré**, highly-regarded Vietnamese food at **Hotel Débo** (the chef is the son of Madame Cat at the Bol de Jade in Bamako – see page 114), and the usual menus elsewhere. Two other restaurants are also worth a try. The **Teranga Bar Restaurant** has generally excellent food, including one or two dishes from Senegal, and comes highly recommended. **Restaurant Mankante** has a limited but interesting menu. Try the 'Mankante', best described as a mutton omelette. **Salon de thé Le Dogon** has a good choice of pastries, while a large **supermarket** run by the ubiquitous Lebanese is next to the Mobile service station at the crossroads.

Nightlife

Sevaré now has a few places to keep you entertained after dinner.

On Fridays and Saturdays after 22.00, the *paillotte* at **Restaurant Mankante** doubles as a dance floor with jazz, disco, hiphop and African music. The cover charge is CFA1,500. **Restaurant Dolce Vita** (tel: 242 08 11) is pretty much deserted during the day, but comes alive during the evenings. It opens every night and serves an expensive special menu (CFA7,500). However, along with the meal comes traditional music (such as *kora, balafon, djembé*; see page 25). On Thursdays to Sundays from 21.30, the adjoining **Nightclub Djiguibombo** opens its doors. This *boîte de nuit* plays African music mostly, but Fridays is reserved for salsa. The admission fee is CFA2,500, which includes one drink. **Discothèque Byblos** opens from 22.00 on Thursdays, Fridays and Saturdays. Apart from loud music, it features a billiard table, flipper games and video games. The entrance fee is CFA1,500 or CFA2,000, except on Ladies' nights (Thursdays), when accompanied ladies get in for free. If you prefer a more passive form of entertainment, check out the **cinema** in the quarter behind the Salon de thé Le Dogon.

Arts and crafts
Next to Restaurant Manakante is **Farafina Tigne** (tel: 242 04 49) – sometimes spelt 'Farafina Tiyen' – a shop-cum-museum specialising in beads and necklaces. Their downstairs collection is truly impressive, but do not forget to visit the upstairs exhibition too.

Practical information
The only place in the area to change **travellers' cheques** is at the BNDA bank on the road to Mopti. Note that the bank closes at 11.00 on Fridays', but is open for a few hours on Saturday between 08.30 and 11.30. **Internet** facilities can be found in the quarter of Tiaboly, near Hotel Flandre. A **police station** and **post office** are along the road to Mopti, opposite the Salon de Thé Dogon.

ELSEWHERE IN THE NIGER INLAND DELTA
The floodplain of the River Niger extends almost as far as the fringes of the Sahara. Sailing north from Mopti, sooner or later you will arrive at **Lake Débo**, the best known of the several seasonal lakes in the inland delta region. Although some 30km in diameter, Débo is shallow and, therefore, difficult for larger vessels to cross, especially on the numerous days and nights when it is windy. On the other hand, this is a popular spot for much of Mali's migratory birdlife, which comes to the Niger floodplain to spend the winter. The best time to see various species of herons, ibises and other Palaearctic waterfowl is around February, when the birds are concentrated on the remaining patches of water.

Continuing downstream, **Niafounké** is the home of the great African bluesman, Ali Farka Touré (see page 22). Not surprisingly, Touré, who still lives here, has a hand in most of Niafounké's pies, and the *campement* or Motel d'Ali Farka Touré is one of his many business concerns. It is quite satisfactory and allows you to break a journey from Mopti to Timbuktu, for example, in this typically Sahelian town. You might even get to meet the great man!

Lake Débo and Niafounké are the two main stops for boats travelling downstream across the inland delta. By the time you reach **Diré**, the next major town after Niafounké, the floodplain has given way to the fringes of the Sahara. Diré has a basic and rather derelict *campement* with rooms and a terrace for camping. There are, of course, many smaller towns and fishing villages throughout the Niger Inland Delta, which are almost always picturesque and which often have their own 'matchbox' versions of the Djenné Mosque. Some tour operators offer river excursions to fishing villages, the lakes and other places of interest (see *Practicalities: Tour operators in Mali* on page 86). Otherwise, getting to these riverine locations will involve renting a pirogue and a decent guide, or travelling by *pinasse publique*, which will cut the cost tremendously (see *Getting there and away: By river* on page 75).

Hippopotamus
(Hippopotamus amphibius)

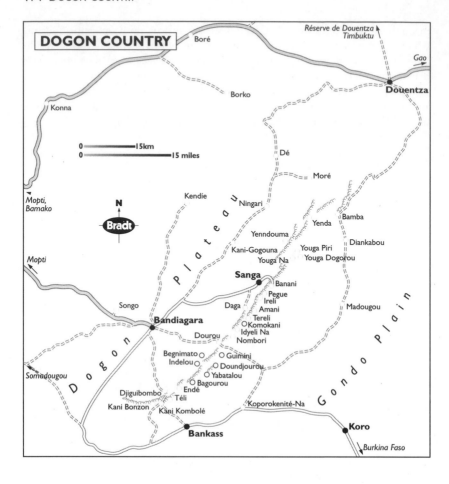

DOGON COUNTRY

Boré

Réserve de Douentza
Timbuktu

Gao

Douentza

Konna

Borko

0 ▭▭▭ 15km
0 ▭▭▭ 15 miles

Dé

Moré

Mopti,
Bamako

Kendíe

Ningari

N

Bradt

Yenda

Bamba

Yenndouma

Youga Piri

Diankabou

Mopti

Kani-Gogouna
Youga Na

Youga Dogorou

P
l
a
t
e
a
u

Sanga

Banani

Pegue
Ireli

Songo

Daga

Amani
Tereli
○ Komokani
Idyeli Na

Madougou

Bandiagara

Dourou

Nombori

Begnimato ○
Indelou ○

○ Guimini
○ Doundjourou
○ Yabatalou

D
o
g
o
n

○ Bagourou

Somadougou

Endé

Djiguibombo

Téli

Kani Bonzon

Kani Kombolé

Koporokenité-Na

G
o
n
d
o

P
l
a
i
n

Bankass

Koro

Burkina Faso

Dogon Country

Tour operators, tourist offices and, indeed, guidebook writers have adopted the term 'Dogon country' (or '*pays Dogon*' in French) to neatly describe the most visited area in Mali. In the interests of convenience, I have followed suit; but at the same time I am embarrassed by the over-generalisation of the term. There are about 350,000 Dogon people living on the plateau, cliffs and plain of an area in the south of the administrative region of Mopti. However, apart from a certain geographical bond and cultural similarities, the Dogon in Dogon country are diverse and different. It is not possible to talk about 'a typical Dogon village', 'a typical Dogon dance' or, worst of all, 'a living museum', where all things are apparently obvious to the visitor's eye and generally understood. On the contrary, this is a place full of surprises. Few things are as they seem and there is always something new to discover. I have an example of my own. It was dusk and I was walking back to Sanga with my guide after a visit to the cliff village of Banani. We had scaled the escarpment and were now on the flat ground of the plateau. In the half-light I saw two old men crouched in the sand with sticks in their hands. I thought that they were simply relaxing and cooling off after another hot day, doodling in the sand to while away the time and to compensate for the lack of conversation between them. Unprompted, my guide explained what they were really doing. Their doodling was not quite as aimless as I had thought, for as we drew nearer I saw that they had been drawing boxes, each with a slightly different design, into which nuts had been placed. These were questions; and the nocturnal tracks of foxes would provide their answers.

HISTORY

The history of the Dogon is based on oral tradition and, as such, is rather muddled. One thing, however, seems clear enough: the Dogon were not the original inhabitants of the Bandiagara escarpment. Their predecessors were known as the **Tellem**, mysterious people who built houses on the rocks of the cliff face, buried their dead in caves high above these houses, and made some of the earliest cloth and wooden objects found in sub-Saharan Africa. These are the concrete facts. Ask the Dogon, however, and they will tell you about the magical powers of these pygmies: how they could fly or transform themselves into giants and climb up to their caves in a single step. The Tellem were probably hunters; the Dogon, on the other hand, were cultivators. When the latter arrived in Tellem country they may have cleared the forest, which at that time covered the plain, so that they could farm the land. The Tellem, thus deprived of their traditional means of survival, deserted the cliffs never to be seen again. Another version of events has the Dogon driving the peaceful Tellem away by force.

Opinions differ as to why the Dogon came to the Bandiagara escarpment in the first place. Some argue that it was to escape drought and the invading Almoravids in the lands of the old Ghana Empire (see page 5). Others maintain that the Dogon were forced to seek refuge in the cliffs in order to avoid being taken as slaves by either the forces of the Songhay ruler, Sonni Ali (see page 8), or bands of Mossi cavalry. Another popular opinion is that the Dogon were once serfs of the *Keita* dynasty of the Mali Empire (see page 7). They were freed during Mali's decline and, deprived of royal protection, needed a safe place to live. Depending on the theory, the Dogon reached the Bandiagara escarpment around the 14th or 15th century. Most agree that four families – the Dyon, Arou, Ono and Domno – were the first to arrive at Kani Bonzon, led there, apparently, by a dog. These families exist to this day and descendants of the forefathers are dispersed in different villages throughout Dogon country.

After the departure of the Tellem, the Dogon's main enemy were the fiercely Islamic Peul, who frequently attacked them on horseback from the Peul heartland on the plain. The former managed to keep control of the *falaise* (escarpment) and the plateau, but only started to spread out on to the plain after the French had conquered the region and pacified the people – both Peul and Dogon – in 1921. By 1937 almost half of the Dogon had left the cliffs to live on the plain where water was more plentiful and the land easier to cultivate.

ECONOMY

The Dogon survive by farming small plots of land on the plateau, plain and wherever else water can be found. Some of what is produced is for personal consumption, while the rest is sold at the market. The main crops are millet, rice, sorghum and onions, which are a common sight – and smell – in Dogon country. When the onions ripen they are pounded into a paste, which is then rolled into balls and dried in the sun. Formerly used as currency, these onion balls are still traded as far away as Bamako and Côte d'Ivoire. Another common sight at the market is millet beer, which is made by the women, lugged up the *falaise* by the women, sold by the women – but drunk by the men. Profits made from the sale of the beer, however, are for the women to keep and dispose of as they see fit. Apart from the one at Bandiagara, there are five main markets in Dogon country – one for each day of the Dogon week, which has only five days. The most important is held on the first day of the week at Sanga. The others follow in order of importance: Ireli, Tireli, Nombori and finally Dourou.

The Dogon raise animals – cattle, goats, sheep, chickens, donkeys etc – for food, sacrifice or work; and small-scale hunting with flintlock rifles made by their own blacksmiths also takes place, although the wild game is minimal and hunters usually have to make do with monkeys, hares, rats, birds and snakes. The other mainstay of the Dogon economy is the revenue derived from tourism: the sale of arts and crafts, village taxes, guides, accommodation etc.

BELIEFS

Although many of the Dogon have now converted to Islam or Christianity, the remainder are still largely animist, a word defined by the *Oxford English Dictionary* as 'one who attributes a living soul to natural objects and phenomena'. This is a useful definition to keep in mind during your stay in Dogon country, for in this world almost everything is infused with meaning and significance. The French ethnologist, Marcel Griaule, was the first European to investigate and discover some of the meanings and ideas behind the complexities of Dogon symbolism and cosmology, and he wrote about them in *Dieu d'eau: conversations avec Ogotemmêli* and *Le Renard Pâle*, the two classics of Dogon literature (see *Appendix 2* on page 282). Read them and the numerous other books on the Dogon for a proper introduction to what these people believe.

In the beginning...

The master of the Dogon universe is **Amma**. Having created the sun, moon and stars, he threw a ball of clay which transformed into Earth – his intended mate. Earth had both male and female organs, the first represented by an anthill and the second by a termite hill. When Amma tried to mate with Earth, access to the termite hill was barred by the masculinity of the female (the clitoris), which he was obliged to cut off before he could copulate. The god's original intention had been to produce twins – the ideal unity of a being is formed by a couple – but the result of this first, disordered attempt was a single birth in the form of the **Jackal** (or fox). Amma and Earth tried again and this time were successful in producing twins, the **Nommo**, who would gradually replace Amma as the arbiter of human affairs. The essence of the Nommo was in water, the source of all life, and they had the torsos of men, the tails of snakes, green skin, red, human eyes and forked tongues. Their first task was to dress Earth, which they did with a grass skirt. The Jackal, meanwhile, wanted to possess Earth and committed incest with his mother. The grass skirt was stained with blood – the origins of women's menstrual blood – and Amma rejected Earth who was now impure. He threw another ball of clay to create the first human couple, who in turn procreated and produced twins. However, after the coming of these two beings, the birth of twins became a rare exception. The Nommo, in order to reduce the impact of this situation – for twins are ideal – took to drawing silhouettes of the male and female souls on the ground. The newborn, once laid on these shadows, absorbs both their male and female souls. If the child is a boy, his female principal will lie in the foreskin; if it is a girl, the male principal will be placed in the clitoris.

THE DOGON & THE DOG STAR

Philip Briggs

In the late 1930s, a quartet of venerable chiefs and priests divulged the most intimate Dogon traditions to the French anthropologist Marcel Griaule. Surprisingly, it emerged that these isolated animists were familiar with several cosmic objects invisible to the naked eye, for instance Saturn's rings and four of Jupiter's moons. More intriguing still were the traditions and beliefs relating to Sirius (aka the Dog Star), the brightest star as seen from earth, and the most venerated celestial object in Dogon culture.

Sirius, the priests explained, is not one star but three, with the bright main star being orbited by two other stars that are invisible from earth – the bright white Pa Tolo (Seed Star) and duller Emme Ya (Sorghum female). Pa Tolo, though relatively small, is the heaviest object in the heavens, and it rotates on its own axis following an elliptical 60-year orbit around Sirius (mirrored in the cycle of the once-in-a-lifetime Sigi Festival).

The odd thing about this was that the existence of Pa Tolo – or Sirius B – had gone unsuspected by Europeans prior to the 1840s, when irregularities consistent with a binary star were noted in Sirius' movements. The corresponding star was seen faintly through a telescope in 1862, but it wasn't until the 1920s that scientists recognised its exceptionally dense nature and classified it as a 'white dwarf', the first such entity known to Western science. So how was it that this remote African tribe had known about the existence of Sirius B centuries earlier?

The traditions recorded by Griaule were initially aired quietly in a rather arcane anthropological journal, but they went into broader circulation in 1977 following the publication of Robert Temple's controversial book *The Sirius Mystery*. Temple postulated that the only credible explanation for the Dogon's knowledge of Sirius B is that the amphibious deity they know as Nommo was in fact a group of spacemen from Sirius who visited earth and passed on information about their home solar system to the Dogon. Temple reckons that the Ancient Egyptians (who also associated Sirius with a deity) were visited by the same extraterrestrials, and that the event occurred about 5,000 years ago, which is when Egypt adopted a new annual calendar that started on the same day that Sirius appeared back in the spring night sky after a three-month winter absence.

The biggest chink in Temple's hypothesis is that it rests so heavily on his assumption that the Dogon possessed ancient knowledge of Sirius' binary nature. And this assumption is itself based solely on Griaule's research. If Griaule got the wrong end of the stick, then Temple's theories amount to groundless speculation. And as it transpires, Griaule's information has yet to be corroborated by any subsequent research. Furthermore, the existence of Sirius B had been confirmed a full 80 years before Griaule collected his information, while other details about the nature of Pa Tolo as supplied by Griaule's informants had been established by astronomers in the 1920s.

Could it be, then, that the ancient knowledge of Sirius B communicated to Griaule was actually information acquired more recently through contact with Europeans and grafted on to existing Dogon legends surrounding Sirius? Well, one tellingly devilish detail is the Dogon assertion that Pa Tolo is the heaviest star in the galaxy – coincidentally, the 'white dwarf' Sirius B was the heaviest celestial body known to Europeans at that time, yet any civilisation sophisticated enough to travel in space would surely have been aware of the many thousands of similar stars subsequently discovered by, um, earthlings! Likewise, the Dogon's supposedly ancient knowledge of the solar system – which omits features such as smaller moons and rings around Jupiter, or of any planets further from the sun than Saturn – is more consistent with European knowledge circa 1930 than information gleaned from extraterrestrials.

Temple and his supporters argue that Dogon Country circa 1930 was too isolated to have learned about Sirius B from Europeans, yet mission schools were established in the area as early as 1910, and it would also have been visited by French colonial administrators and other outsiders. Proponents of the spacemen theory also characterise as absurd the suggestion that an early European visitor would have banged on about the binary nature of Sirius to his Dogon hosts, yet this seems quite plausible considering how important Sirius is in Dogon cosmology. A criticism more worthy of consideration is whether it's realistic for information gleaned from European visitors to have been grafted on to the ancient traditions regarding Sirius in such a short space of time. But surely this scenario – or even one in which Griaule inadvertently conspired with his informants by asking them leading questions – has to rank a notch or two higher on the scale of probability than one in which a bunch of amphibious spacemen appeared on the scene in 3,200BC?

And what of Emme Ya, the third member of the celestial Dogon trinity? Well, it scarcely entered the debate until 1995, when Benest and Duvent's paper entitled 'Is Sirius A Triple Star?' (published in *Astronomy & Astrophysics*) made a persuasive case for the existence of Sirius C based on orbital quirks recorded over the previous 100 years. Soon after, Temple published a revised edition of *The Sirius Mystery*, citing the latter-day emergence of a star that conformed to the Dogon's prescient Emme Ya as proof of the theories he'd expounded first time around. But the notion that Sirius is a trinary star actually predates Benest and Duvent's paper by several decades – it had been quite a talking point in the 1920s when a few astronomers claimed to have glimpsed a third member of the Sirius system.

For further information about *The Sirius Mystery*, visit www.robert-temple.com. Two excellent critiques of Temple's theories are 'The Sirius Mystery' by James Oberg (www.debunker.com/texts/dogon.html) and 'Investigating the Sirius "Mystery"' by Ian Ridpath, published in the *Skeptical Enquirer* of Fall 1978 (www.csicop.org/si/7809/sirius.html).

The first human couple produced **eight ancestors**, four being predominantly male and four predominantly female, but each possessing a male and female soul. These eight ancestors each started their own family – their mortal descendants – and descended from the celestial world to earth one-by-one in order of seniority. The first ancestor, the **Blacksmith**, arrived in an ark containing all that was necessary for man to survive, and he began to teach the eight families how to make tools and plant the seeds which he had brought with him. The remaining ancestors descended in their hierarchical order, each one bringing his or her own particular tools and knowledge. However, the sequence was upset when the eighth ancestor descended before the seventh, the **Master of the Word**. Incensed, the seventh took the form of a snake and sneaked into the granary to steal the grain brought by the Blacksmith. The Blacksmith advised the humans (the eight families) to kill the snake, which they did, eating the body and giving the head to the Blacksmith who buried it under his forge.

However, humans had not yet learnt the word, and the only one who could give it to them, the Master of the Word, was dead. The oldest man in the world, **Lébé**, belonged to the family of the eighth ancestor, who represented the Word itself. Therefore, Lébé was the only human who could be taught the Word, and to be able to learn it he had to die and pass into the same world as the seventh ancestor. (At this point, it must be noted that neither Lébé nor the Master of the Word had *actually* died: for humans, death had not been invented yet, and the seventh ancestor was, in any case, immortal.) Lébé's remains were placed in a field not far from the Blacksmith's forge, his head pointing north towards the interred serpent's head. As the Blacksmith worked, the noise of his anvil and bellows transformed the seventh ancestor into a Nommo, with the trunk of a human and the tail of a serpent. He crawled over to Lébé's corpse, swallowed and regenerated it, vomiting everything up in a torrent of water, the one missing ingredient for human survival.

This is an imperfect précis of what a blind hunter called Ogotemmêli told Marcel Griaule when the latter spoke to him in 1948. The complete interview is recorded in *Dieu d'eau: conversations avec Ogotemmêli*.

Rituals
Cults
Dogon rituals are, naturally, linked to their mythical beliefs, and most are performed in the context of one of the four principal cults. All men – but absolutely no women – are instructed in the cult of the masks or the *awa*, and a select few are chosen to be the keepers of the traditions of the masks or the *oloubarou*. Masks play a major role in Dogon culture and members of the *awa* will dance at ritual ceremonies wearing masks representing various people (old men, young girls, hunters, blacksmiths and thieves, for example); animals (including black-and-white monkeys, crocodiles and antelopes); and the most famous mask of them all, the **Kanaga Mask**, which relates to the creation myth.

Previous page Djenné Mosque, the largest mud building in Africa, after Friday prayers

Above Tuareg drinking tea at homestead in desert, Timbuktu

Right Fula woman with mouth tattoo, Djenné

The cult of *lébé* is associated with several agrarian ceremonies dedicated to the glory and resurrection of the Nommo. There is an altar of *lébé* in the public place of each village and ceremonies are presided over by the high priest or **hogon**, the spiritual leader and the oldest direct descendent of the original ancestors.

The cult of *binou* is pseudo-totemic. Dogon families are linked to one of the eight ancestral groups and the *binou*, which is often in the form of an animal, is taken to represent the ancestor. Each village or clan has its own totem and sacrifices are laid before the *binou* to encourage the immortal ancestors to look favourably on the living.

The cult of the **ancestors** is similar to that of *binou*, the essential difference being that the former relates to individual families. The aim of the cult is to maintain good relations between the living and the dead. Each family household or *ginna* has an altar dedicated to an ancestor and the head of the family or the *ginna bana* presides over sacrifices and other rituals.

The Sigi

Of all the Dogon rituals, the Sigi (pronounced with a hard 'g') is the most important. Originating at Youga (see page 198) and held every 60 years – the next one should be in 2027 – the Sigi is a ceremony of atonement and initiation. It is held to demand pardon for the death of an ancestor after the folly and forgetfulness of some young men at, so the story goes, the village of Youga Dogorou. The grass skirt covered with blood after the incest between the Jackal and Earth had fallen into the possession of a woman, and then of a group of young men who had been frightened by the powers assumed by the woman when she wore the skirt. All of this should have been reported to the oldest man, the guardian of tradition, but was not. As a result, he was transformed into a Nommo and remained on earth in the form of a snake.

A DOGON BONJOUR

Greetings are important all over Africa and Dogon country is no exception. Learn the following exchange and work on getting it up to speed. When two Dogon meet, even if they are simply crossing each other in the road, the oldest begins by saying *aga po* (hello) followed by *séo* (*ça va* or how are you?), to which the other replies *séo* (*ça va*). The first then continues with *oumana séo* (how is the family?), *ounou séo* (how are the children?) and *yahana go séo* (how is the wife?). The latter responds each time with *séo*. When the first has completed his enquiries, the roles are reversed and the second poses the same questions. A shorter version exists whereby *po séo* is replied simply with *ho* and that's all, but it is rarely used. Although a little cumbersome and unusual for the untrained novice, this greeting should eventually sound more like a duet than a verbal exchange, and the words should be sung as much as spoken.

One day he met the young men and began to scold them for not telling him about the skirt. However, in his anger he spoke to them in Dogon, thus breaking the rule which forbids the Nommo to communicate directly with humans in their own language. He was thus impure and died. At each Sigi ceremony a brand new **Great Mask**, carved out of a tree trunk in the form of a serpent and sometimes 10m high, is made and initiated along with a selection of 'impure men' or *oloubarou*, who have the life-long responsibility of preserving the tradition of the masks.

The signal for the commencement of the Sigi is the appearance of a glimmer of red light in the east, leading many observers to link the Sigi with the cycle of a star called Sirius B. Until 1970, when it was photographed by the United States Naval Observatory, astronomers had only suspected the existence of Sirius B. The Dogon seem to have a profound insight into some of Sirius's specific properties, causing wild speculations about the origins of this knowledge. One popular theory, based on Marcel Griaule's published works, is now subject to heavy criticism (see box on pages 178–9).

Death rituals

When a Dogon dies, the soul leaves the body and remains in the village. Before it can leave and proceed to the spiritual world of the ancestors, three separate funeral rites must be performed. The first is the burial itself, performed immediately after the death. In many cliff villages the corpse is hoisted by ropes made from the fibres of the *baobab* tree to its final resting place in the ancient burial caves of the Tellem.

However, the soul of the dead person remains in the family house. Therefore, after a delay of between six months and a year – to allow time for the period of mourning and to give the family of the deceased an opportunity to collect all that is needed for the second ceremony (huge quantities of millet beer, for example) – the death rites continue with a celebration lasting three days and three nights, during which the soul of the deceased is invited to leave the family home. This, however, is not the end of the matter; the soul may have left the house, but it remains in the village. The *dama* takes place five years after the death to ensure that the soul leaves the village for good. Members of the *awa* perform mask dances and follow the soul out of the village and into the bush, from where it continues on its journey to the land of the ancestors.

Circumcision and excision

In the beginning, the rule of procreation was the production of twins and everything was done to provide an individual with two souls, or **kindu kindu**, to compensate for the failure to produce actual twins. Therefore, a newborn child is composed of two spiritual twins, a male and a female, and neither wins over the other until circumcision or excision. By removing the foreskin or clitoris – the material expressions of the opposite sex or other soul – an individual becomes definitely male or definitely female and thus gains his or her urge to procreate. However, the rejected half of the *kindu kindu* is not destroyed. The clitoris turns into a scorpion, while the foreskin turns into a *nay* or a kind of lizard. In this way, the male and female souls of individuals live on in animal twins.

THE DOGON VILLAGE

The layout of a Dogon village is rarely haphazard. Even though the style of the village can vary depending on whether you are along the *falaise*, on the plateau or on the plain, urban planning is always indelibly linked to Dogon spiritual beliefs and symbolism.

Villages are usually divided into several, often quite autonomous quarters, each made up of a grouping of family households or *ginna*. The layout of each *ginna*, which comprises the house of the head of the family, the *ginna bana*, as well as other habitations for his wives and children, storerooms and stables, is considered to represent a man lying on his side in the act of procreation, while the habitations themselves often symbolise a human body. The **granaries** are one of the most distinctive features of a Dogon village. These mud pillboxes with thatched roofs like witches' hats are used to store millet and other worldly possessions: clothes, pottery, jewellery, food for the family etc, depending on whether the granary belongs to a woman or a man. In the centre of each village, or quarter, there is a *togu na*, a shelter reserved for men, where the elders hold meetings, councils and pronounce judgements. Eight posts – symbolising the original ancestors – support a thick, millet-stalk roof which is only 1.2m off the ground. This provides maximum shade – for this is also a place of rest and relaxation – and prevents standing up whilst in the *togu na*. The only circular buildings to be found in Dogon country are the *maisons des femmes* or **menstruation houses**. For reasons already mentioned (see page 177), women are considered to be impure during their period and are banished to these hovels, many of which are decorated with mud carvings of men and women with huge genitals and real pubic hair, until they have finished menstruating.

The *binou* **shrine** (part of the binou cult) is a decorated, single-chambered building. As a spiritual leader of the binou clan, the binou priest is responsible for maintaining a harmonious relationship between the clan-members and the supernatural world. Libations of millet gruel on the façades of the shrine are an indispendable part of the binou cult. The millet leaves clear white marks on the façade. The **house of the** *hogon* is associated with the Lebe cult. The hogon and the binou priest may be considered as complementary counterparts, as they both serve as spiritual leaders. When a hogon dies he is succeeded through election by one of the village elders. After a period of initiation the new hogon has to live by strict rules and taboos. One of these forbids him from leaving his compound and he is not to be touched by anyone – not even his wife and family.

ORIENTATION

Although most people come to visit the cliff villages built on the rocks of the Bandiagara escarpment, otherwise known as the *falaise*, which cuts a 200km swath

RESPONSIBLE TOURISM IN DOGON COUNTRY

One day I was in a Dogon village happily taking photographs of the houses and granaries when something grabbed my attention. I turned my camera on the object of my curiosity – a mound of clay splashed with what looked like white paint – and prepared to take its picture. 'Stop,' cried my guide 'that's an altar. It's sacred. No photo.' I had not even stopped to think; it looked far too ordinary to be sacred.

In a world littered with taboos, fetishes, sacred objects and forbidden areas, using your common sense and good intentions as a responsible tourist will only get you so far before you inadvertently break the rules. For this reason, you should not tramp across Dogon country without the company of a good guide. Follow him at all times, don't touch anything and ask before you take photographs (the general rule is that you can take pictures of the houses and granaries, but not the people and sacred places – unless you pay). It stands to reason that the best guides will normally be Dogon themselves. Try to avoid the numerous *petits guides* touting for business in Mali's tourist towns, who profess expertise in all matters Dogon but, in fact, know very little indeed. On one infamous occasion, an enthusiastic youth employed by a group of travellers eager to 'discover' Dogon country was asked why the women go around barebreasted. 'Because they can't afford to buy clothes,' he answered, with as much confidence as ignorance.

Many other potential tourist blunders can be avoided with a little thought, common sense and respect. For example, you don't have to be a genius to work out that water is in chronically short supply in Dogon country and that, as a result, daily ablutions should be quick and economical. Giving sweets or the

through central Mali, Dogon country actually covers an area of some 4,000km², with hundreds of settlements on the plateau and the vast Gondo Plain, which stretches south from the cliffs into Burkina Faso. The land of the Dogon is divided into four *cercles*: Bandiagara and Douentza on the plateau, Bankass and Koro on the plain. These, in turn, are split into several *arrondissements*.

Bandiagara is the largest town on the plateau and the main base for trekking in Dogon country. Bankass, on the Gondo Plain, is closer to the escarpment, but facilities for visitors here are inferior to those at Bandiagara.

Along the escarpment, the most popular tourist route is between the villages of Banani in the northeast and Kani Kombolé in the southwest. Access to the cliff villages along this route is possible by vehicle from Sanga (for Banani) and Djiguibombo (for Kani Kombolé). Though there is something resembling a road leading down from Dourou to Nombori, this option should be considered only by those with a 4WD and no fear of soft sand. However, since Dourou is roughly halfway between Sanga and Djiguibombo, and accessible by vehicle from Bandiagara, for many visitors it marks the beginning or end of a hiking trip in Dogon country.

ubiquitous *bics* (pens) to children is a thorny issue. I sought the advice of the Mission Culturelle in Bandiagara and a number of senior guides, and the general consensus seemed to be that *bics* should be given to the village school rather than to individual children and that sweets were no good because they caused cavities and the Dogon could not afford to go to the dentist – which all seemed to make sense to me. Another thing often overlooked by visitors is their choice of dress when trekking through Dogon country. Despite the scorching heat on the Bandiagara escarpment, figure-hugging shorts and skimpy vests (or worse) which would turn heads on the Côte d'Azur are obviously not appropriate in Dogon country, where contact with the outside world has been so limited and the people are more easily shocked than in more open societies.

While the Mission Culturelle are keen to re-educate scantily clad backpackers and shutter-happy tourists, their main task is to stop the theft of Dogon and Tellem artefacts. At one end of the scale, professional grave robbers routinely plunder Tellem burial objects from the caves high above the villages on the escarpment and sell them for a small fortune to Western collectors. Meanwhile, tourists walk through Dogon villages, take a fancy to intricately carved doors of millet granaries, masks and statues, offer an irresistible number of dollars for the object of their desire, and walk away with yet another piece of Mali's cultural heritage. To combat the problem the Mission Culturelle are trying to encourage the creation of village museums, where each family donates an exhibit – pots, pans, Dogon underwear – it hardly matters what – instead of selling them to tourists. The money generated by these museums will go back into the village, hopefully creating jobs and the beginning of an infrastructure to support a new way of life – in other words, the tourist boom.

Both Djiguibombo and Dourou have *campements* with prices ranging from CFA1,000 to CFA2,000 per person, while Sanga has better tourist facilities, including some comfortable hotels.

PRACTICAL INFORMATION
Getting around
Trekking in Dogon country involves, by definition, a lot a walking; indeed, the villages along the *falaise* are only accessible by foot. You don't have to be a great climber or super fit, and any guide worth his salt will be quick to evaluate how much you can do in a day. Trust his judgement! Porters are also available at about CFA3,000 a day to carry your bags. It is now possible to stop for a drink and even stay the night at most of the cliff villages, allowing travellers to spend several days exploring Dogon country at a relaxed pace. The distances between the cliff villages are relatively short and easily covered on foot. However, you can also drive along the Gondo Plain – 4WD, motorbikes, and cart and donkey are the preferred means of transport – stopping to visit any village that takes your fancy.

Vehicles are more necessary for tours of the more spaced-out villages on the plateau and for travel between the principal towns in Dogon country – Bandiagara, Sanga, and Bankass (see the *Getting there and away* sections for these towns).

Accommodation

While there are hotels and restaurants in Bandiagara, Bankass, Koro and Sanga, board and lodging in the villages along the *falaise* and on the plateau is predictably rustic. All villages between Kani Kombolé and Banani, and many other popular villages elsewhere, now have at least one *campement*. These should not be compared to others across Mali, for in Dogon country creature comforts are minimal. You must wash with buckets of water, taking great care not to use too much of this precious commodity, and sleep on lumpy mattresses in box-like rooms or on the roof. The majority of *campements* now have something resembling a toilet, and a select few possess a fridge. Bottled drinks are usually available, along with spaghetti, macaroni, rice, couscous and the Dogon favourite, *tô* with gumbo sauce (see *Food and drink*, page 30). The cost of spending the night at one of these *campements* varies from CFA500 to CFA2,000 depending on the facilities available and the popularity of the village.

Several of the tour operators prefer to camp on the Gondo Plain rather than lodge their clients in the villages themselves. There are areas of soft sand not far from the *falaise* which serve as good campsites, although you should be aware of snakes and scorpions! In case you end the day in a village with no *campement*, ask for the *chef du village*. He will find you a place to spend the night, most likely in or near his family compound.

Guides

Guides all over the country purport to have an intimate knowledge of Dogon country. If they are not actually Dogon themselves, they will invariably boast some impressive link to Mali's most popular tourist attraction. Be suspicious of guides who approach you in towns such as Bamako and Mopti offering to take you there. Of course, your suitor might be 100% genuine: knowledgeable, friendly and hard-working. Unfortunately, there is an equally good chance that he will know next to nothing. The general rule is to look for your guide in Dogon country itself. There is no shortage of them in Bandiagara, while at Sanga the Bureau des Guides is reliable and respected (see page 190). If you find your guide in Bandiagara, visit the Mission Culturelle to check out his credentials (see page 190).

It cannot be stressed enough that a guide can make or break your experience in Dogon country, so before making up your mind about a guide, take some time to get to know him a bit. See whether he will be able to give you the kind of information you are looking for and whether his knowledge of French – or occassionally English – suits you. Also try and get a clear picture of what is – and what isn't – included in the price. If meals are included, make sure you know what type of food you are talking about. Some tourists end up living on huge servings of couscous or spaghetti and tomato sauce, but little else. Also check the flexibility of your prospective guide, as certain guides will decide on their own what is best for you, regardless of your expectations and wishes.

Having packed this section – and others in the book concerning guides – with warnings and precautions, I should add that I have heard of more good experiences with guides in Dogon country than bad. A lot depends on the relationship you strike up with your prospective guide. If you warm to a particular person and have a good feeling about him, the chances are that he will not disappoint. Bear the precautions I have mentioned in mind, but also trust your instinct.

Finally, you are not obliged to be with a guide when you trek through Dogon country. However, there is so much to discover in this land, and so many forbidden areas and other traditions to respect, that I strongly advise you to take one (see box on pages 184–5).

Festival of the *Danses des Masques*

If you are planning to visit Dogon country towards the end of December or the beginning of January, ask around if the *Festival des Danses des Masques* is about to take place. This gathering of groups of dancers is staged in a different village every year, and offers a spectacular opportunity to see a whole variety of costumes, masks and dances. It is visited by the Dogon as well as an international public. The entrance fee is CFA4,000 per person, which also buys you the right to take pictures. See also page 89.

BANDIAGARA

Bandiagara is 'base camp' for any visit to Dogon country. Whether you intend to access the cliffs via Sanga or Djiguibombo, or want to see some of the villages on the plateau, Bandiagara is hard to avoid. For this reason, there are several hotels and restaurants, and plenty of guides – but no bank.

You will be disappointed if you come to Bandiagara expecting a picture-postcard Dogon village. Instead, this is a reasonably-sized town which, by Dogon standards at least, is cosmopolitan and busy. The largest market on the plateau takes place here on Mondays, while the smaller *marché des femmes* takes place on Fridays. A picturesque river, the Nyamé, runs along the eastern edge of town. Otherwise, Bandiagara is of limited interest to the sightseer. It is, if you like, a point of transition – a link between the private, spiritual world of the Dogon on the escarpment and the remote plateau, and the rat race 75km away.

Getting there and away

Getting to Bandiagara is simple enough in principle: *bâchées* leave from Mopti and Sévaré and take approximately one hour to cover the smoothly tarred 75km across the Dogon Plateau to Bandiagara. However, if the demand is light – as it tends to be in the afternoons – you might spend hours waiting for your *bâchée* to fill up. With this in mind, ask how many tickets remain to be sold before you hand over your CFA1,500. If there are plenty, it might be quicker to hitchhike. The same is true when you want to leave Bandiagara. On market days (Mondays and Fridays) there is a steady flow of *bâchées* and bush taxis to Mopti, and even a direct (and very slow) bus to Bamako (CFA8,000). On other days, however, the extent of the traffic is hard to predict. You can get to Sanga by public transport (1½ hours, CFA1,500), but try to travel on a market day which, in Sanga's case, is every five days. Alternatively, you might be able to find an *occasion* by going to Restaurant Petit Coin. A ride to Djiguibombo on the back of a mobylette will cost around CFA5,000, while a small car will take you there for CFA11,000.

Where to stay

Designed by an architect flown in from Italy and run by an eccentric Swiss lady, **Hotel Kambary** (tel: 244 23 88) is a little different from the norm. This cluster of futuristic, domed buildings built on an arid piece of land near the road to Mopti looks more like an extra-terrestrial colony in the Star Wars prequel than the most luxurious and expensive hotel in Dogon country. There are two cheaper rooms in the annexe, but otherwise rooms start at CFA17,000 for a single with a fan, rising to CFA30,000 for an air-conditioned double. A small but attractive swimming pool lies well hidden behind the rooms. The Kambary is somewhat overpriced and not half as friendly as the nearby **Hotel Le Village** (tel: 244 23 31). Simple rooms with fans and comfortable bamboo beds cost either CFA2,500 or CFA4,000 depending on the size of the bed; and you can pitch a tent in the garden for CFA2,000. You share washing facilities – note that the water pressure is sometimes very low – and there is a clothes-line in the garden. They will also store luggage while you go trekking along the *falaise*. Two other hotels in Bandiagara are slightly more basic than Le Village, but no less friendly. **Hotel Satimbe** behind the bus yard charges CFA3,000 per person for a bed with a mosquito net, and CFA4,000 with a fan. Prices include breakfast. It might be possible to sleep on the roof and the small *jardin de repos* is, as its name suggests, a peaceful garden in which to relax. The atmosphere at **Auberge Kansaye** (tel: 244 29 04) on the banks of the river is more upbeat, with reggae music and a gregarious Rastafarian manager. You pay CFA3,000 (CFA4,000 with a fan) per person for a bed with a mosquito net. Coming from Mopti, you will pass **Auberge Camping Togona** (tel: 244 21 59) a few kilometres before Bandiagara. The whole setting is pleasant and spacious, as are the rooms with open-air showers (CFA5,000 per person). Camping costs CFA2,000 per person. In 2004, the owner of Le Petit Coin will open a small hotel (and decide on its name) near the market with three ventilated rooms at CFA4,000 per person. CFA2,000 will buy you a mattress on the terrace for the night. **Camping Ogobo** has some basic but adequate rooms with mosquito nets (CFA5,000), while camping costs CFA2,000 per person.

Where to eat

Restaurant Bar Le Cheval Blanc is the official name of the restaurant at Hotel Kambary – which, incidentally, is also known as 'Le Cheval Blanc'.

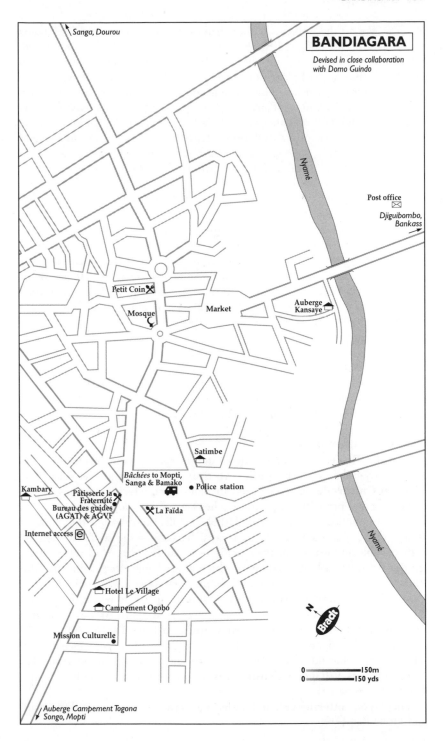

Sanga, Dourou

BANDIAGARA

*Devised in close collaboration
with Domo Guindo*

Nyamé

Post office

Djiguibombo,
Bankass

Petit Coin

Mosque

Market

Auberge
Kansaye

Satimbe

Bâchées to Mopti,
Sanga & Bamako

Police station

Kambary

Pâtisserie la
Fraternité
Bureau des guides
(AGAT) & AGVF

La Faïda

Internet access

Nyamé

Hotel Le Village

Campement Ogobo

Mission Culturelle

Bradt

N

0 ———— 150m
0 ———— 150 yds

Auberge Campement Togona
Songo, Mopti

You eat here for the ambience rather than the great quality of the food. Swiss diners will be disappointed by the one or two Swiss dishes on the menu, while the rest might end up wishing that they had stuck to drinking an aperitif on the cool and pleasant terrace. Meals at **Hotel Le Village** are also taken in a pleasant garden. The servings are not stingy here, but you must order in advance if you want anything out of the ordinary, which effectively means something other than spaghetti. At breakfast, once again taken in the garden, the papaya, guava and other types of jam are home-made and delicious. The same rule applies at the restaurants of the other hotels in town: order in advance. Meals at **Auberge Camping Togona** come recommended by readers.

Restaurant Petit Coin near the market has gained a reputation as *the* travellers' hangout in Bandiagara. As such, guides and hassle are part of the fixtures, but the food is good – especially the *sauce arachide* – and reasonably priced. This can also be a good place to find people to go trekking with in Dogon country or to hitch a lift to Sanga, as many groups stop here for lunch en route to the *falaise*. Near the *gare routiére* is the **Restaurant Pâtisserie La Faïda** with a small terrace around the back, for a limited choice of meals but no pastries. **Pâtisserie La Fraternité** is owned by a Nigerian couple, Moses and Promise, who serve steaks, salads, and tasty fish, sauce and rice dishes.

If you are in Bandiagara on a market day, ask directions to – or stumble across – a *cabaret* or ad hoc bar where men gulp *tchapulo* (millet beer) from calabashes as quickly as the women can make it. It's only CFA125 a litre, so spirits are usually quite high, and rumour has it that *tchapulo* often washes down mouthfuls of the Islamic forbidden fruit – pork.

Practical information

The **post office** is on the other side of the river just past the bridge near the road to Djiguibombo. The **police station** is next to the bus yard. The **Mission Culturelle** (tel: 244 22 63) in Bandiagara, which is responsible for preserving and promoting the cultural heritage of the Dogon, can be found behind the service station next to Hotel Le Village. Although this is not a tourist office – and should not be treated like one – the staff are friendly, approachable and experts in their field. You could ask them to recommend **guides** for treks in Dogon country, which at least guarantees someone who knows what he is talking about – people recommended by the Mission Culturelle have normally taken lessons with them before becoming guides. The guides have now organised themselves, and their **Association des Guides et Accompagnateurs Touristiques au Pays Dogon** (tel: 244 29 05) has its office signposted not far from Patisserie La Fraternité (see above). Their rates should soon be standardised. The **Association des Groupements Villageois Féminins** is located just next to the Bureau des Guides (see page 193).

There is one **internet café** in Bandiagara, between the main road to Sevaré and Hotel Kambary.

BANKASS

Bankass, with its distinctive red *banco* houses, is another base for visits to Dogon country. Situated on the Gondo Plain at the southeastern end of the *falaise*, it is conveniently located for visits to the villages on the 'Kani Kombolé circuit' (see page 193). So is Bandiagara, however, where facilities are more comfortable and numerous. Therefore, unless you are arriving in Dogon country from Burkina Faso – in which case Bankass is the logical stopping point – choose Bandiagara as your main base.

Getting there and away

Most visitors to Bankass are at either the beginning or the end of their stay in Dogon country. The majority of tourist traffic, therefore, is either to the main highway in Mali or to Burkina Faso. During the dry season, the occasional vehicle linking Bankass to any Malian town other than Bandiagara, Mopti or Sevaré may opt for the shorter route via Somadougou. However, until the section between Somadougou and Wo is significantly upgraded, most traffic to Bankass will go by way of Sevaré and Bandiagara. Here you will find *bâchées* and small buses leaving for Bankass, but other than on market day (Tuesdays) they could take very long to fill up. From the *gare routière* in Bankass, look for the occasional vehicle leaving directly for Bamako (CFA6,000) or Sikasso (CFA6,000), again especially on Tuesdays. For Burkina Faso, take a *bâchée* from Bankass to Koro (CFA1,000), from where an excellent daily SOGABAF bus leaves at 15.00 for Ouagadougou (about six hours) via Ouahigouya (3-4 hours).

Bankass is about 10km from Kani Kombolé on the *falaise*. The walk across the sandy Gondo Plain is not the easiest – or the most scenic – but it might be your only option. On market day in Bankass (Tuesdays) hitching a lift from Kani Kombolé is a possibility; otherwise, renting a cart and donkey is the best bet for those who would rather not walk (around CFA4,000–5,000).

Where to stay and eat

The one hotel in Bankass, **Hotel Les Arbres**, has five self-contained doubles/triples at CFA10,000. Check if the water is running before handing over your money; there have been serious problems with the water supply in the past. Camping in the garden costs around CFA2,500. Double rooms with a fan and mosquito nets at the **Campement Hotel Hogon** cost CFA6,000, while a mattress on the terrace costs CFA2,500 per person.

The restaurant at Hotel Les Arbres is overpriced, but it does have the best selection of food in town. One of the few alternatives is at the Campement, where unadventurous chicken and spaghetti dishes must be ordered in advance.

Practical information

The **post office** is opposite Hotel Les Arbres. One *cabine téléphonique* (244 30 02) is the only available **telephone**, serving the whole of Bankass.

KORO

Most travellers going this way are in transit between Mali and Burkina Faso. A recommended place to stay is **Hotel Campement l'Aventure** (tel: 242 01 91), in a pleasant traditional setting built in Sudanese style. Rooms cost around CFA9,000 for a double and camping is also allowed. If you are planning to go to Dogon country, this is a good place to enquire and even book a trip. For more information go to www.aventure-dogon.com, or contact mail@aventure-dogon.com.

SANGA

Sanga is the village made famous by the French ethnologist Marcel Griaule, who spent much of his time here researching Dogon traditions and beliefs. Compared with other villages along the *falaise*, Sanga is better described as a town; it comprises ten villages or quarters which sprawl across the plateau and lie only a couple of kilometres from the escarpment. It is this convenient location – the cliff village of Banani is within easy walking-distance – rather than any intrinsic beauty which has made Sanga so popular with tourists. As a result, some hotels and other tourist facilities have emerged, making Sanga the most convenient of the three 'bases' – Bandiagara and Bankass being the others – for direct access to the *falaise*.

Getting there and away

The only time when *bâchées* are sure to leave for Bandiagara is on market day in Sanga, which is every five days, or once a Dogon week. At other times, departures are entirely dependent on demand. The market takes place behind Campement Sanga near the entrance to town. During high season, 4WDs are always parked outside Campement Sanga, so it might be possible to hitch a lift back to Bandiagara – and perhaps beyond – with returning tour groups.

Where to stay and eat

Campement Hotel Sanga (also known as 'La Guina', tel: 244 20 28) has had an illustrious past: it used to be the Campement Administratif, then Sanga's first school and the home of Marcel Griaulle. Nowadays, it caters for the needs of Sanga's tourists, with self-contained singles/doubles/triples with a fan for CFA15,000/17,500/22,500. Budget travellers have the option to stay in a *paillotte* for CFA6,000, to camp for CFA4,000, or to sleep on the terrace (overlooking the plateau) for CFA2,500 per person. Many of the organised groups stay here, which is why it is overpriced and often full. Independent travellers tend to prefer the **Gîte de la Femme Dogon** (tel: 244 20 13), run by a hospitable, Protestant family. The rooms (CFA7,000 single or double) are basic but friendly and clean, and CFA2,500 per person allows you to sleep on the terrace. There is a nice atmosphere, more intimate than the Campement or than **Hotel Guri Yam** (tel: 244 20 14), which has five basic rooms (CFA3,000/single and CFA5,000/double) and not much else to offer. The nearby **Hotel Nangabanou** (tel: 244 20 42), also at the entrance to town, is equally basic and somewhat pricey at CFA7,500 for a double. However, the pleasant courtyard, which is used by the family and guests alike, makes this a most welcoming place. Give it a try.

Practical information

One of the conspicuously new concrete boxes in the middle of town is the **post office**; another is **Sotelma**.

Guides are available for hire at Campement Sanga and Femme Dogon. The **Bureau des Guides** (tel: 244 20 32) at Campement Sanga has some of the best guides in the country and is recommended by the Mission Culturelle. You can choose from several suggested itineraries or arrange your own tour. The *chef des guides*, Sékou Dolo, will be happy to discuss option with you. The fee for a guide is CFA10,000 per day; food, accommodation, *taxes touristiques* etc are not included. If that sounds like a lot of wages, good guides generally will accept no less than that. A porter charges between CFA1,500–2,500 per day. Some popular excursions have fixed rates with most expenses (but not drinks) included.

Campement Hotel Sanga has a small permanent **exhibition** of Dogon artefacts and pictures. Most of the material has been offered by the Dutch architect Joop van Stigt, who is a frequent visitor to the hotel which serves as a base for his many activities in Dogon country (see box on pages 50–1 and *Charities and NGOs in Mali* on page 48).

CLIFF VILLAGES

Revised by Jolijn Geels

The villages along the *falaise* between Banani in the northeast near Sanga and Kani Kombolé in the southwest receive the most tourist visitors. Here you will find the picture-postcard Tellem architecture, the ancient burial caves, villages built precariously on the rocks of the cliff face and other quintessentially Dogon attractions. The distance between Banani and Kani Kombolé is about 45km and, of course, it is quite feasible to trek from one to the other, eating and sleeping at village *campements* en route. However, the more popular choice – and the one offered by most guides and tour operators – is to visit either the group of villages in proximity to Banani or those near Kani Kombolé. Though it is not impossible to cover the full stretch on foot in a matter of days, it is far more rewarding to cover smaller distances, allowing time to explore the many points of interest and enjoy a siesta during the hottest midday hours. In fact, slowing down is a first requirement to fully appreciate the Dogon pace of life. To walk the full distance between Djiguibombo and Sanga, allow at least a week to ten days. Walking in this direction means having the sun behind you, which is always preferable.

The descent from the plateau at **Djiguibombo** to Kani Kombolé is about 3km if you walk down the *falaise*, but nearer 5km if you take the paved road – which is now suitable for most types of vehicles all year around. On clear days you can see Bankass in the distance. **Kani Kombolé** is not built on the *falaise* itself, but nestles in a shady corner of the plain. However, the lack of cliff-face architecture is made up for by an attractive mosque, built in the traditional Sudanese style and evidence of the increasing number of Dogon who have converted to Islam. At 4km to the southwest, along the *falaise*, and well worth the return trip, **Kani Bonzon** is the place where the migrating Dogon couples first arrived on the *falaise*. The original settlement is halfway up the cliff, where the remains of a former hogon house mark the place where the first four couples chose to stay (see also box on page 198).

At 4km from Kani Kombolé is **Telí**, a picturesque village with former Tellem dwellings – now sometimes used for food storage or as burial sites – Dogon granaries and a well-preserved abandoned village. As in many other villages, the Dogon formerly lived sheltered in the cliffs for security reasons, as they feared both predators (hyenas and lions) that used to roam the plains, and human aggressors. Some 60 years ago, when the French cavalry no longer posed a threat to the Dogon, people started moving to the site of the present village below the cliff. The last families moved out as recently as 10-15 years ago. The abandoned village has since been restored by the villagers and can be visited on payment of a small fee. The view from up above is well worth the climb. Note the new and strikingly ugly church with its corrugated iron roof, which is used by around ten Christian families in and around Telí. The lovely mud-built mosque is testimony to the predominance of Islam. Add to this the few animist families that reside here, and Telí stands out as an example of one of the many Dogon villages that are religiously highly eclectic and tolerant.

Past **Walia** (2km from Telí) is **Endé** (another 2km), which is similar to Telí but considerably larger. The granaries here are even more impressive, but the remains of the old cliff dwellings have seen better days. It is no longer considered safe to climb up to the highest level of the granaries, but you may be taken to visit the hogon who resides well above the village. The old man is one of the few living hogons, the spiritual leaders of the animists. When you visit the hogon, remember that he is not to be touched by anyone, nor should you touch his seat, which also serves as an altar for sacrifices. Bring some money and kola nuts, and leave those in the calabash or clay pot at his feet.

Endé is divided into four quarters, all of which seem to be thriving on tourism. A museum is currently under construction, and will open before the end of 2004. There are several workshops where woodcarvings are being produced and sold, but *bogolans* or mud cloths are what the quarter just below the cliff is about. Observe the different laborious stages of production, from the spinning and weaving of cotton, to the process of decorating the blankets, before you start haggling over prices.

Though Endé has several good *campements*, the one in Endé Toro merits a mention. Whether just for a drink or for an overnight stay, Campement Alakala is worth a visit. So far nine rooms are ready, all of them traditionally built and representing various examples of Dogon architecture (the house of Amma, a *ginna* etc). The owner will gladly give some explanation, so if this is where your trip ends and you haven't come across any similar buildings yet, this is your chance. The tastefully decorated rooms (CFA3,500) are by far the most comfortable ones along the *falaise*, and all come with a washbasin and private bucket shower. Toilets are outside, but who wants an en suite long drop anyway? On busy evenings the *campement* is generator powered.

On leaving Endé in the direction of Bagourou, you will pass below the *pierre unique d'Endé*, locally known as *Endé Touserelé* – with *tou* meaning 'rock', and Serelé being the name of a girl who lived in the area some 300 years ago. One day, the 12-year-old Serelé scrambled up the rocks towards a huge baobab tree to collect firewood. After having chopped off the branches she felt tired, and so she turned away from the tree to quench her thirst from the waterfilled calabash she carried. Then she took a little sleep in the shade of the tree. Refreshed and rested, she turned back to the baobab, only to find that it had transformed into solid rock. Scared and bewildered she ran down to the village, where she barely managed to explain what had happened. Nobody could calm down the girl, no treatment would ease her anxiety. Serelé died 60 years later, never having regained her sanity.

Bagourou (3km from Endé) lies on the plain, with no counterpart along the cliff. In fact, the cliff opposite Bagourou is reserved as a burial place for all the hogon in Dogon country, as well as for the *femmes sacrées* – the very few elected woman who are allowed to see the sacred masks – some important blacksmiths and *griots* (see *Traditional music*, page 25). The bodies are hoisted up with ropes and placed in niches. Obviously, this part of the cliff is sacred, but so are many other sites and objects around the village. Bagourou houses an important family of blacksmiths, and their workshop can be visited.

Following the track along the base of the *falaise* will take you past **Yabatalou** to **Doundjourou**. With the exception of one Muslim family, this village is entirely animist, but is not entitled to have a hogon. Though it is possible to continue walking – and even driving if you like – along the cliff, the track becomes extremely sandy, which makes the going very tough. It is therefore preferable to scramble up the escarpment, gradually reaching the higher levels of the rocky plateau. As a reward, you will get to enjoy stunning views of the Gondo Plain, and see the other type of Dogon villages, built on top of solid rock.

From Yabatalou a steep track winds its way upwards, eventually leading to beautiful **Indelou**. Much of the traditional architecture here is largely intact, as is the deep belief in animism. When visiting Indelou, it is essential to be accompanied by a local guide who is familiar with what might be going on while you are there. Some guides may actually refuse to go anywhere near the village of Indelou, such is the respect for and fear of the power of the animists in this village. Many sites are sacred and certain walls are not to be touched; when fetishists are at work, they should be left to do whatever they do in silence, and care should be taken where blood and millet stains mark the spots where sacrifices have been made not too long ago. Never walk alone, and do not take pictures unless your guide has given clear permission. However, the woman who makes the traditional *dolo* or millet beer will happily put a smile on her face while you taste her brew and take her picture. Life in Indelou is not all about fear.

A somewhat easier way up the *falaise* starts at Doundjourou and takes you to **Begni Mato** (a further 3km), a village very much geared towards tourism and one of the locations where the *danses des masques* regularly take place for tourists' eyes only. Traditionally, the masks were solely meant for ceremonial purposes, and some of the masks still are. These are kept in a place outside the village, and they are for no one to see. However, CFA40,000 will bring out some equally impressive masks and costumed dancers, accompanied by drums, to give a dazzling performance that will stir the dust.

On your way to **Indeli** you will pass (and smell!) the typically checkered onion plots that are repeatedly watered from calabashes filled from streams, ponds or deep wells. The track is sometimes wedged in between huge boulders, but then it opens up totally to offer expansive views of the Gondo Plain. Note the pink and orange sand dunes at the bottom of the *falaise*. Hidden somewhere down there lies **Guimmini**. Once upon a time, when this village was much smaller and home to only a handful of families, it was located between Endé and Bagourou. These two villages were caught up in a serious and violent conflict over landownership. Guimmini was caught in the middle, receiving many attacks from both sides. The families eventually decided they'd had enough, and they chose to move to their present-day location.

Another hour or so past Indeli is **Dourou** (7km from Begni Mato), which can be reached from Bandiagara by car. Many trips either start or end here for obvious reasons, but Dourou isn't the friendliest of places. It seems noisier than elsewhere in Dogon country, and both children and adults alike can come across as rather aggressive. Having said that, it is one of the best places to buy indigo blankets and watch the women as they prepare and dye the cotton cloth. On market days (once every five days) there is a lot of activity, since this is where most of the onions and other produce from a wide area are marketed.

After Dourou, the track leads down again, to the base of the escarpment and **Nombori** (4km from Dourou). On arriving there, it is hard to miss the museum. Inaugurated in December 2002, this was the first museum to be created as part of a programme by the Mission Culturelle to promote sustainable tourism in Dogon country. Its purpose is not only to cater for passing tourists, but also to encourage the local people to conserve, protect and promote their cultural heritage. The locals were heavily involved in the development of the idea and the construction of the museum, and now they enjoy the benefit of the income generated by the museum. It should be open during the daytime, but if it isn't ask any villager to find the museum warden. The exhibition shows numerous artefacts that have been handed in by the people from Nombori, along with some interesting explanations – currently in French only. This is where to find out about the procedure used in Nombori to install a hogon, which involves a year of preparation before the identity of the new hogon is revealed, followed by a period of initiation and finally the actual installation. Nombori boasts not one, but two hogons. The entrance fee to the museum is CFA500. In Nombori there are different groups of dancers who will perform the *danses des masques* on request. Enquire at one of the *campements* and expect to pay CFA40,000 or more, depending on the number of dancers.

Numerous lush gardens spreading out along a dry river bed lead to **Idyeli Na** (2km further on). According to local legend, the founder of the village discovered a waterfall and pond with a big fish in it. After ten days the fish still refused to be caught, so instead the man found an onion not far from the water.

On the eleventh day he found a tomato, and on the following days more edible greens appeared. Thereafter, the man took to planting and harvesting, thus becoming the first farmer of a community of farmers. Pass a few small hamlets before reaching **Komokani** (after 3km). Before walking around the village, make sure to pay your respects to the village elder. Bring some kola nuts, and expect to pay CFA500 if you want to take pictures of the impressive *togu na*.

Tereli (3km from Komokani) must be one of the most spectacular Dogon villages, with the picture-postcard pointed thatched roofs crawling upwards along the escarpment. Not surprisingly, many tour operators visit Tereli, often driving all the way from Sanga and dropping off clients for a short visit, including a performance of the *danses des masques*. Indeed, the section between Tereli and Sanga probably receives more visitors than anywhere else in Dogon country, but given the beauty of these villages this is understandable. Tereli is known for its pottery, though you are not likely to see the potters at work as most of the work centres around the hottest months of April and May, just before the rainy season. The dried clay pots are then placed and fired in huge pits.

Just before entering **Amani** (3km from Tereli), a small pond on the plain harbours sacred crocodiles (locally known as *caïmans*). A visit to the pond costs CFA500, and for CFA1,000 you are allowed to take pictures. Don't expect to see much activity unless they are just being fed, and don't expect the animals to be of an impressive size. Amani is of great importance to the Dogon, since near Amani is where the sacred masks that are used exclusively for the Sigi festival are kept. As you leave Amani, you will pass the local school, which has been designed, financed and built by the Dutch architect Joop van Stigt and his foundation (see box on page 50 and *Charities and NGOs* on page 48).

Ireli (3km from Amani) looks different in scale than most other villages along the escarpment. The cliff looks higher and steeper, and the old Tellem dwellings are spread over an impressively wide section of the *falaise*. Here it is even harder to imagine how the Tellem managed to find their way up, but many Dogon believe they could fly. Some actually believe the descendants of the Tellem are still alive today, and moreover, that they occasionally return to their ancestral sites for offerings and sacrifices. When they do, it is believed they come 'as the wind does', and nobody ever sees them. Traces of blood and millet on their altars and shrines high up the escarpment, however, are considered visible evidence that the Tellem have once again returned.

Banani (4km beyond Ireli) is made up of four rather distinct quarters, and it has a little bit of everything: Tellem architecture, burial caves, plenty of granaries, *togu nas*, *binous* (see *The Dogon Village*, page 183) and a selection of *campements*. This, combined with its proximity to Sanga, makes Banani a good place to visit if you are short of time and want only a 'taste' of Dogon country. When Banani marks the end of a long trek in Dogon country, though, it will probably strike you as overwhelmingly touristy and commercial. In the busy season, you may see cars winding their way along the narrow road to Sanga. When you are trekking the final 3km stretch to Sanga, follow the steep but stunningly beautiful footpath rather than the road.

ANIMISM ALONG THE FALAISE
Jolijn Geels

With many Dogon converting to Islam and Christianity, animism seems to be on the decline in many villages in Dogon country. Indeed, only a few villages now have a hogon (a spiritual leader of the animists), villagers may seek the spiritual advice of a *marabout* (a Muslim religious leader) rather than consulting a fetishist (a potent animist leader, who performs rituals and sacrifices), and a mud-built mosque may be more prominently present than the traditional places of sacrifice. One could easily believe that in some parts of Dogon country animism is all but dead. Officially, the converted consider animism to be an inferior belief, and even they may claim that animism will gradually lose ground altogether. However, just below the thin crust of Islam and Christianity, animist beliefs lay deeply embedded in the minds and hearts of the Dogon people.

During my visit to Kani Bonzon – the cradle of the Dogon presence along the *falaise* – an old Muslim testified that the big mosque in the new quarter on the Gondo Plain had been there for as long as he could remember, and that to this day the mosque serves as much as 40 villages and hamlets on special Muslim days. Though the whole area looked quiet and serene, during those occasions the mosque must be buzzing with religious activity and prayer.

While smoking his pipe, the old man said that he must have been about eight years old when many villagers abandoned their cliff dwellings to move down to the plain and construct the new quarter around the mosque. By then, most of the people had embraced Islam as their religion, creating the predominantly Muslim environment in which he grew up. Around half a century ago, when the last hogon in Kani Bonzon died, nobody took his place and the house of the hogon was left to crumble to a ruinous state. However, at the same time, while the inhabitants of Kani Bonzon would claim to be purely Muslim, and while the outside world had little reason to refute this claim, legendary places continued to be respectfully treated as

Other villages along the *falaise*

About 12km northeast of Banani and accessible by 4WD along the plain, the Youga group of villages – **Youga Dogorou**, **Youga Piri** and **Youga Na** – are actually built on a small hill opposite the *falaise*. Apart from being where the Sigi is supposed to have originated (see page 181), there is also some well-preserved Tellem architecture at Dogorou and Piri, as well as fine views of the plain – the most panoramic being at Dogorou. Finally, a village further north called **Yenda** is also worth mentioning as the place where, according to legend, the sacred crocodiles in Dogon country go to die.

PLATEAU VILLAGES

In all honesty, the average tourist does not come to Dogon country to visit the villages on the plateau. The hardcore Dogon fanatic, however, will find sacred, and, moreover, many animist traditions were still being practised indoors. As part of the cultural heritage that nobody would question or deny, certain customs were simply continued on a smaller scale, and without much fuss.

It is the generation of the old man's sons and grandsons that started to reflect on the meaning of these traditions within their Dogon culture and the Muslim religion. They openly showed a deep interest in animist practices and even requested the elders to pass on their knowledge before it was lost. And they wondered: would life not be much better with the old beliefs restored? Would it not keep the youngest generation from leaving their home villages and straying from their culture? Would harvests not stop failing when the appropriate sacrifices were made in the traditional way? So, while animism seems to be losing ground, Kani Bonzon is preparing itself for the installation of a new hogon. A new dwelling – not far from the original one in the village halfway up the cliff – has been chosen, the future hogon has already been elected, and his installation will take place in the beginning of 2005. He seemed a respectable and sociable man, who will be giving up his present life amongst the villagers in favor of a rather isolated life serving the restoration of animism. To the people of Kani Bonzon, their choice is considered a matter of progress, rather than going back in time.

Though the story of Kani Bonzon may be an extreme example of how animism lived on in hiding through the generations, it is by no means exceptional. All along the *falaise*, from Kani Bonzon to Banani, I met Dogon – animists, Muslim and Christians alike – who were willing to share some thoughts on sacrifices, magic spells and gris-gris, totem animals, sacred and potent places, genies and taboos. I suppose I was lucky, for I walked the *falaise* with a wonderful – Muslim – guide who lifted the veil of animism in a most respectful way. Once again this stresses the importance of choosing a guide carefully. You may always enjoy the beauty of the Dogon country, but you could still miss out on what lies beneath the surface.

much of interest away from the *falaise*, even if the villages themselves are not quite as photogenic as their cliff-side counterparts. There is another, practical reason why the plateau is not as popular as the *falaise*. The distances between villages tend to be greater and trudging across the plateau is not as interesting as walking along the plain. There are also fewer village *campements* and other places to eat and sleep than there are along the *falaise*. For these reasons, hiring a vehicle might be worth considering – which, of course, is expensive and hardly an incentive to spend a great deal of time exploring the plateau.

Having said this, **Songo**, a village 11km from Bandiagara on – or rather 4km off – the road to Sévaré, is well-established on the tourist circuit. It is famous for its grottoes and rock paintings representing different clans of the region; and, although Songo is now almost entirely Islamic, elaborate circumcision rites are held here every three years. This village, more than any other, is held up as an example of how tourism should be developed in Dogon country. The villagers themselves have taken a real interest in – and have directly benefited from – Songo's popularity with visitors. For example, they have built an excellent *campement* which is not privately owned, but belongs to the whole community, and anyone showing you around Songo must come from the village itself, thereby ensuring that tourist dollars are used for local projects. The *taxe touristique* is triple that of most other villages in Dogon country (CFA1,500), but it is put to good use, such as the installation of solar panels, or maintenance of the school and the sandy track leading to the village. A room at the *campement* costs CFA2,000 (single or double), while the rate for camping on the terrace is CFA1,500 per person.

Most of the other villages of special interest on the plateau lie between Bandiagara and Douentza. The following are just a few examples:

Tabitongo Known for its eclectic religious mix – animism, Islam, Catholicism and Protestantism are all tolerated – and for having one of the most beautiful menstruation houses in Dogon country.

Ningari An Islamic village and one of the largest between Bandiagara and Douentza, where each family owns a snake belonging to a species particular to the region, which represents the original ancestors.

Ondougou The village chief was working as an ebonist in Côte d'Ivoire when his father died and he was obliged to return to Ondougou and take up his hereditary responsibilities. This village is also known for the house built by a woman who had taken the unprecedented action of rejecting her husband and living alone until she died.

Moré Home to a massive grotto – allegedly large enough for the entire population of the village to fit inside.

Dé Made famous during the war between the Tukulor Empire and the French when the nephew of the Tukulor emperor arrived here looking for reinforcements to help his uncle. Relics and manuscripts still remain in the village.

Borko This village is located approximately 50km from Douentza, and around one hour off the tarred road. A guide is needed to find the *piste* leading to Borko. Since the valley is rich in water, the area is surprisingly lush with palm trees and gardens. Borko is well-known for its dozens of sacred crocodiles, with which the villagers seem to happily co-exist. Of course it helps that they are being fed almost daily. The downside of a visit to Borko is that tourists are expected to pay extravagant amounts of money to see these crocodiles being fed morsels of chicken. A friendly atmosphere can turn sour rather quickly when you are not prepared to hand over the proposed figure.

Gourma

Gourma is not one of the country's eight official regions. Strictly speaking, it covers the *cercles* of Gourma-Rharous and parts of Ansongo, Gao and Bourem. However, for the purposes of this guide it is the land south of the Niger Bend (Boucle du Niger) in the centre of Mali – in parts Sahelian, in others mountainous, with lakes, ponds and, at the right time of year, elephants – which is made up of parts of the regions of Mopti, Timbuktu and Gao. Much of Gourma is taken up by the Réserve de Douentza, which is home to herds of elephants for several months of the year. The other main feature of this part of the country is the craggy Hombori mountain range, where the Main de Fatma (Fatma's Hand) is the most famous and challenging of several climbable rock formations. However, elephant-spotters and rock-climbers apart, Gourma is not one of Mali's most visited areas and even its larger and more accessible towns, such as Douentza, Hombori and Gossi, have limited facilities for the visitor.

DOUENTZA

Beyond Mopti, the main highway to Gao continues northeast until it reaches Konna, where it gradually veers eastwards, passing Boré before reaching Douentza. Officially the *chef-lieu* (main town) of one of the four *cercles* of Dogon country, Douentza can also be considered the principal town of the Gourma area. This, however, is not saying much. Douentza is a rather bleak town, with maybe three reasons to detain you for a while. First of all, if you want to see the elephants, it might be worth stopping at Douentza for advice on where best to spot them. Secondly, you might want to pay a visit to the nearby attractive Dogon village of Fombori. Lastly, this is the place where many independent travellers look for transport. Looking at a map it may not be that obvious, but Douentza is actually a kind of crossroads. The upgraded dirt road going north is the most commonly used *piste* towards Timbuktu, while two other unpaved roads lead to less explored parts of Dogon country. Starting a journey towards the *falaise* from Douentza is becoming increasingly popular, but the bad state of the roads will ensure that it is for serious hikers only, and not so much for day-trippers.

Getting there and away

Traffic on the highway to Gao dwindles considerably after Mopti. In Douentza, the best place by far to look for transport is Restaurant Express. This is the

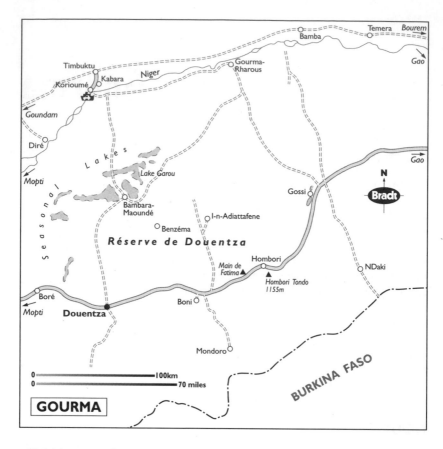

GOURMA

official bus stop for Bani Transport, Binke Transport etc. serving the routes between Bamako/Mopti and Gao. A representative for these companies should be around somewhere. Tickets cost CFA4,000 for Gossi, CFA4,500 for Gao, CFA2,500 for Mopti and Sévaré, and CFA9,000 for Bamako, but bear in mind that buses are often full and places are not guaranteed.

A ticket for public transport – by 4WD – to Timbuktu costs CFA10,000 up to CFA15,000. This is the same fare as when travelling from Mopti, but you will be lucky to find an empty seat for Timbuktu anyway. Hitchhiking, on the other hand, may be cheaper and quicker than public transport.

That is where Dramane – the restaurant owner's son – and his pals come in. They will actively look for a private vehicle that might take you on board, while you are enjoying your meal. Don't expect the ride to be free of charge, and the fee will most likely include some kind of commission. It is well worth it though, because these young men work very efficiently.

To hitch a ride into Dogon country from here would be pot luck. However, *bâchées* for Bamba or Dé and Moré leave when full from the *gare routière* near the market, mostly on Saturdays and Sundays (Sunday being market day in Douentza). Occasionally there are also 4WD vehicles for Dé and Bandiagara.

Where to stay and eat

The most upmarket place to stay is the very decent **Hotel Restaurant la Falaise** (tel: 245 20 95). The rooms are spacious and clean, if rather dark. Rates start from CFA10,000 for a single/double with a fan to CFA15,000 for a self- contained, air-conditioned room. A mattress on the terrace costs CFA3,000 per person. Meals have to be ordered in advance. **Auberge Gourma** (tel: 245 20 54) has basic rooms with *lits Dogon* (wooden or bamboo frames and thin mattresses) at CFA3,500 and CFA4,000 (per person, with or without a fan). Camping is CFA3,000 per person. Meals are filling and quite all right. A very original set up can be found at **Chez Jérôme** (tel: 245 20 50), where accommodation consists of huge airy tents with up to 12 mattresses with mosquito nets. One bed costs CFA5,000, and it is policy to provide guests with as much privacy as possible. If you choose, a small tent will be pitched for you. The *campement* has a friendly bar and restaurant. The only place that is located off the main highway is **Campement Hogon** (tel: 245 20 26). The owner, a jack-of-all-trades, has integrated Dogon elements into the rooms and buildings in ways that are pleasing to the eye. At CFA3,500 per person in a room with a fan, this is a most sympathetic *campement*. The kitchen specialises in local dishes, such as *tô, fouton* (mashed yam) and *sauce arachide* (peanut sauce). At a stone's throw from the Restaurant Express is a brand new **auberge** – with no name yet – with five basic rooms at CFA2,500 per person. Enquire at **Restaurant Express**. This road-side restaurant is designed to cater for travellers who do not want to waste their time waiting for some food to be prepared. Usually you can choose between two meals, both of which are tasty, filling and inexpensive. In the centre of town, **street vendors** sell roasted mutton and several **grocery stores** have sundry items.

Practical information

For many, the most useful address will be that of the **Service de la Conservation de la Nature** (tel: 45 20 29). Run by one of the Mali's pre-eminent elephant experts, Mamadou Baga Samaké, this is the place to come for information about the elephants of Gourma. Samaké will tell you exactly where to find them at any given time, and can also recommend guides. The **Bureau des Guides** at the Auberge Gourma provides guides for Dogon country, Fombori, and quests for elephants. It is possible to rent 4WD vehicles from here, as well as camels for an increasingly popular way to search

for elephants. Guides' fees range from CFA8,000 up to CFA20,000, so clearly there is room for negotiation.

What to see

If you have a few hours to spare, or if a visit to Dogon country is not on your travel agenda, consider a visit to the village of **Fombori**. The location, not far from a rocky cliff, is scenic, the village itself could be described as a characteristic Dogon village, and the villagers are hospitable and friendly. Apart from the *banco* houses, the granaries and the labyrinth-like maze of alleys, there is a small mud-built mosque which you can visit. The **Musée Dogon de Fombori** (entrance fee CFA1,000) is open daily, which in real terms means that someone will open the door for you once the key has been collected. The exhibition is a wonderful hotchpotch of artefacts belonging to local people, who receive some money in return for allowing their items to be displayed. Bring a torch to fully appreciate the museum, since there is a distinct lack of light. The torch will also be useful if you visit the cliff, where a short scramble will lead to **Tellem tombs** with human bones and skulls, and fragments of pottery. It is recommended to take a guide, either from Douentza or from Fombori, though it may be hard to find a villager who speaks good French – not to mention English.

To get to Fombori (4km from Douentza), follow the main highway in the direction of Gao until you cross a bridge. Turn right towards a derelict water tower, and continue on this track, keeping the marshy area to your right. The right turning for Fombori is signposted.

HOMBORI

I met a South African chap at the **Campement Hotel** in Hombori who had spent the past several years constructing wells in Mali. For much of that time he had been in Gourma, so I felt that he was well qualified to give me his opinion of Hombori and the Campement Hotel. 'This place is Las Vegas, man!' he beamed, a bottle of Castle beer in one hand and a scraggy chicken leg in the other. Slot machines and showgirls may not yet have arrived at the Campement Hotel, but, even so, it is a lively place. The CFA4,000 rooms are reasonably clean and the food is well prepared and adapted to Western palates. **Auberge Le Tondanko** (tel: 245 10 02), located behind the Campement Hotel, offers similar accommodation. Meals and chilled drinks are available. The owner, known by the name of Dourcy, can provide information about some good itineraries for rock-climbing and lighter hiking possibilities. Guides can also be arranged by Dourcy. It is possible to rent *charrettes* and bikes at the auberge.

Hombori itself is not an unattractive town – even so, any comparison with Las Vegas can be dismissed as drunken rambling by a South African well-digger. The one – and perhaps the only – thing to do here is climb rocks.

Rock-climbing

Hombori is surrounded on all sides by the Hombori Mountains, the highest range in Mali and a major challenge for serious rock-climbers. Note the word 'serious'. None of the rock formations here is easy to climb, and there is no infrastructure in the area for this type of adventure tourism; in case of emergency, the nearest hospital is 255km away in Gao. Rock-climbers who come to Hombori bring their own equipment and know more or less what they are doing. Beginners beware!

The highest peak in Mali is **Hombori Tondo** (1,155m), the sandstone mesa to the left of the road coming from Gao. This is one of the easier mountains to climb. It takes about four hours to reach the top: two hours walking and two hours climbing. The flat summit covers an area of about 2km and is inhabited by monkeys and other typical forest mammals and birds. There are also remains of old pottery and such like, which should be neither touched nor removed. The most famous rock formation in the Hombori Mountains is *Gami Tondo* or the **Main de Fatma** (Fatma's Hand). Coming from Douentza, the Main de Fatma is the distinctive rock formation looming into view some 10km before you reach Hombori, which, at certain angles, looks like a human hand. Living in the small hamlet next to the rock is a Spaniard, Salvador, who is famous in these parts and well worth consulting before you attempt to climb Fatma – a considerably more challenging proposition than Hombori Tondo.

GOSSI

Gossi is the last town of any note along the main highway before it reaches Gao. Buses cost CFA2,500 for the 156km journey to Gao and stop on the main road – the town itself does not border the highway. Buses to Hombori cost CFA1,000. As at Douentza and Hombori, finding a place on one of these buses is very much a question of luck. If you are travelling to Hombori only, Monday evening and Tuesday morning are your best options. 4WD trucks with merchandise, vendors and passengers then leave Gossi to meet the Tuesday market in Hombori. More 4WD vehicles leave for Gourma Rharous on Wednesday evenings, this time to meet the market on Thursday. In Gossi Sunday is market day, and the options for transport should also work the other way around, since the Gossi market is one of the most important **cattle markets** in the region. Hundreds of camels, cows, goats, sheep, bulls and donkeys are sold to customers who have come from as far afield as Burkina Faso and Niger.

Buses stop at the main road near a cluster of houses and small shops, nearest to the village of Gossi which lies a kilometre off the road. There are two places to stay in Gossi, both of them basic and with only bucket showers to freshen up a bit. Some 200m from the main road, near the signpost for Handicap International, is **Hotel Restaurant Bohanta**, where CFA2,000 per person buys you a mattress on a concrete floor. In the village, the **Campement de Gossi** has six satisfactory – if not luxurious – rooms at CFA2,000 per person. For meals (bring your own drinks – even soft drinks – from Restaurant Bohanta or vendors at the main road) you will be taken to a small restaurant near the market of this typically sandy and windy Sahelian town. A donkey cart will take you and your luggage to the *campement* in town for CFA500–1,000.

Along the way you will pass the **Mare de Gossi** – translated as 'Gossi Pond', but more comparable in size to a lake. It is home to several species of waterbirds and is a popular drinking-spot for the **elephants**, which are probably the main reason for coming to Gossi in the first place. With Gossi being such a small place, you are bound to meet – or at least hear about – **Sister Anne-Marie Saloman** before too long (see *Local charities and NGOs* on page 48). Anne-Marie runs the local **hospital** – many of whose patients are Tuareg nomads – which is on the other side of the Gossi Pond.

THE ELEPHANTS OF GOURMA

Mention of Mali hardly conjures up images of herds of migrating elephants. Yet, for several months of the year, Gourma is home to hundreds of them – apparently the largest elephant species in the world – as they mill around the numerous ponds and waterholes of the **Réserve de Douentza** (Gourma means 'place of the well'). These elephants are something of a contradiction in a country where the wildlife has been hunted so mercilessly. Cohabitation with the human population has been the key to their survival – and, indeed, their popularity. The elephants play an important role in the daily struggle for survival in this harsh Sahelian environment: they trample down

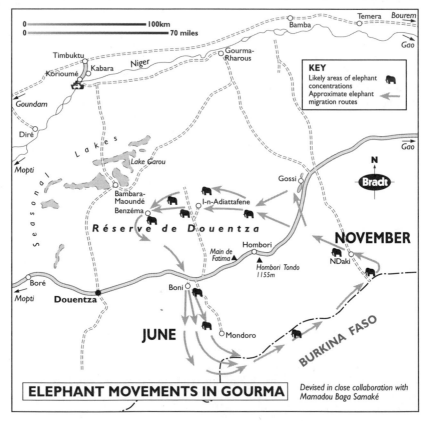

ELEPHANT MOVEMENTS IN GOURMA

Devised in close collaboration with Mamadou Baga Samaké

vegetation, clearing paths for local herders and their cattle, in exchange for which they're spared the hunters' rifles. However, this balance between man and nature is precarious. As bulldozers, the elephants are welcome; but when they start to destroy gardens and eat food intended for human consumption, questions – and rifles – are raised. In short, the future of the elephants of Gourma is uncertain.

Where and when to see them

Like any safari, seeing the elephants is a question of good timing and luck. However, it is not always necessary to travel hundreds of kilometres into the reserve to catch a glimpse of them. Their relatively harmonious relationship with humans means that they are not afraid to install themselves at favourite drinking spots, even if these are quite close to towns and villages.

The elephants of Gourma follow the longest migratory circuit of any elephants in the world. Around November they start to walk north from Burkina Faso to the area south of the Niger Bend in central Mali in search of water. During the dry season, they drink at the ponds and waterholes of the Gourma region – mainly north of the main highway – before returning south towards Burkina after the first rains in June.

Therefore, the best time for travellers to see the elephants is roughly between February and May. During this period, large numbers are often seen around I-n-Adiattafene, Benzéma and other places in the middle of the reserve. However, you might also be able to catch up with the elephants near the main highway not far from towns such as Boni (late May/early June) and Gossi (February/March).

Practical information

Excursions into the Réserve de Douentza require a 4WD, a guide and a couple of days. The cost varies according to the quality of your guide and your own powers of persuasion. Budget on at least CFA50,000 a day for the 4WD vehicle and CFA10,000 for the guide. An increasingly popular way to meet and greet the elephants is by camel. You should at least feel comfortable watching the world from a camels' back, but you don't have to be an experienced rider. Obviously the guides will keep you at a safe distance from the elephants. Rates are around CFA50,000 to CFA125,000 for a guide and camels for one to five clients. Prices obviously drop the nearer the elephants are to your point of departure. In Boni or Gossi, for example, seeing the elephants might be no more than a day or a half-day excursion. Both of these towns are on the main highway and, therefore, accessible by public transport. A good person to speak to about organising excursions, worthwhile guides and the elephants in general is Mamadou Baga Samaké, the director of the Service de la Conservation de la Nature in Douentza (tel: 245 20 29). In Gossi, meanwhile, ask to meet a guide to discuss options and rates. Or better still, give any guide prior notice that you are on your way, so as to give him time to head out and locate the elephants before your arrival. Call one of the *cabines téléphonique* which serve the whole of Gossi (tel: 294 80 00 or 294 80 01) and ask for Aboubacrin Moussa Maïga or one of his fellow guides. Sister Anne-Marie Saloman (see page 206) might also be able to recommend someone to show you where to find the elephants if they are in the vicinity at the time of your visit.

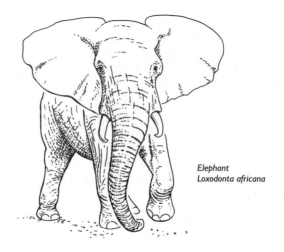

Elephant
Loxodonta africana

Gao

At one time, the region of Gao occupied well over half of the surface area of Mali. Nowadays, three regions – Gao, Kidal and Timbuktu – divide the desert between them, although for the purposes of this chapter, Gao and Kidal will be treated together – indeed, until 1991, Kidal was a *cercle* of Gao. Most of this area of Mali is desert; and even the regional metropolis, Gao, is caught between the banks of the River Niger and a vast blanket of sand. The great droughts of 1970–4 and 1984–5 (see page 16 and 17) exacted a heavy toll in this region, and survival – particularly in undeveloped Kidal – is a constant struggle against the elements. The greenest area is in the south, where the Réserve Partielle de Faune d'Ansongo-Ménaka used to have significant giraffe and ostrich populations before the hunters moved in.

Independent travellers will spend most – if not all – of their time in Gao, which is well linked to the rest of the country by road and river. Most other areas are off the beaten track and require time, patience and stamina to explore. There is also the limited but tangible threat of Tuareg banditry in this part of the country (see page 94). For just these reasons, the best way to explore the Sahara is through a tour operator who is familiar with this region. Organised adventure tourism in the regions of Gao, Kidal and Timbuktu is developing and several tour operators – most of them based in Gao – offer tailor-made excursions to the more interesting and out-of-the-way places such as Kidal and the Adrar des Ifôghas.

GAO TOWN

It does not take long for the visitor to realise that this place was not built with aesthetics in mind: if the architecture is not ugly, it is unspectacular; the layout of the town is slapdash and sprawling; and, apart from the peculiar Tombeau des Askia, antiquity has left Gao only a modest legacy. However, this place can be beautiful and attractive in spite of itself. I particularly like the contrasts: the blinding yellow of the sand under the midday sun and the soothing blue waters of the river, for instance, or the commotion at the port during the day and the dead quiet at night. These qualities alone are not enough to make Gao a highlight of a trip to Mali, but they might persuade you to stop for a while should you be passing through. Not many people, however, are just 'passing through'. Throughout history, Gao has benefited from its strategic location, and what limited prosperity it has today is due to its position as the eastern

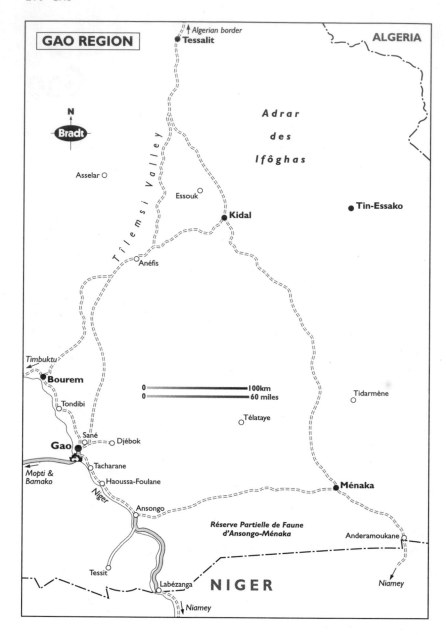

terminus of Mali's main highway and its downstream river traffic. For many travellers, therefore, Gao will be the end of the line.

History

Although it was destined to become the nerve centre of the Songhay Empire (see page 8), Gao was of secondary importance when it was founded by Sorko fishermen around AD650. At this time, Koukia, a settlement to the south between the present-day town of Ansongo and the Niger border, was the Songhay capital. For some reason – perhaps to please the Berber merchants upon whom the Songhay depended for their trade – Dia Kossoï, the 14th king of the ruling Dia dynasty, converted to Islam in 1009, an event which was to prove the making of Gao. The king and his court moved upstream shortly after embracing Islam, and for the next three centuries Gao rivalled Timbuktu and Djenné as the Sudan's commercial and cultural centre *par excellence*. With its excellent strategic location on the banks of the River Niger and the edge of the Sahara, the town was coveted by the Mali Empire and the Tuareg alike – indeed, it was abandoned from 1374 to 1377 while these two forces fought for control of it, until the great dynasties of Sonni and Askia established Songhay dominance in the Western Sudan and Gao became the centre of this empire. Ironically, at this time Gao also started to decline, relinquishing its trading functions to Timbuktu which had been captured by Sonni Ali Ber in 1468. The defeat of the Songhay Empire by the Moroccans in 1591 marked the end of Gao's golden age, the *Arma* of the Moroccan occupation preferring Timbuktu as a base from which to rule.

During its heyday, Gao had a population of nearly 70,000 – double what it is today.

Orientation

The River Niger marks the western boundary of Gao. To the north, south and east, however, there is nothing but desert, and the town has sprawled into it like a large stain on a carpet. In terms of surface area, then, Gao is one of Mali's largest towns – a fact which you will appreciate when looking for accommodation, most of which is found in neighbourhoods some distance from the town centre. In this respect, Gao is Mali's Los Angeles.

The main highway linking Bamako to Gao stops on the eastern bank of the river. A ferry, or *bac*, transports vehicles to the other side where they join Route de Bac, the main road leading into town. Route de Bac runs more or less parallel to the river for several kilometres and ends in Gao's central square, Place de l'Indépendence. This is also where buses from Bamako and Mopti terminate. Another important road runs east from the main square to the airport about 7km away. North of the town centre there is a crossroads called Place des Martyrs: continue straight ahead for Bourem and Timbuktu; turn right for Kidal and the Algerian border.

The town centre is dominated by the port and various markets. Hotel Atlantide, meanwhile, is a large hotel at or near which most of Gao's tourist facilities can be found (post office, banks, guides etc).

Getting there and away
By air
The airport is about 7km east of town. From December to March, **Point Afrique** operates flights between Paris or Marseille and Gao. Enquire at the

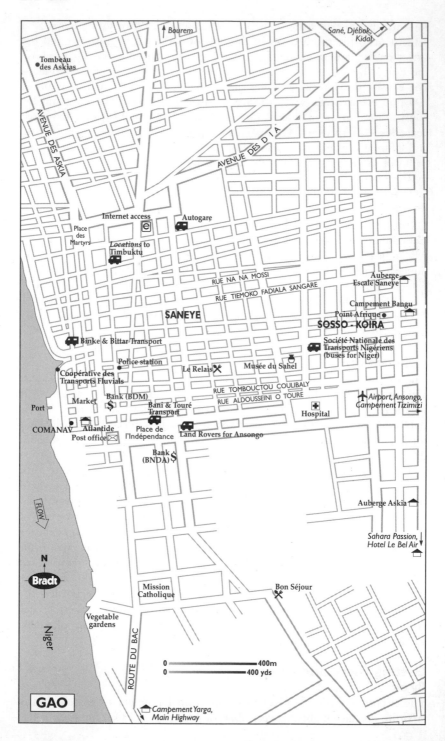

Bourem

Sané, Djébok, Kidal

TOMBEAU des Askias

AVENUE DES ASKIA

AVENUE DES DIA

Internet access

Autogare

Place des Martyrs

Locations to Timbuktu

RUE NA NA MOSSI

RUE TIEMOKO FADIALA SANGARE

Auberge Escale Saneye

Campement Bangu

SANEYE

Point Afrique

SOSSO-KOIRA

Binke & Bittar Transport

Société Nationale des Transports Nigériens (buses for Niger)

Coopérative des Transports Fluvials

Police station

Le Relais

Musée du Sahel

Bank (BDM)

Market

RUE TOMBOUCTOU COULIBALY

RUE ALDOUSSEINI O TOURE

Airport, Ansongo, Campement Tizimizi

Port

Bani & Touré Transport

Hospital

COMANAV

Atlantide

Post office

Place de l'Indépendance

Land Rovers for Ansongo

Bank (BNDA)

Auberge Askia

FLOW

Sahara Passion, Hotel Le Bel Air

N

Bradt

Mission Catholique

Bon Séjour

Niger

Vegetable gardens

ROUTE DU BAC

0 ————— 400m
0 ————— 400 yds

GAO

Campement Yarga, Main Highway

Above Pirogue at sunset, Djenné
Below Pirogues on the River Niger, Mopti

Above Casa palava or *to guna*, where the old men chat all day, Ireli
Right Woman baking bread in a traditional oven, Timbuktu
Below Granary, Sanga, with women carrying millet

Point Afrique/Amawal Voyages office in Gao (tel/fax: 282 02 24) for a flight schedule. Depending on when you travel, fares can be very attractive (see also *Practicalities: Getting there and away* on page 73).

By river

The COMANAV building (tel: 282 04 66) is between Hotel Atlantide and the river. When the steamers are running, two out of three weeks they should arrive in Gao at the end of their voyage downstream on Sunday evening or Monday morning. They return upstream on Monday evening at around 20.00. See *Practicalities: Getting there and away* on page 73 for more information and fares.

At times when the water is too low for the COMANAV boats, you might be able to get to Timbuktu on a *pinasse*. The Coopérative des Transports Fluviale at the port will have all the latest information. Note, however, that the traffic of goods between Gao and Timbuktu is much lighter than between Mopti and Timbuktu, so be prepared to wait some time for a boat. Sailings further downstream to Ansongo, however, are more common. As a rough guide, expect to pay about CFA30,000 to Timbuktu and CFA7,500 to Ansongo. If you have the money, tour operators such as Point Afrique and Sahara Passion operate their own river-trips to Timbuktu. The all-inclusive fare for a four-day trip from Gao to Timbuktu by *pinasse* is from CFA75,000 to around CFA225,000 per person, depending on the number of people travelling.

By road

Gao is about 1,200km from Bamako along the longest stretch of good tar in the country. Bani Transport and Touré Transport both leave from Place de l'Indépendence and charge CFA4,500 for Douentza, CFA6,000 for Sevaré, CFA7,000 for the Carrefour du Djenné, CFA10,000 for Ségou and CFA12,000 for Bamako. Bani Transport has daily departures at 05.00, while Touré leaves for the capital at the same early morning hour on Tuesdays and Fridays. The journey takes approximately 16 hours. There are also buses for Mopti (CFA6,000, 6 hours). Bani Transport has direct buses to Koutiala (CFA9,000) and Sikasso (CFA10,000, 14 hours) on Tuesdays and Fridays at 05.00.

From a bus station near the port, Binke Transport and Bittar Transport also leave for Bamako. Binke leaves daily at 04.00 and 13.00, while Bittar leaves every day but Thursday at 10.00. Note that the last ferry taking vehicles across the river from the outskirts of town to the beginning of the main highway leaves at about 17.00.

Other destinations are only accessible from Gao by 4WD or *camion*. Binke Transport has converted trucks leaving from the same departure point as above for Kidal (CFA8,500) on Tuesdays at 06.00, and returning on Fridays. More transport for Kidal, Tessalit and the Algerian border leaves from the *autogare*. Rather than approach each *camion* individually, ask the Cooperative des Transports Routiers de Gao at the *autogare* for details of who is going where. It is then up to you to fix a price with the driver. *Camions* frequently go to Bourem, 95km north of Gao on the road to Timbuktu, although you can get to Timbuktu directly – most often with Arab merchants on their way to Mauritania. A common departure point is from a building with a large grey door on a road leading off Place des Martyrs. Travel is generally in converted Land Rovers with about 16 places, or 4WD pick ups. The fare depends on the degree of discomfort you have to put up with. On the open back on top of the luggage is cheapest at CFA10,000 to Timbuktu, while the best place is the shared seat in the cabin at CFA15,000. The journey will take at least ten hours, and add another ten hours to continue to Bassikounou in Mauritania (CFA20,000–30,000). The night will be spent camping wherever it suits.

At the eastern end of the Place de l'Indépendance, Land Rovers leave when full for Ansongo, 100km southeast of Gao (CFA2,500, three hours). From Ansongo, you can continue on to Ménaka in the eastern corner of Mali or to Niger, crossing the border at Andéramboukane. Alternatively, you can travel directly from Gao to Niamey, the capital of Niger, going via Ansongo and crossing the border at Labézanga. One company, the Société Nationale des Transports Nigeriens, leaves at 07.00 on Wednesdays for Niamey (CFA8,000) from a quarter called Sosso-Koïra. Other companies leave on Tuesdays, Wednesdays and Fridays for Niger from the *autogare*. Look for *camions* from Erfo-Gaz, Askia Transport and Bahiya Transport.

Where to stay

The only place to stay in the centre of town is the venerable **Hotel Atlantide** (tel: 282 01 30). This old lady has been around since 1932 and must once have oozed colonial charm and elegance. Nowadays, only the shell remains: the rooms have lost their lustre and are overpriced, considering the ramshackle state of furniture and facilities. A shallow promise of planned renovations may or may not materialise. Rooms would then cost CFA10,000 for a single/double with shower and a fan, while an air-conditioned self-contained room will cost up to CFA30,000. Nevertheless, thanks to its excellent location and the limited number of options, Hotel Atlantide should be in business for a few more years to come. Two other hotels have opened in the Chateau Secteur 4 part of town, about 3km from the centre. **Sahara Passion** (tel: 282 01 87) is the guesthouse of the Swiss/Tuareg tour operator of the same name (see *Practicalities: Tour operators in Mali* on page 86). The immaculately clean rooms are quite often full of clients who have also booked tours; otherwise, they cost CFA12,000/15,000 for a single/double with a fan, or up to CFA20,000/22,000 for a self-contained single/double with air conditioning. Camping or a mattress on the terrace costs CFA5,000 per person. **Hotel Le Bel Air** (tel: 282 05 40), also new on the scene, is just down the road. While the Swiss influence is very clear at Sahara Passion, the atmosphere at the Bel Air is much more African: chaotic and friendly. The rooms, all with private showers, start at CFA12,500/15,000 (single/double with a fan) and go up to CFA17,500/22,500 (single/double with air conditioning). They are not as good value, but breakfast is included in the price. Sleeping on the roof is CFA5,000 per person. **Auberge Askia** has spacious, clean rooms at CFA7,500 for a single and CFA10,000 for a double with shared facilities. A place on the terrace is CFA2,500. The friendly **Auberge Escale Saneye** offers beds with mosquito net in the ventilated dormitory or in a *case* – a round hut made of woven mats – at CFA5,500. A mattress on the terrace is CFA2,500. The French-Malian couple who run the place are enthusiasts who organise tailor-made circuits into the desert amongst other trips.

The rest of the accommodation in Gao takes the form of *campings* – cheap and simple rooms which are popular with those who arrive in Gao on the weekly Point Afrique flight from Marseille and with people on various other organised tours. **Camping Bangu** is arguably the most conveniently located, although none of them is close to the town centre. Walk along the road to the airport and turn left at the sign for Hotel Bel Air; Camping Bangu is several blocks down the road. Utilitarian rooms in mud buildings cost CFA3,000 per person – or you can sleep on the roof for CFA1,500. **Camping Yarga** is also a long walk from the centre along Route du Bac. This was the first of all *campements* in Gao, and it has retained an informal kind of hospitality. If you are just passing through and would like to take a shower and freshen up, you can do so here for CFA1,000. Basic *banco* rooms around a shady courtyard are CFA3,000 per person; sleeping on the roof is CFA1,500. **Campement Tizimizi** and its nearby **annexe** (tel: 282 01 94) is far out of town and has rooms ranging from CFA5,000 per person to CFA17,500 for an air-conditioned double. Camping is CFA3,500 per person. There is nothing wrong with **Campement Tila Fanso**, with basic but clean rooms at CFA5,000 per person, but again it is a little too far out of town to be practical.

Where to eat

The quiet garden at **Sahara Passion** is a pleasant place to eat in the evenings, and the restaurant at **Hotel Le Bel Air** is also not bad. The small restaurant at **Camping Bangu** will satisfy undemanding palates, while **Auberge Escale Saneye** serves more refined food and various salads, yoghurts and desserts. On Fridays and Saturdays traditional music is performed in the evenings, at a reasonable cover charge.

In the quarter of Sosso-Koïra, **Le Relais** is primarily a bar but also serves food. **Restaurant de l'Amitié** is next to Musée du Sahel. This is one of the larger restaurants in town, serving international rather than African food. The most exotic menu is probably at the French-run **Restaurant Bon Séjour** next to the water tower, where you can choose from pork sausages, veal escalopes or camel prepared in a Bourguignon sauce, as a paté or filleted. Centrally located near the market is **Restaurant Source du Nord** (tel: 282 03 55) with an ample choice of meals, crispy salads and sometimes fresh fruit juices.

Although Gao is on the edge of the desert and the amount of produce grown locally is limited, the paved highway from the fruit- and vegetable-producing areas of Bamako and Sikasso ensures that the **market** has a good supply of fresh produce – unlike Mali's other main desert town, Timbuktu.

Nightlife

Nightlife in Gao is limited. The aforementioned **Le Relais Bar** plays loud music, while the **Casa Bar**, in a quarter called Saneye, is a local nightclub with three slot machines! **Night-Club Baji**, one block from Le Relais, has a laid-back atmosphere and provocative dancing girls who should be regarded as prostitutes unless you see any evidence to the contrary.

Practical information

The **post office** and one of the two **banks** are just off opposite sides of the Place de l'Indépendance. This BNDA bank changes cash and travellers' cheques. The other bank (BDM) is not far from Hotel l'Atlantide and has a **Western Union** office. The **police**, meanwhile, are a little further down the road. Due to long-standing insecurity in the desert regions in Mali, you should still get your passport stamped by the police as soon as you arrive in town. This is a simple procedure, costs nothing – but you need one photograph – and is intended for your safety. Moreover, passports are sometimes checked when leaving town, and tourists have been sent back because their Gao stamp was missing. There are **internet** facilities not far from the Place des Martyrs.

In 2004, the newly installed Gao representation of **OMATHO** (see page 85) will be relocated to yet another temporary office. See if you can find them behind the lycée in the direction of Restaurant Bon Séjour. Here you can get information about guides and sites around Gao. If you have an interest in history and archaeology, enquire about the **archaeological site** in Gao: in 1325, on his return from Mecca to his Manding Empire, King Kankou Moussa stopped over in Gao and decided to build a mosque and a palace here. The remains of his palace were discovered as recently as December 2003. Excavations may still be in progress. **Guides** in Gao should be members of the Association Askia des Guides Touristiques which is based at Hotel Atlantide (tel: 282 01 30). You can find them milling around the hotel lobby at most times of the day. The best known is a respectable character called Bagna Touré.

For trips into the desert by camel or 4WD, **Sahara Passion** – also represented in Timbuktu – is recommended: a Swiss lady has teamed up with her Tuareg husband to provide desert tours with an emphasis on promoting the local culture and creating jobs. See page 214 for their details. Point Afrique organises many trips through **Amawal Voyages**. Though their main office is in Ménaka, Amawal Voyages are represented in Gao at the Point Afrique office.

What to see

Given the relatively small amount of urban traffic and the endless, sandy streets of this sprawling town, Gao is a good place to see on foot. Indeed, much of your time will be spent wandering about with no fixed destination in mind, because there are only one or two established 'sights' in Gao itself. The most famous is the **Tombeau des Askias** (Tomb of the Askias), which is in the north of town on Avenue des Askia. This strange building might have been inspired by the Egyptian pyramids, as its shape is roughly that of a truncated pyramid, albeit ill-defined and riddled with branches – something resembling a sandcastle, in fact. The mud brick tomb was built in 1495 by the first Askia emperor, Mohamed (see page 8), who is interred inside. Guides will be loitering around outside the tomb – which is surrounded by a wall – and you will have to pay CFA1,000 to be shown around.

The **Musée du Sahel** is three blocks behind the hospital. Despite being small and with descriptions entirely in French, it has some interesting exhibits, particularly about the day-to-day lives of the Tuareg and Songhay people. The museum is closed on Mondays and Saturdays, and open from 08.00 to 12.00 and from 15.00 to 18.00 on other days of the week. Admission costs CFA1,000.

Vegetable gardens are a common feature along the banks of the River Niger as it winds through Mali. Ironically, some of the most lush and fertile are to be found in the desert town of Gao. One of the largest and greenest is opposite the *Mission Catholique* on Route du Bac, where a surprising variety of vegetables, fruits, flowers and other plants grow around ponds and a channel branching off from the river.

Elsewhere, the **port** – the main downstream terminus for river traffic in Mali – is usually quite lively and worth exploring.

Excursions from Gao
La dune rose
From the roof of Hotel Atlantide you can see a huge sand-dune some 60 metres high on the eastern bank of the river, which at sunset glows through several shades of orange and pink before night descends. This is the *dune rose* (pink dune), where, according to legend, sorcerers used to gather to consult their magic and hold conferences. However, it is the peace, tranquillity and great views from the top which make this one of the most worthwhile excursions from Gao.

It is easy enough to arrange a pirogue to take you over to the dune, but try to find other people to share the cost. Bagna Touré at the Association Askia des Guides Touristiques will quote you a fair price. It is also possible to negotiate directly with one of the *piroguiers* in the port, and the owner of Camping Yarga offers very competitive rates also. The dune is best visited at sunset, which means setting off from Gao an hour or so before the sun goes down.

Cattle market at Djébok
For six days of the week, Djébok is a nondescript desert village about 30km east of Gao. On Monday mornings, however, it is a nondescript desert village with one of the most important cattle markets in the region, with plenty of camels and, therefore, plenty of photo opportunities.

Public transport to Djébok departs on Monday mornings from the *autogare* in Gao and costs CFA1,500. Prepare yourself for an early start and a bumpy ride, and be careful not to miss the vehicles returning to Gao after the market – unless you fancy a week in sunny Djébok!

Sané
About 5km along the road to Algeria in the same direction as Djébok, the archaeological site of Sané or ancient Gao is the original location of the

town when it was founded in the 7th century. Arguably the most important findings at the site were several tombstones of Spanish marble with Arabic engravings commemorating some of the first Songhay kings of the Dia dynasty, who migrated to Gao in the early 11th century.

As with many archaeological sites (Djenné-Djeno springs to mind), there is not much to see – let alone recognise – at Sané. There is, however, a reasonable explanation of ancient Gao at the Musée du Sahel (see page 217).

Hippos

Your best chance of seeing some hippos near Gao – and they are quite common along this stretch of the River Niger – is downstream towards Ansongo. The village of **Tacharane** will be your closest vantage point, although the hippos tend to prefer the water around **Haoussa-Foulane**, at a rocky site in the middle of the river which is aptly named *Île des Hippopotames* or Hippo Island.

Pinasses to Ansongo pass both of these towns. This is probably the cheapest way to go hippo-spotting, although it is not ideal if you want to return to Gao on the same day, as *pinasses* will continue downstream all the way to Ansongo (CFA5,000). The alternative, therefore, is to rent a boat for the day. Most guides will charge around CFA60,000 – including lunch – for a trip that will last until early afternoon. However, making arrangements through Camping Yarga may more than halve these rates.

ANSONGO AND THE SOUTHEAST

One of the region's largest towns is Ansongo, 100km downstream of Gao. The *cercle* of the same name is famed for its hippos and at one time was famed for its giraffes and ostriches, which used to cross the stretch of road between Tacharane and Ansongo to drink from the River Niger. Poaching has seen off most of the ostriches, and local experts say that only two giraffes still remain in the area. Your best chances of seeing some wildlife will be within the confines of Mali's second national game reserve, the **Réserve Partielle de Faune d'Ansongo-Ménaka**, which lies between Ansongo, the town of Ménaka and the Niger border. Although you should not count on meeting the pair of giraffes, you might see some antelopes, warthogs, herons and white flamingos. As with the country's other game reserve, the Parc National de la Boucle du Baoulé (see page 272), the appearance of interesting and exotic fauna is the exception rather than the rule. Mali is not, after all, known for its great safari parks. You will need your own 4WD transport and a good guide to explore the Réserve Partielle de Faune d'Ansongo-Ménaka.

Getting to the town of Ansongo, on the other hand, is simple enough by public transport (see *Gao: Getting there and away* on page 211). In fact, most travellers pass through the town – and sometimes stay overnight – on their way to or from Niger, whose border is a further 115km south of Ansongo at Labézanga.

KIDAL AND THE DESERT

The region of Kidal was created in 1991 as a concession to the Tuareg after the end of their rebellion. Unlike the seven other regions of Mali, Kidal enjoys a good deal of autonomy and the mainly Tuareg population exercises a significant amount of local control. After the beginning of the first rebellion in 1962, and before the end of the second, a large contingent of the Malian army was based in Kidal, which was also a popular place to send political prisoners. It was – and still is – the most isolated and inhospitable corner of Mali; a vast expanse of desert in the extreme northeast, where hardly anything grows and hardly anyone goes. It is, however, 'home' for the bulk of the country's Tuareg and Maure populations.

Also, since 1997 the Kidal region hosts **Takoubelt**, a festival celebrating the Tuareg culture. This yearly three-day event takes place in the beginning of January, somewhere in the vast region of Kidal – inadvertently competing for the title of the 'most remote festival in the world'. Unless you join an organised tour or have your own 4WD, finding transport to the location may not be easy. The safest option is to contact the organisation well beforehand, and they will try and find you a seat in any vehicle going to the festival. Travelling to Kidal – or any other town nearest to the chosen location – and hoping to hitch a ride may also work, but may also result in disappointment. You can maximize your chances by travelling to the nearest town days before the festival, since plenty of service vehicles will be going there at some point. Even with your own vehicle, bear in mind that the location will be somewhere deep into the desert and barely – or not at all – signposted. Driving in a convoy is highly recommended. The festival is based on the humbling Tuareg hospitality, and food and shelter can be provided. It is wise, though, to bring some supplies, as on the festival grounds you will not be able to buy much; biscuits, very sweet fizzy drinks and mineral water are available while stocks last (see box on page 220 and also see page 23).

Kidal

The region's largest town is Kidal, which lies about 350km northeast of Gao and has a population of around 2,000. The first impression may be that of a dusty, dormant desert town, but on second sight it is actually a pleasant place to be. People are very friendly and – as Kidal does not receive that many visitors – curious to know who you are. Though the first couple of questions will sound all too familiar, a hidden agenda – to lure you into buying something for instance – is very unlikely. On the contrary: in Kidal you may encounter the heart-warming hospitality of the Tuareg, and this is only the taster of what lies ahead further north, deeper into the desert.

If you are planning to venture out there but still need to organise your trip, an excellent, Kidal-based travel agency is **Affala Voyages Initiatives** (see page 87 for details), which can be contacted through Motel Krutel. It is best to try and contact them before coming to Kidal, but this may prove difficult as telephone lines are hopelessly unreliable. Other agencies include **Azaouad**

Voyages. Even outside the professional circuit you should be able to find all you need for a journey into the desert. However, as you are not going for a Sunday picnic, make sure you are teaming up with the right people: get to know them a little, check that the language barrier does not cause misunderstandings, draw up a contract with all the expenses specified, and talk about the kind of food you will be having – as desert food is usually little else than gritty rice, bread and sometimes meat. If you are travelling independently, consider registering at the **police** station, and do not hesitate to check your prospective guide's credentials, for example at the **OMATHO** or the **Mission Culturelle** (see also page 85). Representations of both these institutions were provisionally set up in 2003, although at the time of writing there were no offices yet. Most local people have never heard of the OMATHO – run by Sidi Mohamed Agaidal – or the Mission Culturelle – temporarily run by Jean Pierre Tita – so you'll have to ask around to find either of these men who are passionate about the Tuareg culture, the archaeological treasures of the Adrar de Ifôghas, and the potential for tourism in the Kidal region.

TAKOUBELT: GATHERING OF TUAREG
Jolijn Geels

Tuareg have been organising gatherings for centuries. These were the occasions where factions of the different families could meet, to catch up with the news, to discuss important matters and to settle disputes. From the 1960s onwards, Tuareg rebellion and droughts impelled these meetings to be discontinued, and it was not until January 1997 that the first Takoubelt (which means 'gathering' in Tamasheq, the Tuareg language) was held again in the region of Kidal. The second Takoubelt took place in 2000, and from then on it has become a yearly event, attracting not only many Tuareg – from as far as away Mauritania and Niger – but also growing numbers of other visitors.

In January 2004 the sixth Takoubelt took place in Essouk, some 60km from Kidal, and for the first time the gathering was officially referred to as a 'festival, dedicated to the Tuareg culture'. It seems to have marked a change in the significance of the event; whereas traditionally the gatherings were a fairly closed event, by choosing the word 'festival' it is obvious that the Tuareg are inviting the public to participate.

The setting of the festival in Essouk was just glorious, with dozens of beautifully decorated traditional tents – to accommodate whoever needed a roof over their head – put up on a sandy ridge in the shape of a crescent. Somewhere in the naturally formed arena were a stage and a tent where discussions took place at set times. It was there – in the open air – that the official opening of the festival took place. What a sight it was, to watch the tribal representatives stride down that sandy slope, all of them immaculately dressed in shiny and starched indigos and whites. Elaborately

In Kidal, you can visit the **fort** and **prison**. This building of historical importance was constructed in 1929 by the French. The prison was in use until 1997, and now there are plans to convert the fort and prison into a museum. The **town gardens** provide a surprisingly green haven in this barren landscape. All kinds of vegetables are cultivated here, and they look their best between November and March. There is also a weekly **camel market**. As for practicalities, Kidal has a **post office** and a BMS **bank** where you can change cash euros and US$. Most of the time, **telephone** lines are down, but theoretically you could make phone calls in one of the *cabines téléphoniques*. Travelling to Kidal by **public transport** is possible by *camion* from Gao (see *Getting there and away* on page 211).

Accommodation is limited to a few comfortable, if not luxurious, places. **Motel Krutel** (tel: 285 00 90) has self-contained rooms with a fan at CFA7,500, while the air-conditioned rooms are CFA15,000. Meals are very good and taste even better when having them on the terrace at the very edge of town; an excellent place for a sundowner! **Hotel Campement Les Dattiers** has rooms starting from CFA5,000 (with a fan and shared facilities)

arranged turbans and piercing, proud looks completed an awesome spectacle.

Throughout the duration of the festival there was much to see of Tuareg culture: almost exclusively Tuareg music and dance; Tuareg poetry; a presentation of camel riders dressed up to the nines; a camel race with camels foaming from their mouths and ridden by young, fearless boys; a beauty contest of Tuareg teenage girls; forum discussions about current issues concerning the Tuareg culture and society; and excursions to nearby historical sites. In between activities there were also periods of quiet and wondering if 'it' was maybe happening out of sight. Quite possibly, as the programme wasn't always too well advertised, but often the invisible programme decreed that factions of Tuareg would hold their meetings somewhere in a tent or in the shade of a thorny tree in the vicinity. It showed that Takoubelt remains to a large degree what it used to be: a gathering of Tuareg.

While Tuareg were the real participants, far outnumbering tourists, this should not imply that the latter were mere spectators. I personally cherish those precious moments where different cultures met and interacted, and not only during forum discussions where ideas were presented and shared on a level that exceeded my expectations. It was those lazy hours in a Tuareg tent, chatting and laughing and discussing life with young Tuareg girls – while they were plaiting their hair and getting ready for the beauty contest – and tourists from different countries that made an impact. Time was a relative notion in that remote desert landscape with young people from another world. Yet it was there that the gap between cultures was naturally bridged.

THE DESERTED MARKETPLACE OF ESSOUK

Jolijn Geels, with thanks to Jean Pierre Tita for his valuable information

One could describe the Adrar de Ifôghas as a desolate landscape of epic beauty. Or as a barren region where any living creature has to struggle for survival. Or maybe as a place where the Tuareg have so little in terms of wordly possessions, while their lives are imbued with a rich history and refined culture. To describe the Adrar as 'one big marketplace' may sound a bit odd at first, but historically that is just what it was. Let us step back in time, to about 100BC. It was still a fairly green environment and there were many – mainly Tuareg – settlements scattered all over the Adrar. The horse had already been introduced to the area, but now a sweeping development took place: the camel first appeared on the scene. It marked the beginning of the prosperous era of the trans-Saharan caravans, trading salt, slaves, gold and ivory. Because water was plentiful and the location was favourable, the Adrar became a crossroads of trading routes and a meeting point for caravans. News and merchandise were exchanged, the local population was thriving, and the Adrar de Ifôghas had become a huge marketplace.

By the 9th century, a particularly popular settlement of at least 3,000 inhabitants was one of those meeting points for caravans. While traders profanely referred to the abundant life that awaited them after the hardships of travelling, chroniclers described it as the most beautiful place of the Adrar. As trading routes were also used for a pilgrimage to Mecca, one day two pilgrims on their way to the holy city reached this town. It exceeded their expectations and they thought it the most beautiful place in Africa! They stayed to rest and stayed some more, and eventually nearly forgot they were actually pilgrims.

'What about Mecca?' asked one of them one day.

'*Tada Mekkat!* (This ís Mecca!)' was the other man's reply. That is how the settlement acquired the legendary name of Tadamakat.

Trade flourished over the next centuries, and at its peak it was not unheard of for one caravan to consist of 12,000 camels. Every morning Tadamakat received at least 200 camels, each of them loaded with four bars of salt from the mines in Taoudenni. Before the sun set, all of that salt was sold. The valuable bars still had a long way to go: to Europe or to the Middle East. It was said that by the end of the day not one grain of salt was left for the *marmite* or cooking pot. Nor was there any water left in all of the 383 wells in Tadamakat. Replenished in the morning, they would be emptied completely by thirsty traders, camel drivers and camels. But the hospitality seemed without limits; the local women – who were said to be the most

up to CFA17,500 (self-contained and air-conditioned). Travellers have recommended both food and accommodation at **Chez Cathérine**, a friendly place run by a French lady. Rooms are CFA7,000.

beautiful women of the Adrar – always went part of the way to meet and welcome the caravans. They provided the weary travellers with water, food and shelter and everything else they could wish for. Really, this was the place to feel at home after an arduous journey! Moreover, it was a place of tremendous religious tolerance, as in two of the three different quarters of the town, Jews, Christians and Muslims alike would happily live together. Just one quarter was reserved for Muslims alone, but still they all co-existed in Essouk, as Tadamakat became known later on.

So what went wrong? Why did Essouk – the Arab word meaning 'market' – perish, almost without a trace? What happened to the 'big marketplace' as a whole? Probably more than one factor contributed to the decline of Essouk and just about all of the other trading places in the Adrar de Ifôghas. One reason must be the shift in importance of the trans-Saharan routes, as traders from Europe established ports along the coast of West-Africa. As a result, slaves were traded and shipped from the coastal towns rather than from the inland Adrar. The region of the Adrar de Ifôghas was faced with more difficulties that affected the towns directly. Natural disaster was creeping in, as the desert advanced and the wells no longer provided enough water for all. Still, while there were profits to be made, greed got the upper hand of many merchants. Sapping the society from within, tolerance became overshaded by fratricide, when even kinsmen stood up against each other. Maybe the towns and settlements in the Adrar de Ifôghas would have stood a chance of survival, had the overall situation of the ruling empires been more favourable. However, by the end of the 14th century, the Mali Empire started to decline as a result of internal power conflicts. The same fate would befall the Songay Empire two centuries later, once again resulting in increased vulnerability and insecurity for the whole region.

Once upon a time the Adrar de Ifôghas was a thriving trading place, with Essouk being the most magnificent town of all. Then it was abandoned, forgotten almost. The remnants have been scavenged for gold, beads and other treasures. Even the rocks and stones with which the ancient town was built were removed and used to build wells and other constructions. In fact, one could now walk past the ruined remains of the three quarters of Essouk barely noticing them, leaving the valley oblivious of all the rock engravings that are testimony to the rich history and the famed eclectical tolerance of the area. Only trained eyes or vivid storytelling can make the site come alive. Then, with some imagination, one can even hear voices and footsteps, the thuds of salt slabs being off-loaded, and the unmistakable growling of camels bickering over water by the well.

The desert

You will need your own 4WD vehicle and someone who knows the territory to explore the rest of the region effectively and safely. Alternatively, one or two tour operators specialise in desert adventures and excursions (see *Practicalities: Tour operators in Mali* on page 70). One possible trip is to the **Adrar des Ifôghas**, an eroded sandstone plateau which forms part of the Hoggar mountain system of the Sahara. Rising to a height of about 500m, the Adrar has a diverse ecosystem which, despite the debilitating effects of drought in the 1970s and 80s, still includes a wide variety of fauna and desert vegetation. There are species of gazelle and antelope, hyenas, jackals and several varieties of snakes and lizards. The vegetation includes acadia trees and cram-cram grass. This is also an area rich in archaeological remains – notably rock paintings depicting men hunting, farming and cattle-rearing. These drawings, along with the fossil of a man discovered to the west of the Adrar at **Asselar**, have been dated back to the Neolithic period (see *Background information: Early times* on page 3) and suggest that the Sahara was once densely populated and relatively rich and fertile. Indeed, the fossilised bed of the river which once irrigated the Sahara, the **Tîlemsi Valley**, stretches along the western flank of the Adrar des Ifôghas. **Essouk**, which hosted the Takoubelt festival in 2004 (see box on page 222), is a site of great prehistorical and historical importance. The hills surrounding the ruined remains of the once prosperous town are scattered with rock engravings, depicting animals and various types of script. One rocky slab shows Hebrew, Roman and Arab script alongside. This is regarded as testimony to the extreme degree of eclectic tolerance between the Jews, Christians and Muslims, all of whom co-existed peacefully in the town of Essouk (see box on page 222).

Elsewhere in the region, travellers en route to Kidal might stop at **Anéfis**, a picturesque village in the first foothills of the Adrar, or **Tessalit**, famous for its ancient salt mines and the border post for the trickle of traffic continuing on to Algeria.

Black-backed jackal (Canis mesomelas)

Timbuktu

As well as being one of the most famous places in the world, Timbuktu is also the name of Mali's sixth region, created in 1977 by clumping together former *cercles* of the Gao region. This effectively makes Timbuktu the country's largest region, stretching from the Niger Bend to the northern frontiers of the Malian Sahara. Virtually all of the human activity takes place in the vicinity of the River Niger, where Timbuktu, Goundam, Diré and Gourma-Rharous are the main towns. The desert hotel at Araouane, 270km north of Timbuktu, is now derclict; and the only other permanent settlement is a further 400km across vast plains, dunes and shifting 'sand seas' known as *ergs*, at the Taoudenni salt mines.

TIMBUKTU TOWN

'...Wide Afric, doth thy Sun
Lighten, thy hills enfold a City as fair
As those which starr'd the night o' the elder World?
Or is the rumour of thy Timbuctoo
A dream as frail as those of ancient Time?'

Alfred Tennyson, *Timbuctoo*, 1829

A year before this poem was published, René Caillié became the first European to visit Timbuktu and live to tell the tale. Previously, this fabled city of gold had been no more than a 'frail dream' in European minds: Mungo Park arrived at the port of Kabara in 1805, but was not allowed up the channel to Timbuktu; and Gordon Laing, the first European to reach the city in 1826, was slaughtered by the Tuareg as he tried to leave. Timbuktu in those days hardly needed a tourist brochure: like a lady playing hard to get, she had men falling over themselves to see her.

In this respect, not much has changed today, and the very name – choose between Timbuktu, Timbuctoo or Tombouctou – still intrigues modern-day travellers. In reality, it may no longer be the most isolated and inaccessible place in the world – nowadays, there is even internet access – but Timbuktu continues to enjoy the *reputation* of being somewhere out of the ordinary. Without this it would be, in René Caillié's words, no more than 'a mass of ill-looking houses, built of earth' – a disappointment, in fact. However, you should not visit

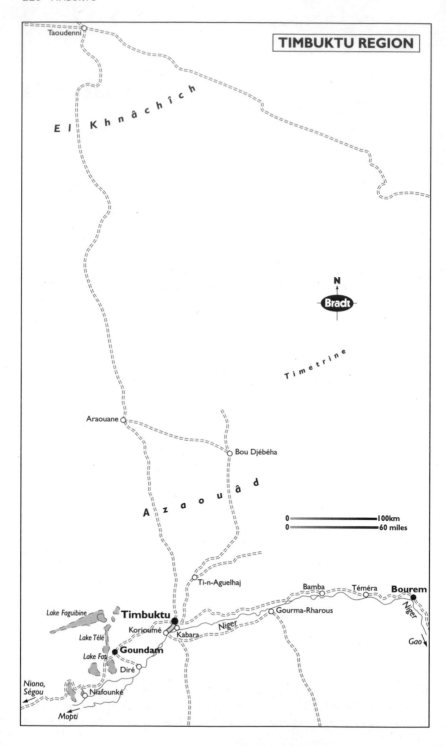

TIMBUKTU REGION

Timbuktu expecting it actually to live up to its reputation. The very fact that you are in a place which was once the nerve centre of trade and learning in the western Sudan, a place men devoted their whole lives to discovering, should be enough to justify a visit.

Three impressive mosques and the houses of explorers, scholars and other VIPs are generally well preserved and protected as World and National Heritage Sites. The other main attraction, of course, is the Sahara. Timbuktu is built in a slight depression or hollow– the Songhay word for which is 'Tombouctou' – and as such the desert surrounds it on all sides. The River Niger, meanwhile, is about 10km to the south.

History

Timbuktu was founded at the beginning of the 12th century by Tuareg nomads, who probably used it as a storage centre for their property and grain whilst they were in the desert. Not much is known of the town's early history, except that it was brought within the Mali Empire around 1275 and was visited by Kankan Moussa on his way back from Mecca in 1325.

At this time, Timbuktu was no more than an oasis for travellers crossing the desert: strategically important, of great potential, but not yet the great trading post it was destined to become. Instead, this role was played by desert towns further west such as Walata and Awdaghust, where gold from the fields of Bambouk and Buré was traded for salt from the mines of Téghaza. However, towards the end of the 14th century gold started to come from the Akan forest east of Bambuk and Buré to satisfy the increasing demand in Europe. Suddenly, Walata and Awdaghust were rather out of the way for traders bringing gold from the Akan forest, and their landlocked positions meant that travel was slow and expensive. Timbuktu, on the other hand, was on the edge of the desert and so accessible to caravans bringing salt from Téghaza, and was also less than 10km from the River Niger, down which gold from the south could be transported quickly and easily via Djenné. But trans-Saharan trade was not restricted to gold and salt; by 1468, when Sonni Ali Ber captured Timbuktu for the Songhay, the market at Timbuktu did a brisk trade in gold, kola nuts, ivory, ostrich feathers and slaves from the south, and salt, copper, tin, cloth and horses from the north.

Timbuktu enjoyed its golden years under the Askia dynasty, which ruled the Songhay Empire from 1493 to 1591. Although Sonni Ali was nominally a Muslim, he cared little for religion, and under his rule many Islamic clerics and scholars fled the town in order to escape persecution. On the other hand, his successor, Mohamed Askia, encouraged the return of the exiles and the development of Timbuktu as a centre of Islamic learning.

In the mid-16th century there were approximately 150 Islamic schools in Timbuktu and students came from as far afield as North Africa and the Middle East, drawn by an academic reputation second to none in the western Sudan. Ahmed Baba was arguably the most famous – and surely the most prolific – of Timbuktu's scholars, producing some 56 works mainly dealing with theological subjects and jurisprudence. Other notable thinkers of the period

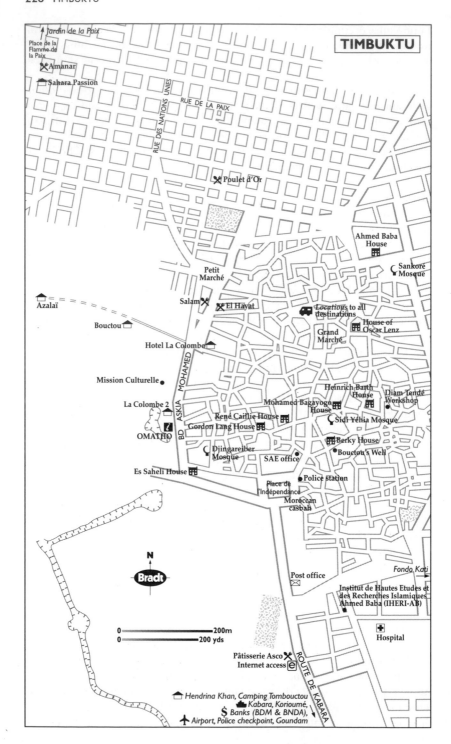

TIMBUKTU

Jardin de la Paix
Place de la Flamme de la Paix
Amanar
Sahara Passion

RUE DE LA PAIX
RUE DES NATIONS UNIES

Poulet d'Or

Ahmed Baba House

Petit Marché

Sankoré Mosque

Azalaï
Salam
El Hayat
Locations to all destinations

Bouctou
House of Oscar Lenz
Grand Marché

Hotel La Colombe

Mission Culturelle

Heinrich Barth House
Diam Tendé Workshop

La Colombe 2
Mohamed Bagayogo House
René Caillie House
Gordon Lang House
Sidi Yéhia Mosque

OMATHO

Berky House
Djingareiber Mosque
SAE office
Bouctou's Well

Es Saheli House
Place de l'Indépendance
Police station

Moroccan casbah

N
Bradt

Fondo Kati

Post office

Institut de Hautes Etudes et des Recherches Islamiques Ahmed Baba (IHERI-AB)

0 ____ 200m
0 ____ 200 yds

Hospital

Pâtisserie Asco
Internet access

ROUTE DE KABARA

Hendrina Khan, Camping Tombouctou
Kabara, Korioumé,
Banks (BDM & BNDA),
Airport, Police checkpoint, Goundam

were Mohamed Kati II, author of the *Tarikh el Fettach*, a chronicle of the western Sudan up to 1599; and Abderrahman Es-Sadi, writer of another important chronicle of the region, the *Tarikh es Sudan*.

Timbuktu slipped into decline when the Moroccans took over in 1591 and established the town as their headquarters. Religious leaders and scholars, including Ahmed Baba, were either arrested or forced into exile, and the town's population – around 25,000 during the Askia period – dwindled due to drought and famine. Under Mali and Songhay rule, the region had prospered through stable and peaceful government; Moroccan control, however, was less effective, and the *pashas* and their descendants, the *Arma*, were unable to protect Timbuktu from Bambara, Peul and Tuareg raids. Eventually, in 1737, the Tuareg had a decisive victory over the *Arma* and became the dominant power in Timbuktu. In 1863 the marauding forces of El Hadj Omar Tall conquered Timbuktu and brought it within the Tukulor Empire, which is where it remained until the French arrived in 1893. The town was in a bad way and the French set about rebuilding some of its depleted infrastructure. However, as with Djenné, Timbuktu had lost its great trading importance and no special effort, such as a railway or a tarmac road linking the town to the south of the country, was expended to restore its past glories. Timbuktu has had its day and, although salt caravans occasionally arrive from the mines at Taoudenni, the town now relies more on tourism than trade to keep the wolves from the door.

Orientation

Timbuktu is, quite literally, on the edge of the desert – walk to the western or northern edges of town, for example, and you can sit on sand dunes with the feeling of being in the middle of nowhere. Although the town itself is not large, getting around can be slow going due to the heat and sandy streets. The old town, where most of your time will probably be spent, is a maze of disjointed streets and alleys, littered with famous places and with the marketplace, or *grand marché*, as its nucleus. The other market, the *petit marché*, is at the northern end of the town's main thoroughfare, Boulevard Askia Mohamed. Many of Timbuktu's tourist facilities (restaurants, post office, banks etc) are on Route de Kabara – the only paved road in town.

Getting there and away
By air

The airport at Timbuktu is no more elaborate than other regional airports, although it seems to function well enough. It is located 4km from the town centre just off Route de Kabara. SAE (tel: 645 39 96) operates two weekly flights from Bamako to Timbuktu, arriving on Tuesdays and Saturdays, and returning to Bamako on Wednesdays and Sundays. SAE does not have a proper office in Timbuktu, but inquiries can be made at Hotel Colombe and at a hardware store (*quincaillerie* Sidi Yéhia), between the Place de l'Indépendance and the Sidi Yéhia mosque (see also *Practicalities; Getting there and away* on page 73).

By river

While flying to Timbuktu is quick and practical, it is also slightly sacrilegious. After all, this place has become synonymous with isolation and inaccessibility and it seems only right to spend days of slow and uncomfortable travel getting here. Getting to Timbuktu by river, therefore, is the romantic – if not always the sensible – option.

Timbuktu itself is a few kilometres from the River Niger. For the big steamers, the main COMANAV office (tel: 292 12 06) is in Kabara. A smaller office is in Korioumé – some 19km from Timbuktu – which is where boats are diverted to when the water level is low and the channel to Kabara is not navigable. However, after 13 years of absence, most COMANAV boats once again dock at Kabara (see *Kabara* on page 240). Here you can buy tickets to go upstream towards Koulikoro (leaving on certain Sundays and Wednesdays) or downstream to Gao (leaving on certain Saturdays). See *Practicalities: Getting there and away* on page 73 for more information and fares.

For travel by *pinasse* and pirogue, see *Mopti: Getting there and away* on page 161; though *pinasses* to Gao sail much less frequently than upstream to Mopti, most of the observations vis à vis journey times and frequency apply. On the other hand, it is a lot easier to arrange a boat in Mopti – where you can deal directly with the owners at the harbour – than it would be in Timbuktu. To negotiate for a river trip directly, you would have to go to Korioumé or Kabara first. The alternative – dealing with boat owners through an intermediary – may prove disappointing: though many guides in Timbuktu are wonderful people, there are also a number of unreliable characters who may well let you down. A form of swindle to be alert for is actually paying for a private *pinasse*, while travelling on a heavily laden public *pinasse*, with your middleman nowhere to be seen.

By road

For those travellers with their own 4WD vehicle, driving to Timbuktu has become much more straightforward than it was before the piste between Douentza and Korioumé was significantly upgraded. Only a few years ago, the piste was sometimes distinct, sometimes rather faint, and all too often consisted of numerous tracks fanning out in all directions, with no signposts telling you which way to go. With little oncoming traffic and only a handful of villages along the way, losing the track altogether posed a serious risk. Those days have gone, however, and even though the surface of the *piste ameliorée* can by no means be described as 'smooth', its outlines are distinguishable from Douentza all the way to Korioumé. At least the present piste seems to be going somewhere, rather than just to be heading out into the desert. For some reason, neither the old nor the new piste appear on the IGN and ITMB maps. The map on page 226 roughly shows the route: heading north from Douentza, skimming the desert town of Bambara-Maoundé, cutting between the seasonal lakes and fording Lac Garou, then turning left where the piste meets the river Niger, towards a causeway and landing place for the ferry. This Korioumé *bac* runs from 06.00 to 18.00 and each crossing costs between

CFA8,000 and CFA16,000, depending on the water level, hence the duration of the crossing. This amount is evenly divided between vehicles, not (foot) passengers.

Travel by road to and from Timbuktu is difficult during the rainy season when much of the Niger Inland Delta is flooded. During the dry season, on the other hand, the section between Douentza and Korioumé now takes only four to five hours. The stretch to Gao can be covered in a day, though most drivers prefer to camp somewhere *en route*. Public transport comes in the form of *locations*: Land Rovers or other 4WD vehicles with space in the back – in theory, at least – for about 16 people. Predicting with any accuracy the volume of traffic and departure times is impossible: it's largely a question of being in the right place at the right time – the right place generally being the marketplace in the middle of the old town, where drivers will hang around waiting for their vehicle to fill up. Land Rovers to Douentza and Mopti cost CFA10,000 and CFA12,500 respectively for a place in the back, while shared front seats cost an extra CFA2,500. Land Rovers to Gourma-Rharous, Bourem and Gao depart less frequently, and cost CFA5,000/6,000 for Gourma and CFA12,500/15,000 for Gao. *Camions* leaving for Gao charge CFA7,500, while those trucks leaving in the opposite direction charge CFA2,000 for a journey to Goundam. From December/January to June, Tikambo Transport offers an interesting weekly option for travellers with stamina: a *camion* to Bamako, via Goundam, Diré, Niafounké, Léré, Niono and Ségou. Departure is scheduled for Mondays around 13.00, and the boldly estimated time of arrival in Bamako is Wednesdays around noon. Note that although the truck stops at regular intervals, it does not halt for a good night's sleep. Be prepared for two rough and bumpy nights on board. The fare is CFA2,500 for Goundam and Diré, CFA12,500 for Niono and CFA15,000 for Bamako.

Hitching a ride with private vehicles or ONG vehicles (ONG is the French version of NGO, or non-governmental organisation) is another feasible option. For Douentza/Mopti, take a *bâchée* from the market to Korioumé (CFA400) and approach drivers while waiting for the ferry. Ignore any mention of fees payable to some sort of association to obtain the right to be looking for transport. For Goundam, stop at the police checkpoint just outside Timbuktu, and police officers will help you to find a vehicle. For Gao, ask around at the marketplace or approach drivers individually .

Where to stay

The most upmarket place, **Hotel Hendrina Khan** (tel: 292 16 81), opened its doors in 2002. All rooms are spotlessly clean and very comfortable, with plenty of amenities, the only drawback being the non-central location of the hotel near the entrance of Timbuktu. However, a courtesy van is available for transfers. Rooms start at CFA19,500 for a single and CFA30,500 for a double. The hotel has a travel agency, as well as an internet service for guests. **Hotel Azalaï** (tel: 292 11 63) on a sandy hillock at the western edge of town was formerly a Sofitel hotel and caters mostly for organised groups. It charges CFA26,000 for a single/double, but standards have slipped and the rooms are

FONDO KATI
Jolijn Geels

During the 15th century, religious intolerance in Spain was the cause of turmoil and violence. People were persecuted and even killed for their convictions, and therefore many preferred to flee the country and live in exile. The Muslim Kati family from Toledo were amongst the fugitives; taking with them the family library, they fled in 1468 to settle eventually in Gumbu in the area of the Niger Bend. Not long after, the Kati family became related to the family of Emperor Askia Mohamed through marriage. This happy conjunction had significant side-effects for the library, as imperial manuscripts trickled into the collection. Through the generations, the collection expanded and eventually consisted of several thousands of manuscripts. Unfortunately, though, after 1648 they got dispersed as the heirs of Mohamed Kati II claimed their share, taking valuable manuscripts with them to their respective places of residence. Some descendants of the Kati family struggled to bring the collection together again, but this proved a difficult task. The final blow was dealt by Peul kings from Macina, as they took the partly rebuilt library into their possession at the beginning of the 19th century, and dispersed it once more.

It took until 1999 before another descendant of the Kati family stepped forward to salvage whatever might be left of the manuscripts. The family, by now very much dispersed along the River Niger, started handing in what they had; sometimes the manuscripts had been cherished and pampered, sometimes they could only be retrieved after a thorough search – as the long-forgotten specimens were stacked in a long-forgotten corner. Only a few years later, over 3,000 manuscripts have been recovered, which is a truly impressive achievement. With funding from different institutions in Andalucía (Spain), a house in Timbuktu has been restored and is dedicated entirely to storing, preserving, cataloguing and studying the manuscripts. Evidently, another objective is to salvage the remainder of the missing

mediocre for the price. Much better and centrally located is **Hotel la Colombe** (tel: 292 14 35) and the nearby annexe which is referred to as **La Colombe 2**, its design and lay-out being a copy of the original establishment. Rooms are comfortable at CFA19,000/23,000 for a single/double. When full – or overbooked in the high season – a villa in the outskirts of town serves as another annexe, with five rather plain rooms with a fan and two communal bathrooms at CFA10,000/12,500 for a single/double. **Hotel Campement Bouctou** (tel: 292 10 12) has a good location, between Hotel Azalaï and Boulevard Askia Mohamed. Rooms here are cheaper and aimed at a broader cross-section of travellers. Consequently, guides and high-pressure Tuareg salesmen choose the Bouctou to sell their wares, keeping a constant vigil outside the hotel. For CFA12,500 (single) and CFA16,000 (double) you get a room with a fan – but not a bathroom – in a very cool and attractive house built manuscripts, and thus to re-unite more of the 7,026 known specimens that were once part of the private library. Sadly, many of them have been destroyed or severely damaged, especially the ones that were written on paper. A truly magnificent and well-preserved specimen, though, is a Koran written on the delicate and hairless skins of unborn lambs. Only a few similar manuscripts exist in the whole world.

Dating from the 12th to the 19th century, the present collection covers a whole array of subjects, including Islam, theology and law, philosophy and logic, medical science and mathematics, and philology and grammar.

Obviously the manuscripts are an invaluable source of information on all these subjects, but perhaps surprisingly a lot of time is spent deciphering and studying the many thousands of notes and comments that have been jotted down in the margins. These notes usually originate from members of the Kati family, and the majority of them can be traced back to Alfa Kati Mohamed and some of his descendants. Many notes have undoubtedly played a crucial role in the forming of the famous chronicle the *Tarikh el Fettach* (see page 229), written by Mohamed Kati II.

Two parallel studies are now taking place in order to understand the full scope and significance of the library: the subject of the manuscript, and the many historical, scientific and (auto)biographical notes. Ismaël Diadié Haïdara – descendant of the Kati family, and founder and director of the Fondo Kati – is dedicating his life to the study, digitalisation and conservation of the library. While the former two are already in progress, conservation is seriously lagging behind due to lack of funds. Though the manuscripts are kept in a secure room and handled as little as possible, many of them are in desperate need of restoration. Visitors to the library and anyone with a heart for the story of this family library are invited to adopt a manuscript and salvage it for future generations.

For more information, check out www.fondo-kati.com, or contact fondokati@yahoo.fr.

in the Timbuktu style. The upstairs shared bathrooms are generally cleaner than the downstairs ones. Self-contained rooms with air conditioning are CFA19,000 (single) and CFA23,000 (double). These rates all include breakfast. You can also pitch your tent in the sandy courtyard for CFA4,500 per person without breakfast. Around the holidays in the high season, when the whole of Timbuktu is probably fully booked, Hotel Campement Bouctou may still have a mattress on the floor in their basic but adequate annexe. The excellent **Sahara Passion** (tel: 942 6947; www.sahara-passion.com) has opened a guesthouse in the northern part of town next to the Place de la Flamme de la Paix. As clean and as friendly as their operation in Gao, singles and doubles start from CFA10,000 and CFA12,000. Camping costs CFA3,000–5,000 per person. Unlike the Bouctou, Sahara Passion has a strict policy of keeping guides and hawkers off the hotel grounds. **Hotel Camping Tombouctou** entrance of town must be considered Timbuktu's budget accommodation. Rates are CFA7,500/10,000/10,500 for a single/double/triple with a fan, or you may opt for the self-contained air-conditioned room at CFA15,000 (single or double). Sleeping on the roof costs CFA2,500/3,500 (with or without mattress). Travellers with scant regard for creature comforts might be attracted by the newly built *banco* rooms and 'African' showers at **Restaurant Poulet d'Or**. It is a welcoming place with no fixed rates.

The odd one out in this listing is actually not located in Timbuktu, but lies at the south side of the River Niger, at 35km from the landing place for the ferry. Coming from Douentza, **Campement Tiboraghene** is the very last settlement – last house, last well – you pass before continuing towards the ferry. The small village is not mentioned on any map, but the *campement* is vaguely signposted. The owner and his family offer basic accommodation in a rural and traditional setting for CFA3,000 per person.

Where to eat

With the exception of the Sahara Passion – where only breakfast is served – all hotels have restaurants or at least the option to order a meal. While **Restaurant Hendrina Khan** has the most sophisticated and expensive menu, most hotels serve good food rather than gastronomic surprises. **Restaurant le Gurey** at Hotel Azalaï is quite expensive but peaceful, while the otherwise pleasant terrace at **Hotel Bouctou** is regularly swarming with guides and salesmen. The terrace at **Hotel la Colombe** on the first floor is certainly attractive, but meals may take a while to be prepared. **Hotel Camping Tombouctou** provides little more than a *plat du jour*, and at the Sahara Passion you will be referred to **Restaurant Amanar** for excellent and inexpensive meals.

The most adventurous food in Timbuktu can be found at **Pâtisserie Asco** (tel: 292 11 68) opposite the post office on Route de Kabara, where traditional Songhay and Tuareg dishes can be prepared for groups of at least four people if you order in advance. The pâtisserie, however, is a disappointment, with only croissants, *pains au chocolat* and meat patties available on a regular basis. Occasionally, the pâtisserie organises *Soirées Gala*, where a CFA5,000 cover charge buys you a soft drink and a set menu accompanied by live traditional music. The owner and chef of **Restaurant Poulet d'Or** used to cater for diplomats in Bamako, but he preferred to return to his hometown to do what he likes best: build his own house to provide hospitality and succulent meals for gourmets. Frankly, the regular menu is quite plain, but talk about food to Dédéou Maïga, and he may propose something out of the ordinary, like an entire sheep from the clay oven in his courtyard, accompanied by various sauces and side dishes.

Three restaurants serve good helpings for little money. **Restaurant du Nord** in the *grand marché* has *riz gras* (fried rice) and *riz sauce* (rice with sauce) available at most times, but for more exotic dishes such as omelette and chips, you must order in advance. **Restaurant Salam**, along the Boulevard Askia Mohamed in the Maison d'Artisanat, is where you join a long table for couscous and rice with meat and sauce. The youngest and most popular kid on the block is **Restaurant El Hayat** opposite Restaurant Salam. El Hayat tends to fill up rather quickly, so despite the fact that the service is highly efficient you may have to wait before finding a seat. The restaurant has a limited choice of pastries, too.

Practical information

The **post office** and three **banks** (BDM, BNDA and BHM) are on Route de Kabara. BDM – with a **Western Union** office – does Visa cash advances and changes travellers' cheques in euros and US$, but not cash. BNDA changes euros, US$ and American Express travellers' cheques only. BHM does not deal with foreign currency.

Télécentre Communautaire Polyvalent – or TCP for short – next to Pâtisserie Asco theoretically provides **internet** access. Open seven days a week until 20.00, they charge CFA2,000/hour. Unless you are passing by anyway, it is recommended to call them first (tel: 292 13 86) and accept that though telephones may work, this doesn't necessarily mean that an internet connection can be established.

If you are heading out to the desert, you are advised to register and get your passport stamped at the **police station** at the Place de l'Indépendance. Given the history of dubious security in the desert regions, this is still considered a logical – but not compulsory – safety procedure. Bring one photograph; it shouldn't take very long and it is free of charge. Many tourists like to have a stamp in their passport just to prove that they have been to Timbuktu – indeed, such a stamp is the rather bizarre entry requirement of a club in New York! If the stamp is what you are after, the new **OMATHO** office (tel: 292 20 86, see also page 85) which doubles as a **tourist office** (*Direction Régionale du Tourism*) issues a stamp at no cost in a minute. Other than a few outdated leaflets, there is little information to be found here, though that may improve over time. The better place to contact is the **Mission Culturelle** (tel: 292 10 77), which is responsible for protecting, preserving and promoting Timbuktu's cultural attractions. Any information about Timbuktu and its environs can be gleaned from the knowledgable, English-speaking director, Ali Ould Sidy.

What to see

In 1992 the old town of Timbuktu, with its mosques, houses of famous explorers and scholars, ancient university and other places of historical interest, was declared a National Heritage Site. You should consult the map on page 228 to help you locate the sights, all of which can be seen quite easily in a day. Next to the Djingareiber Mosque there is a sign, erected by the Mission Culturelle, with an overview of the main places of interest in the old town.

Mosques

There are three mosques classified as World Heritage Sites, only one of which is open to the public. The **Djingareiber Mosque** is the oldest, arguably the most interesting and probably the landmark most closely associated with Timbuktu. Built in 1325 by an Andalucian architect and poet, Es Saheli, on the orders of Kankan Moussa, who had just returned from his pilgrimage to Mecca full of religious zeal, the Djingareiber Mosque is shaped like a pyramid at its base and has conical towers. There is a platform at the top with good views of the city and upon which René Caillié apparently made some of his notes. It costs CFA2,500 to visit the mosque.

The other two mosques were built some time during the 15th century and are not open to tourists. The **Sankoré Mosque** is small and simple, which adds some credence to the story that it was built by a Berber woman to resemble the *Ka'bah* or the house of God at Mecca. During the 15th and 16th centuries, Timbuktu's famous **University of Sankoré** was also based here. The **Sidi Yéhia Mosque**, meanwhile, is the least attractive of the three, although there is wrought-iron door which is as good an example of this feature of the town's architecture as you'll find.

Houses of explorers, scholars etc

In 1512 a fire destroyed much of Timbuktu. Its subsequent reconstruction followed Arab and North African traditions, with rectilinear, flat-roofed houses, often two or more stories in height and built of sun-dried mud, becoming the dominant form of architecture.

A plaque, courtesy of the Mission Culturelle, identifies the house of virtually every famous person who ever spent time in Timbuktu. Many of these houses were used by explorers: Gordon Laing, René Caillié, Heinrich Barth, Oscar Lenz and Berky. The adventures of the first three of these men have been well documented and are elaborated on in *Discovering Mali* on pages 10–11. Oscar Lenz was an Austrian explorer who followed Heinrich Barth (in July 1880) as the next European to visit Timbuktu (his plaque is mounted on the house opposite his original dwelling which now no longer exists); and Berky was the first American to reach the city, which he did in 1913. Most of these houses are now the homes of local inhabitants and should be respected as such – in other words, do not treat them as museums. The one exception is Heinrich Barth's house, which does, in fact, have a small museum with captions in English, French and German. It is run by the lady who now lives in the house and admission costs CFA1,000.

The former dwellings of several other Timbuktu notables are dotted around the old town. There is that of Ahmed Baba, for example, perhaps the city's most famous scholar; Mohamed Bagayogo, a former *iman* and professor at the University of Sankoré; the architect of the Djingareiber Mosque, Es Saheli, and other important figures during Timbuktu's cultural heyday.

Other sights in the old town

The quarter of Badjinde is in the heart of the old town. All that remains today of its glorious past as Timbuktu's bustling trading centre is the ***grand marché***, which was rebuilt in Sudanese style in 2003, and where there is a brisk trade in rotting tomatoes, sour oranges and lumps of salt – for lack of anything more appealing.

The workshop of **Diam Tendé**, whose craftsmen are reputed to be descendants of Es Saheli's companions, still produces traditional doors, windows and other furniture – the door of the restaurant at the Kanaga Hotel in Mopti, for example, is one of theirs. The workshop opens on to the road, so you can usually see the carpenters and other craftsmen at work.

The origins of the name Tombouctou (French spelling) are a contentious issue. However, most go along with the scholar Es-Sadi, who claims in his *Tarikh es Sudan* (1655) that the town owes its name to a distortion of the Targui (Tuareg) word 'tin' and 'Bouctou'. According to legend, a women called Bouctou watched over the Tuareg well or *tin* while the nomads were in the desert. Timbuktu, therefore, means **Bouctou's Well**, the original site of which is supposed to be in the old town.

The statue in the middle of Place de l'Indépendance is of **Al-Farouk**, a legendary figure dressed all in white and mounted on a pure white horse who, according to tradition, was sentenced to 700 years' imprisonment in the waters of the River Bani at Djenné, having been found guilty of misconduct towards the Ulémas of Sankoré.

Nearby, the **Moroccan Casbah** is where Djouder, the leader of the Moroccan expedition which conquered the Songhay, established himself when he arrived in Timbuktu in May 1591. He evicted the local population – primarily merchants from Ghadames in modern-day Libya – and built a fortress in what had previously been considered the smartest part of the city.

Just south of the Moroccan Casbah, is the **Institut de Hautes Études et des Recherches Islamique Ahmed Baba** (or **IHERI-AB**), formerly known as the Centre de Documentation et de Recherches Historiques Ahmed Baba (or CEDRAB). The CEDRAB was inaugurated in 1973 to systematically collect, conserve and exploit the 20,000–30,000 rare and precious manuscripts which are estimated to be at large in northern Mali. These goals still prevail, but since July 2000 – under the new umbrella of the IHERI-AB – the structure of the institute has changed. Not only will the manuscripts be read and listed, they will increasingly be made available for studies in the field of Islamology, history, anthroposociology, Arab-African literature and medicine. The institute already receives many PhD students from abroad. In addition to all this, the extremely laborious process of rescuing and restoring the manuscripts – well over 20,000 by now, the oldest one being from AD1204 – is finally in progress.

The main reason for a tourist to visit the IHERI-AB is to see some of the manuscripts on display and to admire the minute work and the prudent handling of manuscripts in the *atelier de restauration*. Admission costs CFA1,000 and guides are available. If your interest is more than average, make an appointment to see one of the many experts in the field.

Not far from the IHERI-AB are a few private libraries, such as **Fondo Kati** (tel: 292 13 95), open to the public since September 2003. The family are passionate about their collection and will show you the library and an interesting exhibition of facsimiles. For more information, see the box on pages 232–3.

FESTIVAL IN THE DESERT 2004
Jolijn Geels

After three hours of piste, thick sand and shrubs, the festival site comes as a pleasant surprise, if only because it must be the first *cramcram*-free area since Timbuktu (*cram-cram* being the grass with the sharp, barbed seeds that penetrate trousers and socks, even skin). Striking is the moment when the trees of the oasis Essakane open up to an epic vista of pristine white sand dunes. Beyond is a ridge facing the stage, a natural boundary, as the colour of the sand shifts to a soft orangey shade. Then, as far as the eye can see, rolling dunes with no vegetation, no shade and no footprints. It seems the real desert begins here. Turning back to the festival grounds, there is much colour and movement to be seen between the leatherbound and canvas Tuareg tents, areas for meetings and conferences, the souvenir market, and the restaurants and bars. Tuareg dressed in indigo walk back and forth – some of their kinsmen are just arriving by camel. 4WDs with racing engines plough through the sand, while clusters of newly arrived tourists look a bit lost as they try to take it all in at once.

The first Festival in the Desert took place in January 2001. Though the concept as a whole was new to the region, it was clearly based on the traditional Tuareg gatherings – such as *Takoubelt* in the Kidal region and *Temakannit* in the Timbuktu region. The first of these festivals were a rambling open-air celebration of Tuareg culture, music and dance, as well as a stage for other Malian and international perfomances; a meeting place for Tuareg and visitors from all over the world. By 2004, the three-day event had a fixed location at Essakane, some 65km from Timbuktu in the vicinity of Lac Faguibine, with permanent constructions such as ablution blocks, two stages with all the hi-fi and lighting that a rock 'n' roll band

The Flame of Peace

Few places in the world have as much symbolic value as Timbuktu. It was appropriate, therefore, that the symbolic ceremony marking the end of the Tuareg rebellion (see page 17) took place here on March 27 1996. On this day in an open square in the northern quarter of Abaradjou, 10,000 people watched as 3,000 weapons belonging to the Tuareg rebels and Malian Army were burnt in what was dubbed the *'Flamme de la Paix'* (Flame of Peace). Before these weapons were set alight, a certificate was handed to the former Malian president Alpha Oumar Konaré by a representative of the United Nations confirming: 'We have of course checked, Mr President, before laying them on the bonfire, that none of these weapons contain any ammunition and that they can be burned without danger, to make a true "Flame of Peace".' A **monument** commemorating the event has since been constructed in the middle of the Place de la Flamme de la Paix. Its already crumbling marble-tiled arches look rather disproportionate, but on closer inspection the metal, could wish for, some restaurants and bars – serving anything from Nescafé to *pastis* and whisky – and several thousand festivalgoers. Only four years after its inauguration, the Festival in the Desert is suffering from growing pains; it has adopted adult proportions in a very short time. That must be why in the days that followed the 2004 festival there were moments when logistics failed, when it could be sensed that the organisation had maybe solved last year's irregularities, but had not foreseen the new ones.

All in all, it was of minor importance, as magic reigned from the moment the spectators gathered around the stage for the opening ceremony. Tourists sat down on the ridge between groups of Tuareg, while Muslims knelt in the sand for prayer, the colours of their *boubous* (the long, wide cotton robes worn by Tuareg) lighting up in the skimming light of a setting sun. Then dozens of Tuareg on camelback appeared on the scene to keep the public entertained as they were waiting for the Minister of Culture; the festival had begun even before the first opening speech.

These were some of the artists featuring at the 2004 Festival in the Desert:

- The Tuareg ensembles – with mesmerising music, chanting and dancing – like Tinariwen, Tamnana, Awza, Super Onze and Tartit, and many others from Mali, Niger, Mauritania and Morocco, amongst others
- Malian bands and musicians including Habib Koité, Ali Farka Touré, Amadou and Mariam Bagayogo

Activities included camel races, forum discussions, a fashion show with the trendiest *boubous* for men and women, poetry, and arts and crafts displays and demonstrations.

skeleton-like remains of the burnt weapons – imbedded in cement – do leave an impression. As a whole, the monument is much appreciated by the inhabitants of Timbuktu, for both its appearance and significance.

About 400m behind the Place de la Flamíne de la Paix, the **Jardin de la Paix** (Garden of Peace) contains young trees planted by some of the major players in the rebellion and its resolution, including the former president Konaré himself and the United Nations' Resident Representative in Mali, Tore Rose.

Excursions from Timbuktu
Tuareg camps and the surrounding desert
Sand-dunes surround Timbuktu and it never takes very long to walk out to them. The best time for this is at sunset when it is cooler and the desert is at its most beautiful. Apart from the odd camel returning to a Tuareg camp, any wildlife is normally restricted to desert beetles scurrying across the dunes. It is

a good idea to bring a torch with you for the walk back to Timbuktu after the sun has gone down.

Many of the salesman milling around Hotel Bouctou will be trying to sell you camel rides into the desert and visits to Tuareg camps. On the face of it, the idea is romantic, attractive and, when you look out over the dunes from the hotel's terrace as the sun is setting, almost irresistible – which is why the sales pitch is often at its most frantic during the sunset hours! You can choose between trips lasting a few hours or the whole day and night. The former usually involves stopping at a nomad camp for the obligatory cup of tea, while the latter includes dinner, traditional music, staged sword fights and night-time rides in the desert. Prices range from CFA7,000 to CFA30,000, depending on the length of the trip and the number in the party. Although many enjoy this type of excursion, you should realise that they are designed for tourists and not for those who want to visit the Tuareg in their true element. However, it can be a good way of seeing something of the desert, and riding a camel is always an experience!

For those with more time, stamina and a sense for adventure, it is also possible to organise an expedition by camel or 4WD to more remote desert destinations such as Lac Faguibine, Araouane and the Taoudenni salt mines (see *Elsewhere in the region* below). Before making all the necessary preparations, you first of all need an experienced and reliable guide. In this respect, a word of warning is called for, since there have been reports of guides who seemed all too genuine at first, but who have vanished into thin air after a hefty down payment had been made. Do not hesitate to check the identity and credentials of your prospective guide. One place to do this would be at the Mission Culturelle. Since a lot of money may be involved, it is also advisable to draw up a contract, with a clear specification of all the expenses included.

One agency that specialises in camel expeditions only, is Le Mehari or **Mehari Voyages** (tel: 292 11 68), next to Pâtisserie Asco. They offer various *circuits*, lasting from five days (*Circuit des Lacs*, CFA120,000-420,000 for one to four persons, all but mineral water included) to 30 days (*Circuit du Sel*, starting from €1,000 for one person). It could also be worth enquiring at the **Sahara Passion**, which runs a travel agency as well. Alternatively, contact the **Tuareg cameldrivers** from around Timbuktu who have formed an association. They are reliable, charge fair rates and can arrange day trips or long expeditions. Never straying far from Hotel Bouctou, they could be resting in the shade somewhere, having their tea. A respectable and omnipresent guide called Sana Sibily can introduce you to them.

Kabara

Kabara used to be a lively port and the docking place for most freight and passenger boats, including the COMANAV steamers. Then natural disaster struck, and the canal – linking the river port of Korioumé (9km upstream) to Kabara – was blocked with sand. Kabara became a deserted town; in fact, for years it was not far from being a ghost town. The town's new lifeline became land rather than river and the population survived on rice cultivated on the surrounding plains. Then finally action was taken: the canal was dug out and deepened. Imagine the joy of the inhabitants when on October 1 2002, after an absence of 13 years, the first COMANAV boat reached the port of Kabara! Nowadays life has been pretty much rehabilitated, with most of the activities in town centred around the port. *Bâchées* to Kabara leave occasionally from the marketplace in Timbuktu; or squeeze in a *bâchée* for Korioumé and walk the last kilometre after the junction. It is also feasible to walk the 10km during the cooler parts of the day.

ELSEWHERE IN THE REGION
Goundam
Goundam was a thriving town during the period of Songhay domination and many of the salt caravans from the mines further north terminated here – as well as at Timbuktu. The town fell to the Moroccan invaders in 1591, and periods of Peul and Tuareg rule were to follow before the French arrived in 1894. Nowadays, the *cercle* of Goundam – which stretches across the desert to the Mauritanian border – is populated mainly by Tuareg and Maure nomads, some of whom have settled along the shores of the largest lake in West Africa, **Lake Faguibine**, which lies north of the town. At a stone's throw from Lake Faguibine is **Essakane**, the oasis which is the location of the **Festival in the Desert** (see box on pages 238–9 and also see page 90). There are various options to get to Essakane. Joining an organised tour – by camel or 4WD – is obviously easiest but comes at a price. Book well in advance, since the demand is very high. If you have your own 4WD you can join up with service vehicles towards the beginning of the festival, or join the convoy leaving from Timbuktu the first morning of the festival. The convoy is hard to miss, as dozens of cars will be circulating in Timbuktu before heading for the meeting point. Do note that the piste involves a lot of soft sand. When you are travelling independently, finding transport in Timbuktu should be no problem, providing you do not wait until the very last moment. Prices vary considerably and range between CFA5,000 (for some squeezed space in an old and worn out 4WD vehicle) and CFA30,000 (which does not automatically guarantee air conditioning) for one way only. Getting away from Essakane involves a lot of asking around in time or reporting at the water point – where most vehicles will pass sooner or later – before 06.00 in the morning after the festival. Do not worry; you will not be left out there, but prices will go up while the quality of vehicles may plummet, and you may even have to wait for the second round of service vehicles.

Goundam is just under 100km southwest of Timbuktu and is not an unattractive town. It's built on a slight elevation, with more hills about 10km north and two lakes, **Lake Télé** and **Lake Fati**, nearby. Add to this a French-run *campement* (which has a fridge), and Goundam might be worth a visit. Roadworks to upgrade the *piste* linking the town to **Niafounké** (see also page 172) and to the nearest river port at **Diré** had just started at the time of writing the second edition. By the end of 2005, this region should be significantly more accessible, and this may well have a positive effect on the limited existing amenities.

Like Diré, **Gourma-Rharous** is important as the centre of its *cercle*, but has little to detain the tourist for too long. Those travelling to Gourma-Rharous are usually just in transit between the *Réserve de Douentza* or Gossi and Timbuktu. Gourma-Rharous has its own ferry to cross to the northern shore of the Niger, but it is not functional throughout the year. Alternatively, there is a *piste* – heading west from Gourma-Rharous towards the ferry at Korioumé – which is always in a bad condition but even more so during the rainy season. Consequently, it depends on the season and the water level of the Niger whether you should follow the northern or the southern bank. Public transport in this region is erratic, but it does exist (see *Gossi* on page 205 and *Getting there and away: By road* on page 230).

Araouane

The Sahara dominates the remainder of the region of Timbuktu. Apart from the occasional Tuareg camp, there are three permanent settlements in the northern desert region of Mali: Araouane, Boû Djébéha and Taoudenni. There is a vivid description of Taoudenni in Richard Trench's *Forbidden Sands: A Search in the Sahara* (see *Appendix 2*), a book which inspired Ernst Aebi to visit the area and discover Araouane, 270km north of Timbuktu.

When Aebi, a loft-renovator from New York, first passed through Araouane, he discovered a settlement of 125 people living on locusts and waiting for rains which never came: 'Hell on earth', was his immediate reaction. When he returned to Araouane in 1988 – for the loft-renovator had decided to 'save' the town – he brought with him a truck-full of tomatoes, beets, figs and anything else which might stand a chance of growing in the desert. He spent the next three years transforming Araouane into a true oasis in the middle of the desert, with vegetable gardens and even a hotel to accommodate the tourists who had heard about Aebi's social experiment and wanted to see its results. Araouane's good fortune, however, was short-lived. Aebi left to write up his book, *Seasons in the Sand* (see *Appendix 2*), and the town was overrun and destroyed during the Tuareg rebellion.

Today, the gardens have disappeared and locusts are back on the menu. Tourists occasionally visit Araouane on organised excursions and camp in the derelict hotel, though rumour has is that the hotel will be restored to some habitable state. Local people will provide a roof over the heads of smaller parties. By 4WD, it takes at least six hours from Timbuktu to get to Araouane – by camel, about seven days.

Taoudenni

The further north you go, the more dramatic the scenery becomes. Only sand dunes and *ergs*, or shifting 'seas' of sand, disturb the awesome flatness of vast plains such as the Tanezrouft, which spreads across northern Mali and continues into Algeria. In this setting, Taoudenni, some 700km north of Timbuktu, is the remotest human settlement in Mali.

Taoudenni was discovered in the 16th century by the Moroccans as a replacement for the salt fields further north at Téghaza. Salt is still mined at Taoudenni today in large, tombstone-shaped slabs, although the huge caravans or *Azalaïs*, which in their heyday comprised as many as 400 camels and took one month to carry salt to Timbuktu, are now rarely seen. According to Trench (see *Appendix 2*), Taoudenni's 1970s' workforce consisted mainly of political prisoners, common criminals, debtors and other people who were not there by choice. Nowadays miners are paid for their work.

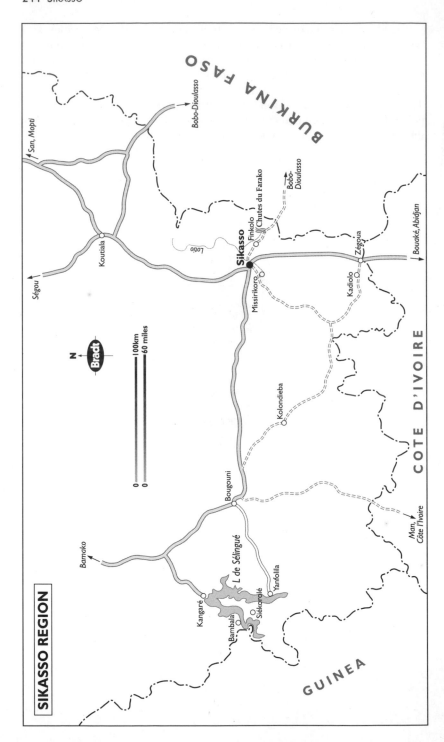

SIKASSO REGION

Sikasso 13

The southern region of Sikasso is Mali's 'bread basket'. Nowhere in the country is greener and, while there is no great river to irrigate the land, the higher rainfall and humidity brought about by a rather more tropical than Sahelian latitude means that the land is rich and fertile. Cotton is a major crop in the *cercle* of Koutiala; tea in Sikasso; and *fonio*, millet and corn grow in abundance almost everywhere else. The region is also something of a 'melting-pot'.

The Sénufo are the indigenous ethnic majority, although Bambara, Peul, Bobo, Minianka, Dioula and Wassalunké groups are also present. However, for all its richness – both agricultural and ethnic – Sikasso is not overrun with tourists and is seldom treated as more than an area of transit between Côte d'Ivoire, Burkina Faso and the better-known regions of Mali.

HISTORY
The Kénédougou kingdom

Just as the Bambara kingdom dominates the history books of Ségou, the Kénédougou kingdom is at the heart of Sikasso's history.

Founded by the Dioula people in the 17th century, Kénédougou began life as a small, disparate kingdom, only developing into an organised state in the mid-18th century under the leadership of the Traoré dynasty. Massa Daoula Traoré (1840–77) is generally credited with being the first of the Kénédougou kings to expand the kingdom, defeating, amongst others, the Ouattara of Kong (in northern Côte d'Ivoire) and Bobo-Dioulasso. However, his successor, Tieba Traoré (1877–93), was the greatest, presiding over the kingdom while it was at its apogee. Under Tieba, the Senufo – the ethnic majority – conquered the Minianka and famously defended the town of Sikasso for 15 months when it was attacked by the forces of Samory Touré (see page 246) in 1887. However, in order to repel Samory's forces, Tieba was obliged to seek French military assistance. The price was a treaty, signed in 1890, which effectively made Kénédougou a French protectorate. Tieba's successor, Babemba Traoré, was bound by the conditions agreed upon by his elder brother and the French, but nonetheless continued to expand the kingdom's borders, and by 1898 the Kénédougou lands stretched into modern-day Côte d'Ivoire and Burkina Faso. Meanwhile, the French were looking for an excuse to invade and take full control of the region, and the proud Babemba, resentful of the French interference brought about by the 1890 treaty, was only too happy to provide it. Early in 1598 the Kénédougou king suddenly refused to send the annual tax of 80 heads of cattle to the French commandant at Ségou, and then antagonised the colonialists further by expelling the French military ambassador from Sikasso. The French response was predictable enough. On April 15 1898 they attacked Sikasso, breached the *tata* (city wall) which had successfully repelled Samory ten years earlier, and took the town on May 1. Babemba decided to shoot himself rather than surrender.

Samory Touré

The other major player in the south of Mali – at least during the second half of the 19th century – was Samory Touré, a Muslim *imam* warrior who established a loosely knit state across lands in what is now Guinea, Mali, Côte d'Ivoire and Burkina Faso. Samory spent most of the 1880s fighting the French on the left bank of the River Niger, until the Treaty of Bissandougou in 1887 marked a break in hostilities, leaving Samory free to attack Tieba Traoré's Kénédougou kingdom. His attempt to take the town of Sikasso failed when the French came to Tieba's assistance, and in 1889 he revoked the Treaty of Bissandougou and moved his armies south as far as present-day Ghana and Sierra Leone. Finally, in 1898, he was captured by the French and exiled to Gabon, where he died in 1900.

SIKASSO TOWN

Many travellers would describe themselves as being 'stuck' in Sikasso rather than being there out of choice. Since it is situated only 100km from Côte d'Ivoire and 40km from Burkina Faso, and is linked to Bamako, Ségou and Mopti by excellent paved roads, travellers might indeed have cause to be passing through en route to Mali's more interesting towns. However, dismiss Sikasso at your peril! It may not be the most attractive and exciting place in the world, but it does represent a slightly different side of life in Mali. For a start, things grow here: the climate is more humid and the countryside certainly greener than the dust bowls in the Sahel. You should also take advantage of the fact that few tourists stop in Sikasso. There are no guides and the people are ready to speak to you normally – that is to say, in the humorous, curious, respectful and gentle Malian way. In this respect, a visit to Sikasso might be worth ten Djenné mosques.

Little is known about Sikasso before Tieba Traoré made it the capital of the Kénédougou kingdom in 1878. The village was probably founded at the beginning of the 19th century on a site in the forest where elephants were abundant – hence the original Senufo name, Solo-Khan or 'village of elephants'. The old city wall, the remains of which are still visible today, played an important part in the two defining moments of Sikasso's relatively short history: in 1887–8 it withstood a 15-month siege by the forces of Samory Touré, only to be breached with relative ease by the French army in 1898. Other than the city wall, there is a hillock in the middle of town and one or two tombs of Kénédougou kings to visit.

Orientation

If you arrive by bus from Bamako, you will be driven through the downtown part of Sikasso before stopping at the bus station which is a couple of kilometres from the centre on the road to Côte d'Ivoire and Burkina Faso. Therefore, if you want to avoid the walk back into town, ask to get off soon after you have passed the arch welcoming you to Sikasso. Remain on the bus if you intend to stay at one of the two hotels near the bus station.

The Mamelon – the sacred hillock in the centre of town – is a good point of reference. The market and much of the town's other activities are close to the roundabout at the foot of this hill. As the main highway passes through Sikasso it splits in two: one road crosses town to the north of the market, the other crosses to the south. These are the two main roads in Sikasso, either side of which are the town's residential neighbourhoods.

Getting there and away

Before the violent crisis in Côte d'Ivoire started, a great deal of traffic passed through Sikasso, since this was, economically speaking, the most important town linking Bamako to its closest port, Abidjan. Virtually all traffic to Abidjan has now been suspended, but Sikasso has never lost its importance as a crossroads town in the proximity of both Burkina Faso and Côte d'Ivoire. Indeed, the majority of tourists tend to be going through the town on their way to and even through Burkina Faso, and a handful of travellers still find their way to Bouaké, the second largest town in Côte d'Ivoire.

Various bus companies have services to Bobo-Dioulasso (CFA3,500) and Ouagadougou (CFA10,000), such as YT and Kénédougou Voyages, each with two daily departures (07.30 and16.30), and Somatrie with one daily departure for Bobo-Dioulasso at 10.00. Bani Transport has direct services all the way to Lomé (CFA22,500), Niamey (CFA22,500) and Cotonou (CFA25,000). YT and CTR have departures for Bouaké at 07.00 and 16.30 (CFA8,000).

For Bamako, companies such as YT, Somatrie, Bittar Transport and Bani transport leave at almost hourly intervals throughout the day (CFA4,000). Note that some companies travel via Koutiala (CFA2,500) and Ségou (CFA4,000), while others travel via Bougouni (CFA3,000). YT has one daily departure at 18.00 for Mopti (CFA5,000), and Bani Transport has two weekly buses leaving for Gao (CFA11,000 on Thursdays and Sundays at 16.00).

All these companies leave from their respective bus yards scattered around Sanabougou, at about 1km from the town centre. A new, central bus station is currently under construction, which means that, before the end of 2004, all big buses in all directions should be leaving from the same location in Sanabougou. For nearby destinations, look for minibuses and *bâchées* leaving from the centre of Sikasso, especially where the market peters out in Avenue Loury and Avenue de France. A shared taxi between Sanabougou and the town centre should cost no more than CFA200.

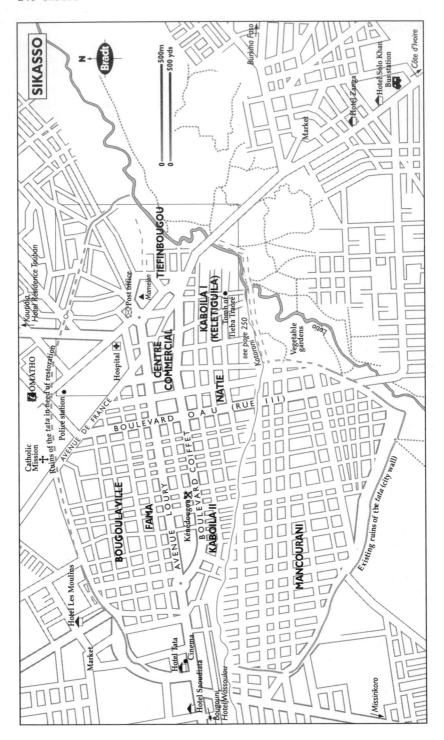

SIKASSO

N

Bradt

500m
500 yds

0
0

Burkina Faso
Côte d'Ivoire

Hotel Zanga
Hotel Solo Khan
Bus station

Market

TIEFINBOUGOU

Koupéla,
Hotel Résidence Toubon

Post office

Mamelon

KABOILA I
(KELETIGUILA)

Tomb of
Tieba Traoré

OMATHO

Ruins of the *tata* in need of restoration

Catholic
Mission

Police station

Hospital

AVENUE DE FRANCE

CENTRE
COMMERCIAL

see page 250

NATIE

Kotoroni

Vegetable
gardens

Lobo

Lobo

BOULEVARD

(RUE III)

BOUGOULA-VILLE

FAMA

AVENUE LOURY

BOULEVARD COFFET OAU

Kénédougou

KABOILA II

Hotel Les Moulins

Existing ruins of the *tata* (city wall)

MANCOURANI

Market

Hotel Tata

Cinema

Hotel Saœdiata

Bougouni,
Hotel Wassoulou

Missirikoro

Where to stay

The most comfortable hotel in Sikasso is arguably **Hotel Wassoulou** (tel: 262 04 24) on the new road to Koutiala, with air-conditioned double rooms (CFA16,000) and twin rooms (CFA19,000). The homely **Hotel Résidence Touban** (formerly known as Hotel Panier de la Ménagère, tel: 262 05 34) on the old road to Koutiala is also quite upmarket. Rooms with a fan are CFA12,000, while air-conditioned rooms are CFA17,000 up to CFA21,000. The considerable distance from the centre of town, however, makes these hotels less convenient unless you have your own transport.

Again not very centrally located are **Hotel les Moulins** – with acceptable rooms with a fan at CFA8,000 – and **Hotel Saoudiata** (tel: 262 19 48), which has rooms at CFA9,000 (with a fan) and CFA15,000 (air conditioned). Rooms at **Hotel Tata** (tel: 262 04 11) next to the entrance to town are similarly priced and within reasonable walking distance from the centre. **Hotel Mamelon** (tel: 262 00 44) is in the heart of town at the foot of the Mamelon. Rooms are CFA17,500/20,000/22,000 for a self-contained single/double/triple. All rooms have air conditioning and television but are a bit shabby for the price. **Hotel Lotio** (tel: 262 10 01) on the main thoroughfare in the centre of town, meanwhile, has singles/doubles with a fan for around CFA6,000/7,000. This is one of the few places to openly advertise a *chambre de passage* (CFA2,000), which is generally used to spend an hour or so *avec une copine*. Of course you could also use that time to have a rest and a shower. Across the road is the **Direction Générale de la Réglementation et du Contrôle du Secteur du Développement Rural**, which is no hotel but nevertheless has three rooms. They provide much better value than Hotel Lotio, since here you can have the same lack of quality for CFA1,500 per person (with a fan) or CFA3,000 per person (with air conditioning) for a full night if you like. Another budget option is the **Complexe Vision 2000** (tel: 262 06 70), located next to the city wall not far from the Mamelon hill, but even at CFA4,000 or CFA5,000 per room, this dark, dirty and depressing accommodation is the antitheses of luxury.

Around 1km out of town towards the bus station is **Hotel Zanga** (tel: 262 04 31). Rooms are bright and kept spotlessly clean and are CFA10,000/14,000 for a single/double with a fan, and CFA19,500/23,500 for a single/double with air conditioning. There is also a good *pâtisserie* on the premises, and a swimming pool that is in desperate need of some attention. Finally, **Hotel Solo Khan** (tel: 262 05 64) is near the bus station, patronised mainly by Malians, very basic with en suite bucket showers, and very cheap (CFA3,000 or CFA4,000 for a room).

Where to eat

Of all the hotel restaurants, the best is **Restaurant Awa Plus** and its excellent *pâtisserie* at Hotel Zanga: an ideal place for breakfast or a snack – perhaps while waiting for a bus at the nearby station. **Hotel Mamelon** and **Hotel Tata** also have restaurants; the ambience at the former is more agreeable, although the choice of food is similar at both.

Other restaurants in town include **Restaurant Kénédougou** and **Restaurant la Vieille Marmite**, both on Boulevard Coiffet, the main thoroughfare. The latter – almost opposite the Shell station – is a small and very popular place which has been run by the same family for over 40 years now. Try the delicious *pintade* (guinea fowl) and sauce! A new and promising place is **Restaurant l'Auberge du Carrefour**, just behind l'Espace Culturelle Handara. The owner has plans to have some rooms ready in 2004. Near the Mamelon hill and overlooking the market, **Pâtisserie Sowlait** is hard to miss. Though the décor isn't all that great, the wide choice of pastries, the fast food, yoghurt and fresh coffee attract many clients. The *pâtisserie* is open all week, but note that the kitchen (for pizzas and such) is closed on Sundays. Meanwhile, the biggest supermarket in Sikasso is at **Hotel Résidence Touban**.

You should try one or two of the region's very large and very tasty **mangoes** while in Sikasso. Otherwise, although much of the country's fruit and vegetables come from this region, the market is not overflowing with fresh produce.

Entertainment and nightlife

At Complexe Tata (which also includes Hotel Tata), a large **cinema** shows Hindu films on Sundays, Tuesdays and Fridays at 21.15. Tickets cost a mere CFA200. The new **Espace Culturelle Handara** (tel: 604 49 06) certainly fills a niche in Sikasso's nightlife, but nobody seems quite sure with what activities. These will most likely include music and dancing, and maybe live performances on weekends. It may become a *boîte de nuit*, or just a place to hang out for a drink and some brochettes. Check it out!

Practical information

Several of Sikasso's public services can be found near the roundabout at the foot of the Mamelon: these include the **post office**, **Sotelma**, the **hospital** and two **internet** cafés – Sicanet next to Pâtisserie Sowlait, and another one next to Sotelma. A third cybercafé, SAM Informatique, is directly opposite l'Espace Culturelle Handara. **L'OMATHO** (tel: 262 18 05, see also page 85) has its office on the premises of the *Haute Commisariat* at the end of Rue Fôh Traoré. There are five **banks** in Sikasso. BIM and BDM both have a **Western Union** office. These banks do not deal with foreign currency, though BDM does Visa cash advances. BCEAO (which is like a fortress), BOA and BNDA (both open on Sundays) change cash euros only.

What to see

While none of the sights in Sikasso will exactly take your breath away, they do reverberate with historical resonance and, with a little imagination, are worth visiting.

The highlight is **Le Mamelon**, a small hill of about 30m in the centre of town. When the Kénédougou kings ruled Sikasso in the 19th century, the top of the Mamelon was covered with lush vegetation – a sacred wood where a *bon génie* (good spirit) looked over the town and protected it. King Tieba Traoré built a two-storied house here where he received royal guests; and a sacred serpent would dispense advice from a well, the opening of which can still be seen today. When the French took Sikasso on May 1 1898, they planted the *tricouleur* on top of the Mamelon – symbolic, perhaps, of the hill's importance. Later, in 1945, they built a tower which served as the town's tribunal and library. In more recent times, water towers and antennae have graced the summit, which is one of the best place for **views** of Sikasso. Another good place for uninterrupted views is the tower – with ladders and platforms – in the market area.

Like other towns in this region of Mali, Sikasso was protected from attacks – first by rival kingdoms, then French colonialists – by the *tata* or city wall. Due to its strategic and commercial importance, three *tatas* were constructed before Sikasso eventually fell to the French. An outer wall built in three months in 1885 was the largest and most recent. It had a perimeter of nearly 9km, an average height of 5m and five *portes* (gates) situated at strategic points around the town. Inside the outer wall, a smaller *tata* protected the merchants, soldiers and nobility. Finally, the smallest and oldest wall encircled the *dionfoutou*, where the king and his family lived. Nowadays, the only part of the *tata* which is being properly conserved skirts around the quarter of Mancourani.

The **tomb of Tieba Traoré**, arguably the greatest Kénédougou king, is in the quarter of Kabiola also known as Keletiguila. Look for an inconspicuous white building covered in graffiti which looks like a transformer kiosk, in the vicinity of a striking *banco* house. Since King Tieba Traoré had many enemies, including in his own family, he feared that after his death his body may be mutilated and bodyparts could be used for sorcery. Therefore he requested to be buried in the protective vicinity of the house of his most trusted warrior, Keletigui Berthe. Up to this day, the oldest living member of the Berthe family, who also happens to be the *chef du quartier*, is the keeper of the key to the tomb. Before disturbing the old man and having the tomb opened up for you, bear in mind that, in all frankness, the interior reveals nothing whatsoever that reminds you of the presence of royalty. More impressive is the nearby *banco* house, which still belongs to the descendants of Keletigui Berthe.

The **tomb of Lieutenant Loury**, who led the French into Sikasso in 1898, is next to a patch of ground which served as a *fosse commune* (communal grave) during the French occupation. Apparently, it is one of many.

If you are craving to see some lush green for a change, walk from Hotel Lotio towards the *banco* house and the king's tomb, and continue onwards until you stumble upon the town's **gardens**. There is always a lot of activity going on here, as the carrots, beetroots, onions etc need daily watering from the minute rivers Lotio and Kotoroni. Follow the Lotio in a southeasterly direction, until you come across a paved road. This road will take you back into town, past a ruined part of the old *tata*.

Excursions from Sikasso
The tomb of Massa Daoula Traoré
If Tieba Traoré is widely considered to be the greatest of the Kénédougou kings, then his father, Massa Daoula Traoré, is generally credited with being the person who established the kingdom as a real force in the region. Before Tieba moved it to Sikasso, the capital of the kingdom was at **Bougoula**, 6km east of Sikasso. This is where Massa Daoula, several members of his family, and an assortment of the king's weapons and fetishes are buried. Introduce yourself to the chief when you arrive at the village. The upkeep of the tombs is the responsibility of a family of Coulibalys who were once slaves of Massa Daoula but who were set free before the king died.

The Stone Mosque
The village of **Missirikoro** 12km southwest of Sikasso owes its name to the nearby grotto, Fara Missiri (Stone Mosque). This natural grotto, complete with stalactites and stalagmites, reaches a height of 50 to 80m and has traditionally been used as a place of worship and sacrifice for both Muslims and animists. A staircase made of cobbles leads to the main entrance of the 'mosque'. *Génies* (guardian spirits) were thought to inhabit the cave and were

always consulted by the Kénédougou kings before any expedition or military exercise. According to another legend, the genies also prepared food and drink for passing travellers until they were spotted by an old woman curious to know the source of the meals. Nowadays the most obvious presence is that of an old cave-dweller who seems to have lived there forever, sharing his grotto with a noisy colony of bats.

There are two other entrances leading into the rocky outcrop. Animist sacrifices take place at the eastern entrance. This corridor is clearly connected to the main grotto, as from inside the 'mosque', when peeping into the right pit, the light and the pile of stones and skulls are visible. On the western side, inside a deep crevasse, Muslim worshippers retreat for months and even years of seclusion. Unless the crevasse is covered with a curtain, you are allowed in. Remember to take off your shoes, and do not disturb the Muslims while they are involved in any sort of religious activity – which is most of the time. A couple of meters inside to the right, there is a small niche which is sometimes used for a kind of seclusion pushed to extremes.

Around the bend you will find ladders and chains, to help you find your way up the rocky hillock for a magnificent view. Beware of snakes around this area.

There is no easy and obvious way of getting to Missirikoro. Unless you fancy walking the 12km, you will probably have to arrange private transportation – a motorbike, for example.

Along the road to Bobo-Dioulasso

The most direct road from Sikasso to Bobo-Dioulasso in Burkina Faso is a track which passes through some of the region's tea plantations. There are one or two places of interest along this road, although you will probably need your own transport to get to them – the buses to Bobo-Dioulasso take the paved road via Koutiala.

About 18km from Sikasso just before you reach the village of **Finkolo** – the capital of the Kénédougou kingdom before Massa Daoula Traoré moved it to Bougoula – there is a picturesque spot in a wooded area at the confluence of two rivers, the Tchintchinko (river of sand) and the Farako (river of stone), known as the **Kofilaben**. Mixing the water from these two rivers in the same container is forbidden, except in extreme cases of drought when it is permitted to encourage rainfall. However, if the first drops of rain hit the person who mixes this water, he will die. Not surprisingly, this is another spot frequented by genies!

A further 10km or so down the road, the **Chutes du Farako** tip into the 'river of stone' – so called because of its limestone bed. This waterfall drops in several tiers, the highest being a modest 3m. Naturally, the best time to see the falls is during the rainy season when the river is at its highest.

ELSEWHERE IN THE REGION
Sélingué

You can travel to Sikasso along a paved road from Bamako, Ségou and Mopti. Coming from the capital, after about 85km there is a turning for Kangaré and

COTTON WOOL AND SOAP
Jolijn Geels

> Mali remains vulnerable to fluctuations in the world market value of cotton, its principal export product (43%).

> In 1998, Mali was second in Africa for cotton production (500,000 tons).

These clinical statistics mean that many Malians must work in the cotton industry. What is it they do – apart from growing cotton? A visit to a *usine d'égrenage* (cotton ginnery) in Bougouni and a group of soap-making women in Koutiala reveal a fragment of the human factor.

Cotton wool
One could almost think the whirling cloud of white fluff consisted of snowflakes, and that the men had covered their heads and mouths to keep out the cold. However, we are in a huge factory building with a tin roof and soaring temperatures; snow would melt and evaporate before reaching the ground. I also cover my mouth to keep out the dust and the cotton fibres, while the foreman shows me around, shouting through the noise of the giant installations: 'This is where the trucks dump their load. Look and touch the raw cotton. Do you feel the seeds and the grit? It is therefore cleaned in steps. First to remove the coarse bits, like small stones and even twigs. Then once more to remove smaller particles.'

He opens a hatch and sticks his hand in, catching some of the cotton wool that is blown through the pipes.

'The seed is still in there, so the cotton passes through the carding engine. See? The blades are so little apart, that the seeds are removed while the cotton is carded. Feel the difference.'

I do, and wonder if the foreman can feel the sweat trickling down his back as I can feel the sweat trickling down mine. Yet my mouth is dry.

'Then the cotton is blown through this pipe to the furnace, where it passes the…well, the drycleaners one could say. Now feel this fluffy cotton wool! Then it passes through here and into this machine, where the cotton is pressed into these bales, each weighing around 230kg. We process appoximately 50,000 tons each year.'

This is where more human labour comes in, with four young men in sweat-sodden shirts preparing the press with iron wires to hold each bale together, handling the heavy blocks of fluff, taking samples of each bale to be tested for quality in a lab, sewing the wrapping by hand and jotting down all the details – date, farmer, truckload and so on – on the wrapping with a marker. Then the bales are wheeled outside, and I follow my guide into the

a dam at Sélingué. Before the completion of the Manantali project (see page 269), the hydro-electric plant at Sélingué was the largest of its kind in Mali, with a capacity of 44.8MW – although when the volume of water flow is low, blinding sunlight. The scorching sun feels refreshing after spending an hour in that furnace. As I dust down my hair and clothes, I seek solace in mathematics in an attempt to make sense of all this labour. It has the reverse effect: 50,000 tons makes 217,391 bales of 230kg. The process of ginning lasts six months or 180 days of non-stop labour in three shifts a day, so that makes 1208 bales per day, 403 per shift or 50 bales per hour. The ginning campaign lasts through the hottest months of the year, which have not even begun yet.

As I take my place on the back of a motorbike, I realise that by the time I get back to the *campement* to replenish fluids and take a shower, these men will have finished another 15 bales, with 200 more to go before the end of their shift.

Soap

The cotton-seeds are pressed into oil, most of which is sent to Koulikoro to be refined and processed into long bars of soap. Neat and shiny, sometimes even perfumed, they're for many purposes. They can be bought all over the country at every market and in many shops. The plant where the seeds are pressed produces a foul and oily waste water. Behind the plant, outside the fence in the open air, women collect the waste water in dozens of rusty oil-drums. After a couple of days, the unrefined oil is scooped from the surface, collected in containers, and carried to the soap-makers – all women – around the corner. At first glance it looks like a busy market square, but there are striking differences: the soil is black and slippery, the women's garments are smothered in various shades of brown, grey and black. Instead of a pleasant odour of spices and fruit, the air is filled with a fatty fragrance. The heat from dozens of fires is everywhere, while thick smoke and fumes hover over the site like a blanket. Who would have thought that a poor man's soap is made in hell? Here comes the recipe:

Pour the oil into huge cauldrons and mix with a potassium solution. Bring to the boil. With wooden spoons the size of paddles, stir and stir the thick grub for hours until it becomes a sort of smooth, creamy brown sludge. Leave to cool, stirring firmly without stopping. Transfer the slippery substance to smaller containers. Wrap your hands in plastic bags. Scoop a handful out of the bowl or bucket and turn into balls. Think of big meatballs. Dozens of them. Leave to dry in the sun. Sell at CFA50 up to CFA150 a piece, depending on size and quality. Ignore the smell; these brown soap balls are meant for cleaning only. They perform miracles on heavily stained clothes, though. They honestly do.

it is sometimes unable to produce any electricity at all. The artificial lake created by the dam has been promoted as a tourist attraction, with *pinasse* rides, traditional dances, several species of waterbirds and places to stay at Kangaré,

Sélingué and Yanifolila. *Bâchées* leave for Kangaré (CFA1,500) – more widely referred to as Sélingué – from near the Gare Routière de Sogoninko, beside the main road opposite the yard from where buses leave for Sikasso. Alternatively, take a bus in the direction of Bougouni, get off at the turning to Sélingué, and look for onward transport from there.

To explore the lake by pirogue, find your way to the village of Carrière – 3km south of Kangaré – first. Pirogues leave from the market, which lies right on the shore of the lake. One option is to take a pirogue to Bambala on the west coast, take a ferry across to Siékorolé, and then take the road to Yanifolila and onwards to Bougouni. In 2003, John Kupiec chose the other option: for CFA2,000, a pirogue took him almost directly to the shore nearest to Yanifolila. From there he walked a pleasant 15km to Yanifolila.

Bougouni

Bougouni is the first major town after Bamako, 160km from the capital and roughly at the halfway point of a bus journey to Sikasso. This is a factory town – economically important, but of little interest to the tourist. There are places to stay should you wish to break your journey here, but note that they cater for business rather than tourist clientele. Another point to bear in mind is the fact that none of the hotels has as a restaurant. Finding a filling meal for little money in one of the small local restaurants, however, should not be a problem.

Coming from Bamako, to the right of the paved thoroughfare, the first option is **Hotel Petit Moulin** (tel: 265 11 88), with air-conditioned rooms at CFA15,000, breakfast included. A little further, again to the right, is **Hotel Piedmont**. Campement Petit Moulin, usually simply referred to as **Le Campement** (tel: 265 11 15) to avoid confusion, is just before the turning to Sikasso to the left of the road. Rooms with a fan are CFA8,400, while rooms with air conditioning are CFA15,000 – breakfast included. Continuing on the same road, ignoring the turning to Sikasso, you'll see another hotel.

When arriving by bus from Bamako or Sikasso, ask to be dropped off at one of the hotels, since the bus station is around 1km off the road and you would have to walk back.

Koutiala

Koutiala is 140km on the other side of Sikasso – that is to say, on the road to Ségou and Mopti. Like Bougouni, it is a factory town, although larger and more important. In fact, the *cercle* of Koutiala is one of the most economically productive areas of Mali and a principal cotton-growing region. For travellers, Koutiala is important as a crossroads for traffic to Bamako, Sikasso, Ségou, Mopti and Bobo-Dioulasso. Buses to all of these destinations can be found at the **bus station** on the road to Sikasso. Between Bani Transport, Bittar Transport, Binke Transport and Somatra, you can choose from at least eight daily departures for Ségou (CFA2,000) and Bamako (CFA4,000), and four daily departures for Bobo-Dioulasso (CFA4,000). Ask around to find out which company is leaving next before purchasing your ticket.

Comfortable TSR Escales buses leave daily for Bobo-Dioulasso, Ouagadougou (CFA9,000), Cotonou (CFA22,500) and Lomé (CFA22,500). However, buses to Sikasso (CFA2,000) or to San (CFA2,000), Mopti (CFA4,000) and Gao (CFA10,000) depart less frequently. Minibuses and *bâchées* to Sikasso, Bla and San leave when full from the departure point opposite the BDM bank.

There are three **banks** in Koutiala. The BDM bank, the BNDA and the Bank of Africa, which changes euros, US$ and travellers' cheques if you can produce the receipt. The **post office** is on the throroughfare to Ségou and Bamako, within walking distance from Pont Lumumba.

Koutiala has a fair selection of hotels. **Hotel la Chaumière** (tel:

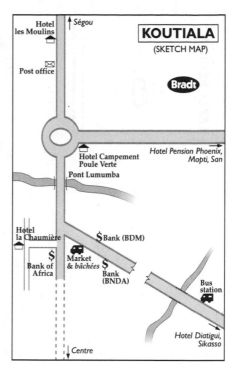

264 02 20) comes highly recommended, with large, clean rooms with a fan at CFA9,500/11,500 (single/double), and CFA14,500/16,500 for a single/double with air conditioning. The restaurant serves excellent food. The quiet **Hotel des Moulins** (tel: 264 01 05) is similar in price and standard. On the road to Sikasso, next to the Huicoma plant, is **Hotel Diatigui** (tel: 264 01 70), a slightly more upmarket place than Hotel la Chaumière. More affordable, and on the road to San, is **Hotel Pension Phoenix**.

For budget travellers with ear plugs, the centrally located **Hotel Campement Poule Verte** (tel: 264 02 38) could be a good choice. It is a drinking place, though, where loud music blasts from speakers on the terrace until late. It is also a place where one wing is reserved for prostitutes, but travellers who want to spend the night get the better rooms and clean sheets. These rooms cost CFA7,000 (with a fan) or CFA10,000 (air conditioned and self-contained). Camping in the garden is allowed, but can hardly be recommended. Meals at the Hotel Campement – like tasty, tender chicken with sauce – are quite good.

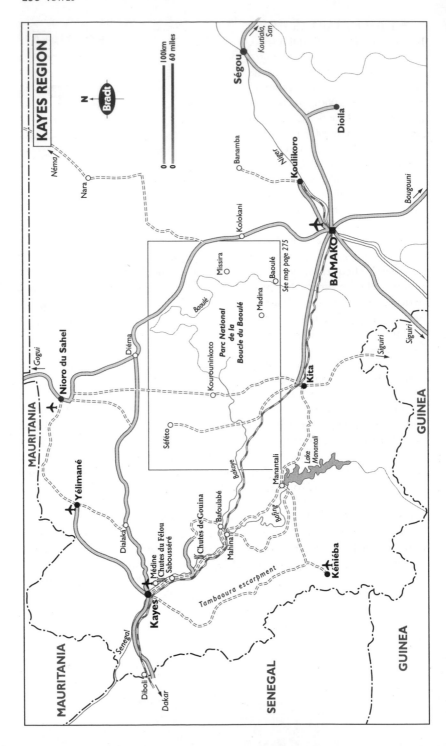

KAYES REGION

Kayes

Most tourists see the western region of Kayes from the window of a train as they travel between Dakar and Bamako. If they do set foot in this part of the country, it is more often than not in the old colonial town of Kayes. Kita also receives the odd visitor thanks to its rail-side location, but otherwise the region is rarely explored. One of the main reasons for this used to be the paucity of good roads in the west of Mali. The Dakar–Bamako railway line has long been seen as a replacement for a sophisticated road network, and as a result access to most of the region used to be difficult and time-consuming. To a great extent, this still applies. However, the decision to construct a tarred road linking Bamako to Kayes must be considered nothing short of revolutionary. That road is a fact now, and more road construction works are under way. In another couple of years, many parts of the region will be more or less accessible just like the rest of Mali, leaving only a few isolated pockets that will receive no more than a handful of tenacious travellers. The Parc National du Boucle du Baoulé is likely to be one of those pockets.

HISTORY

The history of the present-day region of Kayes is not as clear-cut as those of other areas, where one great kingdom or empire has usually stamped its mark and influence. In this part of West Africa regional dominance has always been up for grabs: the French, the Tukulor and the Bambara kingdom of Ségou have all controlled certain parts of it at certain times, while the two indigenous power blocks – the state of Khasso and the kingdoms of Kaarta – have struggled against outside influences.

Khasso

Khasso was originally a Malinké state running along both sides of the River Senegal and extending from present-day Senegal in the west to the Kaarta kingdom in the east. When Mungo Park passed through here in 1796, the Peul were in charge and the capital was at Koniakari.

By the middle of the 19th century, civil wars had divided the state into two important and rival groups. The hereditary ruler, Dyoukou Sambala, had moved the capital from Koniakari to Médine on the right bank of the River Senegal where he and his followers had established themselves, while a few kilometres upstream at Sabousséré on the left bank a group called the Logo opposed him. Meanwhile, the French and the Tukulor had recently arrived in the region and were jostling for power. El Hadj Omar had taken advantage of the state of civil war, and by 1855 the Tukulor had conquered most of the Khasso chiefdoms – including Koniakari – on the right bank of the river. This prompted Sambala to ally himself with the French, who built a fortress at Médine in 1855 ostensibly to protect their own commercial interests in the area. In 1857 this fortress passed its first – and arguably its sternest – test when it successfully repelled a siege by Omar's forces. The French, however, had no desire to be in a constant state of war with the Tukulor, as it disrupted the profitable trade engaged in by the colonialists along the River Senegal. For this reason, the French preferred to remain neutral as the Tukulor fought to maintain their authority in conquered lands. However, when the Logo, led by Niamody, allied themselves with the Tukulor, thus becoming a direct threat on the left bank of the river where the French had their sphere of influence, something had to be done. Sambala was encouraged by Brière de l'Isle, the French governor of Senegal, to invade his old enemy in November 1877; but when the Logo, helped by the Tukulor, were on the verge of victory the French themselves intervened, defeating Niamody and destroying his capital at Sabousséré in September 1878. French commercial interests were secured, and in 1892 the town of Kayes became the capital of Upper Senegal and Niger.

Kaarta

The traditional lands of the Bambara kingdoms of Kaarta – not to be confused with the Bambara kingdom of Ségou (see page 130) – lie north of the River Baoulé. There were, in fact, two Kaarta kingdoms. The first was ruled by the Massassi dynasty and dates from 1650. The Ségou ruler, Biton Coulibaly, was a major thorn in the side of the various Massassi rulers, and in 1753 he finally succeeded in conquering them after several previous attempts. Coulibaly's success spawned the creation of a second Bambara kingdom of Kaarta in 1754 by Sey Bamana Coulibaly, which was to become, unlike its predecessor, an organised political state in the second half of the 18th century. Although battles continued to be lost against Ségou, Kaarta enjoyed military victories over Khasso and reached its apogee under Bodian Moriba (1818–32), whose first capital was at Yélimané, before being moved to Nioro.

The development of Kaarta as a powerful political state was cut short by El Hadj Omar, who brought Nioro under Tukulor control in 1854.

KAYES TOWN

Kayes is apparently the hottest town in Africa. Temperatures in April and May can sometimes reach 50°C and the very slight breeze coming off the River Senegal is about as soothing as a fan heater. One explanation for the heat is that the town is surrounded by hills which contain a lot of iron. As the sun beats down on these hills it warms up the iron and turns Kayes into an oven – or rather a bun in an oven. Be this as it may, the temperature during the cooler months is more tolerable and certainly not too high to put you off visiting this attractive and busy town.

Kayes was – and still is – an important commercial centre. Founded in 1880 when it was a small and irrelevant Khassonké village, it replaced Médine as the capital of the Upper Senegal and Niger colony 12 years later and, thanks largely to the railway, became a major trading centre for gum arabic (a gum produced by certain acacia trees and used in the manufacture of ink, food thickeners, pills, emulsifiers etc). Kayes continued as the undisputed centre of French commercial interests in the region until the railway eventually reached Bamako in 1908. However, although Kayes lost out to Bamako – especially after 1923 when the railway reached Dakar and the Atlantic coast – it remains to this day one of Mali's most important economic centres.

Tourists who are not continuing on to Senegal will ask themselves whether or not it is worth the 1,200km round trip from Bamako to visit the town of Kayes. My answer is an unreserved 'yes'. This place is, at the same time, relaxed and busy, attractive and jaded; it has some of the finest colonial architecture in Mali and also gives visitors the chance to see West Africa's other great river, the Senegal.

Orientation

When you arrive by train, you will be about 2km from the town centre. This part of town is dominated by the railway, which in its heyday in the early 1900s used to terminate near the banks of the River Senegal. Nowadays, the station is in the southeastern part of town on the road to Médine. This road, along with Boulevard de l'Indépendance (the road to Diboli on the Senegalese border) and Avenue Macdeoura (the road running parallel to the river), are the main arteries in a town which is relatively simple to figure out. The new bridge across the River Senegal links the various quarters of old Kayes to Kayes N'Di or Small Kayes, a large, residential quarter built – and still being built – on the right bank of the river, where the roads to Nioro du Sahel and Yélimané begin. Across the River Senegal, 15km from Kayes, is also where the new airport Dacdac, named after a nearby village, is located.

Getting there and away
By air

The new airport of Kayes is located north of the River Senegal approximately 15km from town. **SAE** (tel: 252 31 36/672 93 96) operates flights between Bamako and Kayes, both arriving and departing on Mondays and Thursdays. **STA** offers the same service on Mondays, Tuesdays, Thursdays, Saturdays and Sundays. Both SAE (tel: 674 68 08) and STA (tel: 672 58 97) offices are along the Avenue du Capitaine Mamadou Sissoko. Remember that planes serving Kayes have just 17 passenger seats, and with demand far outstripping supply tickets are at a premium. Also bear in mind that the schedule is subject to change (see *Practicalities: Getting there and away* on page 73).

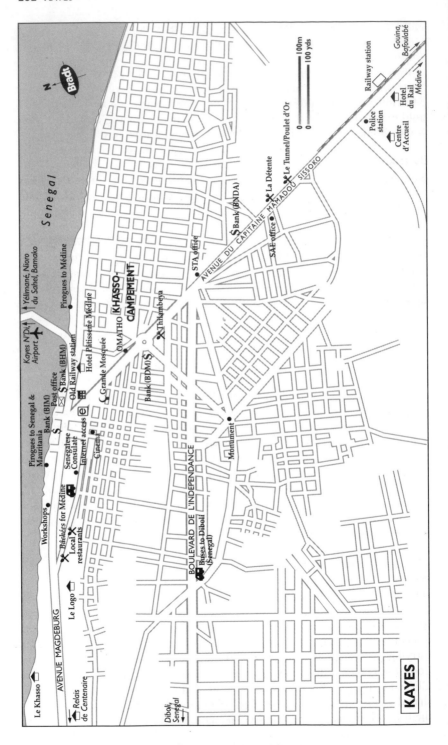

KAYES

Le Khasso

AVENUE MAGDEBURG

Relais de Centenaire

Le Logo

Diboli, Senegal

Workshops

Brochês for Médine

Local restaurants

Pirogues to Senegal & Mauritania

Bank (BIM)

Senegalese Consulate

Internet access

Cinema

BOULEVARD DE L'INDÉPENDANCE

Buses to Diboli (Senegal)

Monument

Yélimané, Nioro du Sahel, Bamako

Kayes N'Dji Airport

Pirogues to Médine

Post office

Bank (BHM)

Old Railway station

Grande Mosquée

Hotel Pâtisserie Médine

OMAITHO KHASSO-CAMPEMENT

Thiambeya

Bank (BDM)

STA office

Senegal

AVENUE DU CAPITAINE MAMADOU SISSOKO

Bank (BNDA)

SAE office

La Détente

Le Tunnel/Poulet d'Or

Railway station

Police station

Centre d'Accueil

Hotel du Rail

Gouina, Bafoulabé

Médine

N

100m
100 yds

By river

Travelling down the River Senegal – which passes through Kayes and continues west along the border between Senegal and Mauritania before emptying into the Atlantic Ocean at the Senegalese town of Saint Louis – is an original and adventurous way to travel to or from Kayes. The best place to ask about pirogues is on the bank of the river, roughly halfway between the bridge and Hotel Khasso. Pirogues also leave daily for Médine from just right of the bridge (see *Excursions from Kayes* on page 267).

By train

Kayes is roughly half way between Dakar and Bamako on the railway linking the two capital cities. Huge delays are commonplace and therefore the train is very unlikely to arrive in Kayes as scheduled, but roughly speaking the Bamako–Dakar express train arrives on Wednesday evenings from Bamako, and returns on Sunday mornings from Dakar. Three more trains run between Bamako and Kayes. For fares and departure times, see *Practicalities: Getting around* on page 73. All local trains have been suspended.

By road

For travellers, a most useful land route is the 92km pot-holed track leading to Diboli on the Senegalese border, from where you can travel to Dakar. Buses and *bâchées* leave every day from opposite the Sad Oil Service station on Boulevard de l'Indépendance (3 hours, CFA3,000). Every now and then – try Saturdays at 17.00 – there is a direct bus to Dakar (at least 15 hours, CFA14,000).

Until recently, travelling by road to Bamako was not an option. Now big buses leave for the capital every morning – to reach their destination late in the afternoon or early in the evening – from the *gare routière* Kayes N'Di across the bridge. At CFA12,000, the fare matches that of a second-class train ticket, but many Malians consider travelling by bus as being far more comfortable than a full day in a second-class train wagon. The road, which does not show on commercially available maps yet, heads east from Kayes to Sandaré (CFA5,000), then to Diema (CFA7,500) and Kolokani (CFA10,500) before reaching Bamako.

Yélimané is also linked to Kayes by tar. Buses leave daily from the same bus station (CFA3,500). Though most maps show a connection by road between Yélimané and Niorno du Sahel, this section of road is in an appalling state. Only *camions* travel between Kayes and Nioro du Sahel, bypassing Yélimané and the impassable section by cutting from the new road to Bamako straight to Nioro du Sahel. The least uncomfortable option is a converted truck which carries passengers only. The alternative is a truck carrying goods and as many passengers as possible on top of the freight. Look for Diema Transport which has daily departures, and expect to pay CFA5,000 for a long and bumpy ride to Nioro. If you are lucky, take a shared cabin seat for CFA7,500. 4WD vehicles to Nioro are CFA7,500 in the back, while a front seat is CFA10,000.

THE BUTCHER OF KAYES

There is a small kiosk opposite Hotel Le Khasso in Kayes selling cigarettes, bottled water, biscuits and various other sundry items. I had got into the habit of purchasing an after-dinner snack at this shop and then whiling away the warm evenings in conversation with its gregarious owner. On one such evening we were installed in our usual chairs solving the problems of the world, shrouded in an atmospheric half-light provided by a lantern which hung on one side of the kiosk. All around us it was pitch-black. During a lull in the conversation, a gentle rattling sound punctuated by heavy scuffs on the ground could be heard in the darkness. We remained silent, obviously more intrigued by the approaching sound than the subject of our suspended conversation. A few seconds later a bicycle crept into our canopy of light and stopped in front of the kiosk. Its rider slipped off the crooked saddle and held the bicycle between his legs as he fumbled in his pocket for some change. In his other hand he held a machete, gleaming like a bar of gold as it caught the light of the lantern. I tried to see his face, but dark shadows obliterated his head and shoulders and they merged effortlessly into the night sky. The stranger purchased one cigarette, slipped it behind what I presume was his ear and rode off into the darkness.

I had just met one of the most important men in Kayes: the butcher. Every night he passes the kiosk on his way to the slaughterhouse, where he spends the night hacking, sawing and slicing so that there can be meat in the market the next day. He works alone and saves his cigarette for breakfast.

Another departure point for *bâchées* and small buses is near the market. Here you may find vehicles for Yélimané, while between Hotel le Logo and the Senegalese consulate vehicles for Médine depart when full.

Kayes is one of the few towns with some kind of public transport service between quarters. The green minibuses, like the Sotramas in Bamako, costs as little as CFA100 for an average ride. A taxi to the airport will charge at least CFA3,000.

Where to stay

When there is a conference in town – which happens quite frequently during the cooler months – the accommodation in Kayes fills up very quickly. The train from Bamako often arrives in the early hours of the morning, so consider making a reservation, at least for the first night.

Hotel Le Khasso (tel: 252 16 66) on the banks of the River Senegal is clearly the best hotel in Kayes. Apart from its location – which benefits from a slight yet significant breeze during the hot season – this well-run, friendly hotel has air-conditioned bungalows with hot running water. At CFA20,000 for a single and CFA27,500 for a double, you get what you pay for. **Hotel du Rail** (tel: 252 12 33) represents the main competition. However, notwithstanding the pretty colonial building opposite the railway station and the charm which inevitably goes with it, this hotel comes off second best. The rooms are rather tatty compared with the immaculate bungalows at the Khasso and, although you pay marginally less (CFA17,880 for a single, CFA27,335 for a double), they are not as good value. The new **Hotel Pâtisserie Médine** (tel: 253 11 09) between the bridge and the post office has clean rooms with air conditioning, hot water and television for CFA20,000 (single/double). **Le Logo Hotel** (tel: 252 13 81) next to the prison has five rooms costing CFA12,500 (single) and CFA17,500 (double) with breakfast included, which makes it relatively good value and worth a try. The budget options in Kayes are as limited as the hotels at the moderate and expensive end of the market. The **Centre d'Accueil** behind the commissariat de police has basic accommodation for around CFA5,000, which fills up just like the smarter hotels at busy times. The **Relais de Centenaire** (tel: 252 18 97), about 200m west of Hotel Khasso as the road turns away from the river is a real gem. There is space here for 50 people, either in tidy dorms with mosquito nets (CFA2,500) or in private rooms with shower (from CFA5,000). The distance from the centre of town is a slight disadvantage, but is more than made up for by the good-value accommodation and friendly welcome. The Relais du Centenaire is part of the *Mission Catholique* in Kayes.

Where to eat
Although this is one of Mali's largest towns, no-one will claim that it is one of its most gastronomic. The restaurant at **Hotel Khasso** is arguably the most popular. The food is OK, even if the ambience is a little depressing. A better choice might be to order *brochettes* and eat them in the garden by the river. The restaurants at **Hotel du Rail** and **Le Logo Hotel** are also not bad: big fish, perhaps, in a small pond. **Restaurant Buvette la Détente** and **Restaurant le Tunnel/Poulet Doré**, both along the Avenue du Capitaine Mamadou Sissoko, are all right, as long as you do not expect anything other than the usual fish, chicken and *brochettes*. **Restaurant Thilambeya**, along the same avenue, and **Pâtisserie Médine**, adjacent to Hotel Pâtisserie Médine (see above), both have a modest selection of pastries. For other options, look around the **market** where a mound of rice ladled with *sauce arachide* should not be too hard to find.

Entertainment and nightlife
Théâtre Massa Mankan Diabaté and the **soccer** stadium are in a large complex behind the airport. The theatre occasionally plays host to some of Mali's best musicians, while at the stadium, Sigui de Kayes – the first regional team to win the national cup competition – play at the weekends. Drama and sport are also activities on offer at **Carrefour des Jeunes**, where dance troupes rehearse and where judo and karate are practised in the evenings.

The garden at **Hotel Khasso** is the nicest place for a drink in the evenings. Afterwards, you could try the hotel's nightclub, **Le Mamery**. Open from Fridays to Sundays, the busiest night is Saturday and the most interesting is Friday, when traditional African music is played and most people come dressed in their most colourful *boubous*. Hotel guests are allowed in for free, while non-guests pay between CFA2,500 and CFA5,000 per person, depending on the day and occasion. The gardens at the **Hotel Khasso**, the **Buvette la Détente** and the **Paillotte** at Hotel du Rail are pleasant places for a drink and *brochettes*.

Not far from the market is a **cinema**, showing violent films for CFA150–250.

Practical information

The **post office**, **Sotelma** and a **bank** (BIM) with a **Western Union** office are all a stone's throw from each other on Avenue Macdeoura, the road running parallel to the river. BIM (closed on Fridays) and BHM banks change euros, while the BDM bank does Visa cash advances. The BNDA bank changes cash euros and US$, as well as traveller's cheques. BDM and BNDA are also open on Saturday mornings.

The **OMATHO** (tel: 252 35 98; see also page 85) office is signposted not far from the BDM bank. Note that the entrance is around the back. The main **police station**, meanwhile, is next to Hotel du Rail. There is also a **Senegalese Consulate** (tel: 252 11 15) between the market and Hotel le Logo. **Internet** facilities can be found not far from the market, and the charge for one hour is CFA1,500.

What to see

It is not difficult to tell that Kayes was once the French capital of Upper Senegal and Niger and a major colonial trading centre. These days, the **colonial architecture** remains largely intact and is frequently used to house government ministries, police commissariats and other public offices. In other cases – the old railway station in the centre of town, for example – these buildings have become children's playgrounds and good places to get out of the sun. Either way, the colonial legacy lives on in Kayes. The most impressive buildings can be found along the river and around the new railway station. Indeed, traditional Sudanese architecture is not at its most striking and beautiful in Kayes. The **grande mosquée**, for instance, is a conventional, white, concrete structure in the market area.

Walk past the post office westwards along Avenue Magdeburg to find **artisans** at work between the road and the riverbank. Look for workshops where calabashes are being cut, scoured and mended, look for craftsmen making urns and pestles used for pounding millet, look for blacksmiths recycling old car parts and see how metal trunks are made out of old oil drums.

The heat and dryness of Kayes make the **River Senegal** a favourite spot for man and beast alike. Walk down to the causeway to see people bathing, washing clothes, animals and cars, or simply sitting under the shade of one of the giant pillars of the new bridge. Across the river and on the right bank in the new quarter of Kayes N'Di there is a **sheep and goat market** in the evenings.

Excursions from Kayes
Médine
Today, Médine is more or less how it started out: a small, quiet Khassonké village on the banks of the River Senegal. The only difference between now and when it was founded in 1826 is the presence of a **fortress** – or at least the ruins of a fortress – built by the French in 1855 to protect important commercial interests in the area. For at this time Médine was the capital of Sambala's Khasso state (see page 259) and one of El Hadj Omar's early military targets as he began his march east from the Fouta Djallon. The fortress proved its worth in 1857 when it withstood a siege by Omar, and later in 1878 it served as base for French troops as they launched a decisive offensive against the Khasso allies of the Tukulor.

The basic structure remains intact, along with several cannons and various other peripheral buildings related to Médine's colonial past – the old railway station and courthouse, for example. Although the village is sparsely populated and few people venture out during the hottest parts of the day, guides have a habit of appearing from nowhere when the scent of tourists is in the air.

Médine is about 12km from Kayes. Walking is an option, but only during the day; hyenas come out after dusk and are known to attack humans. The most pleasant way to get there is by pirogue. They leave in the early afternoon from Kayes and return the next morning. The fare is approximately CFA500. The alternative is a dusty and crowded *bâchée*-ride. Once again, they leave in the afternoons from the marketplace in Kayes and return the following morning (CFA2,000). The problem with public transport to Médine is self-evident: it is difficult to do the round trip on the same day. Perhaps for this reason, and because there are some lovely spots along the river, you might consider **camping** for the night and returning on public transport the next morning. If you do, watch out for waders and small riverbank rodents. Travellers with their own transport often have the same idea, so you may be able to hitch a lift and borrow some water – but don't count on it.

Waterfalls
One of the most popular spots for camping is by the **Chutes du Félou**, a small waterfall created by a hydro-electric project 3km past Médine. The *bâchée* from Kayes passes Félou and continues on to Lontou. Much more impressive, however, are 'Mali's Niagara Falls', the **Chutes de Gouina**, which are about 80km from Kayes. Until the local train resumes its service, allowing travellers to get off at Bagoukou – some 6km from Gouina – there is no easy way to get to the falls unless you have your own reliable 4WD

vehicle. In that case, follow the track which runs roughly parallel to the railway track. After a while, the sandy track becomes a pot-holed tarred road, and where the tar diverts from the river, Gouina (and Mahina and Bafoulabé) is soberly signposted to the right. The track is in a dilapidated state, but word has it that at some point even this stretch will be upgraded. Without a vehicle, you need plenty of time, energy and determination to get to Gouina. If hitching a ride doesn't work – try waiting where the sandy road starts, to the left of the railway track, and keep your hopes up – your only options may be to rent a donkey cart or walk. In either case you should be fully self-supporting.

BETWEEN KAYES AND KITA

Not too long ago, the only feasible way to travel to Bamako by road was via Mahina, Manantali and Kita. It was considered an expedition rather than an ordinary journey. Some stretches of this route have been upgraded since, but the section between Kayes and Manantali must be considered a bottleneck which can only be tackled by 4WD with high clearance. With more comfortable options between Kayes and Bamako to choose from, this route – which still takes up to two days – need no longer be considered an unavoidable obstacle. As things stand, however, you could now opt for this road simply because there is a lot to be seen along the way.

Bafoulabé

One of the principal agglomerations between Kayes and Kita is Bafoulabé. The name of this town ('where two rivers meet') reflects exactly where it is located: at the confluence of the rivers Bafing and Bakoye. The murky waters of the former ('Black River') mix with the clearer waters of the latter ('White River') to produce the grey waters of the Senegal, Mali's second great waterway. Apart from this claim to fame, Bafoulabé is also noted for its large hippopotamus population.

To get to Bafoulabé, choose between the signposted sandy track mentioned above or stick to the pot-holed tar, which is only marginally better. This road eventually leads to a ferry across the Bakoye. The fare per vehicle is around CFA2,500-5,000, depending on the number of vehicles, as the total fare is shared. After 18.00, when the ferry service has stopped, expect to pay at least CFA1,000 to have the ferryman – who lives at the other side of the river – fetched, and another CFA12,000-15,000 to persuade him to take you across.

Campement le Loisir is located at the other end of Bafoulabé, and has basic but adequate rooms at CFA4,000 (single) or CFA6,000 (double). Camping costs CFA2,000 per person. There is an ample supply of chilled beers and soft drinks, but meals have to be ordered in advance. As the *campement* is located on the banks of the River Bafing, the real attraction of this place must be the hippopotamuses that are regularly spotted just behind the premises. They are creatures of habit, so look out for them around 06.00 in the morning and 17.00 in the afternoon.

Mahina

The two roads coming from Kayes merge in Mahina, which is always a lively town, but even more so on market days (Mondays). There are three hotels to choose from: **Hotel Wayowananko**, **Hotel Bafing** and **Hotel Djeneba**. **Bar Dancing Montana**, its entrance hidden between market stalls, also has one room at CFA2,000.

The easiest option to proceed to Manantali is to cross the bridge, which happens to be the railway bridge. Get permission from the *chef de gare* first, as he knows more or less when the next train is due to cross the bridge and you will be using the same single track. He has developed the habit of expecting some money or a gift in return, but officially there is no fee to be paid.

Manantali

Before the completion of the dam in 1988, Manantali was a small village of about 200 people. Nowadays, its population has swelled to around 15,000 and there is a lake here as big as the one at Geneva. Work on the dam was started in 1982 on the River Bafing as part of a wider development plan for the River Senegal. The aim was to provide much of the electricity for Mali, Senegal and Mauritania and, provided that the water is high enough, the hydro-electric plant at Manantali has a capacity of 800MW – which, in laymen's terms, is very, very big!

The lake used to be renowned for its hippopotamus population. However, in recent years the animals have not been spotted anywhere near the dam. While the water may look very appealling for swimming, note that it is very likely to be infected with bilharzia (see page 60).

It is possible to explore the lake by *pinasse*. John Kupiec took a *pinasse* which was equipped with ice chests for fish. For CFA5,000 the *pinassier* took him to the southern end of the lake in about three hours, only to continue pootling about at that far end for another 15 hours. During this time the *pinasse* halted repeatedly to buy and sell merchandise – mainly fish. Since the journey continued throughout the night, falling asleep and waking up by the light of torches, with people wading or paddling around the *pinasse*, created a 'dreamy, mysterious aura' which John Kupiec describes as the best part of this trip. He ended up staying at a family home for a night, and returned to Manatali with the same *pinasse* the following day, at no extra charge.

There are two places to stay in Manatali. **Bar Restaurant Bougouba Sewese** offers basic rooms with a fan at CFA6,000, or a mattress on the floor at CFA5,000. The restaurant serves tender steak and other tasty meals, but they may take a while to be prepared. On Fridays and Saturdays, the nightclub opens its doors and plays disco and African music. The *Mission Catholique* also has some rooms available.

The only **bank** is a BDM bank with a **Western Union** office. Manantali has a **post office** and a **police station**.

As a sign of its contemporary importance, a new road linking Manantali to Kita was completed in 1998, making it one of the first places in the region to be accessible to something other than a train (see *Kita: Getting there and away* on page 271).

Koundian and the Réserve du Parc National du Bafing
Most information provided by John Kupiec
Though there is some sort of public transport from Manantali to Koundian, contributor John Kupiec decided to walk.

> The first part of this walk was composed of many small hamlets/villages each having water. On two occasions I encountered lines of women working in the fields. There was wonderful hootin' hollerin' singing. I stayed on the road until somebody took me to them. I was met with warmth and hospitality along this stretch. Getting closer to Koundian the road curves around and downhill to a tropical setting. I surprised a bunch of brown monkeys who traversed an escarpment. I slept just off the road here (there are two big sandy clearings large enough for vehicles to camp). I heard the screeching and murmuring of the monkeys all night long, along with the sound of fruit dropping to the ground with a thud.

From Koundian, the road goes to **Makandougou**, passing by the villages of Foret and Kofe. There are sections with tricky deviations, which can result in a lot of asking directions and backtracking. From Makandougou it is another 25km to the **Réserve du Parc National du Bafing**, where a ranger may take you in search of chimpanzees. (Though John spotted some chimpanzees near Foret, his quest into the reserve with a ranger was unsuccessful in this respect.) From here continue to **Nanifara** and **Kéniéba**. There is no obvious means of public transport along this route.

For more information on the Réserve du Parc National du Bafing, enquire at the Ministère de l'Environnement (tel: 222 24 98), opposite the National Museum in Bamako.

Kéniéba
The *cercle* of Kéniéba in the extreme southwestern part of the region is known for its picturesque scenery, mesas, mountains and lions, which have been known to venture into the town of Kéniéba itself. This is where Mali's other major chain of cliffs, the **Tambaoura escarpment**, is to be found.

To the west the famous Bambouk gold fields stretch into Senegal. Gold mining still takes place at **Sadiola**, a town on the track linking Kayes and Kéniéba. Public transport from Kéniéba to Kayes usually comes in the form of *camions*. To join the crowd in the back costs CFA5,000, while a shared seat-with-a-view in the cabin costs CFA7,500. The fare for the journey to Bamako – also by truck – is CFA12,000.

KITA
Kita, 185km from Bamako, is a good place to break the train journey between the capital and Kayes. The *cercle* of Kita is of considerable economic importance and consequently its main town is second only to Kayes in terms of the quality of its infrastructure and facilities for visitors. However, Kita offers more than just a comfortable bed for the night – although this alone is an adequate draw after an arduous day on a train!

For one of Mali's main towns, Kita is remarkably calm and guides are conspicuous by their absence. This is also one of the richer and more fertile areas of the region, where the Guinean forests still hold sway over the encroaching sands of the desert.

Getting there and away
By train
Kita is the main stop between Bamako and Kayes. Nearer to the capital (the journey takes about five hours) than Kayes (at least seven hours from Kita), there are four trains passing in either direction every week. The Bamako-Dakar express arrives on Wednesdays from Bamako, and returns from Dakar on Sundays. For more information, the departure schedule and fares, see *Getting around* on page 76.

By road
Thanks to a new road completed by the Germans in 1998, it takes *bâchées* about four hours to cover the 150km to the famous dam at Manantali. They leave when full from two departure points near the Town Hall and near the railway station, and cost CFA3,500. The journey to Kéniéba takes at least 10 hours by 4WD and costs CFA12,500 for a seat in the back and CFA15,000 for a shared front seat. Minibuses and even big *camion* buses (Simbo Voyages) leave at least three times a day for Bamako (5–6 hours, CFA2,500). Simbo Voyages also has some departures late in the evening, for those who do not mind travelling during the night and arriving at inconvenient times.

Where to stay
Hotel Le Relais Touristique 'Kita Kourou' (tel: 257 32 46) is about 200m down the road leading to the railway station. This is quite clearly the best hotel in town and as such is often full. Rooms come with air conditioning or a fan, TVs and cans of insect spray; prices start at CFA7,500 (single) and CFA9,000 (double); there is also a large garden with plenty of shade, and a swimming pool with no water in it. In stark contrast, **Hotel Chat Rouge** – the establishment to which you will be escorted if there is no room at the Relais Touristique – charges about the same price for gloomy rooms with absolutely no appeal. To make matters worse, the discothèque in the courtyard will virtually guarantee no sleep until the early hours of the morning. The budget option in Kita is the **Campement Administratif 'Kita Kourou'** (tel: 257 30 46) next to the Relais Touristique. Basic rooms for CFA2,500 (single) or CFA4,000 (double) are sometimes available, but are normally full of civil servants and government workers. Camping is allowed on the premises. **Hotel l'Auberge** is on the road to Bamako, while **Hotel Dieudonné** is at the other end of Kita, on the road to Manantali.

Where to eat
While there are plenty of places to fill your stomach, you would be wasting your time looking for a gastronomic establishment. Once the restaurant at

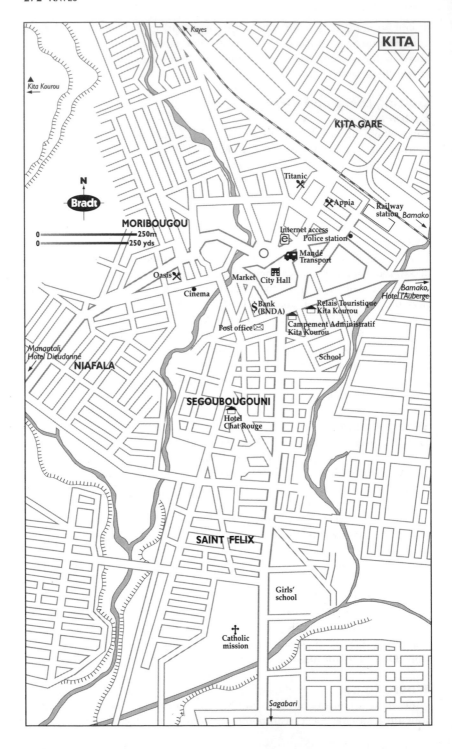

KITA

Kayes

Kita Kourou

KITA GARE

N
Bradt

MORIBOUGOU

0 ——— 250m
0 ——— 250 yds

Titanic ✕

✕ Appia

Railway
station Bamako

Internet access
ⓔ   Police station ●
           Mandé
           Transport

Oasis ✕

Market
Cinema ●   City Hall

Bamako,
Hotel l'Auberge

$ Bank
(BNDA)

Relais Touristique
Kita Kourou

Post office ✉

Campement Administratif
Kita Kourou

Manantali,
Hotel Dieudonné

NIAFALA

School

SEGOUBOUGOUNI
Hotel
Chat Rouge

SAINT FELIX

Girls'
school

✝
Catholic
mission

Sagabari

Hotel le Relais Touristique has been renovated, it could well regain its former position as the most popular place in town. **Restaurant l'Auberge** and **Restaurant Dieudonné** have been recommended by travellers, while **Restaurant l'Oasis** near the market describes itself as having 'un peu de tout' (a bit of everything) – which is not always true. **Restaurant Appia** and **Restaurant Titanic** are two of several places on the road leading to the railway station where you can sit down for a bite to eat. Around the station itself, vendors sell bread, cold drinks and fruit – Kita is noted for its excellent papayas – to the captive clientele of passengers waiting for delayed trains.

Nightlife
When Mali's most popular musicians undertake national tours, Kita is almost always visited and concerts are normally held at **Carrefour des Jeunes** in the centre of town opposite the BNDA. Otherwise, the town's nightlife is centred on the nightclubs at the two main hotels: the **Tropicana** at the Relais Touristique and the **Denver Club** at Hotel Chat Rouge. Both play African music and the cover charge is CFA2,000. On 'ladies' nights' at the Tropicana women get in for free. Meanwhile, the **cinema** in Kita shows violent Indian and Oriental films.

Practical information
The bulk of Kita's business activity takes place in the town's main square north of the marketplace, where the **post office**, a **bank** (BNDA) and the **police station** can be found. Note that the bank only changes cash euros. Sirandou Net provides **internet** access for CFA2,000/hour.

What to see
While Kita itself is a pleasant and relaxing town with no guides, most people come here to go hiking in the surrounding hills and to climb the 617m **Kita Kourou**. On the edge of town and visible from anywhere, Kita Kourou is a rugged and rather unattractive hill, but sacred nonetheless to the town's animist population, who for generations have conducted sacrifices and rituals in its grottoes, some of which have prehistoric wall paintings. People living in the houses at the foot of the hill should be able to show you the correct path to climb Kita Kourou, which is important, not only to arrive safely at the top, but also to avoid trespassing on sacred ground. Note that if you climb the hill in the early morning – the best time to avoid the heat – the rising sun will affect your views of Kita.

ELSEWHERE IN THE REGION
Parc National de la Boucle du Baoulé
The Parc National de la Boucle du Baoulé (Baoulé Bend National Park), which is situated northeast of Kita and overlaps the administrative regions of Kayes and Koulikoro, is Mali's largest **game reserve**. However, before wildlife enthusiasts get too excited, much of the fauna which once roamed around the well-watered forests in the bend of the River Baoulé has

disappeared, largely as a result of indiscriminate hunting, particularly by the military during the Traoré regime. Of the animals still remaining, monkeys are probably easiest to see. Baboons apparently also exist, hippos are found at various spots along the river, and gazelles, hyenas, buffaloes and the occasional lion might also be present. Elephants, giraffes and sadly even chimpanzees have not been spotted in years. In any case, look for wildlife in one of the three reserves within the boundaries of the national park: Kongosambougou, Fina (where the installation of a number of waterholes is planned for 2004) and Badinko; but don't expect an East African-style safari.

In fact, the Parc National de la Boucle du Baoulé is better-known these days for its abundance of **archaeological remains**. Although the area is sparsely populated today, over 200 archaeological sites ranging from the Stone Age to the colonial period prove that it was once densely populated. There are rock paintings and cave dwellings of hunter-gatherers from the Neolithic era (see *Background information: Early times* on page 3), as well as ancient tombs, burial grounds and colonial forts. The map on page 258 indicates the zones where many of these archaeological remains are situated.

Please note that at the time of writing, no updated map to the Parc National was available. However, a new map with more detailed information on the *pistes*, *campements* and the different sections of the National Park should be made availabe from July 2004. To get this map, go to the Ministère de l'Environnement (tel: 222 24 98) which is located opposite the National Museum in Bamako. When not available from stock, it will be printed out for you to be picked up the following day. Expect the charge to be around CFA17,500. If you are planning to go to the National Park de la Boucle du Baoulé, this is the place to go anyway for general information and suggestions on itineraries, as within the boundaries of the National Park you'll find next to nothing in terms of general information.

Most visitors enter the National Park via **Faladié**, but there are other tracks leading into the park where you will have to report at the *Poste de Contrôle*. This is where you must register and pick up a guide; either a local farmer who should know the area inside-out (CFA7,500/day) or an *agent des eaux et forêts* or ranger (CFA4,000/day). The latter has the right to carry a weapon, and this will allow you more freedom: with an armed guide you may roam more deeply into the park, and even camp outside the villages or *campements*.

Four *campements* should be functional by the end of 2004. Rooms cost CFA5,000, while camping is free of charge. **Campement Baoulé** is only 50km from Bamako, and is located in the zone known as Koundou, where there is a French fort and the largest rock dwelling in the National Park. Other *campements* are in **Madina**, **Missira** and **Kourouninkoto**, but access is more difficult. This is not to say that access to any part of the park is easy, and you will need to have or hire your own 4WD vehicle.

Well away from the *campements*, villagers will put you up for the night at a nominal charge. Unless you are happy to eat what they are having, you should bring your own supplies. On leaving the park, you must pay a hefty entrance fee (CFA7,500/day). The reason why you you do not have to pay in advance is to

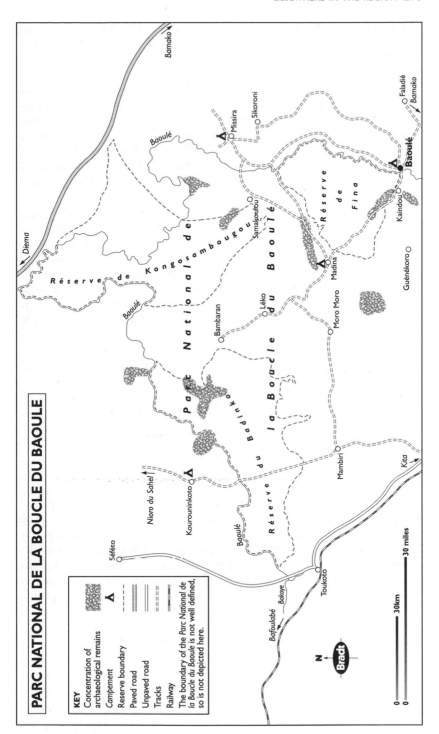

PARC NATIONAL DE LA BOUCLE DU BAOULE

KEY

Concentration of
archaeological remains

Campement

Reserve boundary

Paved road

Unpaved road

Tracks

Railway

The boundary of the Parc National de
la Boucle du Baoule is not well defined,
so is not depicted here.

allow you to make up your mind about the itinerary and the length of your stay. By the same token, you are not obliged to exit the park where you entered.

Yélimané and Nioro du Sahel

Two towns northeast of Kayes, Yélimané and Nioro du Sahel, were both former capitals of the Bambara kingdom of Kaarta (see page 260). Nowadays, they are dusty Sahelian towns kept going by livestock raising and subsistence farming. Although geographically these towns are twinned by remoteness, they could hardly be more isolated from each other. While the roads linking Yélimané and Nioro du Sahel to bigger towns – like Kayes and Diéma – have been upgraded, certain sections between the two towns have been left to deteriorate to such a degree that even walking between them has become problematic.

To get to Yélimané (CFA12,500), look for Diema Transport at the *gare routière du Nouveau Marché Médine* in Bamako. There are two weekly departures (Mondays and Thursdays). Trucks (CFA6,500) and buses or converted trucks (CFA10,000) for Nioro du Sahel leave from the same bus station. Look for Diema Transport and Mandé Transport for departures on Mondays, Thursdays and Saturdays. To travel to both towns from Kayes, see *Kayes: Getting there and away: By road* on page 261. Both **SAE** and **STA** have flights to Nioro du Sahel and Yélimané. SAE are represented in both towns and can be contacted through tel: 253 17 03 and 252 22 62 respectively.

In October 2003, John Kupiec travelled in this region and provided the following information. About 10km before reaching Yélimané, John got off where the road intersects a marshy area, in the village of Diongoulani. He made a complete circuit of the lake (and recommends it for birdwatching), visiting the mud village of Fonga on the way. In **Yélimané**, another good place for birdwatching is past the mosque and the cemetery, where there is a marshy area with trees. You can stay at the Maison de l'Amitié, which has rooms at CFA3,000 (with private shower) and CFA1,500 (without shower). Bar Nightclub le Bambeau is not far from the Mission Catholique, while Buvette Lafia serves chilled beer and not much else.

From Yélimané, John tried to travel to Nioro du Sahel directly: 'There does seem to be a daily vehicle to Kirane, but then it's another 75km to Nioro. This may not even be walkable'; and so he backtracked to Kayes to find transport to **Nioro du Sahel**. This desert town has a mosque, and though you may catch a glimpse of the interior by peering over the wall, it is not open to non-Muslims. There are two *campements*: Restaurant Bar Tamare, with a defunct restaurant but rooms at CFA2,000, and the Complexe Culturelle Jamana, which is frequented by prostitutes. It is located out of the centre on the road to Kayes.

Appendix 1

LANGUAGE
Bambara phrasebook

Bambara is one of several Manding or Mande languages spoken in varying degrees in 11 West African countries. In Mali it is the *lingua franca* of trade and administration, although travellers should note that it is not understood all over the country. In this respect, a working knowledge of French might be more useful than proficiency in Bambara. A smattering of the local language, however, demonstrates respect for your hosts and can be fun to practise on unsuspecting Bambaraphones.

Pronunciation

The Bambara alphabet is a mixture of the French alphabet and the International Phonetic Alphabet conceived by Paul Dassy and Daniel Jones between 1886 and 1900. As far as pronunciation is concerned, the following letters might need clarifying:

c	**tch**é
é	closed (like f**é**e in French)
è	open (like f**ait** in French)
g	**gué**
j	**di**é
ò	closed (like s**aut** in French)
u	c**ou** in French

Some words and phrases

Welcome	*i ni sè*
Hello	*i ni sògòma/i ni ce*
Good evening	*i ni wula*
Good night	*i ni su*
Goodbye	*kambufo* (to a person leaving)
Goodbye	*kambè* (when you are leaving)
How are you?	*i ka kènè wa?*
I am fine/all is well	*toorò té*
All is very well	*toorò si té*
Thank you	*i ni ce*
Yes	*òwò*
No	*ayi*
Okay	*a njé na*
Please	*a ke to*

No, thank you	*akain*
Yes, please	*awò o be dja njè*
Maybe	*a ma don*
Why?	*mun ka ma?*
When?	*uma ju mè?*
Tonight	*bi wula/bi su*
This morning	*bi sògòma*
Today	*bi*
Tomorrow	*sini*
Yesterday	*kunu*
Next week	*dogo kunwèrè*
What is your name?	*i togo?*
My name is …	*n'togo …*
I am British (American)	*ne ye anglais (américain) ye*
I am French (Dutch)	*ne ye français (hollandi) ye*
I am …	*m'bi… /n'bè…*
Do you speak English?	*i bi angèlèkan men wa?*
What time is it?	*leer jumen be yên?/heure jumé be?*
When is the car/bus leaving?	*mobili be taa heure jumé*
We are leaving	*a be taa*
I am going to …	*n'be taa …*
I arrived from …	*n'be bò …*
Where is …?	*… bè min?*
Where is the road to …?	*… sira bè min?*
Where is the bus station?	*mobili sera bè min?*
Where is the train station?	*train gare bè min?*
Where is the bank (toilet)?	*banki (njekèn) bè min?*
There is no water	*ji tè*
Do you have …?	*… bi yan wa?*
How much?	*joli? joli don?*
I don't have any change	*waarime sen tè*
It is too expensive	*a sogo ka cha*
Do you have rice?	*malo be i bolo wa?*
Do you have milk?	*nono be i bolo wa?*
(Do you have) sugar?	*sukara (be i bolo wa)?*
… fruit? … hot water?	*yiri de …? ji kalan …?*
… drinks? … water? …beer?	*boisson …? ji …? dolo …?*
Do you have mineral water?	*tubabu ji b'i bolo wa?*
I don't eat meat/fish	*n'e tè sogo/djègè dun*
I am feeling ill	*n'man kènè*
I have a stomach ache	*n'kònò bè dimi*
I have a toothache	*n'da be dimi*
I am looking for a doctor	*n'be taa docteur so la*
Where is the dentist?	*njigilana be mi?*
Where is the pharmacy?	*pharmacie be mi?*

Numbers

1	*kelen*	11	*tan ni kélén*
2	*fla*	12	*tan ni fla*
3	*saba*	20	*mugan*
4	*naani*	30	*mugan ni tan* or *bi saba*
5	*duurun*	40	*bi naani*
6	*wooro*	50	*bi duurun*
7	*wolonfla*	100	*keme*
8	*seegin*	500	*keme duurun*
9	*kononto*	1,000	*ba kelen*
10	*tan*		

French phrasebook

In terms of getting by and getting things done with your foreign-language skills, French will be more useful than Bambara. Moreover, the fact that it is taught in most Western schools should make it easier to master – or at least mimic! – than a completely alien African language.

Pronunciation

The key to pronouncing French is knowing which letters not to pronounce. Otherwise, a selection of the more important general rules of pronunciation is as follows:

a	c**a**t
c	**s** before e, i and y; **k** before a, o and u
ç	**s**
ch	**sh**oe
é	long **a**
è	short **e**
g	vi**s**ion before e, i and y; **g**un before a, o and u
h	silent
i	m**ee**t
j	vi**s**ion
o	r**o**t
ou	Timbukt**oo**
qu	**k**
r	a mix between an **r** and a **ch** in loch
s	**z** between vowels; silent at the end of words
th	**t**
u	like an Englsh **e** said with pursed lips
w	usually **w**; occasionally **v** (eg 'wagon')
x	**ks** before most consonants; **gz** before most vowels; silent at the end of words

Basics

Hello	*Bonjour (day); bonsoir (evening)*
How are you?	*Comment allez-vous?*
Please	*S'il vous plaît*
Thank you	*Merci*

Goodbye	*Au revoir*
My name is…	*Je m'appelle…*
I am…	*Je suis…*
Where is…?	*Où est…?*
Do you have…?	*Est-ce-que vous avez…?*
Can you…?	*Est-ce-que vous pouvez…?*
Can I…?	*Est-ce-que je peux…?*
I would like…	*Je voudrais…*
I need…	*J'ai besoin de…*
How much?	*C'est combien?*
What time is it?	*Quelle heure est-il?*
Do you speak English?	*Parlez-vous anglais?*

Numbers

0	*zéro*	17	*dix-sept*
1	*un/une*	18	*dix-huit*
2	*deux*	19	*dix-neuf*
3	*trois*	20	*vingt*
4	*quatre*	21	*vingt-et-un*
5	*cinq*	22	*vingt-deux*
6	*six*	30	*trente*
7	*sept*	40	*quarante*
8	*huit*	50	*cinquante*
9	*neuf*	60	*soixante*
10	*dix*	70	*soixante-dix*
11	*onze*	80	*quatre-vingt*
12	*douze*	90	*quatre-vingt-dix*
13	*treize*	100	*cent*
14	*quatorze*	500	*cinq cents*
15	*quinze*	1,000	*mille*
16	*seize*		

Days

Monday	*lundi*	Friday	*vendredi*
Tuesday	*mardi*	Saturday	*samedi*
Wednesday	*mercredi*	Sunday	*dimanche*
Thursday	*jeudi*		

Months

January	*janvier*	July	*juillet*
February	*février*	August	*août*
March	*mars*	September	*septembre*
April	*avril*	October	*octobre*
May	*mai*	November	*novembre*
June	*juin*	December	*décembre*

Other useful words

afternoon	*après-midi*	morning	*matin*
bed	*lit*	passport	*passport*
bread	*pain*	post office	*bureau de poste*
breakfast	*petit déjeuner*	rice	*riz*
bus station	*gare routière*	river	*fleuve*
cheap	*bon marché*	room	*chambre*
chicken	*poulet*	street	*rue*
day	*jour*	thing	*chose*
diarrhoea	*diarrhée*	today	*aujourd'hui*
early	*tôt*	tomorrow	*demain*
eat	*manger*	town	*ville*
egg	*œuf*	United States	*Etats-Unis*
English	*anglais*	very	*très*
expensive	*cher*	water	*eau*
fish	*poisson*	what?	*quoi?*
go	*aller*	when?	*quand?*
good	*bon*	where?	*où?*
how	*comment*	which?	*quel?*
hungry	*faim*	who?	*qui?*
late	*tard*	with	*avec*
man	*homme*	woman	*femme*
money	*argent*		

Appendix 2

FURTHER INFORMATION
Further reading
Background
Griaule, Marcel *Conversations With Ogotemmêli: An Introduction to Dogon Religious Ideas* (Oxford University Press, 1977) and *The Pale Fox* (Continuum Foundation, 1986). The two seminal works about the Dogon.

Imperato, Pascal James *Mali: A Search for Direction* (Westview Press, 1989) and *Historical Dictionary of Mali* (Scarecrow Press, 1996). Everything you ever wanted to know about Mali. The *Dictionary* contains a comprehensive bibliography.

Niané, Djibril Tamsir *Sundiata: An Epic of Old Mali* (Longman, 1965). An English translation of a description of Soundiata Keita by a Malian author (see *History: the Mali Empire* on page 7).

Literature
Condé, Maryse *Segu* (Viking Penguin, 1987)

Ouologuem, Yambo *Bound to Violence* (Harcourt Brace Jovanovich, 1971)

Sembene, Ousmane *God's Bits of Wood* (Presses Pockets, 1960)

The above are three of the best-known contemporary Malian novels translated into English.

Travel
Aebi, Ernst *Seasons of Sand* (Simon & Schuster, 1993). The story of how a loft-renovator from New York transformed the remote desert settlement of Araouane into a reasonably pleasant place to live – for a while!

Barth, Heinrich *Travels and Discoveries in North and Central Africa* (Frank Cass, 1965)

Caillié, Réné *Travels Through Central Africa to Timbuctoo* (Frank Cass, 1968)

Dunn, Richard E *The Adventures of Ibn Batuta: A Muslim Traveller of the 14th Century* (University of California Press, 1986)

Park, Mungo *Travels into the Interior of Africa* (Eland Books, 2003)

Trench, Richard *Forbidden Sands: A Search in the Sahara* (Chicago Academy Limited, 1978). A British journalist describes his journey across the Sahara in the 1970s, with a vivid account of the salt mines at Taoudenni. Influenced Aebi when he wrote *Seasons of Sand*.

Natural history
Borrow, Nik and Demey, Ron *Birds of Western Africa* (Helm Identification Guide, 2001)

Kingdon, Jonathan *The Kingdon Guide to African Mammals* (Academic Press, 2001)

Hutchinson, J and Dalziel, J M *Flora of West Tropical Africa* Volume 1, Part 2 and
Volume 3, Part 1

Health
Ellis, Dr Matthew and Wilson-Howarth, Dr Jane *Your Child's Health Abroad: A Manual
for Travelling Parents* (Bradt, 2004). Indispensable companion for anyone travelling
with children.
Wilson-Howarth, Jane *Healthy Travel: Bugs, Bites & Bowels* (Cadogan, 1995).
Informative and entertaining.

Books in French
Andriamirado, Sennen *Le Mali Aujourd'hui* (Les éditions j.a. 1985). Not really for
practical travel in Mali, but with good pictures and background information on all
of the country's regions.
Bedaux, R et al *L'Architecture de Djenné* (Rijksmuseum voor Volkenkunde Leiden,
2003). Apart from an overview about the architecture of Djenné, this is a revealing
report (in French) on the restoration project that took place between 1997 and
2004.
Benoist, Joseph-Roger de *Le Mali* (Editions L'Harmattan, 1998)
Gardi, Bernard et al *Djenné il y a cent ans* (KIT Publications, 1994). A photograph
album with some of the first pictures and postcards of Djenné from its colonial
period.
Gaudio, Attilio *Le Mali* (Editions Karthala, 1988)

Websites
Africa News On-Line allafrica.com. A pan-African news agency on the internet.
Archaeology www.archaeology.org. Go into search; article index.
Articles www.countrywatch.com/cw_country.asp?vcountry=109. With links to
thousands of articles about Mali.
Books businessafrica.usanethosting.com/africabiz/countries/mali.htm. Facts, figures
and a dozen links to books on Mali.
Culture www.friendsofmali-uk.org. This British organisation promotes Mali and the
Malian culture through information and activities.
Djembé www.djembe.com. All you ever wanted to know about West Africa's most
famous drum, the *djembé*. In French.
Development www.usaid.gov/regions/afr/leland/malindex.htm. With many links to
issues concerning development.
Facts and figures www.cia.gov/cia/publications/factbook/geos/ml.html
General information www.afribone.com. A little bit of everything, including
newspaper articles, bankrates, nightlife in Bamako and much more. In French.
Malian Ministery of Tourism www.malitourisme.com. In French, with many links
to other governmental institutions.
Music www.afromix.or/static/disco/pays/mali/index.en.html. Comprehensive listing
of Malian CDs – which you can also purchase online.
OMATHO www.le-mali.com/omatho/index.htm. In French, about this Office aimed
at promoting and developing tourism.

Photographs mali.pwnet.org/gallery/gallery.htm

River Niger www.nationalgeographic.com/adventure/0301/photo_1.html. Story and pictures about a rivertrip to Timbuktu.

Rockclimbing www.reeladventure.net/mali_story.htm. Story and pictures about the climbing of the Main de Fatma near Hombori.

Yellow pages www.malipages.com. In French, but with a link to the English site.

WIN £100 CASH!
READER QUESTIONNAIRE

Send in your completed questionnaire for the chance to win £100 cash in our regular draw

All respondents may order a Bradt guide at half the UK retail price – please complete the order form overleaf.
(Entries may be posted or faxed to us, or scanned and emailed.)

We are interested in getting feedback from our readers to help us plan future Bradt guides. Please answer ALL the questions below and return the form to us in order to qualify for an entry in our regular draw.

Have you used any other Bradt guides? If so, which titles? . . . .
. . . .
What other publishers' travel guides do you use regularly? . . . .
. . . .
Where did you buy this guidebook? . . . .
What was the main purpose of your trip to Mali (or for what other reason did you read our guide)? eg: holiday/business/charity etc. . . . .
. . . .
What other destinations would you like to see covered by a Bradt guide?
. . . .
Would you like to receive our catalogue/newsletters?
YES / NO (If yes, please complete details on reverse)
If yes – by post or email? . . . .
Age (circle relevant category) 16–25   26–45   46–60   60+
Male/Female (delete as appropriate)
Home country . . . .
Please send us any comments about our guide to Mali or other Bradt Travel Guides. . . . .
. . . .
. . . .
. . . .

Bradt Travel Guides
23 High Street, Chalfont St Peter, Bucks SL9 9QE, UK
☎ +44 (0)1753 893444 **f** +44 (0)1753 892333
e info@bradtguides.com
www.bradtguides.com

CLAIM YOUR HALF-PRICE BRADT GUIDE!

Order Form

To order your half-price copy of a Bradt guide, and to enter our prize draw to win £100 (see overleaf), please fill in the order form below, complete the questionnaire overleaf, and send it to Bradt Travel Guides by post, fax or email.

Please send me one copy of the following guide at half the UK retail price

Title	Retail price	Half price
...	....	....	....

Please send the following additional guides at full UK retail price

No	Title	Retail price	Total
...	....	....	....
...	....	....	....
...	....	....	....

Sub total ....
Post & packing ....
(£2 per book UK; £4 per book Europe; £6 per book rest of world)
Total ....

Name ....

Address...

Tel .... Email ....

☐ I enclose a cheque for £ .... made payable to Bradt Travel Guides Ltd

☐ I would like to pay by credit card. Number: ....

Expiry date: .../... 3-digit security code (on reverse of card) .....

Issue no (debit cards only) .....

☐ Please add my name to your catalogue mailing list.

☐ I would be happy for you to use my name and comments in Bradt marketing material.

Send your order on this form, with the completed questionnaire, to:

Bradt Travel Guides MAL1
23 High Street, Chalfont St Peter, Bucks SL9 9QE
☏ +44 (0)1753 893444   f +44 (0)1753 892333
e info@bradtguides.com   www.bradtguides.com

Bradt Travel Guides
www.bradtguides.com

Africa

Africa Overland	£15.99
Algeria	£15.99
Benin	£14.99
Botswana: Okavango, Chobe, Northern Kalahari	£15.99
Burkina Faso	£14.99
Cape Verde Islands	£13.99
Canary Islands	£13.95
Cameroon	£13.95
Congo	£14.99
Eritrea	£15.99
Ethiopia	£15.99
Gabon, São Tomé, Príncipe	£13.95
Gambia, The	£13.99
Ghana	£15.99
Johannesburg	£6.99
Kenya	£14.95
Madagascar	£15.99
Malawi	£13.99
Mali	£13.95
Mauritius, Rodrigues & Réunion	£13.99
Mozambique	£13.99
Namibia	£15.99
Niger	£14.99
Nigeria	£15.99
Rwanda	£14.99
Seychelles	£14.99
Sudan	£13.95
Tanzania, Northern	£13.99
Tanzania	£16.99
Uganda	£15.99
Zambia	£15.95
Zanzibar	£12.99

Britain and Europe

Albania	£13.99
Armenia, Nagorno Karabagh	£14.99
Azores	£12.99
Baltic Capitals: Tallinn, Riga, Vilnius, Kaliningrad	£12.99
Belarus	£14.99
Belgrade	£6.99
Bosnia & Herzegovina	£13.99
Bratislava	£6.99
Budapest	£8.99
Bulgaria	£13.99
Cork	£6.99
Croatia	£13.99
Cyprus see North Cyprus	

Czech Republic	£13.99
Dresden	£7.99
Dubrovnik	£6.99
Estonia	£13.99
Faroe Islands	£13.95
Georgia	£14.99
Helsinki	£7.99
Hungary	£14.99
Iceland	£14.99
Kiev	£7.95
Kosovo	£14.99
Krakow	£7.99
Lapland	£13.99
Latvia	£13.99
Lille	£6.99
Lithuania	£13.99
Ljubljana	£7.99
Macedonia	£14.99
Montenegro	£13.99
North Cyprus	£12.99
Paris, Lille & Brussels	£11.95
Riga	£6.95
River Thames, In the Footsteps of the Famous	£10.95
Serbia	£14.99
Slovakia	£14.99
Slovenia	£12.99
Spitsbergen	£14.99
Switzerland: Rail, Road, Lake	£13.99
Tallinn	£6.99
Ukraine	£14.99
Vilnius	£6.99
Zagreb	£6.99

Middle East, Asia and Australasia

China: Yunnan Province	£13.99
Great Wall of China	£13.99
Iran	£14.99
Iraq	£14.95
Iraq: Then & Now	£15.99
Kyrgyzstan	£15.99
Maldives	£13.99
Mongolia	£14.95
North Korea	£13.95
Oman	£13.99
Sri Lanka	£13.99
Syria	£14.99
Tibet	£13.99
Turkmenistan	£14.99
Yemen	£14.99

The Americas and the Caribbean

Amazon, The	£14.99
Argentina	£15.99
Bolivia	£14.99
Cayman Islands	£12.95
Colombia	£15.99
Costa Rica	£13.99
Chile	£16.95
Dominica	£14.99
Falkland Islands	£13.95
Guyana	£14.99
Panama	£13.95
Peru & Bolivia: Backpacking and Trekking	£12.95
St Helena	£14.99
USA by Rail	£13.99

Wildlife

100 Animals to See Before They Die	£16.99
Antarctica: Guide to the Wildlife	£14.95
Arctic: Guide to the Wildlife	£15.99
Central & Eastern European Wildlife	£15.99
Chinese Wildlife	£16.99
East African Wildlife	£19.99
Galápagos Wildlife	£15.99
Madagascar Wildlife	£14.95
Peruvian Wildlife	£15.99
Southern African Wildlife	£18.95
Sri Lankan Wildlife	£15.99

Eccentric Guides

Eccentric America	£13.95
Eccentric Australia	£12.99
Eccentric Britain	£13.99
Eccentric California	£13.99
Eccentric Cambridge	£6.99
Eccentric Edinburgh	£5.95
Eccentric France	£12.95
Eccentric London	£13.99
Eccentric Oxford	£5.95

Others

Your Child Abroad: A Travel Health Guide	£10.95
Something Different for the Weekend	£12.99

Index

Page references in bold indicate main entries; those in italics indicate maps